A Blueprint for the Promotion of Prosocial Behavior in Early Childhood

Issues in Children's and Families' Lives

Series Editors:
Thomas P. Gullotta, *Child and Family Agency of Southeastern Connecticut, New London, Connecticut*
Herbert J. Walberg, *University of Illinois at Chicago, Chicago, Illinois*
Roger P. Weissberg, *University of Illinois at Chicago, Chicago, Illinois*

A Blueprint for the Promotion of Prosocial Behavior in Early Childhood

Edited by

Elda Chesebrough
Patricia King
Thomas P. Gullotta
Child and Family Agency of Southeastern Connecticut
New London, Connecticut

and

Martin Bloom
University of Connecticut
West Hartford, Connecticut

Research Assistants

Jessica M. Ramos and Jen Seager
Child and Family Agency of Southeastern Connecticut
New London, Connecticut

and

Jennifer C. Messina
Villanova University, Villanova, Pennsylvania

A Sponsored Publication of the Child and Family Agency of Southeastern Connecticut

Kluwer Academic / Plenum Publishers
New York • Boston • Dortrecht • London • Moscow

Library of Congress Cataloging-in-Publication Data

A blueprint for the promotion of prosocial behavior in early childhood / edited by Elda
Chesebrough ... [et. al.].
    p.   cm.—(Issues in children's and families' lives)
Includes bibliographical references and index.
ISBN 0-306-48186-3
1. Social skills—Study and teaching (Early childhood)   2. Socialization—Study
and teaching (Early childhood)   3. Child development.   I. Chesebrough, Elda.
II. Series.

HQ783.B555   2004
155.42'38—dc22   2003062064

ISBN: 0-306-48186-3

© 2004 by Kluwer Academic/Plenum Publishers
233 Spring Street, New York, New York 10013

http://www.wkap.nl/

10 9 8 7 6 5 4 3 2 1

A C.I.P. record for this book is available from the Library of Congress

Permission for books published in Europe: permissions@wkap.nl
Permissions for books published in the United States of America: permissions@wkap.com

Printed in the United Kingdom by Biddles/IBT Global

Preface

Despite the continued decline in violent crime among young people in the United States, several tragic killings of youth by other youth has made all of us painfully aware of violence. These angry misguided acts against others in schools and elsewhere have made it clear that violence and death are not to be found only on city streets, in city schools, and among city youth but anywhere and everywhere wrathful disenfranchised young people reside. It is this reality and our firm belief that these events can be prevented that brought the Bingham project into being and this book and curriculum to publication.

For Child and Family Agency, this project began more than a decade ago in 1993 with federal funding from a Department of Education "Training in Early Childhood Education and Violence Counseling" center grant. Our partner in that initial venture was the Department of Education at Eastern Connecticut State University, which developed a quality early childhood staff training program. Our work, and more specifically the work of Lynn Andrews, focused on parent and community-based efforts to promote prosocial behavior in young children. Of the several initiatives that arose from that effort, one, "Tips for Parents," held promise for encouraging early childhood prosocial behavior. Sadly, this work and that of the University was placed on hold when the 'Budget Recession Act of 1994' removed funding from this and the other five federally funded centers.

It would be the Columbine tragedy that would bring a rebirth of interest to these efforts of several years past. In a series of discussions with Patricia F. Davidson and Donald M. Barr of the Bingham Trust, I was asked what society might have done to prevent this tragedy. I answered that question by sharing with Pat and Donald one haunting finding from the National Research Council's (Reiss & Roth, 1993) review of the literature on the prevention of violence. What was this finding? Most of the time, often by age 6, we can identify those young people who will be in serious trouble with authorities in adolescence. The defining measurement—very simply put—is can a child play well with others, that is, be kind, express feelings appropriately, respect self and others, cooperate and exhibit self-control. Now, if antisocial behavior in early childhood is such a strong predictor of dysfunctional behavior in later life why do we wait till adolescence to intervene when this pattern of antisocial behavior has had time to become established? Would it not make more sense and be more cost effective to promote prosocial behavior in early childhood? No, push that calculating logic aside. Is it not the right act—the moral act—to help that troubled child succeed? Thankfully, both trustees agreed with this logic.

The informed reader will likely yawn now and think, "So, what's different about this project? Other, effective evidence-based efforts are in existence and are well-known." Both statements are true. What makes the Bingham Early Childhood project unique is its real world origins. By that we mean in its design the group that created this program took into account two critical realities. First, while there are some well-trained early child-hood educators, sadly, they are in the minority. The educational preparation of most childcare staff in childcare settings is minimal. Their experience is based, well, on experience. That is, "I was a child once and I had a parent/guardian who raised me. With that practical 'hands on' job training I'm ready to work and apply that same experience, good or wanting, to others." Clearly, such job preparation leaves much to chance.

Second, it is no surprise to anyone closely connected to the child-caring field to learn that staff turnover averages 40 percent each year. Low salaries and difficult work schedules (early openings and late closings, few if any breaks in the workday) are some of the many reasons for worker flight to other employment opportunities. Thus, even among the most motivated childcare center directors there is little incentive to adopt prosocial pro-gramming that requires lengthy training. Indeed, given the narrow profit margins that nearly all centers operate under and the chronic shortage of staff, any release time to staff for training is hard to come by.

Given these practical realities, the team of advisors whose chapters precede the curriculum and the staff who developed and implemented the program needed to respond differently. So, what's different? First, the group reduced the multitude of prosocial psychological traits to be nur-tured in children to five. These five core behaviors of kindness, feelings, respect, cooperation and self-control, we believe, are essential to the devel-opment of prosocial behavior.

Next, they distilled the wealth of information accompanying these core behaviors into six hours of participatory training. We should note that this "classroom" training introduces the material and is a starting point for the program's implementation and is not by any stretch of the imagination an end in and of itself. 〕◡⸝ ⸜◡◡⸝◠ ⸜◡ ⸜◠⸝

The implementation of the Bingham program is in the classroom with the trainer/coach in attendance. The driving principle is "Practice Makes Permanent," a phrase borrowed from the Federal Emergency Management Act which concretizes a lesson learned long ago in the field of prevention: classroom study and discussion rarely, if ever, translate into lasting practice. The trainer/coach is involved with each site no less than four hours a week and often up to as many as nine hours a week. Like the coach he or she is, this person models the behaviors for the teachers and nurtures similar responses from them for the children in their care. Our classroom observations gathering evaluation data over more than three years and in excess of 3,000 hours tell us that eliciting prosocial behavior from young children is neither easy nor automatic for some child care staff. Authoritarian behaviors occur all too often, and while they may make for an orderly classroom, they do not develop the social emotional intelligence children must have to handle the problems in living with which they will be confronted across their lives. Further, because of staff turnover, the trainer/coach's onsite presence ensures both the necessary fidelity to the program and dosage to obtain results.

Another, unique aspect of the Bingham program is its nontraditional approach to enlisting parents' support of its prosocial objectives. There is an extensive literature supporting the effectiveness of parenting education (Durlak, Chapter 4 this volume; Gullotta and Bloom, 2003). But, for all of its usefulness certain issues remain troublesome. For example, only half of parents in any program attend. Of these, only about three quarters will complete the program (Durlak, Chapter 4). More disconcerting are reports in the literature that parenting education efforts might actually increase negative parenting behaviors (Tolan, 2001 cited in Feinberg & Pettit, 2003). How so?

Imagine rising early to get yourself and your child (or children) ready for the day. Belonging to the working poor, your job assignment does not enable "flex" time in when you arrive and depart. You are expected to be at your station at a particular time, or there will be consequences. Hurried out the door, you rush your child to care and yourself to work. Now, imagine the close of day. Tired, perhaps, frustrated by a thousand and one worries, you want only to pick up your child (or children), go home, and crash. Supper will be found either at a fast food eatery (dollar menu, please) or assembled at home from what's around.

Instead, the child care center expects you to remain at the center or return later that evening for parent education. Emotionally exhausted, the good stuff in that presentation is received in a "Damned if I'll do that attitude." Of note, this reported negative reaction to parenting education was reported most pronounced for mothers with self-reported elevated depression.

Taking this literature into consideration, the Bingham project borrowed from the work done a decade earlier by Lynn Andrews and used "Tips for Parents" as the vehicle for enlisting the all-important support of parents in nurturing social and emotional behaviors in their children.

In the chapters that follow, the reader retraces our journey in the development of this program. In the first chapter, Margaret O'Shea helps us to understand how the preschool child learns. Next, Susanne Denham and Roger Weissberg utilize that information to explain what we know about how children affectively experience the world and the importance of social and emotional intelligence. In Chapter 3, this theme is brought into a practical context as Alice Honig provides numerous examples of how social and emotional learning can be brought into the classroom. This child-centered focus is enlarged in Chapter 4 as Joseph Durlak places this information into a larger ecological context focusing on the family, as does Julia Mendez and her associates in Chapter 5 with the importance of the neighborhood and culture on the preschool child's development. How to interrelate the many separate pieces of empirically supported information found in the Bingham journey into a framework of usable knowledge is examined by Martin Bloom and Thomas Gullotta in Chapter 6. This volume concludes with the Bingham Early Childhood Curriculum by Elda Chesebrough and Patricia King, in which they lay out a systematic training approach for nurturing prosocial behavior in young children.

It is our wish that readers will take the material found within these pages and put it to good use in classrooms. It is our hope that the use of coaches to perfect and maintain performance will become standard practice in the coming years. But most of all, it is our prayer that children will profit from this experience and will grow to lead socially and emotionally enriching lives.

ELDA CHESEBROUGH
PATRICIA KING
THOMAS P. GULLOTTA
MARTIN BLOOM

References

Durlak, J. (2004). How to help families promote optimal development in young children. In E. Chesebrough, P. King, M. Bloom, & T. P. Gullotta (eds.). *A blueprint for the promotion of prosocial behavior in early childhood*. New York: Kluwer Academic/Plenum Publishers.

Feinberg, M. E., & Pettit, G. S. (2003). Parenting, adulthood. In T. P. Gullotta & M. Bloom (eds.). *The encyclopedia of primary prevention and health promotion.* New York: Kluwer Academic/Plenum Publishers.

Gullotta, T. P., & Bloom, M. (eds.) 2003. *The encyclopedia of primary prevention and health promotion.* New York: Kluwer Academic/Plenum Publishers.

Reiss, A. J., & Roth, J. A. (eds.) (1993). *Understanding and preventing violence.* Washington, DC: National Academy Press.

Acknowledgments

Over the years it has taken us to reach this moment, many different staff members were involved. Each member of this large team played a vital and important role. We wish to acknowledge these individuals and the advisors who guided the development of this program. On the Bingham Advisory Committee, which guided the development of the model, this includes Joseph Durlak, Loyola University, Alice Honig, Syracuse University, Margaret O'Shea Saint Joseph's College, Craig Blakely, Texas A&M University; Susanne Denham, George Mason University, Abraham Wandersman, University of South Carolina; and Roger Weissberg, University of Illinois at Chicago.

Lynn Andrews began the initial work to develop a prosocial curriculum, and developed the concept for and wrote most of the "Tips for Parents."

Pam Julian and Deb O'Byrne outlined and provided substance to the text and training outlines.

Jen Seager diligently gathered, tested, modified, and edited activities. Jen contributed the lion's share of activities, and her work with teachers to perfect the activities was a huge contribution to the success of The Bingham Program.

Erin Eckhart and Jen Seager of the Groton School Readiness Program, where this model was first piloted, provided input, which allowed us to develop a training program that is based in the reality of professional development for staff of early childhood programs. They were also instrumental in the standardization of the observation tool.

Clarissa Miles, Grit Francis, Katherine Plantz, and Abigail Miles, staff of the Early Childhood Development Center, where this model was tested, guided the development of the coaching concept and concretized the connection with program supervisors.

Thanks to Deb Fritzsche, Romis Espinal, Mary Beth Reeves, Carly Lutes, Maria Pagan, and Jaime Tulba of the New London Day Nursery Starbright Room, at the site of the third pilot. Their work with this project led us through a complete revision of the text and strengthened the supervision and coaching components of this model.

Janice DelPaine, Tasha Ward, and Wilhelmina Desandre, of the New London Day Nursery Rainbow Room graciously accepted research assistants into their classroom, which served as the control group for the third pilot.

The site managers, coordinators, and community workers of the Early Childhood Department at Child and Family Agency were often called upon to provide technical assistance, brainstorm solutions, and develop activity plans: Cathy Bearce, Erin Eckhart, Deb Fritzsche, Lydia St. Hilaire, Mary Hughes, Judy Lathrop, Lesley Lohr. Clarissa Miles, Bernice Oulundsen, Jen Seager, Christine Riemann, and Mary Ann Root.

Thank you to Pfizer, Inc. and Bright Horizons Family Solutions for your participation in the Bingham program. The faculty of Pfizer Kids warmly welcomed us into their center. A special thank you to Sarah Wills, Gretchen Vogt, Jen Wilson, Nicole Salaun, Catherina Strong, Sharon Feeney and Rose Ciaudelli for their commitment and hard work toward implementing the program. Also, Marianna Grillo, Mary Mickus, JoAnn Santangelo, and Kelly Andersen cordially accepted research assistants into their classroom and implemented the program.

This project would not be complete without the technical assistance of Agency support staff who were often asked to respond quickly to last minute requests for research, typing, and copying: Kim Cotter, Marci Heroux, Mary Hughes, and Jessica Ramos.

The families enrolled in the Groton School Readiness Program, the Early Childhood Development Center, and the New London Day Nursery permitted classroom observations, welcomed the parent and family activities, and participated in the "Tips for Parents."

And, finally, this project was made possible by the patience of our families as we worked nights and weekends to meet deadlines.

On a personal note—to Commissioner Thomas Kirk, to Dianne Harrod, Director of Prevention Services, to Jean King, who thought of us, and for the efforts of Jessica Ramos, Jen Seager, and Jennifer Messina, the project's research assistants, who collected classroom data, tabulated data, and/or assisted in reviewing manuscript. Most of all we express our heartfelt thanks to Patricia F. Davidson and Donald M. Barr of the Bingham Trust for their willingness to support this project. We are pleased to be able to present a program that under real world circumstances works.

Contents

Chapter 1

What Do We Know about How Children Learn? The Social, Intellectual and Cognitive Development of Children
A Guide to the First Five Years

Margaret M. O'Shea

At birth, all of a baby's major organs are fully developed except one—the brain. Each time a baby uses one of the senses—seeing, tasting, touching, hearing, and smelling—a connection or path is made. When a baby has different kinds of experiences, and these experiences are repeated over and over again, the connections in the brain become stronger and stronger. These connections shape the way a child thinks, feels, behaves and learns (Dodge and Heroman, 1999).

The latest neurological findings are providing hard quantifiable evidence of the significance of the early years in the development of the brain. According to Simmons and Sheehan (1997, p. 1), "A child's potential is determined in the early years—from the first moments of life to the many hours spent in home or day care". A 1997 Conference on Early Childhood Development and Learning, hosted by President and Mrs. Clinton, emphasized new scientific research on brain development in very young children, and underscored how critical children's positive early experiences are to ensuring successful beginnings.

According to the Carnegie Corporation (1994), the following are five pivotal discoveries that should strengthen America's efforts to equip and prepare young children to start school ready to learn:

- Brain development that takes place prenatally, and in the first years of life, is more rapid and extensive than previously realized.
- Brain development is much more vulnerable to environmental influence than ever before suspected.
- The influence of early environment on brain development is long lasting.
- The environment affects not only the number of brain cells and the number of connections among them, but also the way these connections are "wired."
- New scientific evidence exists concerning the negative impact of early stress on brain function (Carnegie Corporation, 1994, p. 2).

When a child is born, the brain has 100 billion neurons, which in turn make over 50 trillion synapses (Begley, 1996). Afterwards, especially within the first three years of life, the brain undergoes a series of phenomenal changes. During this period, more connections among neurons are created. Over time those connections that are seldom or never used are eliminated (Nash, 1997). Researchers report that the eliminated connections are not predetermined as once thought. Rather, the manner in which a child is raised affects how the brain chooses to wire itself for life (Simmons & Sheehan, 1997).

Neurological research has shown that there are critical periods for brain development. Recognizing and taking advantage of the various windows of opportunity are paramount to young children's healthy development. A child's brain development suffers if the child is denied the opportunity to live in a stimulating environment (Nash, 1997). The research emphasizes the positive effects of hands-on parenting, which includes talking with and cuddling infants and toddlers, as well as providing them with stimulating experiences (Nash, 1997).

For centuries, parents have understood the newborn's basic need for safety, nourishment, warmth and nurturing. Now, research offers remarkable insights about human development from birth to age three, substantiating the view that parents and other adult caregivers are a vital component in the child's development (Carnegie Corporation, 1994).

Newberger (1997, p. 4), has observed that, "stimulated in part by growing concern about the overall well-being of children in America, the brain research findings affirm what many parents and caregivers have known for years: (a) good prenatal care, (b) warm and loving attachments between young children and adults and (c) positive, age-appropriate stimulation from the time of birth really do make a difference in children's development for a lifetime."

What is important to understand is that parents can make a difference in building their child's brain. "Parents are the child's first and most important teachers" (Nash, 1997, p. 54). When a child is talked to or read to, played with, sang to, touched and nourished the brain is being effected. Taking care of a baby's brain actually begins long before birth when the mother is pregnant. Good prenatal care has a significant effect on the development of a baby's brain.

Infancy

The sequence of brain development is genetically programmed, which is why infants the world over progress through the same general milestones. However, no two infants develop at exactly the same rate. Parents sometimes worry about whether their child is developing at a "normal" rate without realizing that the average ages given for developmental stages can vary as much as six months or more from one child to the next (DeBord, 1996).

While genes program the sequence of neural development, at every turn the quality of that development is shaped by environmental factors (Eliot, 1999 p. 9). The quality of early experience does shape children's brain development in critical ways. Genes and environment are both important, but the fact is that we can do little about our genes and a great deal about the kind of environment we provide for our children (Eliot, 1999 p. 9).

Infants learn about the world through touch, sight, sound, taste and smell. They learn about relationships through how people touch them and hold them, and from the tones of voice and facial expressions people use when caring for them. When babies have their needs met—being fed when hungry, comforted when crying, held and touched gently and kept warm and dry—they begin to trust the adults that care for them. This early sense of trust will help them develop positive relationships for the rest of their lives (Karen DeBord, 1996).

Infants thrive on touch and physical contact, particularly the first few months of life. In many cultures, mothers are almost constantly in contact with their babies, carrying them in slings or pouches by day and sleeping with them by night. The amount of touch, whether it is carrying, massaging, patting, cradling, or caressing is clearly important. But equally important is the emotional significance of that contact, and for most babies, fortunately, loving contact is the norm. Because touch has such ready access to young babies' brains, it offers a significant opportunity and one of the easiest, for molding their emotional and mental well being (Eliot, 1999 p. 144).

From the moment of birth, children love the sensation of motion. Whether it is rocking, jiggling, bouncing or just being carried around the house, babies find comfort in the feeling of repetitive motion and this vestibular stimulation is very beneficial for infants. Newborns often cry less when they are being rocked, carried, jiggled or suddenly changed in position, all actions that activate the vestibular system. Rocking, jiggling, and carrying is not only soothing to a baby but also good for the developing brain (Eliot, 1999 p. 156).

By using their senses to learn about the world, infants "talk" with others through actions and sounds such as cooing and babbling. This is the beginning of communication and language skills. There is a special kind of talk called parentese or motherese, which is a slower, higher-pitched and high-intonated way of speaking that caregivers tend to use when talking to infants and young children. This approach is well suited to stimulate babies sense of hearing because its unhurried cadence is easier for babies to follow. Its louder and more direct style helps babies distinguish it from background sounds and its simpler words and highly intonated structure make it easier for babies to distinguish individual parts of speech. Motherese is one of the most important forms of stimulation a young baby receives (Eliot, 1999 p. 248) because the brain is building the connections for language. It is hearing the sounds of words that wire the brain for language before meaning is connected to the words.

Infants will often cry or fuss which is also part of the learning process. Normal physical development requires that babies cry but the most common reason for a baby's cry is to express that something is needed. Being in tune with a baby's feelings means you show a baby that you know what he is expressing or feeling. When a parent or caregiver is in tune with a baby, they help build the connections in his brain that produce those feelings. Attunement on the part of parents or caregivers helps to wire a baby's brain for understanding feelings and for thinking. As parents respond to a baby's expressions and feelings, babies learn to soothe themselves and relax for sleep by moving about, searching for a finger or pacifier to suck on, or cuddle a blanket as they try to quiet themselves and relax for sleep.

Attachment to the parent or caregiver, which seems to occur around six to eight months, is regarded by many psychologists as the seminal event in a person's emotional development—the primary source of a child's security, self-esteem, self-control and social skills. Through this one intimate relationship, a baby learns how to identify their own feelings and how to read them in others. If the bond is a healthy one, the baby will feel loved and accepted and begin to learn the value of affection and empathy (Eliot, 1999 p. 305).

The Toddler Years

When children learn to walk, they are commonly called toddlers. Usually, this term is applied to one and two year-old children but this is a stage in the growth of a child and not a specific age. The toddler stage is very important and meaningful time in a child's life for it is the time between infancy and childhood when a child learns and grows in many ways.

While children have their own individual timetable, the toddler stage is the time when most children learn to walk, talk, solve simple problems, and relate to others. One major task for the toddler to learn is to be independent which is why toddlers often want to do things for themselves and often have their own ideas about how things should happen. Toddlers, bursting with energy and ideas, need to explore their environment and begin defining themselves as separate people.

Malley (1991) has prepared a series called the "Family Day Care Facts" series in which she has outlined the following general social, emotional and intellectual characteristics of toddlers:

One-Year-Olds

The social and emotional development of one-year-old children is characterized by a need to do things independently, and a view of themselves as the center of the world. They enjoy playing by themselves (solitary play) or beside other children (parallel play) and sometimes have difficulty sharing toys. As one-year-olds become increasingly self-aware, they may begin to express emotions such as jealousy, affection, pride and shame. They also may show increasing fears and often do not wish to be separated from the parents. Toddlers at this stage often have rapid mood shifts showing emotions that are often intense but short-lived.

The intellectual development of one-year-old children can be characterized by a sense of curiosity, an ability to point to objects they want, name familiar people or objects or to imitate animal sounds. Their language skills may enable them to combine two words to form a basic sentence, use the pronoun me and mine, and name body parts and familiar pictures. Their motor skills enable them to use many objects for their intended purpose and hold a pencil or crayon and scribble. They sometimes may begin to include a second person in their play. Generally they are very active and their attention span is short.

One-year-olds seem to enjoy rolling and simply catching large balls, playing with blocks, pushing and pulling favorite toys, filling containers over and over again, looking at themselves in mirrors and playing hide and seek. They also enjoy when parents have them listen to and move to music and allow them to ride wheeled toys without pedals. Parents of this stage child are advised to talk about the size, shape and texture of everyday objects, look at picture books with them and talk about the pictures and talk about cause/effect relationships such as "if you push this block, the whole pile of blocks will fall over."

Two-Year-Olds

The social and emotional development of two-year-olds is characterized by an ability to begin playing simple pretend games, with this fantasy play being very short and simple and often solitary in nature. They are usually surer of themselves than one-year-olds and are still generally very self-centered so sharing is still difficult. They enjoy playing near other children (parallel play) but still not playing actively with other children. Twos endearingly try to assert themselves by often saying "no" and sometimes doing the opposite of what is asked. They like to imitate the behavior of adults and others and often want to help with household tasks. Because they often refuse help, their plans are often not met and they become easily frustrated.

Intellectually, two-year-olds can follow simple directions; use three or more words in combination and express feeling, wishes and desires. They can also memorize short rhymes and enjoy joining in simple songs. While they still have a very limited attention span, they can now use objects to represent other objects and begin to think about doing something before doing it, which is known as executive brain function.

Two-year-olds enjoy playing pat-a-cake, pounding on toy or other workbenches, stacking blocks and other objects and taking things apart and putting them back together (such as pop beads). They also enjoy playing in a sandbox and measuring and pouring water and running, jumping, climbing and swinging outside. Parents of this stage child are advised to sing and act out songs with simple movements, teach them simple finger plays, tell them simple short stories and ask them to name things in the pictures of picture books. Two-year-olds enjoy playing matching games and using simple puzzles as well as art activities such as scribbling, painting with crayons, chalk or paint and using play dough and finger paint.

The opportunity to pretend by using dolls, housekeeping toys, dress-up clothes and toy telephones and household items is very consistent with the cognitive and intellectual needs of two-year-olds.

Preschoolers

Children from three to five years of age are often called preschoolers. During this time, children show improved motor skills and make great strides in language development. Preschool children also become more self-sufficient in caring for themselves and begin to show less attachment to their parents. They engage in more complex play activities, are very curious and want to explore the world outside their familiar surroundings.

The social and emotional development of preschoolers is characterized by an ability to spend more time with people outside their own families. They have a stronger need to be with and accepted by other children of similar ages, and sometimes become quite attached to their playmates. They are generally curious, imaginative and pleased with their own abilities to plan and complete projects, which are primarily carried out in imaginative play activities. They spend much time experimenting with adult roles that they have observed. They often show increased autonomy, although they still move back and forth between their need to be independent and their need to be cared for and helped (called dependence needs). Although the ability to delay gratification of their needs and wants has increased, they still can become easily frustrated, cannot tolerate waiting, and frequently cry when things do not go their way (much of the time exhibiting these behaviors when they are tired). Fear and anxiety can be common emotions during this period also with some preschoolers fearing the dark, unfamiliar animals, and potentially dangerous situation such as fire and deep water (Isenberg & Jalongo, 2001 p. 81).

Cognitively and intellectually, the thinking of preschoolers is often a combination of fantasy and reality and their understanding is based upon their own experiences. Young preschoolers (two and three year olds) usually focus on what they see in their own environments and upon present events. As they become more mature and have more experiences, preschoolers' thinking becomes more realistic. They often ask "why" questions which stem from their strong need to understand their world. This process of asking questions and finding out about things helps them learn. Children of this age enjoy setting up scenarios of stores, farms, villages, rescue workers, etc. and dressing up with play clothes to imitate people in their environment. They also can begin to play simple board games.

Preschoolers' vocabularies increase dramatically and they understand more words than they actually speak. Many preschoolers love to talk and they are curious about words, enjoying such activities as playing with words and rhymes and listening to stories being read frequently. Preschoolers love story time routines that are carried out each day and have special attachment to books that have rhyme and repetition. Children seem to love the predictability that comes from hearing the story, song or nursery rhyme over and over again. By repeating the same words and phrases the neural pathways that link sound and meaning are reinforced. Repetition can become a language game for children by using substitution (inserting different words) or expansion (inserting more words). Preschoolers also enjoy and benefit from the activity of completion or closure where an adult leaves a word off at the end of the sentence and the child fills it in. They also learn from environment print such as signs in the area or print on cereal boxes.

The Importance of Play

Becoming, as they say in the business lexicon, a "major player," is a critical learning task for young children. The developmental stage theories of Erik Erikson (1963) and Jean Piaget (1962), which are basic to early childhood education, emphasize the different tasks to be accomplished at each stage. As has been previously discussed, infancy and toddlerhood offer the opportunity to learn first to trust and then to separate from one's primary caregiver, and to gain sensory-motor knowledge through active exploration of one's own physical self and the physical world. Three to five year olds (pre-school stage) who have mastered these tasks move on to the exercise of initiative, making choices and learning to sustain their play, relationships, and oral language.

To become a master player is the height of achievement for children ages three to five. Master players are skilled at representing their experiences symbolically in self-initiated improvisational dramas. Sometimes alone, sometimes in collaboration with others, they play out their fantasies and feelings about the events of their daily lives. Through their pretend play, young children consolidate their understanding of the world, their language, and their social skills. Children at play are constructing their individual identities as well as their knowledge of the world.

Play, for young children, is active—the child does what he or she is thinking about, using body language as well as words. Such play is open-ended and builds skills in divergent thinking. Such play is also an intermediate stage in the development of complex sequences of which culminates in the child becoming a writer and reader. Children's play develops in a typical sequence, which parallels their physical, cognitive and social development. There are also sequential developmental stages of representation present, which are also often overlapping:

- *Body language* is the mode of representation used by infants.
- *Talk* is next starting with babbling and moving to language.
- *Play* begins as the exploration of the physical world.
- *Image-making* marks a stage in which children explore and then make representations using markers, crayons, etc. Scribbles are given names and move increasingly to recognizable approximations.
- *Writing* evolves when some scribbles are identified as words.
- *Reading* begins as sequence around book knowledge and repetition of remembered text.

The three major modern theoretical models of play are psychoanalytic, supporting emotional development; cognitive-developmental supporting cognitive development and sociocultural, focusing on social development.

Psychoanalytic theory views play as an important vehicle for emotional release (Freud, 1958) and for developing self-esteem as children gain master of their thoughts, bodies, objects, and social behaviors (Erikson, 1963). Play enables children to enact feelings, without pressure, by actively reliving experiences and mastering them in reality. It also provides the caregiver or teacher with clues to children's individual needs (Weber, 1984).

Cognitive theory examines play as a mirror of children's emerging mental abilities (Bruner, 1966; Piaget, 1962; Sutton-Smith, 1986). Piaget (1962) proposes that children individually create their own knowledge about the world through their interactions with people and materials. They practice using known information while consolidating new information skills, test new ideas against their experiences, and construct new knowledge about people, objects, and situations. Bruner (1966) and Sutton-Smith (1986) interpret play as flexible thinking and creative problem solving in action. Because children focus on the process of play they engage in multiple combinations of ideas and solution that they use to solve relevant life problems.

Socio-cultural theory (Vygotsky, 1967, 1978) emphasizes the centrality of the social and cultural contexts in development. Vygotsky (1978 p. 102) believes that pretend play is a leading factor in development and observes "in play a child behaves beyond his average, above his daily behavior; in play it is as though he were a head taller than himself." Because children first encounter knowledge in their social world that later shapes conceptual understanding, play acts as a mental support that enables children to think through and solve problems in new ways. This "zone of proximal development" (Vygotsky, 1978) provides children with the freedom to negotiate reality and do things in play that are often usable to do on their own outside the play setting.

Developmentally appropriate environments for young children have play as the center of the focus. Such play is symbolic, meaningful, active, rule-governed, episodic, pleasurable and intrinsically motivating. Individual choice during extended time periods for play, while physically using available materials, is optimal. The environments should be rich in props for dramatic play, tools for image making and print and many opportunities to be the member of a group. Research indicates that children who engage in pretend and socio-dramatic play increase their literacy skills; cognitive development, particularly problem solving; social competence; and capacity to generate new connections in a creative way (Fromberg, & Bergen, 1998).

As evidenced in this chapter, a child's activities and physical environment are a part of the route to early enrichment but the quality of the interactions between parents and other caregivers are also very important. Parents who are nurturing (physically affectionate, emotionally supportive), involved (consistently spending time in shared activities), responsive (accept their child's individuality) but also demanding (expect appropriate behavior and set clear standards and rules and see that they are followed) seem to foster behaviors that lead to children's academic and intellectual success (Eliot, 1999 p. 451). While it may be difficult to arrive at the "right" balance of these four indicators, researchers agree that some of the "Flynn effect"—the steady IQ rise during this century—is due to improvements in the typical environment and caretaking of young children (Eliot, (1999) p. 455). The Flynn effect is mainly an increase in scores on non-verbal IQ measures and occurs worldwide in all socio-economic groups. Some researchers have attributed this effect to more intellectual flexibility and factual knowledge, better nutrition, and more sensory stimulation. More parents are exposed to information about child development, women are more educated now than at any time in history, and fathers are often more actively involved in child rearing than ever before. While these facts show improvements for many children, the challenge for parents, caregivers, teachers and society in general is to insure that these factors are in place for more children. All of our children deserve the very best families and society can offer.

References

Begley, S., (1996, February 19). Your child's brain. *Newsweek*, 127 (8) 55–61.
Bruner, J.S. (1966). What have we learned about early learning? *European Education Research Journal*, 4(1), 5–16.
Carnegie Corporation. (1994). Starting points: Meeting the needs of our youngest children. [on-line] Available: *http://www.carnegie.org/*

DeBord, K. (1996). *Growing together: Infant development*. Raleigh, NC: North Carolina Cooperative Extension Service.

Dodge, D. & Heroman, C. (1999). Building your baby's brain: A parent's guide to the first five years. Teaching Strategies, Washington, D.C.

Eliot, L. (1999). What's going on in there? How the brain and mind develop the first five years of life. Bantom Books, New York.

Erikson, E.H. (1963). Childhood and society. New York: Norton.

Freud, S. (1958). On creativity and the unconscious. (IF Grant Doff. Trans.) New York: Harper & Row (Original work published in 1928).

Fromberg, D.P. & Bergen, D.M. (Eds.) (1998). Play from birth to twelve: Contexts, perspectives, and meanings. New York: Garland.

Isenberg, J. P. & Jalongo, M.R.(2001) Third Edition. Creative expression and play in early childhood. Merrill, Prentice Hall, Saddle River, New Jersey.

Malley, C. (1991). Toddler development. (Family Day Care Facts series). Amherst, MA: University of Massachusetts.

Nash, J.M. (1997, February 3). Fertile minds. Time, 149(5) 48–56.

Newberger, J. (1997). New brain development research—A wonderful window of opportunity to build public support for early childhood education. Young Children, 52(4) 4–9.

Piaget, J. (1962). Play, dreams and imitation in childhood. New York: Norton.

Simmons, T. & Sheehan, R. (1997, February, 16). Brain research manifests importance of first years. The news and observer [on-line]. Available: http://www.nando.net/nao/2little2late/storiesday1-main.html

Sutton-Smith, B. (1986). The spirit of play. In G. Fein & M. Rivkin (Eds.), The young child at play: Reviews of Research, (Vol. 4, pp. 3–16). Washington, D.C. National Association for the Education of Young Children.

Vygotsky, L.S. (1967). Play and its role in the mental development of the child. Soviet Psychology, 12, 62–76.

Vygotsky, L.S. (1978). Mind in society. The development of higher psychological processes. Boston: Harvard University Press.

Weber, E. (1984). Ideas influencing early childhood education: A theoretical analysis. New York: Teachers College Press.

Chapter 2

Social-Emotional Learning in Early Childhood

What We Know and Where to Go from Here

Susanne A. Denham and Roger P. Weissberg

Four-year-olds Darrell and Jamila are pretending to be Bob the Builder®. They have play hammers and screwdrivers and tool belts and shovels, even a ride-on bulldozer. They are having fun! Darrell moves the bulldozer to the spot that Jamila is pointing to—they are ready to dig the big hole!! But then things get complicated, changing fast and furiously, as interaction often does. Jamila suddenly decides that he should be the bulldozer driver, and tries to pull Darrell off its seat. At the same time, Jimmy, who had been nearby, runs over and whines that he wants to join in. No way!! Darrell, almost falling off the bulldozer, doesn't want Jimmy to join them—he's too much of a baby. Almost simultaneously, Jamila steps on a plastic "bolt," falls down, and starts to cry. And Tomas, the class bully, approaches, laughing at four-year-olds making believe and crying.

Much more than simple playtime was going on here. Imagine the skills of social-emotional learning (SEL) that are needed to successfully negotiate these interactions! For example, Darrell has to know how to resolve the conflict over the bulldozer, react to Jimmy without hurting his feelings too much, and "handle" Tomas safely. More generally, Darrell needs to learn how to communicate well with others (especially to express his emotions in socially appropriate ways), handle provocation, engage with others positively and build relationships. Taken together, these abilities are vital for how Darrell gets along with others, understands himself, and feels good in his world, both within himself and with other people.

Thus, there are important aspects of SEL required as preschoolers attend to important developmental tasks—in this case, learning to interact with agemates. If successful in dealing with Jamila, Jimmy, and Tomas, Darrell shows many indicators of such developmentally appropriate SEL— he is beginning to demonstrate (1) self-awareness; (2) self-management; (3) social awareness; (4) responsible decision making; and (5) relationship management (Collaborative for Academic, Social, and Emotional Learning, 2002; Payton et al., 2000).

At the same time, there are also important adults in Darrell's life who contribute to his SEL. Will he remember what his father told him about being nice to other kids when Jimmy approaches? Will he see his teacher as a resource when confronted by Tomas, who can be a little scary? If things get very tense with any of the other boys, will Darrell's teacher realize that s/he needs to "have a chat" about the feelings and actions of each? That is, does Darrell have adults—his parents and preschool teacher or childcare providers—who can provide a scaffold for his developing SEL?

We are committed to the promotion of SEL skills like the ones Darrell can demonstrate at such a young age, and we see this promotion as focused on both the children in question and the important adults in their lives. In this chapter, we first define our developmental perspective. Then we describe the developmentally appropriate manifestations of SEL during the preschool period. Next, we review current evidence on how caring adults can foster these SEL skills.

Alongside the specific SEL skills that young children can acquire, and the particular ways in which adults can promote this acquisition, are other aspects of the child and his/her environment, which can either promote or make difficult the acquisition of SEL skills. Thus, we subsequently detail important moderators of preschool SEL—processes of risk and resilience. Finally, following directly from our consideration of these issues, we address how early childhood caregivers can intervene in an organized, systematic way to enhance SEL competencies, prevent SEL deficits, and intervene when SEL deficits already exist.

Developmental Perspective on Social and Emotional Learning

All strategies of programming or intervention can be derived from normative theories of child development (Shonkoff & Phillips, 2000). Given this bedrock, we view development through an organizational, bioecological lens, in which different developmental tasks are central to each age level (Waters & Sroufe, 1983; Weissberg & Greenberg, 1998). Transitions from one developmental period to another are marked by reorganization around new tasks, but are also based on the accomplishments of the earlier period. Successful mastery of developmental tasks is supported not only by within-child abilities, processes and biological predispositions, but also by the immediate environment of the child (e.g., interactions of the child with his/her parents or with his/her teacher); transactions between elements of the child's immediate environment (e.g., parent-teacher communication about the child); elements outside the child's immediate environment that nevertheless have an impact on it (e.g., demands on parent's time and energy, even depression and other forms of parent psychopathology); and the broader social/political context of the child's world (e.g., welfare policy). Thus, any programs with the goal of promoting young children's SEL must take into account these levels of influence.

Within this organizational perspective, children's emotions, cognition, and behavior are coordinated in ever more complex ways as they mature (Greenberg, Domitrovich, & Bumbarger, 1999, 2001). Given the nature of brain development, affective development generally precedes cognition and behavior; children experience emotions and react on an emotional level long before they can verbalize their experiences or discern ways to cope (Greenberg & Snell, 1997). An important task of early childhood, then, is to move from primarily lower brain control (where arousal and desire *equal* behavior), to the coordination and self-regulation of emotion, cognition, and behavior via cortical capacities. Such capacities include maintenance of attention, social problem-solving skills, frustration tolerance, and management of affect, all of which are critical to academic, social, and personal outcomes. Language plays a central role as a mediator and tool for establishing cortical control over lower order behavioral and emotional processes (Berk & Winsler, 1995; Nelson, 1996). Thus, it is not merely a truism that the "whole child" is important. SEL is bolstered by each child's cognitive and behavioral skills, and in turn academic success and learning are supported by SEL.

However, as already suggested, these developmental milestones do not unfold automatically; on the contrary, they are heavily influenced, even at the neuronal level, by environmental inputs throughout early childhood (Greenberg et al., 1999; Greenberg & Snell, 1997; Shore, 1997). That is, there are environmental conditions that nurture and reward the application of these skills of SEL. So, SEL programming can directly affect children, but surely also affects them indirectly, via effects on their caregiving environment. The physical and social environments, as well as relationships with primary caregivers, assume pivotal roles in our thinking about SEL programming. Accordingly, our dual focus in this chapter will be on specific SEL skills that preschoolers can acquire, but also on direct SEL-promoting strategies that can be used by adults in their environment.

At the same time, many other factors within the child, family, classroom, and community may moderate the success of any programming. It is the rule rather than the exception, it seems, that child outcomes are a function of interactions between intended programming and these other factors. We will also consider these processes as they affect child- and adult-targeted SEL programming.

Developmentally Appropriate Manifestations of Social and Emotional Learning

In the case of preschoolers, SEL skills are organized around the developmental tasks of positive engagement and managing emotional arousal within social interaction, while successfully moving into the world of peers (Howes, 1987; Parker & Gottman, 1989). These tasks are not easy ones for children just entering the peer arena. Nonetheless, successful interaction with agemates is a crucial predictor of later mental health and well-being, even learning and academic success—beginning during preschool, and continuing during the gradeschool years when peer reputations solidify, and thereafter (Denham & Holt, 1993; Parker & Asher, 1987; Robins & Rutter, 1990).

New empirical research buttresses this view of SEL's importance, for school readiness in particular (Carlton & Winsler, 1999). A number of researchers have shown that children who enter kindergarten with positive SEL profiles also develop positive attitudes about school, successfully adjust to the new experiences there, and demonstrate good grades and achievement (Birch & Ladd, 1997; Ladd, Birch, & Buhs, 1999; Ladd, Kochenderfer, & Coleman, 1996). More specifically, a wide range of varied SEL indicators, including positive interactions with teachers, positive representations of self derived from attachment relationships, emotion knowledge, emotion regulatory abilities, relationship skills, and nonrejected peer status, uniquely predicts academic success (even when other pertinent variables, including earlier academic success, are taken into account; see Carlton, 2000; Howes & Smith, 1995; Izard, Fine, Schultz, Mostow, Ackerman, & Youngstrom, 2001; Jacobsen & Hofmann, 1997; O'Neil, Welsh, Parke, Wang, & Strand, 1997; Pianta, 1997; Pianta, Steinberg, & Rollins, 1995; Shields, Dickstein, Seifer, Guisti, Magee, & Spritz, 2001). We now describe these crucial preschool SEL skills in fuller detail.

Skills of Social and Emotional Learning

EMOTIONAL EXPRESSIVENESS. Self-awareness and emotional expressiveness, especially the recognition and sending of affective messages, are central to SEL. Emotions must be expressed in keeping with one's goals, in accordance with the social context; the goals of self and of others must be coordinated. That is, the self-awareness component of SEL includes experiencing and expressing emotions in a way that is advantageous to moment-to-moment interaction, and to relationships over time. For example, Darrell is well liked, in part, because of his pleasant, happy demeanor.

What, specifically, does the expression of emotions "do for" a child and his/her social group? Most importantly, the experience and expression of emotion signal whether the child or other people need to modify or continue their goal-directed behavior (see Campos, Mumme, Kermoian, & Campos, 1994). Hence, such information can shape the child's own behaviors. An example is happiness—if one boy experiences happiness while playing in the 'block corner' with another, he may seek out the other child during another activity, and even ask his mother if the other child can come to their house to play. The experience of joy gives him important information that affects his subsequent behavior. Additionally, emotions are important because they provide social information to other people, and affect others' behaviors. Peers benefit from witnessing other children's expressions of emotion. When a girl's friends witness the social signal of her anger, for example, they know from experience whether their most profitable response would be to fight back or to retreat.

Thus, preschoolers are learning to use emotional communication to express nonverbal messages about a social situation or relationship—for example, giving a hug. They also develop empathic involvement in others' emotions—for example, kissing a baby sister when she falls down and bangs her knee. Further, they display complex social and self-conscious emotions, such as guilt, pride, shame, and contempt in appropriate contexts. Finally, young children are beginning to realize that a person may feel a certain way "on the inside" but show a different demeanor. In particular, they are learning that the overt expression of socially disapproved feelings may be controlled, while more socially appropriate emotions are expressed—for example, one might feel afraid of an adult visitor, but show no emotion or even a slight smile.

Accumulating evidence suggests that these SEL components contribute to overall success in interacting with one's peers. For example, *positive* affect is important in the initiation and regulation of social exchanges; sharing positive affect may facilitate the formation of friendships, and render one more likable (Denham, McKinley, Couchoud, & Holt, 1990; Park, Lay, & Ramsay, 1993; Sroufe, Schork, Motti, Lawroski, & LaFreniere, 1984). Conversely, *negative* affect, especially anger, can be quite problematic in social interaction (Denham et al., 1990; Lemerise & Dodge, 2000; Rubin & Clark, 1983; Rubin & Daniels-Byrness, 1983). Children who are able to balance their positive and negative emotions: (a) are rated higher by teachers on friendliness and assertiveness, and lower on aggressiveness and sadness; (b) respond more prosocially to peers' emotions; and (c) are seen as more likable by their peers (Denham, 1986; Denham et al., 1990; Denham, Renwick, & Holt, 1991; Eisenberg, Fabes, Murphy, et al., 1995, 1996; Sroufe et al., 1984; Strayer, 1980).

In sum, it is easy to envision why children's patterns of self-awareness and emotional expressiveness provide such potent intrapersonal support for, or roadblocks to, interacting with agemates (Campos & Barrett, 1984). A sad or angry child, sitting on the sidelines of a group, with nothing pleasing her, is less able to see, let alone tend to, the emotional needs of others. It is no wonder when her peers flatly assert, "She hits. She bites. She kicked me this morning. I *don't like* her." Conversely, a happier preschooler is one who can better afford to respond positively to others.

SELF-MANAGEMENT.   Negative *or* positive emotions can need regulating, when they threaten to overwhelm or need to be amplified. Thus, children learn to retain or enhance those emotions that are relevant and helpful, to attenuate those that are relevant but not helpful, to dampen those that are irrelevant; these skills help them to experience more well-being and maintain satisfying relationships with others. For example, Darrell may know that showing too *much* anger with Jimmy will hurt this boy's feelings, but showing too *little* angry bravado with Tomas could make him more of a target.

Early in the preschool period, much of this self-management is biobehavioral (e.g., thumbsucking), and often supported by adults; for example, even though very upset when a younger playmate grabs all the toys, one can use the caregiver's assistance instead of immediately resorting to aggression. As well, because of increased cognitive ability and control of both their attention and their emotionality (Lewis, Stanger, & Sullivan, 1989; Lewis, Sullivan, & Vasen, 1987), children become more independent in their regulation of emotion during the preschool period.

Beginning to attend preschool or childcare is a particularly important transition that taxes young children's emotion regulatory skills. Preschoolers' attention is riveted on success with their friends in this context. Unlike adults, however, these newly important peers are neither skilled at negotiation, nor able to offer assistance in emotion regulation. At the same time, the social cost of emotional dysregulation is high with both teachers and peers. Because play with peers is replete with conflict, this developmental focus demands emotion regulation; initiating, maintaining, and negotiating play, and earning acceptance, all require preschoolers to "keep the lid on" (Raver, Blackburn, & Bancroft, 1999). Thus, because of the increasing complexity of young children's emotionality and the demands of their social world—with "so much going on" emotionally—some organized emotional gatekeeper must be cultivated.

Perhaps because of these converging pressures, preschoolers gradually begin to use specific coping strategies for self-regulation—problem solving, support seeking, distancing, internalizing, externalizing, distraction, reframing or redefining the problem, cognitive "blunting," and denial. Maternal and teacher reports of constructive modes of such emotion regulatory coping are associated with success with peers (Eisenberg, Fabes, Murphy, et al., 1995).

JOINT CONTRIBUTIONS OF SELF-AWARENESS, SELF-MANAGEMENT, AND EMOTIONAL EXPRESSIVENESS.   Emotion regulation and expressiveness often operate in concert. Children with specific SEL deficits—those who experience intense negative emotions, and are unable to identify or regulate their expressions of such emotion—are especially likely to suffer difficulties in social relationships (Contreras, Kerns, Weimer, Gentzler, & Tomich, 2000). In contrast, however, even children who are high in negative emotionality are buffered from peer status problems by good emotion regulation skills, which parents and caregivers can teach them (see emotion socialization section below; Eisenberg, Fabes, Guthrie, et al., 1996; Eisenberg, Fabes, Murphy, et al., 1995, 1996; Eisenberg, Fabes, Shepard, et al., 1997; Murphy, Eisenberg, Fabes, Shepard, & Guthrie, 1999).

SOCIAL AWARENESS.   Key aspects of the social awareness component of SEL are emotion knowledge, the recognition and identification of feelings in others. Young children who understand emotions better have more positive peer relations (Denham et al., 1990). For example, the youngster who understands emotions of others should interact more successfully when a friend gets angry with him or her, and the preschooler who can talk about his or her own emotions also is better able to negotiate disputes with friends. Darrell knows that it can be helpful to tell Jamila, "Hey, I had the bulldozer first. Don't be so mean and make me mad."

More specifically, emotion knowledge yields information about emotional expressions and experience in self and others, as well as about events in the environment. From 2 years of age on, young children are interested in emotions. In spontaneous conversations they talk about and reflect upon their own and others' feelings and discuss causes and consequences of their own and others' emotional experiences and expressiveness (Dunn, 1994).

By preschool, most children can infer basic emotions from expressions or situations (Denham, 1986). They tend to have a better understanding of happy situations compared to those that evoke negative emotions

(Fabes, Eisenberg, Nyman, & Michealieu, 1991). Throughout the rest of the preschool period, children come to understand many aspects of the expression and situational elicitation of basic emotions. They gradually come to differentiate among the negative emotions of self and other—for example, realizing that one feels more sad than angry, when receiving "time out" from one's preschool teacher. They also become increasingly capable of using emotion language (Fabes, Eisenberg, McCormick, & Wilson, 1988)—for example, reminiscing about family sadness when a pet died. Furthermore, young children begin to identify other peoples' emotions even when they may differ from their own—for example, knowing that Father's smile as he comes into the house means his workday was satisfactory, and he probably won't yell tonight. Toward the end of this developmental period, they begin to comprehend complex dimensions of emotional experiences, such as the possibility of simultaneous emotions (Denham, 1998).

Although there are developmental progressions in the various aspects of emotion knowledge, with knowledge of expressions and situations preceding other sorts of understanding, there also are marked individual differences in these developments (Dunn, 1994). Children who understand emotions are more prosocially responsive to their peers, and rated as more socially skilled by teachers, and more likable by their peers (Denham, 1986; Denham & Couchoud, 1991; Denham et al., 1990; Strayer, 1980). For example, if a preschooler sees one peer bickering with another, and correctly deduces that the peer suddenly experiences sadness or fear, rather than intensified anger, she may comfort her friend rather than retreat or enter the fray. Interactions with such an emotionally knowledgeable agemate would likely be viewed as satisfying, rendering one more likable. Similarly, teachers are likely to be attuned to the behavioral evidence of such emotion knowledge—the use of emotion language, the sympathetic reaction—and to evaluate it positively. Emotion knowledge allows a preschooler to react appropriately to others, thus bolstering social relationships.

Recent research by Izard and colleagues (e.g., Izard et al., 2001; Schultz, Izard, Ackerman, & Youngstrom, 2001) corroborates these suggestions. In their study of low-income preschoolers, lack of emotion knowledge predicted both contemporaneous and later teacher reports of overall social functioning (see also Smith, 2001, for similar results predicting peer acceptance). In particular, misattributing anger when other emotions were more correct was related to peer rejection and boys' aggression (Schultz, Izard, & Ackerman, 2000).

RESPONSIBLE DECISION MAKING.   Because thinking and emotion work together in our lives, it is important to address each child's skills in *thinking* about interpersonal interactions, going beyond his or her emotional experience, knowledge, regulation, and expression. Responsible decision making assumes importance as the everyday social interactions of preschoolers increase in frequency and complexity. Young children must learn to analyze social situations, set social goals, and determine effective ways to solve differences that arise between them and their peers. When there is a disagreement or a problem, what can be done (*generation of alternative solutions*)? How do I make a successful solution happen (*means-end thinking*)? How will I know if it works; what solution will work best (*consequential thinking*) (Shure, 1990)? Even preschoolers can begin to learn these important thinking skills, which support their increasingly complex social interaction. Each person involved in interactions that somehow go "wrong"— the actor, the victim, the bystander(s), and the adult caregiver—needs to *understand* how to make interactions go more smoothly for everyone concerned.

Recently the social information processing theory that forms a foundation for training in responsible decision making (Crick & Dodge, 1994)— encoding information about the problem from the social surround, interpreting it, forming goals, selecting and enacting the most favorable response—has expanded to include emotional information and content at every step (Lemerise & Arsenio, 2000). This union of social information processing and emotions illustrates well our thinking about SEL during the preschool period: Children are constantly attempting to understand their own and others' behavior, and emotions play a role in this understanding, conveying crucial interpersonal information that can guide interaction (Dodge, Laird, Lochman, Zelli, & Conduct Problems Research Group, 2002).

Pertinent here, in the *encoding and interpreting* steps, the child takes in the important information of the other's behavior, emotions, intentions, and the likely effect of the others' behavior, as well as his/her own arousal level, the intensity of the emotions felt, and his/her relationship with the other. Darrell sees, accurately, that Jamila is annoyed about who is currently in charge of the bulldozer, that Jimmy is a little scared about asking to play, and that Tomas is looking for a chance to act angry and mean—on purpose.

In the next step, *clarification of goals*, the child formulates goals, which are themselves focused arousal states that function to motivate him or her to produce outcomes. When a child cannot regulate her emotion, she may focus on external goals, such as revenge, or may retreat into passivity, neither of which promotes successful interaction. A child who more successfully regulates emotions is more able to focus on relationship-enhancing goals. Darrell *could* act really mad with Jamila, but he will temper this because they are buddies who play together all the time, and he wants this to continue. He really doesn't want to play with babyish Jimmy, but knows that *sometimes* Jimmy is okay, so won't "come down on him too hard." Finally, he knows that he has to act a bit *macho*-hostile with Tomas, but not too much, or he may regret it.

The child's perception of the other's emotions may also affect goals chosen—for example, a child who showed intense glee at a playmate's distress could render the playmate's revenge or withdrawal more likely. If Tomas acts mean even though Darrell sticks up for himself, Darrell may switch goals and decide that he wants to act really mean back, even to fight.

In the last step, *response generation, evaluation, and decision*, access to and choice of actual behavioral choices differ depending on the child's goals. Self-awareness, self-management, social awareness, and responsible decision making complement one another here: A preschooler who can become emotionally regulated after being pushed, for example, feels better but still might not be able to choose how to act, without responsible decision-making skills; if the child is mired in under-regulated anger and hurt, pre-emptive cognitive processing may take place, rather than the effortful processing needed to choose a behavioral response based on SEL. Conversely, a preschooler who usually has good ideas to solve problems may not have them available while extremely emotionally aroused by being pushed.

If Darrell, who seems rather aware of his own emotional processes, can remain calm enough—perhaps via emotion regulatory strategies listed earlier, such as problem-focused regulation or support seeking—he may choose a response that can further his relationships. For example, even though scared of Tomas, Darrell may say something to defuse the bully's nastiness (and help regulate his own emotions by "fixing" the problem), such as, "Quit laughing, Tomas. Do you want to play or not?" Alternatively, he may seek out his teacher to assist in sorting out the difficulties.

RELATIONSHIP MANAGEMENT. Other relationship skills represent the final component of SEL. These include, for example, making positive overtures to play with others, initiating and maintaining conversations, active listening, cooperating, sharing, taking turns, negotiating, and saying "no" or seeking help when necessary. Extrapolating from our opening story, Darrell may use many such specific skills in the service of getting along with his playmates. He figures out a way to cooperate with Jamila, tries to negotiate some sort of mutually satisfactory solution with Jimmy, and seeks help in dealing with Tomas. Important, distinct abilities such as these enhance the more general strategies of self- and other-awareness, self-management, and responsible decision making.

Fostering Social-Emotional Learning: What Adults Can Do

Thus, young children show SEL strengths (and, sometimes, weaknesses) in self-awareness and self-management, social-awareness, responsible decision making, and other behaviorally specific relationship skills. Promotion of these SEL skills is central to any programming, be it universal prevention programming, targeted intervention, or special services. Much of the variation in these aspects of the SEL skills accrued by individual children derives from experiences within the family and preschool classroom (Denham, 1998; Hyson, 1994). Important adults in each child's life have crucial roles in the development of SEL. So, how do we foster SEL that stands children in such good stead as they move into their school years? We now present these roles in detail.

Attachment to Caring Adults

These tasks of SEL are achieved most readily when young children have caring adults to whom they can turn (i.e., one or more secure attachment relationships). During the first years of life, consistently sensitive caregiving performs a number of important functions—including distress relief, and sharing positive affect. Young children who do not know whether "their special person" will give them these things lack both a secure base for exploration and a secure haven from difficulty and danger. Over time, experiences with caregivers provide the actively social cognizing infant and toddler with fodder to build an "internal working model" of social relationships—"Am I worthy of care?" "Am I important enough to share good times with?" "Is the world a safe place?" "Are people predictable, responsive, and readable?"

Emotional security and its attendant working models form a foundation for SEL (e.g., Laible & Thompson, 1998; Sroufe et al., 1984). In contrast, emotional insecurity can render a child less willing and able to learn about emotions, and more apt to be "flooded" by aversive emotions. Not only do secure relationships with adults predict concurrent SEL, but they also predict later ability to relate to peers (Howes, 2000). In any SEL classroom-based programming, building secure relationships between teacher and child is a key foundation (Pianta, 1997; Pianta & Walsh, 1998). Naturally, promotion of secure parent-child attachment relationships can also be a goal of SEL programming.

Adult caregivers can use their knowledge of attachment in their teaching and interaction with children, by purposefully fostering strong positive relationships with children, and by really *knowing* each child. Knowing each child includes observing her/him to detect patterns of strengths and weaknesses that can be supported by adults, and promptly attending to individual needs. A perceptive preschool teacher, for example, would know that Jimmy was often on the sidelines of peer play, as he was with Darrell and Jamila. This teacher could make efforts to give Jimmy more one-on-one time to enhance his security when in her presence.

Positive Guidance

Preschoolers are learning what it means to be part of a group for the very first time. Along with secure attachment relationships, young children need guidance from adults with regard to the rules for behavior in dyadic and group situations. They need to learn the life skills necessary to function alone or interact responsibly with others, caring for their own and others' needs.

Hence, young children learn SEL skills best when they have clear rules and limits set for them by the important adults in their lives, when they receive both indirect and direct guidance from them. Indirect guidance focuses on making the children's environment conducive to positive emotion and behavior (Gartrell, 2003; Greenberg, 1992). In using these techniques, adult caregivers take a proactive stance to maximize not only the smooth workings of each day, but also the children's development in all domains.

But direct guidance of specific children's behaviors is necessary, too. The indirect guidance techniques that fit well for all children need to be supplemented by direct guidance techniques tailored to the behaviors and needs of, and one's relationship with, a specific child. Such direct guidance typically emphasized for parent and early childhood programs includes abundant supervision that flexibly utilizes specific techniques (Bergin & Bergin, 1999; Cataldo, 1987; Greenberg, 1992).

Current theorizing and empirical findings converge on three socialization techniques that promote young children's SEL: socializers' emphasis on teaching about emotions and behaviors, modeling positive emotional expression and behaviors, and accepting and helpful reactions to children's emotions and behaviors (Denham, Grant, & Hamada, 2002; Eisenberg, Cumberland, & Spinrad, 1998; Gottman, Katz, & Hooven, 1997; Tomkins, 1991).

TEACHING ABOUT EMOTIONS AND BEHAVIOR. Teachers' and parents' tendencies to discuss children's feelings, thoughts, and behaviors, if nested within a warm relationship, assist the child in acquiring SEL competencies. The central aspect of this teaching is providing reasons or *inductive* explanations for events in the child's life, including correction of their mistaken behaviors. Highly inductive guidance strategies coach children to perceive the social consequences of their digressions (e.g., "Johnny will not want to play with you again if you keep taking away his toys") and to empathize or consider another's viewpoint (e.g., "That hurt Toby's feelings—look, he feels sad"). Low inductive strategies, in contrast, assert power over the child without any explanations related to the social environment (e.g., "Give that toy back now, or else").

More specifically, adults who are aware of emotions and talk about them in a differentiated manner (e.g., clarifying, explaining, pointing out responsibility for others' feelings when necessary, but not "preaching") assist children in self-management, as well as in formulating other-awareness (Denham & Auerbach, 1995; Denham & Grout, 1992; Denham, Renwick-DeBardi, & Hewes, 1994; Dunn, Brown, Slomkowski, Tesla, & Youngblade, 1991; Eisenberg et al., 1998; Gottman et al., 1997; Zahn-Waxler, Radke-Yarrow, & King, 1979). When adults discuss and explain their own and others' emotions, young children also are more capable of empathic involvement with peers (Denham, Zoller, & Couchoud, 1994). The same general trend also holds true for low-income, minority children (Garner, Jones, Gaddy, & Rennie, 1997).

MODELING APPROPRIATE BEHAVIORS AND EMOTIONS. Children constantly observe the behaviors of adults, and incorporate this learning into their social behavior, often via affective contagion in the case of emotions. Through their emotional expressiveness, adults also teach children what emotions are acceptable in which contexts. Their emotional displays tell children about the emotional significance of differing events, behaviors that may accompany differing emotions, and others' likely reactions. Thus, adults' emotional expressiveness is associated with children's understanding of emotions as well as their expressive patterns (e.g., Denham & Grout, 1993; Denham, Mitchell-Copeland, Strandberg, Auerbach, & Blair, 1997; Denham, Zoller, et al., 1994).

A mostly positive emotional climate makes emotions more accessible to children. Thus, when children have experience with clear but not overpowering parental emotions, they also may have more experience with empathic involvement with others' emotions (Denham & Grout, 1992, 1993; Denham, Renwick, & Holt, 1991; Denham, Renwick-DeBardi et al., 1994; see also Parke, Cassidy, Burks, Carson, & Boyum, 1992). As well, low-income preschoolers' emotion regulation is facilitated by mothers' appropriate expressiveness (Garner & Spears, 2000). However, several factors suggest potential negative contributions of adults' expressiveness. Though well-modulated negative emotional expression can contribute to children's understanding of emotion (Garner, Jones, & Miner, 1994), frequent and intense negative emotions may disturb children, making SEL more problematic (Denham, 1998). For example, children whose mothers self-report more frequent anger and tension also are less prosocial, and less well liked than children of more positive mothers. Further, adults whose expressiveness is generally limited impart little information about emotions. Finally, positive parental interaction has been found to relate to young children's sociometric status (Cohn, Patterson, & Christopoulos, 1991; Putallaz, 1987); presumably, parents who are emotionally and behaviorally positive are modeled by their young children, who then become preferred playmates.

CONTINGENT REACTIONS TO CHILDREN'S EMOTIONS AND BEHAVIOR. Adults' contingent reactions to children's behaviors and emotional displays are also linked to children's SEL. Contingent reactions include behavioral and emotional encouragement or discouragement of specific behaviors and emotions (Tomkins, 1991). More specifically, adults who dismiss emotions may punish children for showing emotions, or ignore the child's emotions in an effort to "make it better" (Denham, Renwick-DeBardi, et al., 1994; Denham, Zoller, et al., 1994). In emotion-evoking contexts, children who experience such adult reactions have more to be upset about—not only their emotion's elicitor, but also the adults' reactions (Eisenberg et al., 1998; Eisenberg, Fabes, Shepard, et al., 1999).

Positive reactions, such as tolerance or comforting, convey a very different message—that emotions are manageable, even useful (Gottman et al., 1997). Good emotion coaches accept children's experiences of emotion and their expressions of emotions that do not harm others; they empathize with and validate emotions. Emotional moments are seen as opportunities for intimacy (Eisenberg & Fabes, 1994; Eisenberg, Fabes, Murphy, et al., 1996; Eisenberg, Fabes, Shepard, et al., 1999; Gottman et al., 1997).

As well, adults who best promote SEL may use other guidance techniques in response to children's behaviors and emotions, such as (a) distracting the child and assisting her/him in choosing substitute behaviors, rather than asserting power; (b) ignoring inappropriate attention-getting behavior when there is no threat of harm to the child, other people, or inanimate objects; and (c) telling the child what *to* do (rather than what *not* to do)—persistently persuading the child toward compliance (Bergin & Bergin, 1999).

These various optimal responses assist children in integrating emotions, cognitions, and behavior—that is, their application of SEL skills in everyday situations (Denham & Grout, 1993; Zahn-Waxler et al., 1979). For example, when mothers show certain benevolent patterns of reactions to children's negative emotions, children are friendlier, showing less egoistic distress and more sympathetic concern to the distress of others. They have warm, empathic, nurturant templates to follow in responding to others' distress (Barnett, King, Howard, & Dino, 1980; Denham, 1993; Denham & Grout, 1993).

THE SPECIAL ROLE OF LANGUAGE.   Many of these direct techniques take advantage of the preschooler's new sophistication in language. Adults can *talk* to use direct guidance techniques to solve many difficult behavioral episodes with children. They can enunciate clear, simple, essential rules. Before any difficult behaviors occur, adults can state expectations clearly. When an "incident" does arise, language that promotes responsible decision making can be used within direct guidance. For example, if Tomas walked up and destroyed the block constructions that Darrell and Jamila had been making, and even savvy Darrell "lost it," the astute preschool teacher could engage the boys in a dialogue about everybody's feelings, their goals for the interaction, and the behavioral choices that they made. Teacher support in such conversations could make possible more sophisticated SEL processes than the children would be capable of alone.

SUMMARY: HOW ADULTS SOCIALIZE SEL SKILLS.   Thus, there is a growing body of knowledge regarding the contributions of adults to young children's SEL. Secure attachment and positive behavior management via guidance are two important foundations for SEL that derive from relationships with caring adults. Also, although cultural values and variations must be acknowledged, a more detailed, generally positive picture emerges of "emotion coaching" and inductive, proactive discipline replete with references to, and explanations of, emotion. These elements will be useful in building adult roles in any successful SEL programming for young children.

Using Developmental Knowledge: Going from "What Is Known" to "What Is Done"

Although normative views of SEL and its promotion are crucially important, the daily context of young children's lives must also be understood. Such understanding is central to accurate perceptions of how particular children have progressed developmentally, and how they will continue to progress. We must understand their specific needs, the processes of risk and resilience that operate in their lives. This view of the child is pivotal in SEL programming.

Each child has unique life circumstances. For many, SEL skills unfold easily, but, in our society with its fragmentation and violence, all children can benefit from clear attention to SEL. Universal programming (i.e., to which all children are exposed) with individualization is the *sine qua non* of such a view. Theoretical and empirical evidence strongly suggests the utility of universal SEL prevention in lowering the incidence and prevalence of related problems (e.g., aggression, depression, anxiety, impulsiveness, antisocial behavior) and increasing the probability of successful management of social-emotional developmental tasks (Weissberg & Greenberg, 1998).

Nonetheless, there are children who, by virtue of compromised development and the presence of risk processes, or the absence of resilience, require more than universal programming. Their behaviors are already challenging themselves and others; they are already taxed to develop age-appropriate SEL skills. These children will benefit from more targeted intervention to assist them and those in their environment to maximize the probability of SEL.

Finally, for those with the most pressing difficulties, integration of the primary prevention, intervention, and mental health services will be necessary. Because we need to be able to respond to such individualized needs, we now turn to a consideration of risk and resilience processes as important moderators of SEL.

Intrapersonal/Contextual/Interpersonal Processes Affecting SEL Development and Programming

A chair sailed through the air, narrowly missing three children playing in the "house corner" and the classroom aide who was gathering materials for circle time. Tomas had thrown the chair in anger.

Tomas' teachers were desperate for ways to help him improve his behavior, and others', to make the classroom a place where children and teachers could work, learn, and play productively and in peace. Even when teachers work to promote attachment relationships with children, and apply the guidance and socialization techniques just discussed, promoting SEL for some children may be difficult. Conversely, there may be some children whose lives are marked by special processes that enhance our abilities to promote SEL.

As outlined earlier, when we consider processes that facilitate or hinder SEL development and programming, we must include aspects of these children's personal makeup, the immediate environment of the child, transactions between elements of the child's immediate environment, elements outside the child's immediate environment that nevertheless impact it, and the broader social/political context of the child's world.

RISK PROCESSES. Many risk processes can thwart preschoolers' SEL (Davis, 1999; Peth-Pierce, 2000). These include both intrapersonal and interpersonal/contextual risks. Intrapersonal risk processes include gender-related vulnerabilities: Starting from four years of age, boys are more likely than girls to engage in physical aggression and antisocial behavior. In contrast, girls show more continuity of internalizing symptoms even during early childhood. Cognitive deficits also play a role, both those that are more general, such as low IQ and delayed language development, and those that are more specific, such as deficiencies in planning and problem-solving abilities.

Another intrapersonal risk, related to emotional expressiveness, involves temperament. Early temperaments characterized by high levels of negativity when aroused, or behavioral inhibition and shyness, place young children at risk for externalizing and internalizing difficulties, respectively. Temperamentally difficult 3-year-olds show heightened probability of growing up impulsive, unreliable, and antisocial, with more conflicts in their social networks and at work. Temperamentally inhibited 3-year-olds are more likely to be unassertive and depressed, with fewer sources of social support. Lack of attentional control (i.e., attention focusing and shifting), especially in interaction with temperamental negativity, is associated with long-term social dysfunction.

Davis (1999) specifically cites SEL deficits, including emotion regulation, as intrapersonal risk processes. Similarly, lack of relationship skills— e.g., the abilities to recruit support when needed, to be well thought of in the peer group, and to make and sustain friendships—renders the important tasks of grade school more difficult to attain. Children already rejected in kindergarten are the least adjusted to school by sixth grade; peer rejection is one of the strongest predictors of eventual school dropout (Gagnon, Craig, Tremblay, Zhou, & Vitaro, 1995).

Contextual risk processes also are many and varied. Low socioeconomic status is a marker for multiple risk processes—including lower maternal education, homelessness, unexplained separations from parents, hunger, chronic exposure to violent and otherwise unsafe, chaotic neighborhoods, maltreatment or neglect (Bolger, Patterson, Thompson, Kupersmidt, 1995; Huston, McLoyd, & Garcia Coll, 1994). Persistent family instability, including residence change, lack of daily routines, marital conflict, lack of social support, and other negative life events predict concurrent and later behavior problems, particularly when these stressors are cumulative, and even with other factors controlled (Ackerman, Kogos, Youngstrom, Schoff, & Izard, 1999).

Several interpersonal risk processes map directly onto the important SEL promotion techniques already outlined here. For example, absence of a secure attachment relationship with a caregiver or multiple caregivers leaves a young child at a distinct disadvantage. Such children have no one person on whom they can count in times of distress, as a fundamental support for learning and growing, and to aid them in forming a positive view of their own worth. Parents' own punitive or inconsistent parenting practices, and/or their own psychopathology, are related to SEL problems among children. Moreover, these risk processes may be especially salient among impoverished children because of their exposure to chronic stress and less-than-optimal emotion socialization (Cutting & Dunn, 1999; Garner & Spears, 2000; Shields et al., 2001), making it especially important to bolster their SEL.

There is some evidence that intrapersonal and interpersonal risks, in combination, are also important; in particular, aspects of emotionality may moderate or mediate the risk/outcome relation (Ackerman, Izard, Schoff, Youngstrom, & Kogos, 1999). For example, the interaction of the child's emotionally negative temperament and parental negative emotion, conflict, or punitiveness may be a particularly potent predictor of behavior problems at the end of the preschool period.

PROTECTIVE PROCESSES.   Thankfully, protective processes also exist, which can moderate the deleterious effects of existent risk factors. These also include intrapersonal and interpersonal/contextual factors, and parallel the enumerated risk processes. Intrapersonally, the confident child with an "easy" temperament, who exhibits relatively high cognitive functioning, is relationally competent enough to have friends (or be able to make them when exposed to peers), and has an early history of functioning well with respect to developmental milestones, has a better chance of also marshaling the component skills of SEL by kindergarten entry.

Regarding interpersonal and contextual protective processes, social support for the child and parents also can be crucial and adds to the benefits of positive parenting practices. Moreover, parental and other adults' investment and involvement in the child's development are key advantages. Concomitant with positive involvement is the presence of the child's caring relationship with at least one adult; Mitchell-Copeland, Denham, and DeMulder (1997) have found, for example, that when attachment with mother is insecure, a secure attachment relationship with one's preschool teacher may support positive development of SEL.

SUMMARY: USING INFORMATION ON RISK AND PROTECTIVE PROCESSES.   In general, we seek to promote the positive, rather than to prevent disorder; we believe this to be a broader and more basic approach to primary prevention than risk-driven attempts (Elias et al., 1997; see also Battistich, Schaps, Watson, Solomon, & Lewis, 2000). Knowing the child—what risk processes s/he has been exposed to, what protective processes are operative—allows us to not only understand behavior better, but also to individualize treatment, whether it be part of a universal prevention program, targeted intervention, or mental health services. It is to these most pressing practical matters that we now turn.

Social and Emotional Learning Programming: What Is Needed? What Has Been Done? Where Do We Go From Here?

We already have some ideas of how to evaluate programs as effective in their promotion of social and emotional foundations for learning (Collaborative for Academic, Social, and Emotional Learning, 2002; Durlak & Wells, 1997; Payton et al., 2000; Ramey & Ramey, 1998; Shonkoff & Phillips, 2000). For example, in order to maximize programs' effectiveness, they must be of sufficient duration and intensity; change takes time. Further, children need to receive direct intervention if SEL is to be enhanced. Because children's profiles of SEL strengths and weakness are extremely heterogeneous, individualization of service delivery is needed. The most effective SEL programs are comprehensive and multifaceted, with SEL, cognitive, and health components for child and family. Finally, initial benefits will diminish in absence of environmental supports. We must not consider that offering SEL programming in preschool "inoculates" children thereafter.

More specifically, Payton et al. (2000) offer the following as criteria for successful SEL programming:

- Individual lesson plans or activities need to be consistent in providing clear objectives and activities, as well as a clear rationale for their contribution to the overall program goals. That is, teachers and parents need not only to acknowledge the program goals, but also understand how each lesson furthers these goals. There is nothing more sure to lessen the momentum of programming than a lesson or series of lessons that "don't make sense" to the teacher or parent.
- SEL skills must be reinforced through infusion across subject areas and by creating opportunities for skill application throughout the day, and rewarding students for using SEL in daily interactions. Effective programs provide structure for the infusion and application of SEL instruction across other subject areas within the school curriculum, and encourage teachers to model SEL skills and to prompt and reinforce students' social and emotionally competent behavior.
- Quality of program implementation, too often overlooked, must be assessed as it relates to SEL outcomes. Classroom or parenting group

implementation assistance must exist, in the form of formal training and technical support, as well as guidelines, procedures, and instruments for planning and monitoring program implementation. We need to be able to see whether programming is proceeding as expected, and if not, why—so that we may modify and improve our programming.

- Assessment measures need to be included to measure individual mastery of SEL objectives. We need to be able to see whether our programming works! This need raises the issue of the paucity of such assessment tools.

Furthermore, these authors point out another vital aspect of SEL programming, that it is not isolated in the classroom. As noted earlier, all the adults and all the environments, both proximal and distal, in a child's life must be involved in SEL programming, for the most positive, long-lasting results. Hence, Payton et al. (2000) enumerate the following guidelines to ensure such involvement:

- School-wide coordination is necessary; that is, the program includes structures that promote reinforcement and extension of SEL instruction beyond the classroom and throughout the school.
- School-family partnerships are similarly crucial. Programming must include strategies to enhance communication between school and families regarding SEL, involving parents in their children's SEL education both at home and at school.
- Finally, school-community partnerships are needed. Community members can be involved in school-based SEL instruction and embrace as an overarching goal.

Early Childhood Social-Emotional Learning: "Best Bets" in Programming

Beginning from these premises, we can already identify several preschool SEL "best bets"; that is, we have some information about evidence-based programs (e.g., CMHS Promising Programs, 1999; Denham, 2003). Several SEL programs exist that meet many of the above requisites, and have met with some success.

Three programs share some basic similarities in approaches. Denham and Burton's program (1996; Burton & Denham, 1999) includes teacher training on attachment and guidance issues, lessons on self- and other-awareness, self-management, responsible decision making, and relationship skills. Children who experienced this universal program, especially those with the largest initial deficits, showed improvements in self-management and relationship skills.

The downward extension of the Promoting Alternative Thinking Strategies (PATHS) program to preschoolers, applied in Head Start classrooms (Greenberg et al., 1999, 2001; Greenberg, Kusché, & Mihalic, 1998; Kusché & Greenberg, 1994) includes emphases on self- and other-awareness, as well as self-management and responsible decision making. Early evaluations indicate that program participants improved on emotion knowledge and multiple reporters' views of their social skills; they also demonstrated decreased internalizing problems (Domitrovich, Cortes, & Greenberg, 2002).

The recently updated Preschool/Kindergarten version of Second Step (Frey, Hirschstein, & Guzzo, 2000), a self-named "violence prevention" program, prominently includes promotion of empathy, social problem solving, impulse control, and anger management. An evaluation of the previous version showed that program children's knowledge of each of these program elements increased, and their problem behaviors decreased (McMahon, Washburn, Felix, Yakin, & Childrey, 2000). Izard's Head Start program (Izard & Bear, 1999), as yet not evaluated, focuses on emotion knowledge and regulation. Other similar programs with promising results are reported by Dubas, Lynch, Galano, Geller, and Hunt (1998), Sandy and Boardman (2000), and Serna, Nielsen, Lambros, and Forness (2000).

Working from slightly different perspective, the bimodal prevention program for disruptive kindergarten boys includes social-problem-solving and cognitive-behavioral training for children, thus focusing on responsible decision making and self-management. It also has a significant programming component on parent training in child development and parenting practices, suggestive of positive guidance practices as described here (Tremblay, Pagani-Kurtz, Masse, Vitaro, & Pihl, 1995). This program has shown beneficial effects, in terms of desistance from aggression, delinquency, and other problems, well into adolescence.

Webster-Stratton's combination of training mothers about positive guidance and other effective parenting skills, and training their Head Start teachers to work with 4-year-olds regarding social skills, has been evaluated through several replications (Webster-Stratton, 1998; Webster-Stratton, Reid, & Hammond, 2001). Overall, we consider the rudiments of all these programs to include many core elements in ways that foster young children's SEL, as follows.

Creating Attachment Relationships

The development of a positive, consistent, emotionally supportive relationship with the child is primary (Burton & Denham, 1999; Greenspan. 1992; Mardell, 1992, 1994). Children may actually seek psychological proximity to teachers when their prior attachment history is insecure. Such relationships are promoted through use of "floor time," a means of building a warmth and intimacy between caregiver and child. Teachers can use this technique during play by observing the child, opening communication, continuing the communication process by following the child's lead in play, and then by helping the child to expand that play one step further through gestures and words (see also Howes, Galinsky, & Kontos, 1998, for teachers' training in sensitivity). Burton and Denham (1999) report that the inclusion of these techniques was central to the success of their programming.

Positive Behavior Management: Guidance

For teachers and caregivers of young children who are already demonstrating signs of SEL deficits, behavior management must be an integral portion of SEL programming. Of course, even children who are showing no difficulties need guidance. Fortunately, positive guidance can also further the goals of SEL (Galambos, 1978). Bergin and Bergin (1999) advocate the use of persistent persuasion until the child complies, without increasing the level of power assertion or using coercive threats. The overuse of power assertion can damage adult-child relationships and fails to promote the child's internal motivation. In fact, power assertive behavior management can actually teach the child aggression and raise the expectancy level for coercion.

In the use of persistent persuasion, coercive elements are veiled, if not nonexistent. Such ambiguity increases the child's tendency to attribute their compliance to self-motivation. The affective component of such guidance is also quite important. Committed compliance is rooted in long-term relational qualities, so that some anxiety inducement, in the context of the warm relationship, motivates the child to reciprocate by complying. Furthermore, self-assertion and negotiation on the child's part are not antithetical to compliance. Such behavior management also takes some time to carry out, giving the child time to regain self-control. Along with persistent persuasion, inductive guidance that focuses on the consequences of the child's behaviors on others, particularly others' feelings, is very effective. Such inductive guidance techniques—explaining to the child why one is pleased or displeased with their behavior, with feeling—are associated with SEL (Berkowitz & Grych, 2000).

As a central component of their programming, Denham and Burton (1996) trained preschool childcare providers in positive guidance techniques. Webster-Stratton (1998) and Tremblay et al. (1995) also implement similar concepts in parent training to increase preschoolers' SEL.

Self-Awareness, Social Awareness, and Self-Management

Young children may not have been exposed to language to express their feelings. Without emotion language and understanding, no distancing occurs between their own feelings and their actions. Thinking about the effect of one's actions upon others also requires that the child understand her or his feelings. Emotion knowledge is, then, the next component of "best bet" programs. With such knowledge, children have a vehicle with which to regulate emotions by attaching a label to feelings inside and bringing feelings to consciousness. Children can recognize their own feelings; they also can begin to empathize with feelings seen in others. Programming emphasizing enjoyable didactic activities in understanding and labeling emotions provides the child with the exposure to feeling words, ability to use words to label affect in themselves and in others, and recognition that actions can cause emotions (Denham, 1998; Denham & Burton, 1996; Izard & Bear, 1999; Jensen & Wells, 1979). Second Step, as well as Greenberg and Domitrovich's downward extension of the PATHS curriculum, and Izard's Head Start curriculum, all include numerous lessons involving aspects of SEL skills.

In both Denham and Burton's and Greenberg's programs, children learn a validated method of controlling negative feelings called the Turtle Technique (Robin, Schneider, & Dolnick, 1976; somewhat similar techniques are used in Second Step and Izard's Head Start programming). In this technique, children are encouraged to imagine that they are turtles, retreating into their shells when they feel scared or hurt or angry actually pulling their arms close to their bodies, putting their heads down, and closing their eyes. They then relax their muscles to cope with emotional tension. This gives them time to regulate their feelings, reflect on them, and decide how they will react to the cause of these feelings. Qualitative results in Burton and Denham (1998) suggest that this is indeed a very powerful technique.

Responsible Decision Making

Because understanding and regulating affect are such important parts of social relationships, experience in talking through affect-laden social problems and concerns also enhances the child's ability to solve problems that occur with peers. Thus, the next component of "best bet" programs—including Denham and Burton's program, Head Start PATHS, and Second Step—is promoting responsible decision-making and social interaction skills (Shure, 1990). This approach improves an individual's ability to think through interpersonal conflicts; the learner is guided to develop the habit of generating multiple options, evaluating these options, and using systematic means to reach their goal. Denham and Almeida's (1987) meta-analysis of then-extant evaluation research on SEL promoting programs revealed that these programs do result in successful skills acquisition in preschool-aged children. Moreover, on average, children's behavior changes in a prosocial direction through such programs.

Individualization of Program Techniques

As repeatedly reiterated here, the complex interplay of factors that influence development is unique to each child. Accordingly, it is important for optimum transfer, and efficient use of time and resources, for work with each child to be individualized in a way that utilizes all program components, but tailors information from each to meet the child's particular needs. Teachers can be taught to investigate the history of the child and use that information to facilitate effective interactions. They can tailor the use of floor time, the "turtle technique", and "dialoguing" to work one-on-one through emotional and social events with a child.

In particular, the technique of dialoguing involves identifying the problem "in vivo" (e.g., two children who want to play with the same toy), talking about feelings of all parties related to the problem, generating alternative solutions to the problem, associating likely consequences to each solution, and then choosing an appropriate action. Denham and Almeida (1987) found the use of dialoguing to be related to success of SEL programs. The critical aspect is to include discussion of feelings in the dialoguing process, both one's own and those of the other parties involved (although if young children are *too* upset, immediate discussions may not work). Techniques also can be expanded to include emphasis on prosocial solutions with aggressive children (i.e., because aggressive children can sometimes come up with *many* aggressive solutions to social problems, to show children with such SEL deficits that not just any solution to a problem is called for, but that prosocial solutions are preferable in both the short and long run).

Infusion Throughout the Early Childhood Classroom Day

SEL programming is not an isolated entity. Other programs or program components also may have salutary effects on SEL. For example, several large-scale early childhood education programs include some, but not all, aspects deemed crucial for SEL programs (e.g., High/Scope, Schweinhart & Weikart, 1997; see also Greenwood, Model, Rydell, & Chiesa, 1996; Mendel, 2000). Further, several well-known constructivist early childhood models have much to offer in the way of infusing a positive climate, and a socio-moral atmosphere throughout the curriculum (DeVries, Reese-Learned, & Morgan, 1991; Marcon, 1993, 1999; Stipek, Daniels, Galuzzo, & Milburn, 1992). Some of these elements should be incorporated into comprehensive SEL programs; for example Denham and Burton's (1996) program was nested within the overarching High/Scope curriculum.

Conversely, SEL concepts should be generalized across children's daily activities and integrated with other "themes" of learning deemed important for children's development. SEL can be infused into all parts of a preschooler's day, into almost every corner of the curriculum, and into the most mundane activity at home, since many of the practices involve the adult appropriately labeling, discussing, and scaffolding/working through the child's emotions during everyday interactions and activities. SEL "teachable moments" abound! For example, children benefit from learning how to express their feelings appropriately during not only center time play, but during snack time, waiting in line, and transitions from one activity to another. SEL also can be integrated into themes such as nutrition (e.g., some foods are good for us and make us feel happy), and safety (e.g., wearing a safety belt in the car makes one feel safe). Finally, SEL programming is not restricted to "lessons" or didactic aids, such as displaying pictures of different feeling faces and situations that elicit feelings throughout the classroom; teachers also can create environmental spaces that support SEL (e.g., a "peace" table or "feelings" corner, where children can go to calm down or have quiet time to reflect on their feelings).

Classroom Climate, School Ecology, and Neighborhood Context

Classroom climate, school ecology and neighborhood issues also are very important to the success of SEL programming (e.g., Brooks-Gunn, Duncan, Klebanov, & Sealand, 1993; Frey et al., 2000; Hawkins, Catalano, Morrison, O'Donnell, Abbott, & Day, 1992). Preschool programs can become "caring communities," in which affective bonds develop between the child and the community, promoting acceptance and internalization of community mores (Battistich et al., 2000). But, because there are few empirical evaluations of successful preschool SEL programs and thus few accounts of the role of early childhood classroom climate, school ecology, and neighborhood context in program implementation and effectiveness, much of the information related to these contextual issues is in the form of anecdotal "lessons from the field" (Yoshikawa & Knitzer, 1997). For example, creators of the Head Start PATHS and Second Step programs for preschool children have identified criteria that they believe are important for SEL at the classroom, school, and community levels.

First, interventions should be designed to provide a safe and supportive school climate that fosters SEL. This includes training of teachers and all key adults in the school environment with whom children have contact (e.g., center directors, bus drivers, teachers' aides), and parents, in positive emotion coaching strategies (Elias et al., 1997). Training teachers and parents to provide greater opportunities for children to be active participants in the classroom and the family, and to be recognized for positive involvement, along with providing children with SEL skills, should strengthen children's bonds of commitment to education, as well as attachment to family and school (Hawkins & Weis, 1985). In turn, stronger bonding to school and family improves children's academic achievement, and decreases the likelihood that they engage in behaviors disapproved of by school personnel and family members.

School-Family Partnerships

School-family partnerships produce more positive outcomes for children than school programs or family programs conducted in isolation (Epstein, 1996; Webster-Stratton & Taylor, 2001; Weissberg & Greenberg, 1998). When parents and teachers work together, programming is enhanced, school climate can be more focused on positive SEL, and it is easier to coordinate community resources—an auspicious fusion of effects obtain (Webster-Stratton et al., 2001). However, such an approach needs systematic inclusion and evaluation in early childhood SEL programs (e.g., Tremblay et al., 1995). At this point, most extant programs address compliance and oppositionality problems common in families with preschool children.

Several programs that focus on such issues have very salutary effects. For example, mothers who experienced Webster-Stratton's program, in comparison with those who did not, made fewer critical remarks and commands, used less harsh discipline and more positive parenting, and were more involved in their children's education. Their children, also exposed to a program to strengthen their prosocial and social skills, exhibited fewer conduct problems, less noncompliance, less negative affect, and more positive affect. These improvements were largely maintained after one year.

In Webster-Stratton's program, home-school consistency and parent involvement in school programming are also promoted. Training includes a 4-day workshop for parents, with ongoing weekly supervision, with vignettes on video, role-plays, activities and stories, and homework. Implementation of the parent training program is tracked via weekly checklists of group process, parent interest, and participation. Importantly, such school-parent partnerships have been effective specifically in strengthening parents experiencing multiple risk processes (Catalano, Haggerty, & Gainey, 2002).

Parent training centering even more specifically on all aspects of preschoolers' SEL is also necessary, and requires more scientific development. One of the recent efforts in this regard includes "The Heart of Parenting" (Gottman & Declaire, 1997). Other books on the mass market hold possibilities for kernels of "emotion coaching" information that could be tailored.

In addition, the *Bingham Early Childhood Program* employs many of the components found useful in other studies, but presents them in innovative and potentially useful way. This program will be discussed at length in this book, but fits particularly well in this discussion of school-family partnership. The staff at Child and Family Agency, in consultation with a national advisory group, undertook a review of the early childhood literature on promoting prosocial behavior. From this review, they identified five key behaviors that should be nurtured: kindness toward others; awareness of feelings in self and others; respect for others and for property; cooperation; and self-control.

The Child and Family Agency recognized the industry-wide fact of life that child care workers frequently had inadequate educational preparation, lacked time for continuing education, and exhibited a high staff turnover. Consequently, the Agency developed a brief training curriculum (that could be repeated, as needed for new staff). Key to this curriculum was the use of the curriculum instructor as a coach in the preschool classroom on a continuing basis for several hours a week. The presence of the coach in the classroom was a reminder to staff of the prosocial training materials that needed to be actively practiced with their young pupils. The coach also acted as a positive evaluator for teachers—so that behaviors helpful to the development of prosocial behaviors in early childhood could be strengthened, and detracting teacher behaviors minimized.

The Bingham curriculum enlisted parent involvement in nurturing prosocial behavior, reflecting best practice ideas from the literature. Through a series of short, single-page handouts called "Tips for Parents," the staff created a communication path between the classroom and the home. A behavior that the child care staff wished to encourage as part of the planned curriculum was described in the "Tips." However, "Tips" also contained a space in which the teacher wrote an example of their child displaying that behavior in the classroom. With great enthusiasm, the child care teacher presented "Tips" to the parent when he or she was picking up the child after class, praised the child's behavior to the parent, and encouraged the parent to read the handout and look for like praiseworthy behaviors at home. Happily, many of these "Tips" found their way onto the refrigerator door, and positive discussions around the child's good behaviors are reported to increase.

Evaluation of the Bingham project is reported elsewhere. Based on live classroom observations of child and teacher interactions, and an analysis of parent questionnaires, the overall results are very encouraging.

SUMMARY. The active engagement of educators, parents, and community leaders can provide opportunities to facilitate SEL across many domains of the child's environment, such as the home environment, a domain that is particularly relevant for preschool children whose social world is only beginning to expand. In summary, we need to reach beyond the classroom to influence the lives of all of the adults with whom children have contact.

The Importance of Culture

In maximizing the success of school-family and school-community partnerships, we must not overlook the role of culture. Culture provides young children with a sense of identity and a frame of reference that helps them understand their worlds; every interaction between young children and others is a cultural experience. When young children experience programming that may be cognitively, linguistically, and emotionally disconnected from the language and culture of their home, it is the responsibility of caregivers to develop the skills and understandings to work with children and families in a culturally responsive manner. This injunction requires professional preparation and development in the areas of culture, language, and diversity (Tabors, 1997), as well as understanding of one's own unique cultural lens (Sánchez, 1999).

Adults working with culturally and linguistically diverse young children and families are often unaware that they bring their own cultural lens that is unique and plays a role in their interactions with others (Ballenger, 1999; Garcia Coll & Magnusson, 2000). This lack of awareness is particularly critical when practitioners apply their own cultural lens to assess, assign meaning, or interpret SEL of diverse young children, thus failing to account for roles, rituals, and expectations which may be different from their own (de Melendez & Ostertag, 1997; Kalyanpur & Harry, 1999). We can seriously misunderstand the SEL needs of the child if we do not understand the child's culture and our own cultural perspective (Hudley, 2001).

Specifically, we must guard against inappropriate or intrusive programming based on faulty assumptions, such as: (1) the caregiving environment necessarily requires modification, and (2) the family and the program necessarily agree on desired outcomes. Thus, programming approaches must also be culturally relevant, empowering children within their unique cultural contexts. This tenet includes the possibility that certain definitions of SEL may be unique to the child's home culture.

Therefore, to better know a child, practitioners must get to know the family. Building relationships with families can provide practitioners with the insight needed to understand the decisions, behaviors, and values exhibited by the child and their family (Thorp, 1997). Family activities show an outsider how that family transmits knowledge, and can serve as resources to tap into children's SEL while simultaneously addressing cultural and linguistic continuity for young children (Moll & Greenberg, 1990). Family routines, mother's games and lullabies, family stories, and the family's way of interacting and questioning could be sources to help caregivers to provide emotional continuity in a culturally responsive and caring manner (Sánchez, 1999; Sánchez & Thorp, 1998).

Promoting Reflective Training, Supervision, And Consultation

Reflective methods also have emerged as vital components to the success of the program documented in Burton and Denham (1998; Denham & Burton, 1996). When rapport is achieved between SEL consultants and teachers, teachers are hungry for someone to observe in their classrooms, someone who cares and understands, and is knowledgeable, someone who will listen and engage them in a true dialogue. For example, Fantuzzo, Childs, Stevenson, Coolahan, Ginsburg, Gay, Debnam, and Watson (1996) showed that collaborative training, in which Head Start teachers and parent volunteers were involved conjointly in experiential training that included receiving guided practice and feedback from exemplary peers, resulted in teachers' and parents' greater levels of active involvement in and satisfaction with the training, as well as significantly greater levels of parent classroom activity. With respect to adult-child classroom interactions, teachers demonstrated significantly more positive initiations and praise with children. Active investment in the process yields positive results for all involved. Truly collaborative alliances with teachers, other school personnel, and preventionists ensure that everyone is "on the same page" (Hunter, Elias, & Norris, 2001).

Integration and Conclusion

In this chapter, we have attempted to give a full overview of the importance of SEL during early childhood—from attachment, guidance, and positive socialization, to self- and other-awareness, self-management, responsible decision making, and relationship skills. Given the centrality of these components of SEL to concurrent success in the early years, but perhaps even more importantly, to later academic, interpersonal, and intrapersonal success, it behooves us to consider universal and targeted prevention programming in this area. We have outlined promising research-based evidence for such programming, from specific SEL instructional techniques, to considerations of individualization, infusion into the fabric of the entire early childhood program, classroom climate, school ecology, and family-school partnerships, cultural sensitivity, and reflective supervision. We consider also that better assessment of SEL skills is needed for the early childhood years.

Thus, many kernels of effective SEL programming in early childhood have been introduced. Making these possibilities explicit within early childhood education, rather than implicit, is a priority that we can no longer postpone. Although there is evidence-based research supporting the importance of early SEL, as well as growing support for specific SEL practices during early childhood, more focused attention on successful SEL programming is needed to advance sound practice that enhances children's success in schools and life. As well, we need to take Ramey and Ramey's (1998) admonition seriously, and seamlessly unite preschool SEL programming with SEL programming for older children, both in school and family.

Where will Darrell, Jamila, Jimmy, and Tomas be at age 15? If we provide them with continued SEL-enhancing programming and adult support in home, school, and community, the results will be well worth our efforts.

References

Ackerman, B. P., Izard, C. E., Schoff, K., Youngstrom, E. A., & Kogos, J. (1999). Contextual risk, caregiver emotionality, and the problem behaviors of six-and seven-year-old children from economically disadvantaged families. *Child Development, 70*, 1415–1427.

Ackerman, B. P., Kogos, J., Youngstrom, E. A., Schoff, K., & Izard, C. E. (1999). Family instability and the problem behaviors of children from economically disadvantaged families. *Developmental Psychology, 35*, 258–268.

Ballenger, C. (1999). *Teaching other people's children: Literacy and learning in a bilingual classroom.* New York: Teachers College Press.

Barnett, M. A., King, L. M., Howard, J. A., & Dino, G. A. (1980). Empathy in young children: Relation to parents' empathy, affection, and emphasis on feelings of others. *Developmental Psychology, 16*, 243–244.

Battistich, V., Schaps, E., Watson, M., Solomon, D., & Lewis, C. (2000). Effects of the Child Development Project on students' drug use and other problem behaviors. *Journal of Primary Prevention, 21*, 75–99.

Bergin, C., & Bergin, D. A. (1999). Classroom discipline that promotes self-control. *Journal of Applied Developmental Psychology, 20*, 189–206.

Berk, L. E., & Winsler, A. (1995). *Scaffolding children's learning: Vygotsky and early childhood education*. Washington, DC: National Association for the Education of Young Children.

Berkowitz, M. W., & Grych, J. H. (2000). Early character development and education. *Early Education and Development, 11*, 56–72.

Birch, S. H., & Ladd, G. W. (1997). The teacher-child relationship and children's early school adjustment. *Journal of School Psychology, 35*, 61–79.

Bolger, K. E., Patterson, C. J., Thompson, W. W., & Kupersmidt, J. B. (1995). Psychosocial adjustment among children experiencing persistent and intermittent family economic hardship. *Child Development, 66*, 1107–1129.

Brooks-Gunn, J., Duncan, G. J., Klebanov, P. K., & Sealand, N. (1993). Do neighborhoods influence child and adolescent development? *American Journal of Sociology, 99*, 353–395.

Burton, R., & Denham, S. A. (1998). "Are you my friend?": A qualitative analysis of a social-emotional intervention for at-risk four-year-olds. *Journal of Research in Childhood Education, 12*, 210–224.

Campos, J. J., & Barrett, K. C. (1984). Toward a new understanding of emotions and their development. In C. E. Izard, J. Kagan, & R. B. Zajonc (Eds.), *Emotions, cognition, & behavior* (pp. 229–263). Cambridge: Cambridge University Press.

Campos, J. J., Mumme, D. L., Kermoian, R., & Campos, R. G. (1994). A functionalist perspective on the nature of emotion. *Monographs of the Society for Research in Child Development, 59* (2–3), 284–303.

Carlton, M. P. (2000). Motivation and school readiness in kindergarten children. (Doctoral dissertation, University of Alabama, 1999). *Dissertation Abstracts International Section A Human and Social Sciences, 60(11-A)*, 3899.

Carlton, M. P., & Winsler, A. (1999). School readiness: The need for a paradigm shift. *School Psychology Review, 28*, 338–352.

Catalano, R. F., Haggerty, K. P., and Gainey, R. R. (2002). Children of substance abusing parents: Current findings from the focus on families project. In R. D. Peters & R. J. McMahon (Eds.), *Children of Disordered Parents*. New York: Kluwer Academic/Plenum Publishers.

Cataldo, C. Z. (1987). *Parent education for early childhood*. New York: Teachers College Press.

Center for Mental Health Services (CMHS). (1999, February 26). Examples of Exemplary/Promising Programs. Retrieved January 19, 2003, from http://www.mentalhealth.org/schoolviolence/initiative.asp

Cohn, D. A., Patterson, C. J., & Christopoulos, C. (1991). The family and children's peer relations. *Journal of Social and Personal Relationships, 8*, 315–346.

Collaborative for Academic, Social, and Emotional Learning (2002). *Safe and sound: Educational leader's guide to evidence-based social and emotional learning programs*. Retrieved on July, 18, 2002, at http://www.casel.org/progrevfr.htm

Contreras, J. M., Kerns, K. A., Weimer, B. L., Gentzler, A. L., & Tomich, P. L. (2000). Emotion regulation as a mediator of associations between mother-child attachment and peer relationships in middle childhood. *Journal of Family Psychology, 14*, 111–124.

Crick, N. R., & Dodge, K. A. (1994). A review and re-formulation of social information processing mechanisms in children's social adjustment. *Psychological Bulletin, 115*, 74–101.

Cutting, A. L., & Dunn, J. (1999). Theory of mind, emotion understanding, language, and family background: Individual differences and interrelations. *Child Development, 70*, 853–865.

Davis, N. J. (May 28, 1999). *Resilience: Status of the research and research-based programs*. Working draft. Rockville, MD: Center for Mental Health Services. Retrieved on January, 19, 2003, at http://www.mentalhealth.org/schoolviolence/5-28Resilience.asp

Denham, S. A. (1986). Social cognition, social behavior, and emotion in preschoolers: Contextual validation. *Child Development, 57*, 194–201.

Denham, S. A. (1993). Maternal emotional responsiveness and toddlers' social-emotional functioning. *Journal of Child Psychology and Psychiatry, 34*, 715–728.

Denham, S. A. (1998). *Emotional development in young children.* New York: Guilford Press.

Denham, S. A. (2003). Social and emotional learning in early childhood. In T. P. Gullotta & M. Bloom (Eds.), *The encyclopedia of primary prevention and health promotion.* New York: Kluwer Academic/Plenum Publishers.

Denham, S. A., & Almeida, M. C. (1987). Children's social problem-solving skills, behavioral adjustment, and interventions: A meta-analysis evaluating theory and practice. *Journal of Applied Developmental Psychology, 8*, 391–409.

Denham, S. A., & Auerbach, S. (1995). Mother-child dialogue about emotions. *Genetic, Social, and General Psychology Monographs, 121*, 311–338.

Denham, S. A., & Burton, R. A. (1996). A social-emotional intervention for at-risk 4-year-olds. *Journal of School Psychology, 34*, 225–245.

Denham, S. A., & Couchoud, E. A. (1991). Social-emotional contributors to preschoolers' responses to an adult's negative emotions. *Journal of Child Psychology and Psychiatry, 32*, 595–608.

Denham, S. A., Grant, S., & Hamada, H. (2002, June). *"I have two 1st teachers": Mother and teacher socialization of preschoolers' emotional and social competence.* Paper presented in symposium 7th Head Start Research Conference, Washington DC.

Denham, S. A., & Grout, L. (1992). Mothers' emotional expressiveness and coping: Topography and relations with preschoolers' social-emotional competence. *Genetic, Social, and General Psychology Monographs, 118*, 75–101.

Denham, S. A., & Grout, L. (1993). Socialization of emotion: Pathway to preschoolers' affect regulation. *Journal of Nonverbal Behavior, 17*, 205–227.

Denham, S. A., & Holt, R. (1993). Preschoolers' likability as cause or consequence of their social behavior. *Developmental Psychology, 29*, 271–275.

Denham, S. A., McKinley, M., Couchoud, E. A., & Holt, R. (1990). Emotional and behavioral predictors of peer status in young preschoolers. *Child Development, 61*, 1145–1152.

Denham, S. A., Mitchell-Copeland, Strandberg, K., Auerbach, S., & Blair, K. (1997). Parental contributions to preschoolers' emotional competence: Direct and indirect effects. *Motivation and Emotion, 27*, 65–86.

Denham, S. A., Renwick-DeBardi, S., & Hewes, S. (1994). Affective communication between mothers and preschoolers: Relations with social-emotional competence. *Merrill-Palmer Quarterly, 40*, 488–508.

Denham, S. A., Renwick, S., & Holt, R. (1991). Working and playing together: Prediction of preschool social-emotional competence from mother- child interaction. *Child Development, 62*, 242–249.

Denham, S. A., Zoller, D., & Couchoud, E. A. (1994). Socialization of preschoolers' understanding of emotion. *Developmental Psychology, 30*, 928–936.

DeVries, R., Reese-Learned, H., & Morgan, R. (1991). Sociomoral development in direct-instruction, eclectic, and constructivist kindergartens: A study of children's enacted interpersonal understanding. *Early Child Research Quarterly, 6*, 473–517.

Dodge, K. A., Laird, R., Lochman, J. E., Zelli, A., & Conduct Problems Prevention Research Group (2002). Multidimensional latent construct analyses of children's social information processing patterns: Correlations with aggressive behavior problems. *Psychological Assessment, 14*, 60–73.

Domitrovich, C. E., Cortes, R., & Greenberg, M. T. (2002, June). *Preschool PATHS: Promoting social and emotional competence in young children.* Paper presented in symposium 7th Head Start Research Conference, Washington DC.

Dubas, J. S., Lynch, K. B., Galano, J., Geller, J., & Hunt, D. (1998). Preliminary evaluation of a resiliency-based preschool substance abuse and violence prevention project. *Journal of Drug Education, 28*, 235–255.

Dunn, J. (1994). Understanding others and the social world: Current issues in developmental research and their relation to preschool experiences and practice. *Journal of Applied Developmental Psychology, 15*, 571–583.

Dunn, J., Brown, J. R., Slomkowski, C., Tesla, C., & Youngblade, L. (1991). Young children's understanding of other people's feelings and beliefs: Individual differences and their antecedents. *Child Development, 62* 1352–1366.

Durlak, J. A., & Wells, A. M. (1997). Primary prevention mental health programs for children and adolescents: A meta-analytic review. *American Journal of Community Psychology, 26*, 115–152.

Eisenberg, N., Cumberland, A, & Spinrad, T. L. (1998). Parental socialization of emotion. *Psychological Inquiry, 9*, 241–273.

Eisenberg, N., & Fabes, R. A. (1994). Mothers' reactions to children's negative emotions: Relations to children's temperament and anger behavior. *Merrill-Palmer Quarterly, 40*, 138–156.

Eisenberg, N., Fabes, R. A., Guthrie, I. K., Murphy, B. C., Maszk, P., Holmgren, R., & Suh, K. (1996). The relations of regulation and emotionality to problem behavior in elementary school children. *Development & Psychopathology, 8*, 141–162.

Eisenberg, N., Fabes, R. A., Murphy, B., Karbon, M., Smith, M., & Maszk, P. (1996). The relations of children's dispositional empathy-related responding to their emotionality, regulation, and social functioning. *Developmental Psychology, 32*, 195–209.

Eisenberg, N., Fabes, R. A., Murphy, B., Maszk, P., Smith, M., & Karbon, M. (1995). The role of emotionality and regulation in children's social functioning: A longitudinal study. *Child Development, 66*, 1360–1384.

Eisenberg, N., Fabes, R. A., Shepard, S. A., Guthrie, I., Murphy, B. C., & Reiser, M. (1999). Parental reactions to children's negative emotions: Longitudinal relations to quality of children's social functioning. *Child Development, 70*, 513–534.

Eisenberg, N., Fabes, R. A., Shepard, S. A., Murphy, B. C., Guthrie, I. K., Jones, S., Friedman, J., Poulin, R., & Maszk, P. (1997). Contemporaneous and longitudinal prediction of children's social functioning from regulation and emotionality. *Child Development, 68*, 642–664.

Elias, M. J., Zins, J. E., Weissberg, R. P., Frey, K. S., Greenberg, M. T., Haynes, N. M., Kessler, R., Schwab-Stone, M. E., & Shriver T. P. (1997). *Promoting social and emotional learning: Guidelines for educators.* Alexandria, VA: Association for Supervision and Curriculum Development.

Epstein, J. L. (1996). Perspectives and previews on research and policy for school, family, and community partnerships. In A. Booth and J. F. Dunn (Eds.), *Family-school links: How do they affect educational outcomes?* (pp. 209–246). Hillsdale, NJ: Lawrence Erlbaum Associates.

Fabes, R. A., Eisenberg, N., McCormick, S. E., & Wilson, M. S. (1988). Preschoolers' attributions of the situational determinants of others' naturally occurring emotions. *Developmental Psychology, 24*, 376–385.

Fabes, R. A., Eisenberg, N., Nyman, M., & Michealieu, Q. (1991). Young children's appraisal of others spontaneous emotional reactions. *Developmental Psychology, 27*, 858–866.

Fantuzzo, J., Childs, S., Stevenson, H., Coolahan, K. C., Ginsburg, M., Gay, K., Debnam, D., & Watson, C. (1996). The Head Start teaching center: An evaluation of an experiential, collaborative training model for Head Start teachers and parent volunteers. *Early Childhood Research Quarterly, 11*, 79–99.

Frey, K. S., Hirschstein, M. K., & Guzzo, B. A. (2000). Second Step: Preventing aggression by promoting social competence. *Journal of Emotional and Behavioral Disorder, 8*, 102–110.

Gagnon, C., Craig, W. M., Tremblay, R. E., Zhou, R. M., & Vitaro, F. (1995). Kindergarten predictors of boys' stable behavior problems at the end of elementary school. *Journal of Abnormal Child Psychology, 23*, 751–766.

Galambos, J. (1978). *Positive discipline.* Washington, DC: NAEYC.

Garcia Coll, C., & Magnusson, K. (2000). Cultural differences as sources of developmental vulnerabilities and resources. In J. P. Shonkoff and S. J. Meisels (Eds.), *Handbook of early childhood intervention,* 2nd ed. (pp. 94–144). New York: Cambridge University Press.

Garner, P. W., Jones, D. C., Gaddy, G., & Rennie, K. (1997). Low income mothers' conversations about emotions and their children's emotional competence. *Social Development, 6*, 37–52.

Garner, P. W., Jones, D. C., & Miner, J. L. (1994). Social competence among low-income preschoolers: Emotion socialization practices and social cognitive correlates. *Child Development, 65*, 622–637.

Garner, P. W., & Spears, F. M. (2000). Emotion regulation in low-income preschoolers. *Social Development, 9*, 246–264.

Gartrell, D. (2003). *A guidance approach for the encouraging classroom* (3rd edition). Clifton Park, NY: Delmar Learning.

Gottman, J. M., & Declaire, J. (1997). *The heart of parenting: Raising an emotionally intelligent child.* Los Angeles, CA: Audio Renaissance.

Gottman, J. M., Katz, L. F., & Hooven, C. (1997). *Meta-emotion: How families communicate emotionally, links to child peer relations, and other developmental outcomes.* Mahwah, NJ: Lawrence Erlbaum Associates.

Greenberg, M. T., Domitrovich, C., & Bumbarger, B. (1999). *Preventing mental disorders in school-age children: A review of the effectiveness of prevention programs.* State College, PA: CMHS.

Greenberg, M. T., Domitrovich, C., & Bumbarger, B. (2001). The prevention of mental disorders in school-aged children: Current state of the field. *Prevention & Treatment, 4*, Article 1. Retrieved March 30, 2001, from *http://journals.apa.org/prevention/volume4/pre0040001a.html*

Greenberg, M. T., Kusché, C., & Mihalic, S. F. (1998). *Blueprints for violence prevention, book 10: Promoting alternative thinking strategies (PATHS).* Boulder, CO: Center for the Study and Prevention of Violence.

Greenberg, M. T., & Snell, J. L. (1997). Brain development and emotional development: The role of teaching in organizing the frontal lobe. In P. Salovey & D.J. Sluyter (Eds.), *Emotional development and emotional intelligence* (pp.93–119). New York: Basic Books.

Greenberg, P. (1992). How to institute some simple democratic practices pertaining to respect, rights, roots, and responsibilities in any classroom (without losing your leadership position). *Young Children, 47*(5), 10–17.

Greenspan, S. (1992). *Floor Time,* a videotape. New York: Scholastic, Inc.

Greenwood, P., Model, K. E., Rydell, C. P., & Chiesa, J. (1996). *Diverting children from a life of crime: Measuring costs and benefits.* Santa Monica, CA: RAND.

Hawkins, J. D., & Catalano, R. F., Morrison, D. M., O'Donnell, J., Abbott, R. D., & Day, L. E. (1992). The Seattle Social Development Project: Effects of the first four years on protective factors and problem behaviors. In J. McCord & R. E. Tremblay (Eds.), *Preventing antisocial behavior: Interventions from birth through adolescence* (pp. 139–161). New York: Guilford.

Hawkins, J. D., & Weiss, J. G. (1985). The social development model: An integrated approach to delinquency prevention. *Journal of Primary Prevention, 6*, 73–97.

Howes, C. (1987). Peer interaction of young children. *Monographs of the Society for Research in Child Development, 53* (1, Serial No. 217).

Howes, C. (2000). Social-emotional classroom climate in child care, child-teacher relationships and children's second grade peer relations. *Social Development, 9*, 191–204.

Howes, C., Galinsky, E., & Kontos, S. (1998). Child care caregiver sensitivity and attachment. *Social Development, 7*, 25–36.

Howes, C., & Smith, E. W. (1995). Relations among child care quality, teacher behavior, children's play activities, emotional security, and cognitive activity in child care. *Early Childhood Research Quarterly, 10*, 381–404.

Hudley, C. (2001). The role of culture in prevention research. *Prevention & Treatment, 4*, Article 5. Retrieved March 30, 2001, from *http://journals.apa.org/prevention/volume4/pre0040005c.html*

Hunter, L., Elias, M. J., & Norris, J. (2001). School based violence prevention: Challenges and lessons learned from an action research project. *Journal of School Psychology, 39*, 161–175.

Huston, A. C., McLoyd, V. C., & Garcia Coll, C. (1994). Children and poverty: Issues in contemporary research. *Child Development, 65*, 275–282.

Hyson, M. C. (1994). *The emotional development of young children: Building an emotion-centered curriculum.* New York: Teachers College Press.

Izard, C. E., & Bear, G. (1999). *Head Start/ECAP emotions curriculum.* Newark, DE: Instructional Resources Center, University of Delaware.

Izard, C. E., Fine, S., Schultz, D., Mostow, A., Ackerman, B., & Youngstrom, E. (2001). Emotions knowledge as a predictor of social behavior and academic competence in children at risk. *Psychological Science, 12*, 18–23.

Jacobsen, T., & Hofmann, V. (1997). Children's attachment representations: Longitudinal relations to school behavior and academic competency in middle childhood and adolescence. *Developmental Psychology, 33*, 703–710.

Jensen, L. C., & Wells, M. G. (1979). *Feelings: Helping children understand emotions.* Provo, UT: Brigham Young University Press.

Kalyanpur, M. & Harry, B. (1999). *Culture in special education: Building reciprocal family-professional relationships.* Baltimore, MD: Brookes Publishing Co.

Kusché, C. A., & Greenberg, M. T. (1994). *The PATHS curriculum.* Seattle, WA: Developmental Research and Programs.

Ladd, G. W., Birch, S. H., & Buhs, E. S. (1999). Children's social and scholastic lives in kindergarten: Related spheres of influence? *Child Development, 70*, 1373–1400.

Ladd, G. W., Kochenderfer, B. J., & Coleman, C. C. (1996). Friendship quality as a predictor of young children's early school adjustment. *Child Development, 67*, 1103–1118.

Laible, D. J., & Thompson, R. A. (1998). Attachment and emotional understanding in preschool children. *Developmental Psychology, 34*, 1038–1045.

Lemerise, E., & Arsenio, W. F. (2000). An integrated model of emotion processes and cognition in social information processing. *Child Development, 71*, 107–118.

Lemerise, E. A. & Dodge, K. A. (2000). The development of anger and hostile interactions. In M. Lewis & J. M. Haviland-Jones (Eds.), *Handbook of emotions* (pp. 594–606). New York: Guilford.

Lewis, M., Stanger, C., & Sullivan, M. (1989). Deception in three-year-olds. *Developmental Psychology, 25*, 439–443.

Lewis, M., Sullivan, M., & Vasen, A. (1987). Making faces: Age and emotion differences in the posing of emotional expressions. *Developmental Psychology, 23*, 690–697.

Marcon, R. (1993). Socioemotional versus academic emphasis: Impact on kindergarteners' development and achievement. *Early Child Development and Care, 96*, 81–91.

Marcon, R. (1999). Differential impact of preschool models on development and early learning of inner-city children: A three-cohort study. *Developmental Psychology, 35*, 358–375.

Mardell, B. (1992). A practitioner's perspective on the implications of attachment theory for childcare professionals. *Child Study Journal, 22*, 201–232.

Mardell, B. (1994). How understanding attachment theory can help make us better teachers. *NHSA Journal, 12*, 39–47.

McMahon, S. D., Washburn, J., Felix, E. D., Yakin, J., & Childrey, G. (2000). Violence prevention: Program effects on urban preschool and kindergarten children. *Applied and Preventive Psychology, 9*, 271–281.

Mendel, R. A. (2000). *Less hype, more help: Reducing juvenile crime, what works—and what doesn't.* Washington, DC: American Youth Policy Forum.

de Melendez, W. R., & Ostertag, V. (1997). *Teaching young children in multicultural classrooms.* Albany, NY: Delmar Publishers.

Mitchell-Copeland, J., Denham, S. A., & DeMulder, E. (1997). Child-teacher attachment and social competence. *Early Education and Development, 8*, 27–39.

Moll, L. C., & Greenberg, J. (1990). Creating zones of possibilities: Combing social contexts for instruction. In L. C. Moll (Ed.). *Vygotsky and education: Instructional implications and applications of sociohistorical psychology* (pp. 319–348). Cambridge, England: Cambridge University Press.

Murphy, B. C., Eisenberg, N., Fabes, R. A., Shepard, S., & Guthrie, I. K. (1999). Consistency and change in children's emotionality and regulation: A longitudinal study. *Merrill-Palmer Quarterly, 45*, 413–444.

Nelson, K. (1996). *Language in cognitive development: The emergence of the mediated mind.* New York: Cambridge University Press.

O'Neil, R., Welsh, M., Parke, R. D., Wang, S., & Strand, C. (1997). A longitudinal assessment of the academic correlates of early peer acceptance and rejection. *Journal of Clinical Child Psychology, 26*, 290–303.

Park, K. A., Lay, K., & Ramsay, L. (1993). Individual differences and developmental changes in preschoolers' friendships. *Developmental Psychology, 29*, 264–270.

Parke, R. D., Cassidy, J., Burks, V. M., Carson, J. L., & Boyum, L. (1992). Familial contribution to peer competence among young children: The role of interactive and affective processes. In R. D. Parke & G. W. Ladd (Eds.), *Family-peer relationships: Modes of linkage* (107–134). Hillsdale, NJ: Erlbaum.

Parker, J. G., & Asher, S. R. (1987). Peer relations and later personality adjustment: Are low-accepted children at risk? *Psychological Bulletin, 102*, 357–389.

Parker, J. G., & Gottman, J. M. (1989). Social and emotional development in a relational context: Friendship interaction from early childhood to adolescence. In T. J. Berndt & G. W. Ladd (Eds.), *Peer relationships in child development* (pp. 95–131). New York: Wiley.

Payton, J. W., Wardlaw, D. M., Graczyk, P. A., Bloodworth, M. R., Tompsett, C. J., & Weissberg, R. P. (2000). Social and emotional learning: A framework for promoting mental health and reducing risk behaviors in children and youth. *Journal of School Health, 70(5)*, 179–185.

Peth-Pierce, R. (2000). *A good beginning: Sending America's children to school with the social and emotional competence they need to succeed.* Chapel Hill, NC: The Child Mental Health Foundations and Agencies Network. Retrieved December 3, 2002, from *http://www.nimh.nih.gov/childhp/fdnconsb.htm*

Pianta, R. C. (1997). Adult-child relationship processes and early schooling. *Early Education and Development, 8*, 11–26.

Pianta, R. C., Steinberg, M., & Rollins, K. (1995). The first two years of school: Teacher-child relationships and deflections in children's classroom adjustment. *Development & Psychopathology, 7*, 295–312.

Pianta, R. C., & Walsh, D .J. (1998). Applying the construct of resilience in schools: Cautions from a developmental systems perspective. *School Psychology, 27*, 407–417.

Putallaz, M. (1987). Maternal behavior and children's social status. *Child Development, 58*, 324–340.

Ramey, C. T., & Ramey, S. L. (1998). Early intervention and early experience. *American Psychologist, 53,* 109–120.

Raver, C. C., Blackburn, E. K., & Bancroft, M. (1999). Relations between effective emotional self-regulation, attentional control, and low-income preschoolers' social competence with peers. *Early Education and Development, 10,* 333–350.

Robin, A. L., Schneider, M., & Dolnick, M. (1976). The Turtle Technique: An extended case study of self-control in the classroom. *Psychology in the Schools, 13,* 449–453.

Robins, L. N., & Rutter, M. (1990). *Straight and devious pathways from childhood to adulthood.* Cambridge, England: Cambridge University Press.

Rubin, K. D., & Clark, M. L. (1983). Preschool teachers' ratings of behavioral problems: Observational, sociometric, and social-cognitive correlates. *Journal of Abnormal Child Psychology, 11,* 273–286.

Rubin, K. D., & Daniels-Byrness, T. (1983). Concurrent and predictive correlates of sociometric status in kindergarten and grade 1 children. *Merrill-Palmer Quarterly, 29,* 337–352.

Sánchez, S. Y. (1999). Learning from the stories of culturally and linguistically diverse families and communities: A sociohistorical lens. *Remedial and Special Education, 20,* 351–359.

Sánchez, S. Y. & Thorp, E. K. (1998). Policies on linguistic continuity: A family's right, a practitioner's choice, or an opportunity to create shared meaning and a more equitable relationship? *Zero to Three, 18(6),* 12–20.

Sandy, S. V., & Boardman, S. K. (2000). The Peaceful Kids conflict resolution program. *The International Journal of Conflict Management, 11,* 337–357.

Schultz, D., Izard, C. E., & Ackerman, B. P. (2000). Children's anger attribution bias: Relations to family environment and social adjustment. *Social Development, 9,* 284–301.

Schultz, D., Izard, C. E., Ackerman, B. P., & Youngstrom, E. A. (2001). Emotion knowledge in economically disadvantaged children: Self-regulatory antecedents and relations to social difficulties and withdrawal. *Development & Psychopathology, 13,* 53–67.

Schweinhart, L. J., & Weikart, D. P. (1997). *Lasting differences: The High/Scope preschool curriculum comparison study through age 23* (High/Scope Educational Research Foundation Monographs No. 12). Ypsilanti, MI: High Scope Press.

Serna, L., Nielsen, E., Lambros, K., & Forness, S. (2000). Primary prevention with children at risk for emotional or behavioral disorders: Data on a universal intervention for Head Start classrooms. *Behavioral Disorders, 26,* 70–84.

Shields, A., Dickstein, S., Seifer, R., Guisti, L., Magee, K. D., & Spritz, B. (2001). Emotional competence and early school adjustment: A study of preschoolers at risk. *Early Education and Development, 12,* 73–96.

Shonkoff, J. P., & Phillips, D. A. (2000). *From neurons to neighborhoods: The science of early childhood development.* Washington, DC: National Academy Press.

Shore, R. (1997). *Rethinking the brain: New insights into early development.* New York: Families and Work Institute.

Shure, M. B. (1990). *ICPS problem-solving techniques for preschool age children for use by teachers* (2nd edition). Philadelphia: Hahnemann University.

Smith, M. (2001). Social and emotional competencies: Contributions to young African-American children's peer acceptance. *Early Education and Development, 12,* 49–72.

Sroufe, L. A., Schork, E., Motti, F., Lawroski, N., & LaFreniere, P. (1984). The role of affect in social competence. In C. E. Izard, J. Kagan, & R. B. Zajonc (Eds.), *Emotions, cognition, & behavior* (pp. 289–319). Cambridge, England: Cambridge University Press.

Stipek, D., Daniels, D., Galuzzo, D., & Milburn, S. (1992). Characterizing early childhood education programs for poor and middle-class children. *Early Childhood Research Quarterly, 7,* 1–19.

Strayer, J. (1980). A naturalistic study of empathic behaviors and their relation to affective states and perspective-taking skills in preschool children. *Child Development 51*, 815–822.

Tabors, P. O. (1997). *One child, two languages: A guide for preschool educators of children learning English as a second language.* Baltimore, MD: Brookes Publishing Co.

Thorp, E. K. (1997). Increasing opportunities for partnership with culturally and linguistically diverse families. *Intervention in School and Clinic, 32*, 261–269.

Tomkins, S. S. (1991). *Affect, imagery, and consciousness, Vol. III. The negative affects: Anger and fear.* New York: Springer.

Tremblay, R. E., Pagani-Kurtz, L., Masse, L. C., Vitaro, F., & Pihl, R. O. (1995). A bimodal preventive intervention for disruptive kindergarten boys: Its impact through mid-adolescence. *Journal of Consulting and Clinical Psychology, 63*, 560–568.

Waters, E., & Sroufe, L. A. (1983). A developmental perspective on competence. *Developmental Review, 3*, 79–97.

Webster-Stratton, C. (1998). Preventing conduct problems in Head Start children: Strengthening parenting competencies. *Journal of Consulting and Clinical Psychology, 66*, 715–730.

Webster-Stratton, C., Reid, J., & Hammond, M. (2001). Preventing conduct problems, promoting social competence: A parent and teacher training partnership in Head Start. *Journal of Clinical Child Psychology, 30*, 283–302.

Webster-Stratton, C., & Taylor, T. (2001). Nipping early risk factors in the bud: Preventing substance abuse, delinquency, and violence in adolescence through interventions targeted at young children (0–8 years). *Prevention Science, 2*, 165–192.

Weissberg, R. P., & Greenberg, M. T. (1998). School and community competence-enhancement and prevention programs. In I. E. Sigel & A. Renninger (Eds.), *Handbook of child psychology* (5th ed.). *Volume 4: Child psychology in practice* (pp. 878–954). New York: John Wiley.

Yoshikawa, H., & Knitzer, J. (1997). *Lessons from the field: Head Start mental health strategies to meet changing needs.* New York: National Center for Children in Poverty, Columbia School of Public Health and the American Orthopsychiatric Association Task Force on Head Start and Mental Health.

Zahn-Waxler, C., Radke-Yarrow, M., & King, R. A. (1979). Child rearing and children's prosocial initiations toward victims of distress. *Child Development, 50*, 319–330.

Chapter 3

How Teachers and Caregivers Can Help Young Children Become More Prosocial

Alice Sterling Honig

Children show prosocial behaviors as they empathize with a hurt peer or adult, as they comfort, share, help, forgive, wait patiently, donate to charity, act kindly to protect or defend a sibling or a pet. Prosocial behaviors are defined by their "intended consequences for others" (Eisenberg & Mussen, 1990, p. 3). But children may be generous and thoughtful in the hope that their parents or Santa will give them a present in return. *Altruism* refers to a special subset of prosocial behaviors that are purely voluntary without any thought of personal gain. Prosocial behaviors have been observed even in infants.

> Held in arms, 12-month-old Benjy watched his mother wince and cry out as the doctor tried to see way down her throat. Benjy swiped his hand to push the doctor away to "protect" his mom from being hurt.

> A toddler's mom was babysitting her neighbor's baby. Her toddler picked up a cracker dropped by the neighbor's wailing baby onto the floor from his high chair. "No cry baby!" the worried toddler reassured the crying baby as he gave back the cracker, which the toddler himself usually loved as a snack.

> Shoshie picked up a sponge at the art center where her four-year-old peer Harold stood staring uncertainly and shyly at the sponges, poster paints, and egg cartons set out on the table at the childcare center. "See honey it's easy" she reassured Harold. "You just dip a piece of sponge in the paint and press

down to make a color at the bottom!" Shoshie proceeded to demonstrate and smiled up at Harold, who gathered courage and then tried creating a blob of color inside one of the cardboard egg cups of the carton.

Children learn social norms of *reciprocating helpfulness* and of *responsibility for helping others less fortunate*. This knowledge is learned by 8 or 9 years. Children may even endorse the norm when questioned; and they can explain it to other children. Yet this knowledge or agreement with social "norms per se does not ordinarily instigate prosocial actions" (Eisenberg & Mussen 1990, p. 5). Prosocial behaviors need to be distinguished from *moral judgment*, which refers to reasoning about moral issues and dilemmas rather than actual behaviors.

For many years, child development research focused far more on children's aggression than on their prosocial behaviors. Then, in March 1964, a terrible event galvanized national awareness about the importance of caring about what happens to others. In Queens, New York, a nurse, Kitty Genovese, was fatally stabbed many times in the parking lot near her apartment. Dozens of people heard her screams and from their windows even watched her being murdered. Not one person called the police or did anything to help. Press coverage of this shocking revelation of civic unconcern led to a spurt in social research on when and how and why people learn to be concerned and kind and helpful.

During the 1990's, TV coverage on incidents where children killed other children in public schools re-awakened public shock and concern about the quality of social interactions within schools. This awakening concern with a school climate of violence broadened to include attention to violence in media fare for children. Thus, recent headlines on the front page of the New York Times informed readers that Japanese "anime" style TV cartoons for children show extremely vivid and sadistic fight scenes. One example is when a pug-nosed thug kicks in an elderly storekeeper's face. Then he punches a young heroine in the eye and cracks her in the small of the back with a heavy bar stool. Her limp frame collapses to the ground as he stands over her with his gun drawn and pointed at her head.

Although the "Mighty Morphin Power Rangers" TV program had caused teacher concern in the 1990's (Levin & Carlsson-Paige, 1995), as did the Nintendo video game and Pokemon TV episodes, little protest is currently heard about these "anime" violent cartoons. Some experts believe that nowadays parents are "desensitized," since they themselves grew up with violent TV cartoons.

Clinicians daily hear graphically how schools are riddled with bullying and sneers, with jeering and put-downs and rejections. Not only schools, but neighborhoods also provide daily episodes of violence. When children are exposed to acute violence, they show a range of internalizing problems, including anxiety, depression, somatic symptoms (such as tics, nail biting, self-scratching, crying jags) and fears, but more often there is a stronger relationship with externalizing behaviors, such as child aggression and conduct disorders (Buka, Stichick, Birdthistle, & Felton, 2001). Often school personnel urge parents to "talk with their children." But at an antiviolence forum on "Warning Signs for Parents" (WSP), one mother related that in school "My son is a victim of teasing and bullying. He's told me, 'Mom, I'm gonna blow'." A tearful mother said she does talk with her son, but he feels desperate because kids are mean and call him "retard" (Zabriskie, 2001). The American Psychological Association Practice Directorate has developed a written pamphlet "Communication tips for parents."7 made available at WSP forums. The importance of planning and programming to decrease violence, child loneliness, rejection, and social insensitivity and to increase sensitive and responsive awareness of others' needs and feelings, as well as techniques of defusing and resolving conflicts becomes evident daily as we read the deadly and sorrowful consequences of our inattention to prosocial goals.

Bullying is a serious problem in schools, summer camps, and other group settings for children. What is bullying?

> Bullying is when one person is repeatedly hurtful to another. It can be physical, verbal, or psychological. In its obvious form, one child is taunting another with put-downs or shoving or hitting. But bullies are often more subtle. Bullying happens when six girls are sitting at a table in the dining hall and girl number seven shows up: the six girls spread out just enough so there's no room for her to sit down. Nothing is said . . . . Bullies tend to be smart, socially aware kids who know enough to wait till the grownups aren't watching. At school they wait until recess or lunch time, and at camp they wait until free time, when the counselors take breaks. As if to aid and abet the bullies, victims keep quiet. Squealers are victimized tenfold. (Kates, 2001, p, 7)

Some nations are more advanced in their attention to bullying. In Norway, the admirable work of the psychologist Olweus has resulted in national laws that teachers are responsible for preventing bullying in school and in the production of videos and handbooks so that teachers can implement programs to decrease bullying in schools (Olweus, 1993).

Until recently a philosophical awareness in society that implementation strategies to create prosocial classrooms should become an urgent social priority for preschoolers and school age children was not a general belief. Advocating prosocial behaviors has been generally considered the domain of faith communities and of specialized parent training programs such as PET (Parent Effectiveness Training, Gordon, 1970) and STEP (Systematic Training for Effective Parenting, Dinkmeyer & Dinkmeyer, 1982).

Horrors such as the Columbine School massacre as well as violence in school corridors and in neighborhoods where youthful gang "turf" wars make citizens fearful, increase our sense that we need to galvanize our efforts to help our youngest citizens to become more caring and peaceful in their relationships as early in life as possible.

Who Are the Earliest Teachers of Prosocial Interactions?

Fundamental work to promote prosocial behaviors has traditionally belonged to parents. *Attachment theory* has been foremost in the past decades in illuminating how closely parental care patterns influence baby altruism and an early sense of caring about others' feelings (Honig, 2002b).

Attachment researchers make it abundantly clear that when parents are attuned to infant distress, prompt in meeting distress with caring, appropriate nurturing, and generous with body loving and comforting, then their babies and young children are far more likely to be more positive and cooperative with the parents in turn, but also more friendly and prosocial with others (Bretherton & Waters, 1985; Grossman, Zimmerman, & Steele, 1999). The securely attached infant or toddler is far more likely to grow up to be friendly and cooperative with peers as Sroufe & Fleeson (1986) discovered. Infants rated as avoidant, insecurely attached (their mothers did not provide enough body loving and intimate nurturing and the infants had learned to avoid asking for nurturance) were more likely to behave as bullies years later when placed in a preschool classroom. Another group of preschoolers had experienced some cuddling, but also narcissistic and inconsistent mothering, and as infants they had been rated as insecurely "ambivalently" attached. In the preschool classroom, these children were more likely to act immature with each other in play and to be victimized if they were at play with a preschooler whose initial attachment classification in infancy had been "avoidant."

The most cogent finding of these researches was that the teachers gave more leeway for misbehavior and more nurturance to the "victim" preschoolers. Toward the preschoolers who had been securely attached to mother in infancy, teachers showed the highest expectations for compliance and gave the least attention! No teacher knew about the assessment of the children's attachment classifications in infancy, whether "secure", or insecure ("avoidant" or "ambivalent"). Although they were highly trained professionals, the teachers did show anger, but only with the preschoolers more likely to be bullies—those children who had been avoidantly attached in infancy, years before entering the preschool.

Compared with peers, college students who scored high on an empathy scale recollected their parents as more empathic and affectionate when they were children (Barnett, Howard, King, & Dino, 1980). Longitudinal researches report more bullying, more accusing peers, more tattling, more angry or isolated children when there has been lack of early family cherishing of infants and young children (Egeland & Sroufe, 1981).

In today's world, the majority of mothers of infants and preschoolers are in the work force (Honig, 2002a). Thus, group care settings for very small children are now critical places where children need to learn compassionate ways to interact with peers and teachers.

Prosocial classrooms flow from the harmonious synergy of family loving, together with teacher cherishing and teacher skills. So the urgent question becomes: "How can we create classrooms as well as home climates that emphasize empathic concern, kindness, cooperation, generosity, and helpfulness for young children, as early as infancy?"(Honig, 1982; 1996; 2002b). Some techniques teachers use are for the whole school. For example, child-friendly safe schools will display a variety of children's work on the walls. Principals walk the hallways and interact with the children every day. Classes are small and so is the school (about 300 to 400 children). "Albert Shankar, who led the American Federation of Teachers, once said that if the principal knew only the top students and the troublemakers, the school was too big" (Morrow, 2002, p. 58).

Suggestions in this chapter address teacher concerns for the entire classroom, for engaging small groups with each other, and for interacting with individual children and pairs of children to promote peaceable play.

Child-Centered, High-Quality Care Promotes Prosocial Behaviors

Classroom ambience and philosophy make a difference in creating a climate for prosocial interactions. Developmentally appropriate programming (DAP) enhances cooperation (Bredekamp & Rosegrant, 1992). Teacher training increases the probability that DAP philosophy will be implemented. One researcher noted that both teacher-rated and observed preschool aggression scores were *lower* when staff was more highly trained and stable, although the preschoolers had quite varied histories of full-time or part-time nonparental care during infancy and toddlerhood (Park & Honig, 1991).

Four-year-olds from a constructivist classroom (who had been encouraged to make choices and devise social problem-solving strategies) performed with higher social-cognitive skills at board games compared with their peers from a different preschool program (Devries & Goncu, 1990).

Adult-directed preschool classrooms are less likely to provide active support for prosocial behaviors than classrooms where child-initiated learning is encouraged (Huston-Stein, Friedrich-Cofer, & Susman, 1977). Longitudinal follow-up into young adulthood of children from low-income households who had attended either a high adult-directed preschool or a program that emphasized high child-initiations, revealed more social competence in the latter (Schweinhart, Weikart & Larner, 1986).

Children who experienced both high quality care and supportive parents were rated as more adept at decoding and regulating emotional signals in peer play. Such regulation is a good indicator for positive peer relationships (Howes & Stewart, 1987). Sadly, these researchers noted that the most stressed families chose the lowest quality childcare and were more likely to change care arrangements; their children had the lowest levels of competence during social play with peers. Such results point to the fact that a three-pronged concerted effort is needed to enhance prosocial competence. Efforts must be directed to educate parents, educators, and community planners.

Community-wide Supports for Quality Care

Community help is often available through a Resource and Referral (R&R) agency or Child Care Council. These agencies are often a fine source of materials and information to help families recognize and choose high quality childcare and to inform parents about centers that have NAEYC accreditation. Unfortunately only about 7% of centers in the United States are NAEYC accredited, and estimates of unregulated care cited in Congressional testimony ranges from 60% to 90% (Honig, 2002a).

Federally, through the Child Care Technical Assistance Network (CCAN) of the Child Care Bureau, a few projects have begun to address community needs to provide more coordinated partnership delivery systems of care to include staff training and supports for working families (Azer & Elliott, 1998).

Ideas for Classrooms

Provide a Teaching Model of Firm Calmness

Some children and their folks live in angry households, and the anger is acted out in the preschool. How can a teacher of young children "tame the dragon of anger?" (Eastman, 1994). Calmness and caring radiate like warm sunshine through a classroom. Be sure to show by example the value of self-control as well as how to act fairly and with consideration. See problems with an angry child as an opportunity for you to practice finding the strength to set limits and consequences for inappropriate expressions of anger. Adults need a good deal of strength to deal firmly and directly with an angry child hurting another rather than ignoring the incident for example, by saying "Oh, you must be tired." Teachers instigate considerate behaviors and reward them when they occur (Lickona, 2000). But they must also learn how to use a lowered voice tone, look directly at a child at eye level, stay calm, continue to give the message that the child is cherished, and still provide clear, effective consequences when faced with a child's angry hurtful behaviors.

Use Inductive Reasoning

Maternal use of "explanations with emotional loading (e.g., "Look what you did! Don't you see that you hurt Amy! Don't ever pull hair!) has been linked with high levels of reparations and altruism" (Eisenberg & Mussen, 1990, p. 83). In contrast, a high use of power-assertive discipline ("Don't do that!") is associated with low levels of consideration for others. "Simple explanations of cause and effect ('Tom's crying because you pushed him') had no effect" on children's altruism. Thus, emotionally-toned explanations when coupled with clear explanations of rules and strong modeling of consideration for others can arouse empathy in very young children, stimulate role taking, and also give a clear message that children are responsible for their behaviors.

Emphasize Cooperation Rather Than Competition in School Learning

Dear to the heart of each experienced preschool teacher is the wish that the young children in her or his classroom will be prepared for successful learning careers as well as social adeptness with peers and adults. Competitive classrooms result in some children becoming tense, fearing failure, and becoming less motivated to persist at challenging tasks. In *cooperative interaction classrooms*, the emphasis is on children working together to accomplish mutual goals (Aronson, Bridgeman, & Geffner, 1978).

Even toddlers can work together in cooperative play. For example, if each toddler grasps the opposite ends of a towel, both can joyfully keep a beach ball bouncing on the towel by coordinating their efforts together.

Every child has an essential and unique contribution to make to class learning. One teaching tool has been called the *jigsaw technique* because the teacher provides each school child with one piece of information about a lesson. Then the children must work cooperatively with each other to learn all the material and information necessary for a complete presentation by the small group (Aronson, Stephan, Sikes, Blaney & Snapp, 1978).

Engage Children In Peaceful Sports and Games

Caregivers who ingeniously devise cooperative sports promote peace in the classroom (Kreidler, 1985). Variations of traditional children's games will encourage cooperation rather than competition (Orlick, 1978, 1982, 1985; Prutzman, Sgern, Berger, & Bodenhamer, 1988). Play musical chairs so that each time a chair is taken away, the "left-over" child must find a lap to sit on rather than be out of the game. Then no child feels "left out" or a "failure". Bev Bos (1990) provides examples such as "Spider swing". One child, with legs hanging out the back of the swing, sits on the lap of another. Bos uses the term *coaction* when children play cooperatively together to create pleasure and fun in their games.

Arrange Classroom Spaces to Boost Prosocial Play

How you arrange learning centers and play corners, such as the block play area, affect whether children's play will become more aggressive or sustain a peaceful atmosphere. Give children enough space to feel friendly and unthreatened by others as they build with blocks. Small, cluttered play areas often lead to child confrontations and fights. Where preschoolers are crowded together in a narrow area with large blocks, there is greater pressure to use the blocks as missiles or pretend guns.

Choose equipment that requires joint activity. A group see-saw, a tire-bouncer, or a nylon parachute encourage group cooperation since the children need each other to maximize their enjoyment. More prosocial responses were given by young children attending daycare or nursery school programs when (1) a variety of age-appropriate materials were available and (2) space was arranged to accommodate groups of varying sizes (Holloway & Reichhart-Erickson, 1988). Children who played with large hollow and unit blocks in a large block area of their preschool learned and practiced positive social problem-solving skills rather than aggression (Rogers, 1987).

How can you use classroom layout to promote traffic patterns that will ensure more peaceful interactions? You may want to try to decrease clutter, create clearly defined and well-supplied interest centers, and provide duplicate materials (Honig & Wittmer, 1992). Four toddlers will march around to music much more happily if each one is able to march with a toy instrument.

Actively Use Aesthetics and Visualizations

Give attention to *aesthetics* to boost happiness and peaceful play in the classroom. Try soothing colors, wall decorations, banners, displays of children's art work, posters of classic fine paintings (such as Renoir's picture of two sisters at the piano), intimate relaxing spaces with soft cushions for snuggling down with a favorite picture book, and occasional soft waltz music to enhance calmness and harmony in the classroom. At lunch or snack time, use aesthetic touches such as a vase of silk flowers on the table and a lovely tablecloth easily tossed in a washing machine. Aesthetic touches give pleasure to children's eyes and spirits. They infuse eating time with positive feelings. One three-year-old said when a teacher forgot the tablecloth one day at lunch "Where is the table's blanket?"

Lead your children in imaginative *visualizations* as they lie resting on their mats. Each can pretend to be an ant or a fly busily walking on the ceiling How would the resting children appear to the fly?

Conjure a warm summer day near a stream. Ask the children to close their eyes and listen to birds singing and leaves rustling gently. Let them pretend they feel the warm dappling sunshine on their skin as they peek through the trees and watch a shy fawn coming to drink at the stream. Visualization experiences are soothing. They give children an imaginative way to calm themselves and take a "breather" when life seems full of grumpiness or stress (Honig, 2001).

Bibliotherapy: Books Are Powerful Teacher Allies

Daily reading affords teachers many opportunities to enhance empathy and caring. Choose literature that clearly emphasizes prosocial themes and altruistic characters. Children's literature can give a boost to prosocial and moral development (Krogh & Lamme, 1985). Below are some examples of such books for younger and for older children.

Persis, the little doll in *The Little One* (Dare Wright, 1959) lives with Cross Bear and with Nice Bear. Worried that maybe grumpy Cross Bear does not love her, she enlists her friend Turtle and then Crow to help her find a way to make Cross Bear happy. When she falls from a tree while trying to gather honey for him, Cross bear is so concerned that he blurts out that he does indeed love Persis and would never let her get hurt.

Hiawatha, in *Hiawatha's Kind Heart* (Walt Disney, 1986), is a young Native American boy who sets out on a hunting trip adventure to prove how brave he is by shooting an animal. Instead, he proves how courageous he is by not killing a baby squirrel or other animals he meets. In turn, his new friends help him escape safely by quick action when Hiawatha is chased by an angry bear.

Percy the park keeper (in a series of books by Nick Butterworth, 1996) proves to be a kind and ingenious friend. In *The Hedgehog's Balloon* Percy comforts a crying little hedgehog who longs for a balloon of his own. But balloons always burst on his prickly spines! Percy fastens a cork to each spine. Now the hedgehog can set off carrying his very own balloon without it breaking right away.

Two Good Friends (Delton, 1974) relates the charming story of two friends—Bear who is messy but a fine cook, and Duck who can keep everything tidy but can't cook well—who care for each other lovingly and generously. Lobel's, (1979) *Frog and Toad Are Friends* also recounts the story of two friends' gentle times together.

Dr. Seuss's Horton the Elephant is a loyal and trustworthy friend as a character in the books *Horton Hears a Who* (Dr. Seuss, 1954) and *Horton hatches an egg* (Dr. Seuss, 1991). So is the king's young page boy in Seuss's *The King's Stilts* (1967). So is *The Little Engine That Could* (Piper, 2001), as she chugs courageously up and over a very tall mountain to bring toys to boys and girls whom the little engine does not want to disappoint. Jack Keats' (1972) *The Pet Show* demonstrates how generous adults can be with children. Every child who brings a pet to the neighborhood show is made to feel proud as his or her pet gets some prize. There is even a prize for the quietest ant!

Something from Nothing (Gilman, 1993) reaffirms the gentleness and caring of Joseph's grandpa as over and over, during the preschool years, he refashions new clothing items from material in the old blanket he had initially and lovingly stitched when Joseph was a little baby and reaffirms the child's trust in his grandpa's kindness.

When an elderly lady tells him that she has lost her memory, the young boy, *Wilfred Gordon McDonald Partridge* (Mem Fox, 1984) sets out to find it for her. His loving search and caring friendliness open the way to the sharing of private memories between the boy and the old woman. *Mrs. Katz and Tush* by Patricia Polacco (1994) is another tale of intergenerational friendship and caring between an African-American boy and an elderly Jewish widow.

For elementary school age children, the Value Tales (a series of books published by Value Communications) by Spencer Johnson (1976a; 1976b; 1076c; 1979) emphasize loyalty, courage in the face of disappointments, sticking up for a peer, and other prosocial actions. Each book tells the story of a real person whose actions were truly altruistic. *The Value of Kindness* (1976c) relates the story of Elizabeth Fry, who taught the children of women prisoners in England to read and write. She also taught the mothers literacy and crafts so that they could earn a living when they left prison.

SOCRATIC QUESTIONS ENHANCE STORY TIME.   As you read stories with small groups, try to *use open-ended questions* (McMath, 1989). "Socratic" questions stimulate children to think about and better understand the motives and actions of story-book characters. As you read stories with kind and helpful animal and human characters, children are better able to understand in a practical every-day action sense what we adults mean by "kind" ways or "helpful" actions (Dreikurs, Grunwald, & Pepper, 1982). Set up a special place in your room for your *prosocial library*.

STORIES ABOUT WORRIES. Some of the children in your care may be dealing with painful family issues, such as loss of a parent because of divorce, death of a beloved pet, jealousy over the birth of a younger sibling, scared feelings about a harsh adult or an alcoholic parent. Try to add to your "Bibliotherapy" collection some books that can help a child identify with the character in the story who is going through similar troubles and finds ways to cope. Some examples of such books are: *Nobody's perfect, not even my mother* (by Norma Simon, 1981), which helps kids understand that everyone makes a mistake, like spilling milk, some of the time, and we all need to remember that everyone is good at some things!

In Russell Hoban's (1994) *Best Friends for Frances*, the badger Frances first rejects her little sister as a playmate. Then, realizing how it feels to be excluded from a "no-girls" ball game and how good it feels when everybody (even little sister!) can be invited to play, Frances organizes all the animals to play together and to enjoy a picnic too!

In *The Boy Who Could Make His Mother Stop Yelling*, Sondheimer (1982) tells the story of a little boy who is very careless with his toys. Finally, he communicates with his mom how scared he is of her loud "lion" voice. They both agree to try harder to be patient and remember what upsets the other.

Children who miss their fathers may feel real empathy with the boy in Norma Simon's (1983) book *I Wish I Had My Father*. Idealized solutions are not given. But longings and thoughts about men who *are* kind to the boy help him deal with his sorrow.

Don't touch (by Suzy Kline, 1987) perfectly captures the frustration of a little boy yelled at for messing with a freshly baked pie or with Grandpa's fishing tackle. He goes down to pound and pull and poke and stretch his playdough. Having worked out his need to touch in sundry actions with the playdough, Dan then puts up a big sign of his own that says "Don't touch!"

Annie Stories (by Doris Brett, 1988) provide a way for caregivers to make up a scenario when a child has something bothering him. The adult conjures characters very similar to the little boy or girl with the problem. Working out an ending that brings resolution to a worry or a resentment or an estrangement the child himself feels, the adult tells the child the "story" so that the worrier identifies with the story child and can better see how he too may positively resolve his distressing issue.

INCLUDE BOOKS ABOUT CHILDREN WITH DISABILITIES.   Extend your prosocial bibliotherapy collection so that the children hear stories that increase friendly, accepting, feelings about children with disabilities. *Nick joins in* (by Joe Lasker,1980) tells the story of a boy with a physical handicap who must use a wheelchair. When the children's ball at playtime gets stuck way up out of reach in the school gym, Nick cleverly thinks of a solution to the problem. He wheels his chair over to where the custodian keeps the long pole to open the gymnasium windows. With the help of that long pole, the ball is now retrievable and the children rejoice that with Nick's help the game can go on.

Introduce Prosocial Songs into Singing Circle Time

Some circle time songs give each child a chance to introduce himself or herself. The Russian preschool song "There will always be sunshine" ends with reassuring peaceful affirmations by the singing child that there will always be peace, mama, and me. Cassettes with songs to build a peaceable classroom through music and movement are also available (Pirtle, 1997). If children come into class angry, you can help them deal with their feelings by singing words that inspire awareness and impel self -control and alternate outlets for angry feelings. For example, use the melody to the song "If you're happy and you know it clap your hands" and vary the words:

If you're angry and you know it, take a breath;
If you're angry and you know it, breathe out slow;
If you're angry and you know it, you surely do not have to show it;
If you're angry and you know it, count to ten!

Children and teachers can think up other words that reflect the need to deal with angry feelings so that nobody gets hurt and the angry child finds a way to calm down and to deal in more socially appropriate ways with those feelings.

As they drift into nap time, sing lullabies whose melodiously murmured tones reassure your little ones that you are keeping them safe. Make daily soothing rituals of lullaby songs. Sing slow waltz songs as you dance with a baby in arms to calm her and sing soothing songs you make up that repeat her name often to reassure her after she wakes up cranky from her nap (Honig, 1995).

Establish Group Times to Talk about Prosocial Interactions

Sometimes adults think that children will pick up positive social rules for friendly interactions on their own. Young children often want what they want right away. They need help from adults in thinking about others' feelings as well as their own strong wishes (Fugitt, 1983; Sapon-Shevin, 2000). So *create classroom conversation times* when you and your group talk about fusses and problems and how to solve these so each person will feel better. Role playing scenarios help young children take the point of view of others, such as Goldilocks or baby bear! Role-plays help children become aware of how hurtful name calling and verbal put-downs feel to the other person. Role-plays challenge children cognitively and emotionally to feel how others feel when they are treated or not treated with courtesy. Teachers themselves are powerful role models of social courtesies as they listen to each child's ideas and give each child a turn to talk during group sharing times.

Bessell & Palomares (1973) suggested that teachers set aside time each day for *Magic Circle* activities. Two circles are formed. Children can choose to sit in the inner circle where they participate, or in the outer circle until they feel more comfortable about sharing. The teacher asks simple questions at first and each child is invited to take a turn answering. Some simple questions would be: "Tell us about a time when you made another child feel happy" or "Tell us about a time when another child made you feel glad". Questions move to more complex feelings when "sad" or "scared" or "angry" are substituted for the positive adjectives. Sometimes a child will copycat what another child has said. But each child feels *safe* in responding during such nonjudgmental sessions. These fifteen minutes daily are a special time when children know they are not been graded or judged as they share emotions and personal memories and listen to the feelings other children express about their significant emotional situations.

Sometimes children are unclear about the reasons why they need to behave cooperatively. In a nursery in China, the teachers told me that one preschooler was quite cooperative in the class. Teachers were puzzled when the parents came to complain that the child was not helpful when asked to do simple chores at home. Next day, the teacher took the 4-year-old aside and quietly asked him about this. He explained. "Well, in school I get a red star every time I help out. My parents do not ever give me a star!". The teacher then explained patiently that at home children and parents help each other because of their special love and caring closeness as a family.

Teachers cannot always assume that children will make such reasoning connections on their own. Many times, a preschooler will understand about rules for cooperation much better when teachers talk about and explain with homey, real-life examples, how we all have to help each other out to get along to have the most fun together in preschool.

When teachers gave preschool children explanations as to *why* sharing was important and *how* to share (Barton & Osborne, 1978), then sharing did increase. In another school-based research, second grade teachers set aside brief classroom time daily to encourage children to describe specific incidents relating how they and their classmates were being helpful and kind with one another that day. After one month, prosocial interactions increased about two-fold among these youngsters compared with a randomly assigned classroom of control children (Honig & Pollack, 1990).

Whitin (2001) motivated the children in her class for prosocial awareness and actions by creating a policy of writing down children's acts of kindness on slips of paper and then putting them in a "kindness jar". Whitin explained during her first kindergarten class meeting:

> Children, in our class we are going to watch for kind and helpful things that people do for one another. Already I have noticed people being kind to one another. Before our meeting, I saw Nicholas help Kai find the right puzzle piece and I wrote down Nicholas's kind act on this pad of paper in my pocket. I am sure that I will be able to write down many kind acts this morning. Then I will read them aloud before we go to lunch. (p. 18)

The teacher made her intentions explicit by talking aloud: "Oh, Shakura is sharing the dishes with Brittaney. I'd better write that down" (p. 18). Within a few days, the children were pointing out kind acts to the teacher and reminding teacher to write them down! A decorative canister was labeled "Kindness Jar" and a small box with slips of paper was used to keep all the kindness acts. Soon children were drawing their own pictures of kindness acts and earnestly trying to print a few letters to explain or announce the action of the picture. The children made the Kindness Jar their own to share with each other during circle time. Some teachers call this receptacle for the kindness actions and children's drawings a "Sunshine Basket".

Clarify Concepts of Fairness and Equity

During group discussion times try to increase young children's awareness of a concept difficult for preschoolers to grasp. *Distributive justice* refers to how goods and benefits are distributed justly among people with varying needs, temperaments, talents, and troubles. Of course you will not use such a fancy term. But you surely have lots of experience with young children's intense interest in what seems to them "fair" or not so fair. Children between 4 and 8 years are busy learning rules for games and rules for social relations. They are often concerned about fairness and who gets "more". Perhaps you could talk about a class where one child came to school without breakfast most of the time and wanted extra crackers at snack time because he felt so hungry. *Fairness* sometimes means giving extra generously to someone who has special needs (Damon, 1977). A child with a disability may need help from classmates and teacher or extra time to finish a project.

This special way of viewing fairness will be particularly important if you work in an inclusive classroom that integrates typical and atypical children. Children with disabilities sometimes need direct teacher assistance in learning to make friendly gestures to playmates and respond to playmates' friendly overtures. They may well need special coaching to enter and sustain friendly play with peers (Gresham, 1981; Honig & McCarron, 1990; Honig & Thompson, 1994).

Young children also need you to talk about how each person gets special attention at different times in different ways. Adults give extra special tender attention to little children when they are sick or scared. When mama is nursing the new baby, the preschool sibling in your class may tell you that she feels "they love the new baby more." During "circle time" the class may want to take turns talking about how a new baby gets special attention such as nursing when hungry and rocking on lap when crying. But the child in your class received the same loving special bodily care when he or she was a little baby. Also, the preschooler does get special attention! Mama reads him a bedtime story and invites him to roll the dough and cut out animal shapes while they bake cookies together. Baby does not get those special privileges. Dad escorts the preschooler to a friend's house for a birthday party, but baby does not get that special treatment. Your discussions will heighten young children's awareness of the complex nature of "fairness".

A prosocial curriculum, like the *Bingham Early Childhood Program*, is likely to increase acceptance of children from families who differ in ethnicity, language, or family background (Derman-Sparks & the A.B.C. Task Force, 1989). Emphasize how children are alike as much as possible. Kids like to eat pizza, visit the zoo, build a block tower with a friend, sit on a parent's lap for a story, play a circle game with hands held together as they chant. Discovering how alike child's wishes and favorite activities are will increase comfort with a child who may look different from others in the class.

Enlist Preschoolers to Pitch in Eagerly and Help with Chores

Anthropologists, studying six different cultures, noted that when children helped care for younger siblings and interacted socially with a cross-age variety of children in nonschool settings, they gained more nurturing skills and acted more responsible for the welfare of the group (Whiting & Whiting, 1975).

Give children responsibility, commensurate with their abilities, to care for and help teach younger children or children who may need extra personal help in the classroom. Children who carried out caring actions of *"required helpfulness,"* in a long term study of at-risk infants born on the island of Kauai, were more likely 32 years later to be functioning positively as family members and as community citizens (Werner, 1986).

Development occurs best in the context of an enduring, reciprocal relationship of play, love, and work. Around the world, very young children feel very safe and truly belonging within the family because they are intimately engaged in chores that help the family to function well. There is a vast difference between child "slave labor" and those chores that help children feel they truly belong to and contribute to the well-being of both their household and their classroom. Tasks and jobs to promote peaceful pride and helpfulness include:

- cleaning a gerbil's cage
- setting out magic markers at an art table
- squeezing soapy sponges to help clean up after an art project
- watering plants and feeding fishes
- sweeping under a table to clean up crumbs after snack or lunch
- comforting a young child in the childcare facility who seems scared or lonesome or has taken a tumble
- sorting and putting away scattered toys
- decorating gingerbread boy cookies during baking time
- sharing a picture story book with a younger sibling or child
- cutting wild weeds in the play yard to feed the class bunny

Children themselves may enthusiastically enjoy chiming in with more ideas for tasks that confirm the feeling they "belong" securely in their group. Their contributions are important and vital to the harmonious workings of the group. "When asked to move a heavy table . . . an entire classroom of preschoolers grab hold of the table's edge and wrestle it to its desired destination (Readdick & Douglas, 2000, p. 70).

As children engage in daily chores and jobs in the classroom, be sure to use your encouraging words and smiles to express appreciation and instill pride for each child's helpfulness.

Feed the birds. Taking care of classroom pets can be supplemented with taking care of wild creatures during the winter time. If parents in your center set up a pole with a bird feeder station right outside a picture window, the children can keep the feeder filled, put out suet, save up crumbs from dinner time to bring to the bird feeder station, and enjoy with delight the many birds that will gratefully flock to the feeder during the winter. This is a great time to watch social behaviors of other creatures too! How many children can spot a scarlet cardinal or a blue jay or a chickadee? Feeding the birds as a cooperative class activity can also result in children developing keen observation skills and a passion for naming wild birds they spy outside. This activity will not only promote prosocial actions, but increase child skills at naming, counting, and categorizing!

Galvanize Class Interest in Donating to Needy Others

Getting in the habit of giving to others in need or less fortunate is something children can learn very early. When a jar of collected pennies in your classroom is full, the children can count out how much money they have and dictate to you a joint class letter to the persons to whom they are contributing.

The children themselves may think up and volunteer to work on helpful projects, such as: school-yard clean-ups, drawing pictures for pen pals in other lands, collecting toys or food for poor persons, and singing songs for elderly residents during visits to a home for the aged.

Promote Specific, Active Peacemaking Techniques

Shure's (1992) ICPS (I Can Problem Solve) curriculum provides daily lesson plans throughout the school year for teachers. Preschoolers learn that the feelings or wishes of one child may be the same OR different from those of another child ("Ofira wants to go bike riding with you and you want to play dress up. Do you have the SAME or DIFFERENT ideas about what to play?")

ICPS challenges children to think of the consequences of their behaviors and to think up alternatives to resolve social differences or choose more appropriate peacemaking in order to solve a social problem. These lessons in emotional language skills are also available for parents (Shure, 1994). ICPS gives children tools to understand how to talk about scuffles or disagreements they have and how to generate ideas themselves to resolve disputes. Research using this *Interpersonal Cognitive Problem Solving* program found that after daily use of ICPS techniques for three months, aggressive children decreased such behaviors, and shy children were more positively assertive.

First you will want to make sure your children know basic ICPS concepts. "The concept of "AND" can be taught in real-life situations: "Can I comfort Tamar who is crying AND read you a story book at the same time?". The concept of "FAIR/NOT FAIR" can also be taught be referring to a real life scenario. If teacher has five cookies at snack time and there are six children seated at the table, is it fair or NOT fair to give one whole cookie to five of the children and leave the last child with none.

Use ICPS concepts of "WHY/BECAUSE" in discussing a fight between two children and guiding the children to think further about an incident.

Harry hit James *because* James knocked him over and took away the toy car he was playing with. Teacher can first ask: "Was knocking Harry down (or hitting James) a good idea or NOT a good idea. Given the children's actions, the teacher might also use the word pairs "IF/THEN" to guide the children to think further about the *consequences* of hurtful or helpful actions.

Another ICPS pair of words children need to learn are "ALL/SOME." Preschoolers often want a playmate to go along with their idea for a game *all* of the time. Many group discussions with real examples can help the children understand that other children want to do what one child proposes only *some* of the time, but not *all* of the time. ICPS encourages teachers to get children themselves to find out about the wishes of others—for example what another child *might* like or *might not* like to do with you right now but *may* want to play later on. ICPS techniques sharpen children's thinking skills about the feelings and wishes of others, about possible consequences of behaviors they engage in (such as hitting to take a toy) and about alternatives they could use to get their needs met (such as offering another toy in exchange for the one you want to play with now).

Have Children Play Out Story Dictations

Tolerance of other children must be proactively taught. Bullying may include not only verbal jeering and physical intimidation, but verbally shutting out children who want to join in play. Story telling can promote positive child interactions (Smith, 1986). Systematic rejection of a particular child can cause smoldering anger or self-hatred. Paley (1992) has created a dramatic play-acting technique. Daily she asks a child to tell a story. As the child dictates, the teacher writes down the child's play scenario. The author child has to choose others to play each story role in a small staging area. Paley's classroom rule "You can't say you can't play" means that all children will be chosen sometime and get a chance to act in the playlet.

Support the Learning of Group Entry Skills

Some children are rejected in a group because they lack *group entry skills* for joining in play or skills for extending a play interaction. Teachers need to support toddlers and preschoolers still struggling with rudimentary social skills. Harlan sidled up to a boy building with blocks. He wanted to join in. Not knowing how to ask to play, he kept moving until he bumped the boy who was busy building. " Hey, don't crowd me!" the builder said indignantly. Harlan needed a boost from teacher in order to learn ways of offering to join in play (Honig & Thompson, 1994).

Naffy was dragging his wagon around the playroom. Tenisha shyly held out her teddy bear toward the wagon. The teacher coached Naffy cheerfully: "Tenisha would love you to take her Teddy for a ride." Thank you for being such a good driver and riding Teddy slowly around. On her own, Tenisha was not able to ask for "taxi" service for her Teddy. With teacher's help, the two children could give her toy bear a ride.

Your perceptive observations will help you decide when a child needs you to "scaffold" positive play participation. Suppose Gerry needs help with group entry skills. He stares longingly at the children as he lingers near the housekeeping area where each preschooler already is playing an assigned role. Suggest that the family will be receiving lots of packages for a birthday that is coming soon. Gerry can be the mailman who drives the mail truck, delivers these packages, and has the children "sign" for each package. Your ingenious ideas to help each child be included in play are essential ingredients for barring the grim twins—rejection and loneliness— from the preschool classroom.

Establish Special Ceremonies for Solving Social Spats

When children are aware of the class goals of trying really well to interact prosocially and when teachers provide the tools for children themselves to achieve these goals, then children will be more likely to know what procedures will regain peace after social tussles. Children feel more secure when they can anticipate and understand rules, routines, consequences, and customs designed to keep your classroom a safe and peaceful environment for play (Carroll, 1988; Cartledge & Milburn, 1992).

THE PEACE ROSE.   Use of the *peace rose* is a powerful technique practiced in Montessori classrooms (Paulsen, 1998 p. 42).

> When two children are beginning to have a conflict or a difficulty, one of them (or sometimes a third child who notices what is going on) goes to get the peace rose. This rose is a silk flower beautifully displayed in a prominent place in the classroom in a crystal vase. The child getting the peace rose gives it to one of the participants and that child may speak to the other. The child then hands the rose to the other participant and she may speak. Each child says (1) what happened, (2) how he feels about what happened, and (3) what he thinks should be done about it. The peace rose is handed back and forth between the two children as long as they want to talk about their difficulty. Only the child holding the rose may speak. When they feel that everything has been expressed between them, both children . . . hold the stem of the peace rose and say, "We declare peace."

Prepare "Emotion" Pictures and Puppet Skits

Many preschoolers need help in recognizing and naming emotions. "Sad", "mad," and "happy" are easy for toddlers. But you may have to teach other emotions more directly through puppet work and by displaying pictures of people expressing a variety of emotions, such as "proud," "worried," "scared," and many others. The more that preschoolers learn the words for feelings, the more likely they will be to be able to comply when you firmly request that they "Use words" rather than hit out at a peer.

Preschool children often need help in understanding that they can hold two conflicting feelings. A child may be happy to go to his friend's 5th year birthday party. He may feel grumpy and jealous when the friend receives as a birthday gift just the toy the preschooler himself has been wishing for. A toddler may love his grandpa very much. But when he is longing to see his mom at the end of a long day in childcare, the toddler may turn his head away and say "I angry" when his beloved (and now bewildered) grandfather shows up to take the toddler home.

Launch Group Art Projects

Encourage cooperative in-classroom activities that require several children's joint productive efforts. Some ideas are: drawing a group mural (maybe of the sea, with boats and whales and fishes galore); building a large "boat" or "space station" with blocks and tinker toys; planning and producing a puppet show; and sewing a yarn picture with a peer. Working together, two children with large yarn needles embroider a picture outlined on both sides of a stretched burlap cloth.

Plan for Increased Peacefulness during Transition Times

Transitions are stressful times. Use your creative talents to set in place specific procedures so that children can come back to the classroom and settle more peacefully after running and shouting noisily in outdoor play. Some teachers remind preschoolers: "Use your indoor voices". Some teachers arrange an orderly way for preschoolers to get to or from their outdoor play area by singing songs. "We are marching to Pretoria!" with its vigorous stresses on syllables is a favorite with some three-year-olds, who lustily sing out that chorus as they march to the door.

Ease "graduation" to a new group in your center. Other school transitions, too, need careful planning to increase calmness and cooperation. When toddlers are moved to a next age group classroom, they adjust more comfortably when they "move up" with playmates. Children who stayed in the same child care center with the same peer group developed more complementary and reciprocal peer play compared with children who changed peer groups although they stayed in the same center (Howes, 1987). Children need the *security of continuity of care*. More and more centers are experimenting with keeping infants and toddlers together for the first three years (Essa, Favre, Thweatt, & Waugh, 1999). This plan allows teachers to get to know each child deeply. In turn, toddlers feel more secure and safe as they interact comfortably with friends. Very young children are extremely sensitive to change. They will indeed feel safe and have more emotional resources to focus on your curriculum as they grow up in childcare with familiar cherishing and cherished caregivers.

Arrange Occasional Viewing of Prosocial Media

Children's cartoons are mostly violent. Major effects of viewing TV violence have been documented. "The aggressor effect consists of increased mean spiritedness. Children who are most susceptible ... are often those who identify most strongly with the aggressive characters and those who perceive the portrayed violence as realistic" (Slaby, Roedell, Arezzo, & Hendrix, 1995, p. 166). These researchers refer to three other outcomes. The *victim effect* involves increased mistrust and fearfulness toward others. The *bystander effect* occurs when children are desensitized and indifferent to real life violence. The *increased appetite effect* means that children increasingly desire to see more violence. This desire may spill into classroom play and teachers will need to wrestle with how they can more effectively respond to "war play" in the classroom (Carlsson-Paige, & Levin, 1987).

When young children view prosocial videos and television programs, they increase their social contacts as well as smiling, praising, and hugging (Coates, B., Pusser, & Goodman, 1976), their sharing, cooperating, turn-taking, positive verbal/physical contact (Forge & Phemister, 1987), and their willingness to help puppies (Poulds, Rubinstein & Leibert, 1975). Some TV programs for young children, such as Arthur or Dragon Tales or Clifford the Big Red Dog, regularly address prosocial and moral issues and try to teach lessons such as being courageous and honest. So, for example, a TV character learns that he should not "hide" the fact that he broke something that belonged to someone else and should not try to blame the breakage on another. In an episode from Dragon Tales, the little boy learns that everybody gets mad sometimes (he is mad because he can't win in a race with the others) but "how" we handle a mad feeling is so important to learn, so that we can live and play with our friends more happily.

Regular viewing of prosocial television, particularly Mr. Rogers' neighborhood, has resulted in higher levels of task persistence, rule obedience, and tolerance of delay of gratification. Children from low socioeconomic families who watched this program daily showed increased cooperative play, nurturance, and verbalization of feelings (Friedrich & Stein, 1973). Children who were exposed to aggressive video games donated less to needy children than those children who played prosocial video games by themselves (Chambers, 1987).

Invite Moral Mentors to Visit the Class

Teachers need supportive others to broaden the message of prosocial interactions as an admirable goal for community members, not just for in-school participants. Actively recruit *moral mentors* to visit your classroom (Damon, 1988). Children may be especially pleased and proud to see relatives come in to tell about their volunteer work. Perhaps Aunt Madeleine sets hair and polishes nails for elderly ladies in a local nursing home or Uncle Richard volunteers time to coach a children's sports team. Maybe Uncle Larry sometimes serves soup in a kitchen for the homeless, or Aunt Genia volunteers to tutor a child with reading difficulties after school. Moral mentors can broaden young children's ideas of the endless array of helpful and kind actions that people can offer to those in need.

Further Class Resources

More ideas for classroom activities to promote friendship and peaceful relations are available in many early childhood publications (Adcock & Segal, 1986; Crary, 1984; Edwards, 1986; Fox, 1980; Marcus & Liserson, 1978; Smith, 1982; Wichert, 1989; Wolf, 1986). Kreidler's (1997) activity guide gives tips for teachers to develop a peaceable program. There is a section on how to eliminate bullying and name-calling. Activities include use of a parachute, hand puppets, musical instruments, and a Polaroid camera. Levin (1994) provides a guide to practical activities for creating a peaceable classroom through the use of puppets, play, class charts, curriculum webs, and charts to help young children resolve conflicts peacefully and respect each others' differences.

Sunrise Books (P.O. Box B, Provo, Utah 84603) is a commercial source of book and video materials for teachers and parents to promote positive discipline and conflict resolution. One of their books by Nelson (undated) features the use of *class meetings*, a technique through which children share in the class work of assisting each other to cooperate more, communicate more positively and openly, and problem solve so that classmates' mutual respect and accountability increase.

Watkins & Durant (1992) provide preK to 2nd grade teachers with specific classroom techniques for prevention of antisocial behaviors. They suggest the right times to *ignore* inappropriate behavior and specify situations when the teacher absolutely must instead use *control*. Teachers are taught to look for signs that they may actually be rewarding socially inappropriate behavior by their responses. The use of subtle, nonverbal cues of dress, voice control, and body language are recommended in order to promote children's more positive behaviors. Beaty (1995) provides ideas to convert preschool conflicts into more peaceful interactions. Dreikurs, Grunwald, & Pepper (1982) provide advice for teachers: establishing mutual respect and confidence takes time, observing skills, patience, planning, and a repertoire of specific techniques.

Techniques with Individual or Pairs of Children

Greeting Rituals

Loving morning rituals can include a group greeting song that names and welcomes and addresses each child *individually* every morning to show how you personally value each child. At naptime, leisurely and soothing back rubs, while soft soothing songs are provided by you (or a tape) *establish a personal climate of caring in the classroom.*

Since you know each individual child best in your classroom, sometimes you will have to tailor a special way to handle a particular child's experiences with anger, aggression, lonesomeness, rejection, or frustration. First, you will want to marshal up all your understanding of that particular child's temperament style and then make a plan for individualized helpfulness to promote peace within and between children.

Teach to a Child's Temperament Style

Temperament is a partly genetically determined personality characteristic. Temperament traits must be taken into consideration. They will influence how well your personality and those of the children mesh. A highly active enthusiastic teacher may enjoy the high spirits and constant whirl of motion of a high-energy youngster. That teacher may be less attuned to the special needs of a cautious, shy preschooler who rarely participates voluntarily in class.

What are the nine temperament traits you need to tune into for each child? Children have higher or lower levels of activity; mood; rhythmicity (in daily routines of eating, voiding, and sleeping); sensitivity to stress/distress; ability to try the new or withdraw from the new (e.g., events, persons, foods); intensity of response to frustration or pain; comfortable adaptability eventually to change; attention span; and persistence.

Temperament traits cluster into three major styles: easy, difficult/feisty/irritable, and cautious/slow-to-warm up (Honig, 1997). Australian researchers discovered that "easy" toddlers were more overlooked than difficult children in high quality centers, and especially so in low-quality centers. Withdrawn children tended to attract more teacher attention in high compared with low quality centers. Easy and withdrawn toddlers received the least attention (up to 98%) especially in poor quality centers (Watson & Kowalski, 1999). Self-reflective teachers will monitor their own emotional reactions so that in the child care facility they do not "re-create" negative interactions learned earlier in home environments (Wittmer & Honig, 1988). Teacher warmth and genuine attentiveness can ensure that, regardless of infant temperament vulnerability or attachment classification vulnerability, young children do receive nurturing, personalized, positive care.

Sharpen Your "Noticing Skills"

Teachers' wonderful powers of observation provide a strong support for individualizing interactions in their work toward creating a peaceful classroom. Without these "X-Ray" noticing skills, sometimes adults miss seeing or hearing bullying that goes on in classrooms.

> In the four-year-old classroom, Jerry , still clutching his toy car from home, climbed onto a teeter totter that could hold several youngsters. Ralph climbed up behind him and knocked the toy car out of Jerry's hands. On hearing Jerry's wailing cries, the teacher came over and remarked "Now what are you crying about Jerry?" Jerry kept on sobbing. Nobody had noticed Ralph's unkind and bullying action.

Teach Victims to Stand up Assertively to Aggression

Instead of submitting, crying or telling the teacher, some children need coaching in standing up to an aggressor. Assertiveness training includes teaching children to ask each other directly for what they want.

> When a child whines to the teacher, "She's in my way." the teacher can say, "Then you need to ask her to move over." If the other child starts to move beforehand, the teacher can stop her and say ,"Wait! He needs to practice asking you first". Thus the teacher encourages social self-reliance, rather than rewarding dependency on adults to solve the problem.

> Sometimes a child readily allows an aggressor to take something from her forcefully. When urged to resist, she may say, "That's OK. He can have it." The teacher can then explain, "It's OK to give it to him, but first he needs to practice asking you for it". This practice helps the aggressor learn that

he must ask nicely to get the object ... Even two-year-old children can be taught to look straight at a child who hurt them and tell the aggressor firmly, "No hitting! " or "No kicking!" (Slaby, Roedell, Arezzo, & Hendrix, 1995, p. 138–139).

Teachers also have to watch for those few bright youngsters who understand how to use empathy and insight into others' feelings in order to manipulate other children into playing "victim". Some children use their emotional knowledge in a "Machiavellian" way for their own gain and power to manipulate others to do their bidding (Barnett & Thompson, 1985).

Enhance Personal Self-Esteem

Because you know each child as an individual, you will be able to craft special ways to compliment and cheer on each child's new tries and efforts. Be certain each child has satisfying and successful experiences in group games, art work, and in your activity areas.

Let each child know that you like him, by telling him, by your actions, and by your attitudes. If you are exasperated at a child, often your irritated voice tone, your tightened mouth, frowning eyes, and body stance give strong negative messages to a child about himself.

Start the "Helping Coupon" Habit

Teachers learn about each child's individual family situation. These special insights can be very useful as you help children generate personal ideas for sharing kindness and caring in each one's own family. In class, children can draw their own "Helping Coupons." Each child's gift book contains large, hand-drawn coupons. Every coupon promises a helpful act to a parent or family member. Let each child dictate to you what to write on each illustrated coupon. "Setting the table for supper" or "Playing with my baby brother while daddy does the dishes" or "Helping find socks to make pairs in the laundry basket" are some possibilities. Go over each coupon and express your admiration of the good ideas your children express in creating their Helping Coupons, which will be personal gifts to family members. Rice (1995) provides some ready-to-copy coupons.

Birthday Rituals

On a given child's birthday, go around the festive table at your child-care and ask each child to tell something special about her or his relationship to the birthday child. Write down positive "birthday stories" into a personal book for each child. This positive social ritual creates a climate of affirmation where children feel secure, accepted, and loved (Salkowski, 1991). Use ingenuity in creating special rituals for holiday celebration times, such as Thanksgiving, Abraham Lincoln's birthday, Father's Day, or Mother's Day. How many ideas can you think up so that children can express caring and thankfulness at such holiday celebrations?

The Great Predictor Game

Rice (1995 p. 57) suggests that you plan a personalized variation on classroom group discussions. Choose one child at a time to wear a costume turban with a large feather plume. That child will be the "great predictor." The teacher asks questions such as" What will happen if we are polite and friendly in school?" "What will happen if we get angry and hit someone?", or "What will happen if we share?". Each turbaned child gets a chance to be the great predictor and figure out answers regarding social interactions in their classroom.

Elicit Positive Attributions as You Focus on the Child of the Week

Sometimes preschoolers label one child in a group as a "bad boy" or tell the teacher "I don't want to sit next to Ollie. He pushes and hits." As you work at rewarding new positive social behaviors in the child who needs to learn more positive skills with peers, you will also need to find ways to overcome rejection and resentment from the other children who may not be giving the new learner a chance. Spend time with your class "discussing how it feels (good!) when people say positive things about us" (Wolf, 1986, p. 75). To foster positive attributions of others, choose one child as "Child of the Week" each week. Make sure that the child just starting to learn new, more prosocial ways, gets chosen too. Seat each "Child of the Week" in a special chair during circle time and have the other children cheer "Hip, hip hooray" for that child. Go around the table each day of the week and have each child make a positive comment about the chosen child. Print each comment on a large piece of paper. Gradually, preschoolers will find ways to think up positive things to say about each designated "Child of the week". At the end of that week, send home a chart or folder with all the positive sayings. Every child "needs a pat on the back to brighten the day. That's what friends are really for!" (Wolf, 1986, p. 76).

Positive attributions have been used as powerful tools in work with older youth also, in ART (Aggression Replacement Training) programs, which use the Skillstreaming techniques created by Goldstein and his colleagues (Goldstein, Glick, & Gibbs, 1998). In Yakima county, for four weeks prior to Mardi Gras, youth who had been in a program to address conduct disorders were nominated by fellow students and teachers. Weekly, at a "Beads for Deeds" school-wide rally, students were given red beads for anger management, blue beads for empathy, green beads for character education, and gold beads for skillstreaming. At the monthly meeting, positive attributions were then enthusiastically bestowed:

> "Let's give it up for Kyle who demonstrated great anger management on the bus Tuesday morning!" "Great self-talk on the basketball court during Thursday's game, Brandon!" "Way to go with empathy, Elizabeth! Thanks for being so supportive when Mrs. Smith had a headache last Monday! (Dowling-Urban, 2002 p. 5).

Personalize a Magic Ritual

With young children, magical reassurance sometimes soothes and calms. Kissing a child's "Bo-bo" after he has taken a tumble in your classroom may magically make the sore place feel better. A baby who comes into childcare from a very stressful home situation may find it hard to settle into your peaceful classroom routines unless you hold him cheek-to-cheek and murmur reassuringly at arrival time.

Some children find it hard to control their own tensions, sadness, and anger. One teacher keeps her "Magic Feather Duster" prominently displayed on the wall near the entry door. Often in the morning she must "brush off" upsets from children with tensions and stress.

> Natalie Bess arrived in childcare upset and aggravated. "Teacher," she announced, "I think you better get the Magic Feather Duster to brush off all the "bad vibes"! After the teacher carefully and tenderly used her Magic Feather Duster, Natalie Bess sighed, smiled, relaxed, and felt ready to enter into the atmosphere of a caring and peaceful preschool classroom.

Conjure your own favorite "magic touch" (perhaps a back rub, a pat on the shoulder, gentle stroking of hair, an arm-around-the child as you sit him near you) to renew a child emotionally. Your refueling loving gestures keep a child feeling safe, calm, and cooperative. With a fussy baby, offer generous lap time, so the little one can sink into that somatic certainty that banishes separation anxiety and renews the baby's feeling of emotional well-being.

When a child is very tense, sometimes rubbing "Magic lotion" on his hands in a slow thorough way assists the child to become soothed. One teacher uses lotion with tiny bits of glitter that sparkle in the lotion. Mr. Jonathan assures his little ones that this is magic lotion and whoever has it rubbed on the hands becomes more gentle! The power of magic to promote kindliness should not be underestimated by a creative teacher!

Pair a Withdrawn Preschooler with a Sociable Peer

Teachers who pair a withdrawn child with a gregarious child during play sessions have noted an increase in sociability as well as more helping, giving, sharing, and participating in cooperative play after these one-on-one play sessions were arranged. Peers can be effective change agents in the classroom to raise the level of cooperative classroom play.

Introduce Pairs of Children to Body Cooperation Games

Many preschoolers learn best while actively engaged in body movement. Have two children hold hands together and smile into each others' eyes. Then they close their eyes and count slowly under their breath. When both feel ready, they bend their knees slowly so that they are both going down together into a deep knee bend. Even though each cannot see when the other is "ready", they do manage to harmonize their bodies when they start deep-knee bending and then rising up in synchrony!

> In another cooperating game, ask the children to form partnerships. Tell them that you would like to see how well they can cooperate. Ask partners to sit back-to-back. When they are ready, ask them to stretch out and interlock their arms with their partner's. [Then] ask them to work together to stand without letting go of their partner's arms. When the children are finished, ask them to sit facing each other with their legs slightly bent and their feet touching. They should then take hold of each others' hands. Can they pull each other up to a standing position? (Smith, 1993, p. 112)

Plan Sensory Awareness Experiences for Preschool Pairs

In order to help children make gentle rather than rough contacts with one another, ask each preschooler to find a partner. Put a small blob of hand lotion in each child's (clean) hand. First the children experience rubbing the lotion on their own hands. Then they join hands and massage palms together (Smith, 1993). Use words like "Rub your hands gently together". The children can knead a soft wad of playdough into a smoothly colored blob by mixing in a few drops of color thoroughly as they work cooperatively.

Work Closely with Families toward Prosocial Goals

Families need to know that prosocial interactions are an integral curriculum component of your child care program. Then they are more likely to respond positively when you reach out to enlist their help in actualizing these goals. As a practicing professional, you use your prosocial skills to support and affirm family members of each child in your classroom. When you develop friendly contacts with parents, they are more likely to provide insights and clues to help you individualize your emotional support for each of the children in your class. On the other hand, parents need you to explain the importance of a prosocial as well as a more "cognitive" curriculum. During informal greetings at the beginning of the day or at end-of-day pick-up times, be sure to communicate to parents what an empowering role they play in young children's development of empathic caring and kind deeds (Barnett, Howard, King, & Dino, 1980). Yarrow and colleagues revealed that parents who exhibited tender concern when their very young children experienced fright or upset, and who also firmly forbade their children to act aggressively to solve their squabbles, had children who showed very early signs of concern and empathy for others' troubles. These personal examples of "baby altruism" persisted into elementary school as rated by teachers who knew nothing of the earlier findings (Pines, 1979).

When interviewed ten years after graduation from a program that emphasized caring and prosocial development (through outreach with families as well as in high quality group care), teenagers and their families reported that they felt more family support, closeness, and appreciation than did control youth. The program adolescents also had far lower rates of juvenile delinquency compared with control youngsters (Lally, Mangione, & Honig, 1988).

Establish a Parent Lending Library of Prosocial Materials

Interested parents will appreciate being able to browse through prosocial articles in your child care facility. Photocopy brief articles and tack them to a bulletin board. Choose articles from *Young Children, Scholastic Parent and Child, Childhood Education Journal, Montessori Life* (see Honig, 1999), and *Zero to Three*, to name a few good resources. Parents will enjoy Kobak's (1979) description of how she embeds caring and awareness of positive social interactions in all classroom activities, dialogues, and projects. Her concept of a *Caring Quotient* (CQ) classroom motivates parents to realize that promoting CQ is as precious as promoting IQ skills. Social problem-solving by Kobak's students takes into consideration that the child whose problem is being brainstormed has to feel that the class *cares* about him or her as they explore ways to resolve a problem—such as chronic truancy, or a book borrowed from a teacher and never returned.

You may also want to display some brief easy-to-read reports of research articles on the parent bulletin board. Findings from the *Abecedarian* program provide powerful research "ammunition" to support the importance of a prosocial curriculum (Finkelstein, 1982). Children who had attended the high quality infant and preschool ABCedarian childcare program that emphasized cognitive development, later on were fifteen times more aggressive with kindergarten peers than a control group of children. A prosocial curriculum was then instituted for future waves of children in the program. When those preschoolers reached kindergarten, there were no longer any differences in aggression rates compared with controls.

Become Familiar with Structured Curriculum Packages Designed to Promote Prosocial Development

To complement the materials in the Bingham Early Childhood Prosocial Program (see Chapter 7), you should consider the following programmatic packages for enhancing prosocial behaviors in the classroom.

Communicating to make friends (Fox, 1980) provides 18 weeks of planned activities to promote peer acceptance. The Dinkmeyer and Dinkmeyer (1982), *Developing Understanding of Self and Others (Rev. DUSO-R)*, provides puppets, activity cards, charts, and audiocassettes to promote children's awareness of others' feelings and social skills. The Abecedarian program instituted *My friends and me* (Davis, 1977) and thereby promoted more prosocial development among participants. The *Second Step* program is designed for use with elementary school children (Frey, Hirschstein, & Guzzo, 2000).

Arrange Bessell and Palomares' (1973) *Magic Circle* lessons so that each day the children, during a safe, non-judgmental circle time, feel *secure enough to share their stories*, their feelings and memories about times they have had troubles with others, times when they have been helped by others, and times when they have been thoughtful and caring on behalf of others.

Commercial sources provide some materials that directly support teacher attempts to introduce peace programs and conflict resolution programs in their classrooms. Some school-based materials include separate workbooks and videos for all grades. The Peace Education Foundation (2627 Biscayne Boulevard, Miami, Florida 33137) has materials for conflict resolution (for example, *Creative Conflict Solving for Kids*: Grades 5–9) and mediation (*Mediation for Kids: A New Way to Handle Student Conflicts* for grades 4 through 9) that teachers can use in classrooms. Also available with teacher's guide is a video "Fighting fair: Dr. Martin Luther King, Jr. for Kids". A coach is seen helping a group of angry youngsters resolve a conflict on the basketball court. The video uses vivid scenes of the civil rights movement to motivate young people to tune into the dynamics of nonviolence.

Video training programs for early violence prevention efforts are available from Educational Productions (email: custserv@edpro.com). Some titles are "Understanding difficult behaviors," " Nurturing responsible behavior," and "Building a prevention strategy."

Implement a Comprehensive School-Based Prosocial Program That Emphasizes Ethical Teaching as Important as Academic Teaching

Wood (1991) has suggested that teachers try to implement a more ethical style of teaching he calls "maternal teaching". He cites John Gatto, who was given the New York City Teacher of the Year award in 1990 who lamented: "The children I teach are cruel to each other, they lack compassion for misfortune, they laugh at weakness, they have contempt for people whose need for help shows too plainly" (Wood, p. 7).

Despite educator's disapproval of such interactions, bullying, put-downs, and prejudiced talk and behaviors are common even in early grades. One adopted youngster with a swarthy complexion was just starting school in an upper middle class suburb. A peer asked him "Do you believe in Jesus as the Lord?". When the six-year-old said he didn't think so, the other child replied contemptuously "Then you're not as good as my family or me!" During the next years, other children taunted this child about his dark skin as much as his family's faith beliefs. Teachers must become more alert to endless bullying. Wood suggests that teachers develop routines of positive morning meetings including singing together. Help each child feel personally valued when you greet each child by name as she or he enters your class. Wood further urges that teachers "figure out a way to teach recess and lunch . . . When children come in from recess, the teacher often can spend another half hour of instructional time sorting out the hurt feelings and hurt bodies and hurt stories she wasn't even there to see or hear" (p. 8).

Role playing helps children become aware of how hurtful name calling and verbal put-downs feel. Keep on helping children to feel how others feel when they are not treated with courtesy. Teachers are powerful positive model of social courtesies as they listen to each child's ideas and give each child a turn to talk. Help children feel all-school ownership. Use artistic and aesthetic touches, such as flowers on lunchroom tables and a lovely tablecloth as incentives for children to make lunchtime a friendly and positive experience.

Systems approaches may be needed to deal directly with violence and victimization in schools (Institute for Urban and Minority Education, 1999). The Child Development Project (Battistich et. al., 1989; Battistich,

Watson, Solomon, Schaps, & Solomon, J., 1991b; Brown & Solomon, 1983) has translated prosocial research for application throughout school systems in the Bay Area in California. The features of this comprehensive program carried out in several elementary schools in order to increase children's prosocial attitudes and behavior are the following:

1. Children from about age 6 onward, with adult supervision, take responsibility for caring for and helping younger children, doing classroom chores, and participating in peer-tutoring and "buddies" programs.
2. "Cooperative activities" requires that children work with each other in learning teams within classes. Teachers explicitly encourage children to try to be fair, considerate and socially responsible. Teachers give training in group interaction skills.
3. Classroom management techniques promote internalization of prosocial norms and values. Self control is encouraged through the building of positive interpersonal relationships within the classroom. Teachers involve children in setting rules and making decisions. Teachers emphasize the principles that underlie rules and they use non punitive control techniques that challenge children to reason inductively about a social conflict.
4. Children are involved in structured programs of helpful activities that will be useful, such as visiting shut-ins, making toys for others, visiting the elderly, cleaning up or gardening in nearby parks and playgrounds.
5. Children of mixed ages engage in activities.
6. With parental approval and cooperation, children help with home chores on a regular basis.
7. Children regularly role-play situations where persons are in need of help in order to experience feelings of "victim" and "helper".
8. Spontaneous class occurrences, such as interpersonal conflicts or having a visitor from another culture, are used to enhance children's awareness of and understanding of others' perspectives, feelings, and needs.
9. Activities programmed to promote social understanding include class meetings and discussions of stories and TV programs and films.
10. The entire elementary school recognizes and rewards caring, helping, responsibility, and other prosocial behaviors whether they occur at home or at school.
11. Children watch for adult prosocial models on TV and in the news; they clip newspaper articles about prosocial persons; they invite models to tell their stories in class.

12. Empathy training includes children's exposure to examples of animals or children in distress, in real life, or in staged episodes; they hear adults comment on how to help someone in trouble and they get to watch examples of helpfulness.
13. Continuity and total saturation in a school program create a climate, in the demonstration schools and families, that communicates prosocial expectations and supports children's learning and enacting prosocial behaviors.

How well has this program worked when children are compared with those in matched schools without the program? Student outcome data for kindergarten through sixth grade indicate that program students engage in more spontaneous prosocial behaviors, such as giving affectionate support, cooperation and helpfulness, and concern for others' needs (Solomon, Watson, Delucci, Schaps, & Battistich, 1988). Self-report data by the children in fourth through sixth grade indicates that they perceive the classroom social environment as more caring and supportive than children in the comparison schools. Social competence also was enhanced. The children demonstrated greater perspective-taking skills and showed more consideration for classmates' needs in problem situations. They were "more likely to consider the consequences of their actions and anticipate obstacles to effective resolution, and use more cooperative and prosocial strategies (e.g. discussing the problem, explaining their position, sharing or other compromise solutions) than comparison children." (Battistich, Schaps, Solomon, & Watson, 1991a, p. 111). By fourth grade, the children also scored higher on beliefs that each group member has a right to be involved with and influence group decisions as well as expressing democratic values and showing greater willingness to compromise. By fifth grade, children were named as friends by a greater percentage of their classmates than students in comparison classrooms. By sixth grade, the program students responded on questionnaires with significantly lower scores for loneliness and social anxiety than comparison students.

Despite the long-term nature of this all-embracing program to enhance prosocial skills, findings suggested that implementation by program teachers was not uniformly high. Thus, program initiations must be particularly concerned about how to enhance teacher motivation, participation, and creativity in implementing a prosocial curriculum. Further, no differences were evident outside the classroom in assessments of program children's interpersonal behaviors in small-group activities. This too raises the troubling question of the generalizability of prosocial learning outside of the carefully monitored settings in which these skills are taught. Commitment to community-wide implementation of prosocial programs in all school settings and neighborhoods, rather than just in a few "demonstration" schools requires political and cultural decisions by families and communities that building prosocial skills is a crucial educational goal.

Civic Literacy Training

Flanagan & Faison (2001) note the importance of teachers emphasizing "civic literacy". *Civic skills* include socially adept ways of actively listening to another's point of view and pitching in to achieve group goals. They report that in many communities, projects for school age children promote character education. The *Giraffe Project* initiated in the state of Washington in 1982 is a story-based curriculum that encourages children to be active and compassionate citizens, teaches them about people with vision and courage who are willing to stick their necks out, take a stand, and solve their community's problems (Flanagan & Faison, 2001 p. 11).

Peer Mediator Training

Some schools in New York City and elsewhere implement the *Resolving Conflict Creatively Program (RCCP)*. The RCCP program trains fifth graders as peer mediators. These youngsters move into a situation of social conflict, such as a playground fight, and help the children resolve their conflict. RCCP rules require the peer mediator to give each child in a conflict a chance to describe and explain how the problem seems from her or his viewpoint and then both parties must try to agree on how to settle the conflict. The peer mediators are coached to use nonviolent and creative ways of dealing with social conflicts (RCCP: 163 Third Avenue # 239, New York, NY 10003).

Materials for training students as peer counselors for middle schools are available through the Peace by Peace program (http://www.peacebypeace.org/pxp/) which includes a peer mediator's guide and handouts to explain the program to all students and parents. The Bureau for At Risk Youth (2000) also publishes *Let's work it out* workbooks for grades K-3 and 4–6 as well as *Peace Talks*, a 10-part violence prevention video series for grades 6–12. Their "Peace Talk" posters for classroom walls cover teasing, bullying, and how to work out problems by hearing others' feelings and by standing up for yourself and negotiating.

Empathy Training

The *Empathy Training Program* was designed for third and fourth graders (Feshbach & Feshbach, 1983). The idea behind this program was that children's increased empathic understanding will be more likely to lead to more prosocial interactions. The teachers carried out classroom exercises to enhance recognition and discrimination of others' feelings, role playing, and increasing one's ability to be aware of and experience one's own emotions. Teachers carry out these sessions for one hour three times a week for 10 weeks. Results from teacher and peer ratings of aggressive and prosocial behaviors (helping, sharing, generosity, and sympathy) showed that in the classes that received the empathy training (compared with control classes who did not receive the training), prosocial actions increased and social understanding was enhanced.

Small-Group Teaching (SGT) Project

The SGT project (Sharan & Hertz-Lazarowitz, 1981), carried out in low-income schools in Israel, restructured classrooms into small learning groups. The children provide each other with mutual support and help, exchange ideas, and are mutually accepting of each other as they work on sub-units of a task. Tension and conflict were significantly reduced for children in the SGT program compared with youngsters in control classrooms. For example, the SGT children worked more helpfully together to construct new words from letters in an anagram.

Conclusion

Together, parents and teachers are priceless partners in nurturing the flowering of prosocial values and behaviors. The more cherished a child is, the less likely he or she is to bully others or be rejected by other children. The more nurturing parents and caregivers are, the more positive affection and responsive, empathic care they provide, the more positively children will relate in social interactions with teachers, caring adults, and peers and in cooperating with classroom learning goals as well (Honig & Wittmer, 1996).

References

Adcock, D., & Segal, M. (1986). *Play together, grow together.* Mt. Ranier, MD: Gryphon House.

Aronson, E., Bridgeman, D., & Geffner, R. (1978). Interdependent interactions and prosocial behavior. *Journal of Research and Development in Education, 12* (1), 16–27.

Aronson, E., Stephan, C., Sikes, J., Blaney, N., & Snapp, M. (1978). *The jigsaw classroom.* Beverly Hills, CA: Sage Publications.

Azer, S., & Elliott, K. (1998, November/December). States move toward systems that encompass training, compensation, and program quality. *Child Care Bulletin, 20.*

Barnett, M., Howard, J., King, L., & Dino, G. (1980). Empathy in young children: Relation to parents' empathy, affection, and emphasis on the feelings of others. *Developmental Psychology, 16,* 243–244.

Barnett, M. & Thompson, S. (1985). The role of perspective-taking and empathy in children's Machiavellianism, prosocial behavior, and motive for helping. *The Journal of Genetic Psychology 146,* 295–305.

Barton, E.J. & Osborne, J.G. (1978). The development of classroom sharing by a teacher using positive practice. *Behavior Modification, 2,* 231–251.

Battistich, V., Schaps, E., Solomon, D., & Watson, M. (1991a). The role of the school in prosocial development. In H. E. Fitzgerald, B. M. Lester, & M. W. Yogman (Eds.) *Theory and research in behavioral pediatrics* (pp. 89–121). New York: Plenum Press.

Battistich, V., Watson, M., Solomon, D., Schaps, E., & Solomon, J. (1991b). The Child Development Project: A comprehensive program for the development of prosocial character. In W. M. Kurtines & J. L. Gewirtz (Eds.), *Handbook of moral behavior and development. Vol. 3. Applications.* Hillsdale, NJ: Lawrence Erlbaum.

Beaty, J, (1995). *Converting conflicts in preschool.* Ft. Worth, TX:; Harcourt, Brace.

Bessell, H. & Palomares, U. (1973). *Methods in human development: Theory manual.* El Cajun, CA: Human Development Training Institute.

Bretherton, I., & Waters, E. (1985). Growing points of attachment theory and research. *Monographs of the Society for Research in Child Development, 50*(1–2, Serial No. 209). Chicago: University of Chicago Press.

Bos, B. (1990). *Together we're better: Establishing a coactive learning environment.* Roseville, CA: Turn the Page Press.

Bredekamp, S., & Rosegrant, T. (1992) (Eds.), *Reaching potentials: Appropriate curriculum and assessment for young children. Volume 1.* Washington, DC: National Association for the Education of Young Children.

Brett, D. (1988). *Annie stories.* New York: Workman Publishing Company.

Brown, D. & Solomon, D. (1983). A model for prosocial learning: An in-progress field study. In D.L. Bridgman (Ed.) *The nature of prosocial development: Interdisciplinary theories and strategies.* New York: Academic Press.

Buka, S. L., Stichick, T. L., Birdthistle, S. M., & Felton, J. E. (2001). Youth exposure to violence: Prevalence, risks, and consequences. *American Journal of Orthopsychiatry, 71*(3), 298–310.

Bureau for At Risk Youth (2000). *Peace by peace. conflict resolution through peer mediation.* Plainview, NY: Author.

Butterworth, N. (1996). *Percy the Park Keeper.* Scarborough, ON, Canada: Harper Collins Publishers.

Carlsson-Paige, N., & Levin, D. E. (1987). *The war play dilemma: Balancing needs and values in the early childhood classroom.* New York: teachers College Press.

Carroll, J. A. (1988). *Let's learn about getting along with others.* Carthage, IL: Good Apple.

Cartledge, G., & Milburn, J. F. (Eds.) (1992). *Teaching social skills to children: Innovative approaches* (2nd edition). New York: Pergamon Press.

Chambers, J. (1987). The effects of prosocial and aggressive video games on children's donating and helping. *The Journal of Genetic Psychology, 148,* 499–505.

Chesebrough, E. & King, P. (2004). Bingham early childhood prosocial behavior program. In E. Chesebrough, P. King, M. Bloom & T.P. Gullotta (Eds.). A blueprint for prosocial behavior in early childhood. NY: Kluwer Academic/Plenum Publishers.

Coates, B., Pusser, H. & Goodman, I. (1976). The influence of "Sesame Street" and "Mr. Rogers' Neighborhood" on children's social behavior in the preschool. *Child Development, 47,* 138–144.

Crary, E. (1984). *Kids can cooperate: A practical guide to teaching problem solving.* Seattle, WA: Parenting Press.

Damon, W. (1977). *The social world of the child.* San Francisco, CA: Jossey-Bass.

Damon, W. (1988). *The moral child: Nurturing children's natural moral growth.* New York: Free Press.

Davis, D.E. (1977). *My Friends and me.* Circle Pines, Minn: American Guidance Service.

Delton, J. (1974). *Two good friends.* New York: Crown Publishers.

Derman-Sparks, L., & The A.B.C. Task Force (1989). *Anti-bias curriculum: Tools for empowering young children.* Washington, DC: National Association for the Education of Young Children.

DeVries, R. & Goncu, A. (1990). Interpersonal relations in four-year-old dyads from Constructivist and Montessori programs (pp. 11–28). In A. S. Honig (Ed.), *Optimizing early child care and education.* London: Gordon & Breach.

Dinkmeyer, D. & Dinkmeyer, D. Jr. (1982). *Developing understanding of self and others (Rev. DUSO-R).* Circle Pines, MN: American Guidance Service.

Dr. Seuss (1954). *Horton hears a who.* Mississauga, ON: Canada: Random House of Canada.

Dr. Seuss (1967). *The king's stilts.* New York: Random House.

Dr. Seuss (1991). *Horton hatches an egg.* Mississauga, ON: Canada: Random House of Canada.

Dowling-Urban, G. (2002, Summer). Pathways school livens ART curriculum. *Communicator,* p. 5.

Dreikurs, R., Grunwald, B. B., & Pepper, F. C. (1982). *Maintaining sanity in the classroom: Classroom management techniques.* New York: Harper & Row.

Eastman, M. (1994). *Taming the dragon in your child.* New York: John Wiley.

Edwards, C.P. (1986). *Social and moral development in young children: Creative approaches for the classroom.* New York: Teachers College Press.

Egeland, B. & Sroufe, A. (1981). Developmental sequelae of mal- treatment in infancy. *Directions for Child Development, 11,* 77–92.

Eisenberg, N., & Mussen, P. H. (1990). *The roots of prosocial behavior in children.* New York: Cambridge University Press.

Essa, E., Favre, K., Thweatt, G., & Waugh, S. (1999). Continuity of care for infants and toddlers. *Early Child Development and Care, 148,* 11–19.

Feshbach, N. D. , & Feshbach, S. (1983). *Learning to care: Classroom activities for social and affective development.* Glenview, IL: Scott Foresman.

Finkelstein, N. (Sept. 1982). Aggression: Is it stimulated by day care? *Young Children, 37*(6), 3–13.

Flanagan, C. A., & Faison, N. (2001). Youth civic development: Implications of research for social policy and programs. *Social Policy Report, 15*(1), 3–14.

Forge, K.L., & Phemister, S. (1987). The effect of prosocial cartoons on preschool children. *Child Study Journal,17,* 83–88.

Fox, L. (1980). *Communicating to Make Friends.* Rolling Hills Estates, CA: B.L. Winch.

Fox, M. (1984). *Wilfred Gordon McDonald Partridge,* New York: Kane/Miller Publishers.

Frey, K., Hirschstein, M., & Guzzo, B. (2000). Second Step: Preventing aggression by promoting social competence. *Journal of Emotional and Social Disorders, 8*(2), 102–112.

Friedrich, L.K., & Stein, A.H. (1973). Aggressive and prosocial television programs and the natural behavior of preschool children. *Monographs of the Society for Research in Child Development, 38*(4), Serial No. 151.

Fugitt, E. (1983). "He hit me back first!" Creative visualization activities for parenting and teaching. Rolling Hills Estates, CA: Jalmar Press.

Gilman, P. (1993). *Something from nothing.* New York: Scholastic.

Goldstein, A.P., Glick, B., & Gibbs, J. C. (1998). *Aggression replacement Training: A comprehensive intervention for aggressive youth.* Champaign, IL: Research Press.

Gordon, T. (1970). *P.E. T. Parent Effectiveness Training. The tested new way to raise responsible children.* New York: Wyden.

Gresham, F. (1981). Social skills training with handicapped children: A review. *Review of Educational Research, 51,* 139–176.

Grossman, K., Zimmerman, P., & Steele, H. (Eds.) (1999). Internal working models revisited. In *Attachment and human development. Special issue, 1*(3).

Hoban, R. (1994). *Best friends for Frances.* New York: Harper Collins.

Holloway, S. D., & Reichhart-Erickson, M. (1988). The relationship of day care quality to children's free-play behavior and social problem-solving skills. *Early Childhood Research Quarterly, 3,* 39–53.

Honig, A. S. (1982). Prosocial development in children. Research in review. *Young Children, 37*(5), 51–62.

Honig, A. S. (1995). Singing with infants and toddlers. *Young Children, 50*(5),72–78.

Honig, A. S. (1996). *Behavior guidance for infants and toddlers.* Little Rock, AR: Southern Early Childhood Association.

Honig, A. S. (1997). Infant temperament and personality: What do we need to know? *Montessori Life, 9*(3), 18–21.

Honig, A. S. (1999). Creating a prosocial curriculum. *Montessori Life, 11*(2), 35–37.

Honig, A. S. (2001). Promoting creativity, giftedness, and talent in young children in preschool and school situations. In M. Bloom & T. Gullotta (Eds.), *Promoting creativity across the life span.*(pp. 83–126). New Haven: Child Welfare League of America.

Honig, A. S. (2002a). Choosing child care for young children. In M. Bornstein (Ed.), *Handbook of Parenting, Vol.5* (pp. 375–405). Hillsdale, NJ: Lawrence Erlbaum.

Honig, A. S. (2002b). *Safe and secure: Nurturing infant/toddler attachment in childcare settings.* Washington, D. C: National Association for the Education of Young Children.

Honig, A., & McCarron, P. (1990). Prosocial behaviors of handicapped and typical peers in an integrated preschool. In A.S. Honig (Ed.), *Optimizing early child care and education.* London: Gordon & Breach Science Publishers.

Honig, A., & Pollack, B. (1990). Effects of a brief intervention program to promote prosocial behaviors in young children. *Early Education and Development, 1,* 438–444.

Honig, A. S., & Thompson, A. (1994). Helping toddlers with peer entry skills. *Zero to Three, 14*(5), 15–19.

Honig, A. S. & Wittmer, D. S. (1992). *Prosocial development in children: Caring, sharing, and cooperating: A bibliographic resource guide.* New York: Garland Press.

Honig, A. S., & Wittmer, D. S. (1996). Helping young children become more prosocial: Part 2. Ideas for classrooms, families, school, and communities. *Young Children, 51*(2), 61–70.

Howes, C. (1987). Social competence with peers in young children: Developmental sequences. *Developmental Review, 7,* 252–272.

Howes, C., & Stewart, P. (1987). Child's play with adults, toys, and peers: An examination of family and child care influences. *Developmental Psychology, 23*(8), 423–430.

Huston-Stein, A., Friedrich-Cofer, L., & Susman, E. (1977). The relation of classroom structure to social behavior, imaginative play, and self-regulation of economically disadvantaged children. *Child Development, 48,* 908–916.

Institute for Urban and Minority Education (1999). Improving school violence prevention programs through meaningful evaluation. Developing social competence in children. Exposure to violence and victimization at school. Cooperation, conflict resolution, and school violence: A systems approach. School strategies for increasing safety. *Choices. Briefs* (No. 2, 3, 4, 5, 6). Columbia University, New York: Teachers College.

Johnson, W. (1976a). *The value of believing in yourself. The story of Louis Pasteur—A Value Tales Series*. La Jolla, CA: Value Communications.

Johnson, W. (1976b). *The Story of the Mayo brothers—a Value Tales Series*. La Jolla, CA: Value Communications.

Johnson, W. (1976c). *The value of kindness. The story of Elizabeth Fry—a Value Tales Series*. La Jolla, CA: Value Communications.

Johnson, S. (1979). *The value of curiosity. The story of Christopher Columbus—a Value Tales Series*. La Jolla, CA: Value Communications.

Kates, J. (2001, May 17). Bully-proofing your child at camp. *Syracuse Jewish Observer*, 6–7.

Keats, J. (1972). *The pet show*. New York: MacMillan.

Kline, S. (1987). *Don't touch*. Morton Grove, IL: Whitman and Company.

Kobak, D. (1979). Teaching children to care. *Children Today, 8*, 6–7, 34–35.

Kreidler, W. J. (1985). *Creative conflict resolution*. Evanston, IL: Scott Foresman.

Kreidler, W. J. (1997). *Early childhood adventures in peacemaking*. Cambridge, MA: Educators for Social Responsibility.

Krogh, S.., & Lamme, L. (1985). "But what about sharing"? Children's literature and moral development. *Young Children, 40*(4), 48–51.

Lally, J. R., Mangione, P., & Honig, A. S. (1988). The Syracuse University Family Development Research Program: Long range impact of an early intervention with low-income children and their families. In D. Powell (Ed.), *Parent education as early childhood intervention: Emerging directions in theory, research, and practice* (pp. 79–104). Norwood, NJ: Ablex.

Lasker, J. (1980). *Nick joins in*. Morton Grove, IL: Albert Whitman and Company.

Levin, D. E. (1994). *Teaching young children in violent times: Building a peaceable classroom*. Cambridge, MA: Educators for Social Responsibility.

Levin, D., & Carlsson-Paige, N. (1994). Developmentally appropriate television: Putting children first. *Young Children, 49*(6), 80–84.

Levin, D., & Carlsson-Paige, N. (1995). The Mighty Morphin Power Rangers: Teachers voice concern. *Young Children, 50*(6), 67–74.

Lickona, T. (2000). *Educating for character*. New York: Random House.

Lobel, A. (1979). *Frog and Toad are Friends*. Scarborough, ON, Canada: Harper Collins Children's Books.

Marcus, R. F., & Liserson, M. (1978, September). Encouraging helping behavior. *Young Children, 33*(6), 23–34.

McMath, J. (1989). Promoting prosocial behaviors through literature. *Day Care and Early Education, 17*(1), 25–27.

Morrow, J. (2002, January 13). Taking the measure of a school. *Education Life*, 57–58.

Nelson, J. (undated). *Positive discipline in the classroom featuring class meetings*. Provo, UT: Sunrise Books, Tapes & Videos.

Olweus, D. (1993). Bullies on the playground: The role of victimization. In C. Hart (Ed.), *Children on playgrounds* (pp. 85–128). Albany: State University of New York Press.

Orlick, T. (1978). The cooperative spirit and games book: Challenge without competition. New York: Pantheon Books.

Orlick, T. (1982). *Winning through cooperation: Competitive insanity—cooperative alternatives*. Washington, D.C.: Acropolis.

Orlick, T. (1985). *The second cooperative sports and games book*. New York: Pantheon Press.

Paley, V. (1992). *You can't say you can't play*. Cambridge, MA: Harvard University Press.

Park, K. & Honig, A. (1991). Infant child care patterns and later teacher ratings of preschool behaviors. *Early Child Development and Care, 68*, 80–87.

Paulsen, J. (1998). Active peacemaking n the Montessori classroom. *Montessori Life, 10*(1), 42–43.

Pines, M. (1979). Good samaritans at age two? *Psychology Today,13,* 66–77.

Piper, W. (2001). *The little engine that could.* New York: Penguin Putnam Books for Young Readers.

Pirtle, S. (1997). *Linking up! Building a peaceable classroom through music and movement.* (Audiocassette) Cambridge, MA: Educators for Social Responsibility.
    This audiocassette for children three to nine years old has 46 easy-to-learn songs that promote caring, cooperation, and communication. Some songs are bilingual in English and Spanish.

Polacco, P. (1994). *Mrs. Katz and Tush.* New York: Dell Publishing.

Poulds, R., Rubinstein, E., & Leibert, R. (1975). Positive social learning. *Journal of Communication, 25* (4), 90–97.

Prutzman, P., Sgern, L., Berger, M.L., & Bodenhamer, G. (1988). *The friendly classroom for a small planet: Children's creative response to conflict program.* Philadelphia, PA: New Society.

Readdick, C. A., & Douglas, K. (2000). More than line leader and door holder: Engaging young children in real work. *Young Children, 55*(6), 63–70.

Rice, J. A. (1995). *The kindness curriculum. Introducing young children to loving values.* St. Paul, MN: Redleaf Press.

Rogers, D. (1987). Fostering social development through block play. *Day Care and Early Education, 14*(3), 26–29.

Salkowski, C. J. (1991, Spring). Keeping the peace: Helping children resolve conflict through a problem-solving approach. *Montessori Life,* 31–37.

Sapon-Shevin, M (2000). *Because we can change the world.* Syracuse, NY: Syracuse University Press.

Schweinhart, L.J., Weikart, D.P., & Larner, M.B. (1986). Consequences of three curriculum models through age 15. *Early Childhood Research Quarterly, 1,* 15–45.

Sharan, S., & Hertz-Lazarowitz, R. (1981). Changing schools: The small-group teaching project in Israel. Tel-Aviv: Israel.

Shure, M. (1992). *I can problem solve: An interpersonal cognitive problem-solving program.* Champaign, IL: Research Press.

Shure, M. (1994). *Raising a thinking child. Help your young child to resolve everyday conflicts and get along with others.* New York: Henry Holt.

Simon, N. (1981). *Nobody's perfect, not even my mother.* Morton Grove, IL: Albert Whitman.

Simon, N. (1983). *I wish I had my father.* Morton Grove, IL: Albert Whitman.

Slaby, R. G., Roedell, W. C., Arezzo, D., & Hendrix, K. (1995). *Early violence prevention: Tools for teachers of young children.* Washington, DC: National Association for the Education of Young Children.

Smith, C. A. (1982). *Promoting the social development of young children: Strategies and activities.* Palo Alto, CA: Mayfield.

Smith, C. A. (1986). Nurturing kindness through story telling. *Young Children, 41*(6), 46–54.

Smith, C. A. (1993). *The peaceful classroom. 162 easy activities to teach preschoolers compassion and cooperation.* Mt. Rainier, MD: Gryphon House.

Solomon, D., Watson, M.S., Delucci, K.L., Schaps, E., & Battistich, V. (1988). Enhancing children's prosocial behavior in the classroom. *American Educational Research Journal, 25*(4), 527–554.

Sondheimer, I. (1982). *The boy who could make his mother stop yelling.* New York: Rainbow Press.

Sroufe, L. A., & Fleeson, J. (1986). Attachment and the construction of relationships. In W. W. Hartup & Z. Rubin (Eds.), *Relationships and development* (pp. 51–71). Hillsdale, NJ: Lawrence Erlbaum.

Walt Disney (1986). *Hiawatha's kind heart.* New York: Bantam Books.

Watkins, K. P., & Durant, L.(1992). *Complete early childhood behavior management guide.* West Nyack, NW: Center for Applied Research in Education.

Watson, J., & Kowalski, H. (1999). Toddler-caregiver interaction: The effect of temperament. *Early Child Development and Care, 159,* 53–73.

Werner, E. (1986). Resilient children . In H.E. Fitzgerald & M.G. Walraven (Eds.), *Annual editions: Human development.* Sluice-Dock, CT: Dushkin.

Whitin, P. (2001, September). Kindness in a jar. *Young Children, 56*(5), 18–22.

Whiting, B., & Whiting, J. (1975). *Children of six cultures: A psychocultural analysis.* Cambridge, Mass: Harvard University Press.

Wichert, S. (1989). *Keeping the peace: Practicing cooperation and conflict resolution with preschoolers.* Philadelphia, PA: New Society Publishers.

Williams, L.K. (2000, Fall). If you're angry and you know it.*Teaching Tolerance,* No. 18. p. 6

Wittmer, D. S., & Honig, A. S. (1988). Teacher recreation of negative interactions with toddlers. In A. S. Honig (Ed.), Optimizing early child care and education (Special Issue). *Early Child Development and Care, 33,* 77–88.

Wittmer, D. S., & Honig, A. S. (1994). Encouraging positive social development in young children. Part 1. Strategies for teachers. *Young Children, 49*(5), 4–12.

Wolf, P. (Ed.) (1986), *Connecting: Friendship in the lives of young children and their teachers.* Redmond, WA: Exchange Press.

Wood, C. (1991, Summer). Maternal teaching: Revolution of kindness. *Holistic Education Review,* 3–10.

Wright, D. (1959). *The little one.* New York: Doubleday.

Zabriskie, J. (2001, Winter). APA anti-violence programs spark lively dialogue. *Practitioner, 13*(1), 5, 15.

Chapter 4

How to Help Families Promote Optimal Development in Young Children

Joseph A. Durlak

There have been thousands of studies of the effects of family life on child development. Because it is impossible to do justice to this huge literature in a single chapter, the intent here is to highlight several representative issues around which a consensus has emerged regarding their importance and their impact. In doing so, some liberties have been taken in the terminology used to describe theoretical issues, variables or constructs, and research findings. This is necessitated by the diverse terminology used by different researchers who nevertheless seem to be describing or studying similar phenomena.

This chapter is divided into four main sections. The first offers a theoretical perspective for viewing families and child development, and the remaining sections describe selected successful interventions targeting parenting practices, the family system, and community and neighborhood-level influences on family life.

An Integrated Theoretical Perspective

Two paradigms that can be easily integrated and offer a useful perspective for considering the well-being of children are ecological theory and the risk, protective, and promotive factor model. Each of these paradigms has several variants, but often most of the following issues are considered important.

Ecological Theory

The foremost principle in various ecological theories is that behavior cannot be considered apart from the context or environment in which it occurs (Bronfenbrenner, 1979). While the remaining discussion concentrates on the psychosocial environment, this does not deny the corresponding importance of the physical environment on behavior. There are several corollaries and implications to the first major tent of ecological theory. First, environments are known to have strong effects on individual behavior; environments vary in their norms, expectations and feedback mechanisms and can elicit and reinforce behavior that would normally not be emitted in the absence of such influences. Second, the adaptiveness or maladaptiveness of specific behaviors depends on the environment in which behaviors occur. What is appropriate in one setting may not be appropriate in another setting. Third, the same environment can produce different effects on individuals; not everyone reacts the same way to situations. Fourth, even young children can affect their environment. For example, a demanding, temperamental infant can put strain and stress on parents and thus modify the care giving process. The bi-directional effects of individuals and environments lead to a constantly evolving series of behavioral-environmental transactions. In these transactions, for example, children and their parents are continually behaving in ways that influence each other, including attempts at anticipating what the others' reactions might be and modifying their usual behavior accordingly.

Moreover, ecological theory recognizes that multiple environments influence children. One should not only consider parents and other members of the family system, but also peers, major social institutions such as schools, and the local neighborhood and larger community. These latter systems can affect children directly or indirectly via their effect on family members. Furthermore, different systems of influence can interact with each other to affect child outcomes in positive or negative ways. For example, when family members and schools work together to promote learning, the positive effects on children's school performance are often greater than would be produced by the influence of either family or school operating separately (Durlak, 1997).

Finally, with respect to children in particular, a developmental perspective should be maintained. Among other things, a developmental perspective stresses the critical importance of timing. The relative degree or nature of behavioral change often depends on when during the course of development influences are present. Prior development must also be considered because the behaviors, abilities, and limitations that a child brings to the present context will affect future functioning.

Risk, Protective, and Promotive Factor Paradigm

A second useful paradigm for understanding child development centers on the importance of risk, protective and promotive factors. A risk factor is any variable associated with an increased likelihood of a future negative outcome, whereas protective factors are variables associated with a decreased likelihood of negative outcomes. With growing recognition that good mental health is not simply the absence of problems, researchers have also focused on promotive or positive factors, which are variables that increase the likelihood of decidedly positive outcomes such as high self-esteem, good coping skills, effective problem solving skills, and so on.

There are several important principles connected to risk, protective and promotive factors (Coie et al. 1993; Durlak, 1997; Gullotta & Bloom, 2003; Institute of Medicine, 1994). These factors can be attributes of an individual (e.g., a physical disability) or the environment (e.g., a cold, rejecting parent or a violent neighborhood); can be demographic characteristics which would not be the focus of change (male gender), or behaviors that are quite amenable to influence (the amount of reinforcement parents provide their children). Although risk and protective factors are conceptually linked because of their effects on negative outcomes, they are not simply the opposite of each other. Aggressive behavior in a young child is a risk factor, but the lack of aggression is not a protective factor. Moreover, most factors do not exist as all-or-none phenomena, but in degrees along a continuum. Although it is difficult to identify the cut-point or threshold at which different factors become crucial, it is not necessary to completely eliminate a risk factor or maximize a promotive factor to produce an effect. For example, occasional, mild forms of aggression are unlikely to put a child at risk, and a child's problem-solving skills do not have to be excellent or perfect to be helpful.

Typically, multiple risk, protective or promotive factors operate to influence outcomes. In other words, a single risk factor is rarely responsible for a negative outcome; rather, it is the accumulation or interaction of several risk factors that leads to negative effects. The same usually holds for protective or promotive factors. Finally, the same factor (be it a risk, protective or promotive factor) can be associated with multiple outcomes.

Aggression is a risk factor for school and peer problems, or drug abuse, as well as a variety of psychological problems such as depression or low self-esteem. Correspondingly, parental warmth can protect against any of these outcomes.

Finally, confusion can result because the same construct can be identified as a protective factor in one context, but a promotive factor in another. It helps to keep the ultimate goals of the intervention in mind. Protective factors operate under conditions of risk to reduce the later prevalence of negative outcomes. For example, we could focus on increasing levels of parental warmth to reduce or eliminate the potential risk of marital conflict on children. However, a movement which has recently gained momentum focuses on the development of decidedly positive abilities, strengths or competencies in children. This literature uses different terms, such as wellness, health promotion, positive psychology, or positive youth development to distinguish its emphasis on promoting positive aspects of development or functioning (Catalano, Berglund, Ryan, Lonczak & Hawkins, 2002; Cicchetti, Rappaport, Sandler & Weissberg, 2000; Roth & Brooks-Gunn, 2003). The focus is on positive outcomes for their own sake, because such outcomes improve the quality of life for children, and thus increase the chances that young people will maximize their potential and talents and develop into independent, competent, and contributing members of society. In these cases, processes or variables that enhance well being and healthy functioning are identified as promotive or positive factors in children's lives.

So, how do the two above paradigms help us understand ways to promote child development? Regardless of whether or not the same terminology is used, psychosocial interventions and relevant policy initiatives can be viewed as attempts to reduce or eliminate risk factors in the child's multiple environments and/or to increase or establish protective or promotive factors in their lives. Often, multiple factors might be targeted to increase the possibility of success, and intervention would occur in multiple environments for ecological reasons. As one might expect from research findings that environments affect individuals differently and individuals have been exposed to a diverse array of influencing factors, effective interventions take many forms. There is not a single approach that works, but a variety of efforts that have been successful depending on the target population, its developmental history, its ecological setting, and the composition of relevant risk, protective and promotive factors. Hopefully, the ensuing discussion on effective interventions will illustrate these points more specifically.

In the remainder of this chapter, interventions occurring in three overlapping areas are discussed: 1) parenting; 2) other aspects of the family system; and 3) factors outside the family system that influence child development. Relevant risk, protective and promotive factors are briefly presented in each section before specific interventions are discussed. Such a presentation should help place the described programs in a broader, common perspective. Space limitations do not permit a detailed description of all the relevant factors in each area, but several sources provide detailed information on the relevant literatures (Durlak, 1997, 1998a; Gullotta & Bloom, 2003; Institute of Medicine, 1994).

Parenting Interventions

What are effective parenting practices? Although the answer to this question has been debated for decades, it is possible to identify the value of different parenting practices by conceiving of them as risk, protective, or promotive factors in reference to child development. Although the terminology varies somewhat across research studies, there is now fairly consistent evidence that certain parenting practices are much more likely to be associated with negative child outcomes (i.e., are risk factors) whereas others are more closely linked with fewer negative outcomes (are protective factors) or more positive outcomes (are promotive factors). Table 1 contains a listing of several of these factors, which are identified as such in terms of the consistently and intensity of their occurrence. That is, parent hostility is a risk factor when it occurs frequently and at moderately high degrees. This is important because it relieves parents (appropriately enough) of having to be perfect. What parents could claim they have never expressed any anger or hostility toward their child? In other words, all parents will make some "mistakes" in child rearing (i.e., emit parenting behaviors that are risk factors), but what is most helpful is to focus as much as possible on the positive dimensions of parenting. Practically speaking, this means that parents should focus on maximizing the extent to which they use child-rearing techniques that qualify as protective or promotive factors while simultaneously minimizing their use of strategies seen as risk factors. This is precisely what effective parenting interventions do.

Among the factors listed in Table 1, *demandingness* might give pause, but this research term reflects the extent to which parents establish realistic standards of behavior for their children that become increasingly more challenging and growth-oriented as the child develops. Parents high on demandingness tend to raise children who are mature, self-confident, and independent, whereas parents who have lax standards produce children who lack self-confidence, are more dependent, and lack initiative (Baumrind, 1989).

Table 1. Typical Influence of Selected Parenting Practices on Children

	Type of Factor	
	Risk	Protective/Promotive
Practices		
Demandingness		
Lax	X	
Demanding		X
Involvement		
Distant/neglectful, unaware	X	
Involved, monitors closely		X
Responsiveness		
Unresponsive, insensitive to needs	X	
Responsive, sensitive to needs		X
Acceptance/Nurturance		
Rejecting, hostile	X	
Warm, supportive		X
Disciplinary Style		
Punitive, harsh, inconsistent	X	
Firm consistent behavioral limits		X
Communication Patterns		
Vague, commanding, few explanations	X	
Clear and specific with explanations for rules and requests		X
Support and Reinforcement		
Infrequent support and reinforcement; attention paid to negative behaviors	X	
Frequent support and reinforcement; focus on the positive		X

Successful Parent Training Programs

By far, the most outcome research on any topic related to family life has been devoted to helping parents in the difficult and demanding task of raising children. Fortunately, an extensive body of research has confirmed the value of parent training programs. Such programs have been quite effective in improving child development both in terms of reducing problems when they are present and in increasing developmental competencies (Serketich & Dumas, 1996; Taylor & Biglan, 1998).

Programs with the strongest empirical support share two central features. One is associated with the theoretical approaches guiding these interventions (e.g., behavioral and social learning theories), and the second relates to the procedural aspects of these programs. According to behavioral and social learning theory, children's adaptive behaviors, as well as their maladaptive behaviors, are learned and largely shaped by the environment (i.e., by the supports, feedback, reinforcement, and prompting provided by the environment). Parents are seen as educators for their children, who, as the case may be, can teach children adaptive behaviors, eliminate undesirable behaviors, and help them realize their potential and talents. While some parents are naturally gifted in the nuances of child rearing, many can learn more effective child rearing techniques. In fact, the research literature is very clear that merely providing information to parents is not effective; it does not significantly change or improve child functioning. Similarly, changing parental attitudes about their children or child rearing also does not lead to improved child functioning; nor does letting parents discuss their family situations in an unstructured fashion. Changing parenting practices means changing behavior, and such changes usually result in concomitant positive changes in parental feelings and attitudes. For example, among other things, parents should carefully and clearly explain to their children what is expected (i.e., use good communication skills which is a protective/promotive factor); they may also need to model or demonstrate more complicated behaviors and skills so their children can see what is expected. Most important, effective parents establish high but realistic standards for their children's behavior (i.e., are demanding) but also deliver plenty of positive feedback and reinforcement as the child learns a new behavior (using responsiveness, involvement, warmth, support and reinforcement; all protective/promotive factors). Moreover, in many cases, the new skills parents are learning are designed to replace ineffective practices they previously may have used (i.e., risk factors). It is not possible to be warm, supportive and reinforcing to a child and hostile at the same time. Indeed, outcome studies confirm that ineffective parenting practices decrease while effective ones increase during the course of successful parent programs (Eisenstadt, Eyberg, McNeil, Newcomb & Funderburk, 1993; Kosterman, Hawkins, Spoth, Haggerty & Zhu, 1997; Schrepferman & Snyder, 2002). In other words, risk factors in relation to parenting are being reduced or eliminated at the same time that protective/promoting factors are being increased or established.

The second distinguishing feature of effective parent training involves the procedures used in these programs to develop parenting skills. Consistent with the principle that behavioral change is crucial to success, these programs use behavioral change methods that are known to alter behavior. It is no coincidence that successful programs use many of the same techniques to change parents' behaviors that they expect parents to use to change their children's behavior. For instance, many programs first define parenting skills carefully and clearly, demonstrate their use in vivo or using videotapes, ask parents to practice the skill in role-playing scenarios and then provide immediate supportive feedback about the parents' performance. In sum, parents learn behaviors in a step-by-step fashion in a similar way they are expected to teach their children new behaviors and skills. Some parenting programs whose effectiveness has been consistently confirmed in programs evaluations include those developed by Patterson and his colleagues (Patterson & Guillion, 1968), Eyberg (Eisenstadt et al. 1993), and Webster-Stratton (Webster-Stratton, 1998).

While most of the parent training programs that possess the two distinguishing features noted above have been successful, the general limitations that must be addressed in further research should be mentioned. Attendance and level of participation is far from ideal. It is common to have only half of all eligible parents attend any sessions and to have only between two-thirds to 3/4 of attendees complete the full program (Durlak, 1998b). Furthermore, it is generally more difficult to enlist the cooperation of fathers in many programs. Finally, co-occurring issues limit program impact for some families (e.g., single, low-income parents, parents with serious adjustment problems of their own, cases of severe marital conflict, and so on).

Some researchers have responded to the challenge of dealing with the general limitations of parent training initiatives. For example, they have developed specialized interventions that combine more traditional parent training with additional components that address economic or general stress, personal psychopathology or marital distress; worked collaboratively with community leaders to offer more culturally sensitive interventions and thus more effectively engage participants, and brought interventions directly into the home instead of conducting them in preschools or mental health clinics. (e.g., see Olds & Kitzman, 1993; Podereksky, McDonald-Dowdell, & Beardslee, 2001). Other examples of successfully engaging more parents include conducting parenting workshops in the workplace (Colan, Mague, Cohen, & Schneider (1994) and reaching out to parents through day care centers (Gross et al. 2003; see also Chesebrough & King (Chapter 7) in this volume).

The Family System

Table 2 lists selected risk and protective/promotive factors that have identified in the family system apart from specific parent practices. Both marital conflict and economic strain have received the most research attention as risk factors, and have been associated with a wide variety of negative outcomes in the early childhood period, such as behavioral problems, social isolation and withdrawal, and poor school performance. Later

Table 2. Typical Influence of Selected Features of the Family
System on Children

Features	Risk	Protective/Promotive
		Type of Factor
Marital conflict	X	
Domestic violence	X	
Parental psychopathology	X	
Parental well-being		X
Economic strain	X	
Marital satisfaction		X
Positive parent-child relationship		X
Supportive sibling relationship		X
Aspects of the family environment		
Conflict	X	
Cohesion		X
Structured, organized environment		X
Problem solving/coping skills		X

in development, outcomes might include school drop out, delinquency, substance use, and adolescent pregnancy (Brooks-Gunn & Duncan, 1997; Cummings & Davies, 1994). If marital conflict escalates into domestic violence, then it produces an additional risk to optimal development. In fact, both marital conflict and economic strain can have a cascading effect throughout the family system by affecting other factors. Each of these factors (and in particular their combination) may undermine parental well-being, disrupt parenting practices, contribute to parental psychopathology, and damage parent-child relationships. Keep in mind, however, that it is the combination and interaction of relevant factors that determines the likelihood of different child outcomes. For example, the negative effects of marital conflict or low income status (economic strain) on the child can be mitigated by a positive relationship with one parent, with siblings or through social support provided by extended kin and neighbors. All of the latter are possible protective factors as noted in Tables 2 or 3. Because both marital conflict and economic strain are potent risk factors, interventions for each are emphasized. This section discusses interventions for marital conflict while economic issues are treated in the next section, mainly in the context of social policies to help poor families.

INTERVENTIONS FOR MARITAL CONFLICT. Research has identified at least three successful strategies for combating marital conflict. One is marital

Table 3. Typical Influence of Selected Features of Neighborhood and
Community on Children

Features	Type of Factor	
	Risk	Protective/Promotive
Supportive Relatives and neighbors		X
Aspects of work		
Role Strain	X	
Challenging, varied work environment		X
Supportive supervisors and co-workers		X
Pro-family work policies		X
Aspects of various community services (medical, social, psychological, child care)		
High quality, accessible, and affordable services		X
Poor quality, difficult to access, or unaffordable services	X	
Social policies to assist the poor		X

therapy. Marital therapy is successful for about half of all distressed couples in the sense of greatly reducing or eliminating major conflict; another 25% of couples show some improvement although some serious distress and disagreements remain. The remaining 25% demonstrate few major changes (Jacobsen & Addis, 1993). These are encouraging findings, but many distressed couples never seek therapy, and when they do, their problems are often relatively long-standing, suggesting their children have been exposed for some time to marital strife.

A second strategy targeting marital conflict is to prevent its occurrence in the first place. One of the most promising approaches in this arena has been the Premarital Relationship Enrichment Program (PREP), a relatively brief but effective intervention that trains newly married or engaged couples in basic communication and problem solving skills including how to identify "trigger points" and defuse potential problems when they first arise in a relationship. Program evaluations indicate PREP has been very effective in improving marital satisfaction and decreasing marital conflict. In one case, PREP couples had a 32% lower divorce rate at a 12-year follow-up point compared to control couples who received no intervention (Stanley, Markman, St. Peters & Leber, 1995). Because one of the main limitations of PREP has been that many couples do not wish to take advantage of its services, the original developers of PREP are now disseminating the program through churches. The benefit of this approach is that several religions encourage or require their faithful to participate in some type of preparation program before marriage. That is, the legitimacy that church sponsorship lends to PREP could lead to higher recruitment rates of couples.

A third and final successful strategy has been to expand the scope of traditional parent training programs to focus on marital issues. Modification have been made in several parent training programs to target marital difficulties when necessity, and both researchers and practitioners are beginning to realize that a failure to attend to marital conflict when it is present can diminish the impact of child-oriented services.

This is nicely illustrated in a study by Dadds, Schwartz and Sanders (1987) in which couples with chronic marital discord were assigned to a regular training program designed to improve child rearing, or to a program that also helped couples deal with their conflicts through better communication and problem-solving. All participating couples had young children with conduct problems. Children in both conditions improved significantly by the end of treatment, but only the children of parents whose marital problems were targeted and treated maintained their treatment gains six months later.

Influences Outside the Family System

Table 3 lists selected risk and protective/promotive factors that exist outside of the family system at the neighborhood and community level. Indeed, it is essential to look beyond the family system because of the potency of many these other factors in influencing family life and thus child development. This final section discusses three related issues: 1) work, 2) community services impacting physical health, and 3) ways to help poor families.

Work

The impact of work on family life should not be underestimated. There is, of course, the necessity of stable employment and good wages to insure an adequate standard of living, but as noted in Table 3, other work-related factors are also relevant. The type and variety of job activities, the supportive climate of the work environment, and the role strain that may ensue affecting both work and family life are all important factors (Crouter & Helms-Erikson, 1997; Greenberger, O'Neil & Nagel, 1994) Role strain refers to instances when the intersection of roles (in this case work and family) produces stress, pressure and dissatisfaction. Role strain is felt to some extent by all individuals fulfilling multiple roles, but can increase in intensity to the point at which it can undermine well being and lead to adjustment difficulties (Greenberger, O'Neil & Nagel, 1994). The ability of marital partners or single parents to deal with role strain is important, but the discussion focuses on employer policies that reduce such strain and promote family life. Three pro-family employment policies that can substantially ease worker stress and enhance general well being are (1) flex time arrangements, (2) provision of work-based child care, and (3) supportive family leave policies. Flex time generally refers to the possibility of adjusting the hours (and sometimes the place) of one's work schedule. Many workers appreciate the opportunity to negotiate their working hours to suit their personal and family lives. Changes in many fields now allow for more employees to work at least in part from their homes, but this possibility usually exists only for those with certain technical expertise. Surveys indicate a significant minority of workers would work fewer hours at the expense of reduced pay so they could have more free time. Others in this text have already focused on the importance of child care (Honig, Chapter 3); relevant here is the value of having child care available at work which can eliminate the stress of finding good child care in the first place and then the transportation hassles that frequently occur when traveling to and from work and child care. The parameters of family leave policies in many businesses fall far short of the need. For example, pregnancy leave is often brief and allowances are not made for the necessity of caring for ill or incapacitated family members and relatives. The family and medical leave bill passed in 1993 does provide for up to six months leave for such situations, but many employers offer no financial compensation for such leaves placing many lower income families in a quandary.

Physical Health

It is extremely important to prevent physical health problems in young children. Good physical health is a central component of children's overall well-being, whereas poor health, particularly chronic medical conditions or disability, places a child at additional risk for social, cognitive and psychological problems (Lavigne & Faier-Routman, 1992). Although much more needs to be done, especially for low-income and minority populations, the following discussion highlights three success stories in the health area: smoking during pregnancy, teenage pregnancy, and home visiting programs. Although national trends reflect decreases in both smoking during pregnancy teenage pregnancy, the incidence of each is still too high and the developmental consequences for children can be severe.

For example, an estimated 20% of women who become pregnant each year smoke during pregnancy although such behavior incurs serious fetal, infant and maternal risk. The major health risks include low birth weight, prematurity, miscarriages, infant respiratory illnesses, and various birth and delivery complications that can lead to death for the infant or the mother (Floyd, Rimer, Giovino, Mullen & Sullivan, 1993). Fortunately, reviews indicate that smoking cessation programs are effective. Sound evaluations suggest that smoking can be reduced by 50% or more with concomitant improvements in perinatal and postnatal outcomes for both mother and infant (Dolan-Mullen, Ramirez, & Groff, 1994). This has been accomplished through very brief interventions requiring only a few face-to-face and phone contacts coordinated with routine physician visits. In fact, the effects of smoking during pregnancy are so pernicious, that it has been demonstrated that programs that reduce smoking rates by only 14% can nevertheless yield lifetime benefits for the family and society of over $45.00 for every dollar spent on the program (Windsor et al. 1993).

Teenage pregnancy, particularly for young single women who have not finished high school, also carries multiple risks for both mother and child. Early childbearing increases the likelihood that the mother will not finish her education (less than half of teen mothers ever complete high school), will not marry, will not begin a marriage that will last, and will not secure a good paying job (Sawhill & Kane, 2003). As a result, notice how different risk factors can easily accumulate in the child's family over time. Just as with smoking during pregnancy (which by the way is more likely in younger pregnant women), teenage pregnancy can also produce a variety of perinatal and postnatal health problems for infant and mother.

One program that has received considerable national attention for its positive impact on teenage pregnancy is Teen Outreach (Philliber & Allen, 1992). Teen Outreach attempts to create viable long-term life options for youth by innovatively combining community- and school-based activities. In the community component, high school students participate in volunteer opportunities of their own choosing which may be in nursing homes, social service agencies, or schools. The intent is to connect youth with positive role models in the community and increase their self-confidence by placing them in helping roles. The school component consists of a specially designed class that focuses on real-world issues facing teens (e.g., dating, career plans, work, sexuality, and stress). The class is led by a specially trained teacher or guidance worker who helps the youth develop effective goals, communication skills and decision-making abilities. In one evaluation involving over 2000 teens, Teen Outreach was successful in reducing pregnancy rates by 41% and also reducing school suspensions by 23% and grade failures by 16% (Allen, Kuperminc, Philliber & Herre, 1994). Teen Outreach's success despite its small attention devoted to pregnancy issues per se illustrates quite nicely the importance of a ecological perspective. Teen Outreach seems to work by enhancing young people's school and community environments in ways that radiate through their psychological and sexual lives.

Home Visiting Programs

Home visiting programs deserve special mention because they have become a popular form of health intervention that often extends its reach to target other domains discussed in this chapter. As the name implies, home visiting programs bring services directly into the home, but beyond this feature, programs vary considerably in scope and implementation. Home visits often begin when the mother becomes pregnant and continue after the birth of the baby. Usually, home visitors focus their attention first on good prenatal care, then on daily infant care after the birth, and eventually on the infant's behavioral, social and cognitive development. Most important, several programs for teenage mothers also simultaneously target maternal adjustment and growth, particularly educationally and vocationally. For example, home visitors may help mothers plan to continue or complete their education and learn needed job skills. Finally, because the intervention occurs in the natural setting of the home, home visiting tends to be an ecologically valid intervention. Home visitors often tailor their services to each family's unique situation.

Evaluations have indicated that the most successful programs share four common features. They (1) are more comprehensive in nature, offering services to target the needs of both mothers and their infants; (2) are more intensive and longer in duration, *sometimes, lasting for several years*; (3) use well-trained personnel (often nurses) as home visitors; and, finally (4), concentrate on serving families at elevated risk, which often means families in which the mother is young, unmarried, of low income, and a member of a minority group.

Successful home visiting programs have yielded many positive outcomes including substantial improvements in young children's physical health and their social and cognitive development. Mothers have also profited in meaningful ways in terms of staying in school to finish their education, avoiding early repeat pregnancies, and becoming employed. Two special issues of the *Future of Children* devoted to home visiting provide excellent analyses of many issues related to these interventions (Behrman, 1993, 1999).

Poverty

Although economic issues directly affect the family system, they are discussed here because the most effective solutions for family poverty are in large part determined by broader social and community forces and initiatives. Many families cannot become economically self-sufficient without some outside assistance.

In 1995, over one-fifth (20.8%) of all U. S. children were poor and more than 5 million of these children were under the age of six. During childhood and adolescence, poor children are at elevated risk for many negative outcomes such as poor health including early death, low academic achievement, school dropout, early pregnancy, behavioral problems, and becoming perpetrators and/or victims of crime and violence. Furthermore, poor children are much more likely than higher income children to end up as poor adults and be vulnerable to another series of negative outcomes in terms of marital, social, and vocational functioning (Brooks-Gunn & Duncan, 1997).

Admittedly, it is difficult to disentangle the effects of the array of factors that often accompany poverty such as various life stresses, reduced educational and vocational opportunities, exposure to adverse neighborhoods, and the availability and affordability of needed medical, mental and social services. Some of these factors are listed as separate risk factors in Table 3. Although money per se does not cause happiness, increasing the financial resources of low-income families improves their access to needed material resources. Children need minimum levels of resources to survive and develop their talents. Research indicates that when families do not have much, increasing their income can promote family well being and improve critical young children's outcomes related to physical health, cognitive ability, and school achievement (Brooks-Gunn & Duncan, 1997).

Individual service programs certainly have merit, but in the grander scheme of things, social policies, broadly defined to also include laws and stable funding streams for needed services have better prospects for reaching and improving the lives of many more people. Indeed, many initiatives have benefited the poor such as direct government cash payments, consumer product legislation to protect the physical health and safety of young children, different food, housing and medical insurance programs, and alterations to the federal tax system (Cowen & Durlak, 2000; Durlak, 1997; Plotnick, 1997). The public health impact of these efforts is considerable. In 1995, the effective implementation of various policies raised the incomes of more than 7 million families to above the poverty line (Plotnick, 1997).

Because the poverty rate of children is still over 20%, much more needs to be done. Although political debate always swirls around this topic, there is consensus among several experts that governmental efforts to help the poor through government programs and policies must not only continue, but also in many cases be intensified or modified to reach more individuals more effectively. Lewit, Terman and Behrman (1997) have offered a useful analysis and set of recommendations in this regard.

Poverty and Divorce

Poverty is an-all-too-frequent fate for custodial parents and their children following a divorce. Although the popular press often paints "deadbeat dads" as the main culprit, referring to fathers able to pay child support but who find various ways to avoid doing so, a more fundamental problem appears to be states' policies regarding child support payments. Three related aspects of current policies place custodial parents and their offspring at undue economic risk: 1) the decision to make an award in the first place; 2) the amount of any established award; and 3) collection rates. Improvements are needed in all three areas (Garfinkel, Miller, McLanahan, & Hanson, 1998).

First, awards are made to only 60% of eligible children (excluding those situations when the noncustodial parent is poor and truly cannot offer financial support). Second, the level of the award is set too low and not indexed to inflation in those cases when the noncustodial parent could afford to pay more. Third, and finally, states only collect about 63% of awarded payments on average. Two statistics summarize the dreary current status of child support payments. Over $34 billion more in child support could be provided *each year* if the current system were operating ideally (Sorensen, 1997). Translating 1992 figures (Garfinkel et al. 1998) into 2002 dollars, annual average child support payments in the United States are only $1475, or only $4.04 a day. Improvements in child support policies are certainly one way to promote the economic well being of families and children.

Concluding Comments

This chapter has provided a survey of issues affecting family life and offered examples of effective evidence-based programs and policies that brighten the prospects for optimal child development. It has combined ecological theory with the risk, protective, and promotive factor paradigm to provide a perspective for considering the goals and outcomes of different family-oriented interventions. It is beyond the scope of one chapter to detail all possibly relevant influences and their interactions, or to detail all family-related programs. Therefore, a few success stories in each section were highlighted.

The emphasis has been to view family life in multi-dimensional ecological terms. Although improving parenting practices has been a popular choice for promoting child development, it is also possible to help children by positively modifying different aspects of the family system such as the parents' marital relationship, and by recognizing factors outside of the family system that impact family members' functioning such as work and the medical care system. In the latter cases, social policies and initiatives are likely to reach many more who can benefit from services and support than one-on-one efforts with families.

This chapter concludes on a hopeful note. Although there still is a long way to go, definite progress has been made in helping families. We now have a more realistic and complicated view of family life and its processes. Most important, research conducted mainly over the past two decades has confirmed the value of several programs that can help families in various ways depending on their circumstances. There are still formidable obstacles in dealing with family poverty, disseminating sound interventions to reach more people, and deciding how to modify intervention for different family circumstances. Yet the successes achieved to date hold promise for the future, and depend on our continuing commitment to achieve a high quality of life for our nation's children.

References

Allen, J. P., Kuperminc, G., Philliber, S., & Herre, K. (1994). Programmatic prevention of adolescent problem behaviors: The role of autonomy, relatedness, and volunteer service in the Teen Outreach Program. *American Journal of Community Psychology, 22*, 617–638.

Baumrind, D. (1989). Rearing competent children. In W. Damon (Ed.), *Child development today and tomorrow* (pp. 349–378). San Francisco: Jossey-Bass.

Behrman, R. E. (Ed.). (1993). Home visiting. [Special Issue]. *The Future of Children, 3.*

Behrman, R. E. (Ed.). (1999). Home visiting: Recent program evaluations. [Special Issue]. *The Future of Children, 9.*

Brooks-Gunn, J., & Duncan, G. J. (1997). The effects of poverty on children. *Future of Children, 7*, 55–71.

Bronfenbrenner, U. (1979). *The ecology of human development: Experiments by nature and design.* Cambridge, MA: Harvard University Press.

Catalano, R. F., Berglund, M. L., Ryan, J. A., Lonczak, H. S., & Hawkins, D. (2002). Positive youth development in the United States: Research findings on evaluations of positive youth development programs. *Prevention and Treatment, 5.* http://journals.apa.org/prevention/volume5/pre0050015a.html

Cicchetti, D., Rappaport, J., Sandler, I. & Weissberg, R. P. (2000). *The promotion of wellness in children and adolescents.* Washington, DC: Child Welfare League of America.

Coie, J. D., Watt, N. F., West, S. G., Hawkins, J. D., Asarnow, J. R., Markman, H. J., Ramey, S. L.,

Shure, M. B., & Long, B. (1993). The science of prevention: A conceptual framework and some directions for a national research program. *American Psychologist, 48*, 1013–1022.

Colan, N. B., Mague, K. C., Cohen, R. S., & Schneider, R. J. (1994). Family education in the workplace: A prevention program for working parents and school-aged children. *Journal of Primary Prevention, 15*, 161–172.

Cowen, E. L., & Durlak, J. A. (2000). Social policy and prevention in mental health. *Development and Psychopathology, 12*, 815–834.

Crouter, A. C., & Helms-Erikson, H. (1997). Work and family from a dyadic perspective: Variations in inequality. In S. Duck (Ed.), *Handbook of personal relationships* (2nd ed.) (pp. 487–503).

Cummings, E. M., & Davies, P. (1994). *Children and marital conflict: The impact of family dispute and resolution.* New York: Guilford.

Dadds, M. R., Schwartz, S., & Sanders, M. R. (1987). Marital discord and treatment outcome in behavioral treatement of child conduct disorders. *Journal of Consulting and Clinical Psychology, 55*, 396–403.

Dolan-Mullen, P., Ramirez, G., & Groff, J. Y. (1994). A meta-analysis of randomized trials of prenatal smoking cessation interventions. *American Journal of Obstetrics and Gynecology, 171*, 328–334.

Durlak, J. A. (1997). *Successful prevention programs for children and adolescents.* New York: Plenum.

Durlak, J. A. (1998a). Common risk and protective factors in successful prevention programs. *American Journal of Orthopsychiatry, 68*, 512–520.

Durlak, J. A. (1998b). Why program implementation is important. *Journal of Prevention and Intervention in the Community, 17*, 5–19.

Eisenstadt, T. H., Eyberg, S., McNeil, C. B., Newcomb, K. & Funderburk, B. (1993). Parent-child interaction therapy with behavior problem children: Relative effectiveness of two stages and overall treatment outcome. *Journal of Clinical Child Psychology, 22*, 42–51.

Floyd, R. L., Rimer, B. K., Giovino, G. A., Mullen, P. D., & Sullivan, S. E. (1993). A review of smoking in pregnancy: Effects on pregnancy outcomes and cessation efforts. *Annual Review of Public Health, 14*, 379–411.

Garfinkel, I., Miller, C., McLanahan, S. S., & Hanson, T. L. (1998). Deadbeat dads or inept states? A comparison of child support enforcement systems. *Evaluation Review, 22*, 717–750.

Greenberger, E., O'Neil, R. & Nagel, S. K. (1994). Linking workplace and homeplace: Relations between the nature of adults' work and their parenting behaviors. *Developmental Psychology, 30*, 990–1002.

Gross, D., Fogg, L., Webster-Stratton, C., Garvey, C., Julion, W., & Grady, J. (2003). Parent training of toddlers in day care in low income communities. *Journal of Consulting and Clinical Psychology, 71*, 261–278,

Gullotta, T. P., & Bloom, M. (eds.) (2003). *The encyclopedia of primary prevention and health promotion.* New York: Kluwer Academic.

Institute of Medicine. (1994). *Reducing risks for mental disorders: Frontiers for preventive intervention research.* Washington, DC: National Academy Press.

Jacobsen, N. S., & Addis, M. E. (1993). Research on couples and couple therapy: What do we know, where are we going? *Journal of Consulting and Clinical Psychology, 61*, 85–93.

Kosterman, R., Hawkins, J. D., Spoth, R, Haggerty, K. P., & Zhu, K. (1997). Effects of a preventive parent-training intervention on observed family interactions: Proximal outcomes from Preparing for the Drug Free Years. *Journal of Community Psychology, 25*, 337–352.

Lavigne, J. V., & Faier-Routman, J. (1992). Psychological adjustment to pediatric physical disorders: A meta-analytic review. *Journal of Pediatric Psychology, 17*, 133–157.

Lewit, E. M., Terman, D. L., & Behrman, R. E. (1997). Children and poverty: Analysis and recommendations. *Future of Children, 7*, 4–24.

Olds, D. L., & Kitzman, H. (1993). Review of research on home visiting for pregnant women and parents of young children. *The Future of Children, 3*, 53–92.

Patterson, G. R., & Guillion, M. E. (1968). *Living with children: New methods for parents and teachers*. Champaign, Il: Research press.

Philliber, S., & Allen, J. P. (1992). Life options and community service: Teen Outreach Program. In B. C. Miller, J. J. Card, R. L. Paikoff, & J. L. Peterson (Eds.), *Preventing adolescent pregnancy: Model programs and evaluations* (pp. 139–155). Newbury Park, CA: Sage.

Podereksky, D. L., McDonald-Dowdell, M., & Beardslee, W. R. (2001). Adaptation of preventive interventions for a low-income culturally diverse community. *Journal of the American Academy of Child and Adolescent Psychiatry, 40*, 879–886.

Plotnick, R. D. (1997). Child poverty can be reduced. *Future of Children, 7*, 72–87.

Roth, J. L. & Brooks-Gunn, J. (2003). What is a youth development program? Identification of defining principles. In F. Jacobs, D. Wertlieb, & R. M. Lerner (Eds.), *Handbook of applied developmental science. Vol. 2: Enhancing the life changes of youth and families* (pp. 197–223). Thousand Oaks, CA: Sage.

Sawhill, I. V., & A. Kane, A. (2003). Preventing early childbearing. In I. V Sawhill (Ed.), *One percent for the kids: New policies, brighter futures for America's children*. New York: Brookings Institution.

Schrefperman, L., & Snyder, J. (2002). Coercion: The link between treatment mechanisms in behavioral parent training and risk reduction in child antisocial behavior. *Behavior Therapy, 33*, 339–359.

Serketich, W. J., & Dumas, J. E. (1996). The effectiveness of behavioral parent training to modify antisocial behavior in children: A meta-analysis. *Behavior Therapy, 27*, 171–186.

Sorensen, E. (1997). A national profile of nonresident fathers and their ability to pay child support. *Journal of Marriage and the Family, 59*, 785–797.

Stanley, S., M., Markman, H. J., St. Peters, M., & Leber, B. D. (1995). Strengthening marriages and preventing divorce: New directions in prevention research. *Family Relations, 44*, 392–401.

Taylor, T. K., & Biglan, A. (1998). Behavioral family interventions for improving child-rearing: A review of the literature for clinicians and policy makers. *Clinical Child and Family Psychology Review, 1*, 41–60.

Webster-Stratton, C. (1998). Preventing conduct problems in Head Start children: Strengthening parenting competencies. *Journal of Consulting and Clinical Psychology, 66*, 715–730.

Windsor, R. A., Lowe, J. B., Perkins, L. L., Smith-Yoder, D., Artz, L., Crawford, M., Amburgy, K., & Boyd, N. R. (1993). Health education for pregnant smokers: Its behavioral impact and cost benefit. *American Journal of Public Health, 83*, 201–206.

Chapter 5

Neighborhood and Community Influences Favoring the Growth and Development of Young Children

Julia L. Mendez, Lindsey Stillman, Doré R. LaForett,
Abraham Wandersman, and Paul Flaspohler

Neighborhoods and communities are important contexts that influence the lives of young children. The purpose of this chapter is to present an overview of features of larger community contexts that have been associated with favorable outcomes for young children. We strive to offer a broad perspective that organizes variables that have been studied by psychologists using an ecological orientation, including neighborhood characteristics and the socio-cultural factors that comprise the macrosystem of the child. Following the review, we feature several school readiness initiatives in order to illustrate how research on neighborhoods and communities can inform the design of state and national policy in support of early childhood development.

Use of an Ecological Perspective

The United States continues to experience tremendous growth in diversity of cultural background and family composition. National indicators of child well being (Federal Interagency Forum on Child and Family Statistics, 2002) reveal that 64% of children were of white, Non-Hispanic background, 15% of children were African American, 4% were Asian Pacific

Islander, 1% were American Indian or Alaskan native. Nearly 16% of U.S. children were of Hispanic background, constituting the fastest growing ethnic group in the United States. With respect to family arrangements, 61% of children received some regular childcare from caretakers other than parents prior to kindergarten entry. Worldwide, the development of mass media, Internet access, and other communication technology is resulting in an increasing globally connected society. An ecological framework offers a useful roadmap for guiding psychologists in their study of how changing community contexts shape the development of young children.

Many theoretical approaches have been offered for conceptualizing environmental influences on children (Holohan & Wandersman, 1987; Wandersman & Nation, 1998; Wilson, 1987). A chapter in the National Academy of Science volume, Neurons to Neighborhoods (2000), lists four predominant theoretical views including stress theory, social organization theory, institutional explanations, and epidemic theories. While stress theory and institutional explanations focus on the neighborhood institutions, physical structures, and exposure to toxins, the remaining theories emphasize the interactions that occur among residents of particular neighborhoods. In general, the study of neighborhood and community can be conceptualized as comprising the exosystem of Bronfenbrenner's person-time-context model of human development. Broader societal attitudes and cultural beliefs are also captured within the macrosystem level of Bronfenbrenner's (1999) framework. Although the mechanisms of community influence continue to be debated, there is some consensus as to particular conditions that positively and negatively affect the development of young children.

While a number of chapters in this volume address the impact of family and school contexts, this chapter addresses how the neighborhood and community may influence child development. Figure 1 depicts the neighborhood context most proximal to the family that includes characteristics of residents, their physical surroundings, and the quality of neighborhood institutions (e.g., healthcare, childcare). Studies of these variables typically involve observable structures present within neighborhoods or investigations of differences among groups of residents (e.g., demographic characteristics, socioeconomic status). An intermediary level of contextual influence involves variables that characterize relationships among people and neighborhood institutions within local communities. Two variables that meet this definition and have received attention are the degree of social cohesion or social bonding in a community and the problem of community violence and crime. Next, the macrosystem level consists of cultural values and beliefs that may be present within particular settings. The degree of poverty is also studied as a macrosystem influence, as some communities are identified solely by their lack of resources (e.g., ghetto or inner

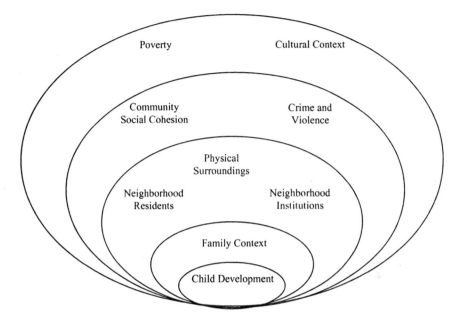

Figure 1. A Conceptual Framework for Reviewing Existing Literature on Neighborhood and Community Influences on Early Childhood Development *Note.* Important contextual influences on child development include the family, neighborhood residents, neighborhood surroundings and institutions, social cohesion of the community, community violence, and broad macrosystem factors including poverty and cultural context. Other contextual factors could be placed into this framework according to their level of proximity to the developing child. Factors at the neighborhood level may have a more direct impact on families, where factors at the broad macrosystem level of the framework may have a more indirect impact. State and national influences may operate at any level of the ecology.

city neighborhood). State and national influences also tend to be associated with the macrosystem level; however, their impact on individuals may often operate by affecting institutions (e.g., schools, health care services) at the more proximal levels of the ecology. Presently, the majority of studies examine neighborhood influences on adolescent and adult populations; our knowledge base regarding early childhood is extremely limited (Klebanov, Brooks-Gunn, Chase-Lansdale & Gordon, 1997). Also, the literature is just beginning to uncover and document the relative importance of neighborhood characteristics and their contributions to prosocial development for children (Gephart, 1997).

In using an ecological perspective, it is crucial to examine research that may capture the bidirectional nature of contextual influences. This perspective is also described as a transactional approach (Cicchetti & Lynch, 1993; Lewis, 2000; Sameroff, 1975) that reflects the study of how individuals and their unique characteristics interact with and are influenced by the community surroundings. For example, a transactional model is well-understood within the child maltreatment literature; children with difficult temperament typically are at greater risk for experiencing negative parenting, which thereby increases their risk for disruptive behavior that may lead to escalating child maltreatment over time (Belsky, 1980; Cicchetti & Lynch, 1993). At the neighborhood level, researchers have difficulty disentangling the characteristics of one's neighborhood with characteristics of the families who choose to reside in a particular community. These selection effects may help explain why some studies detect limited variance at the neighborhood level. For example, Klebanov et al., 1994, found that only 4% of variance in depression, social support and coping among mothers of preschool children was accounted for by neighborhood conditions.

In sum, the use of an ecological perspective involves examining a range of environmental factors and their influences on child development. With recent changes in the demographics of our children, attention to cultural and community context is more relevant and necessary for a deeper understanding of development. Finally, a sophisticated understanding of ecological influences must acknowledge that children and their ecology mutually influence one another.

Definitional and Measurement Issues

An important issue in evaluating the quality of research on contextual influences is the ambiguous use of terms like 'neighborhood' and 'community'. Earls and Buka (2000) note that multifaceted notions of community are so broad that research designs tend to select particular neighborhoods in order to operationalize meaningful variables to study. According to Coulton, Korbin, & Su (1996) measurement of neighborhood environments relies upon the use of three major strategies to designate boundaries: 1) phenomenological information, 2) interactional information, or 3) statistical information. A phenomenological approach involves determining meaningful boundaries that residents draw for their neighborhoods, while an interactional approach attempts to use patterns of social interaction to define a physical space (Coulton et al., 1997). Statistical information, often drawn from census tracts or zip codes, has frequently defined specific neighborhood environments. Critics of the census approach have recommended the use of a smaller unit of analysis, namely block group data, to more closely approximate the more immediate influence of neighborhood on families with younger children in particular (Coulton et al., 1997; Tienda, 1991).

Although a comprehensive treatment of these theoretical and methodological issues is beyond the scope of this chapter, we emphasize that refining measurement is a crucial step towards a fuller understanding of neighborhood influences, and how these influences change over time. For example, the Project on Human Development in Chicago Neighborhoods (Project on Human Development in Chicago Neighborhoods, n.d.) has been examining a set of neighborhoods over time to capture how composition and structural conditions interact to influence children's development. Other researchers have examined longitudinal data sets in order to tease apart the relative influence of neighborhood characteristics and family environments (Klebanov et al., 1997). In one effort, researchers examined the influence of five characteristics of the neighborhood environment with two different data sets, the National Longitudinal Survey of Youth (NLSY) begun in 1979, and the Infant Health and Development Program (IHDP), conducted between June and October of 1985 (Chase-Landsdale, Gordon, Brooks-Gunn, & Klebanov, 1997). This research showed that exposure to neighborhood characteristics for young children is often controlled by family practices. Therefore, in order to test causal relationships between neighborhood factors and early child development, more large scale and longitudinal efforts are needed (Klebanov et al., 1997).

Proximal Influences at the Neighborhood Level

As shown in Figure 1, our review of the literature on community contextual influences is organized from the most proximal and observable characteristics of neighborhoods to broader, macrosystem influences that may define communities. We begin by examining the proximal features of neighborhoods, which includes characteristics of residents, characteristics of physical surroundings, and characteristics of community institutions.

Characteristics of Residents

The socioeconomic status (SES) of residents in a neighborhood, beyond the influence of family income, has received significant attention in discussions of child well being. Growing up in high SES neighborhoods has been associated with higher IQ's, better achievement outcomes, higher scores in reading, and more play with peers in the home or at the home of peers (Chase-Lansdale & Gordon, 1996; Duncan et al., 1994; Kupersmidt, Griesler, DeRosier, Patterson, & Davis, 1995; Leventhal & Brooks-Gunn, 2000). In contrast, children growing up in low SES neighborhoods have been found to display more externalizing and internalizing behaviors, higher rates of child injury, and worse physical environments inside the home (Chase-Lansdale & Gordon, 1996; Duncan, Brooks-Gunn, & Klebanov, 1994; Klebanov, et al., 1994; Durkin, Davidson, Kuhn, O'Conner, & Barlow, 1994). Kupersmidt and colleagues (1995) found that 2nd through 5th grade African American boys from low-income single-parent homes living in high SES neighborhoods displayed less aggression than their counterparts living in low SES neighborhoods. Crane (1991) found that when the percentage of adult residents employed in managerial or professional positions dropped to a particularly low level, that area was characterized by higher school drop-out rates and higher rates of problem behavior.

Neighborhood SES is also associated with differences in the caregiving behavior of residents. For instance, mothers living in high SES neighborhoods displayed higher levels of warmth and more appropriate and consistent discipline (Pinderhughes et al., 2001). In contrast, mothers living in low SES neighborhoods were found to display less warmth and higher frequency of harsh interactions with their children (Klebanov et al., 1994; Pinderhughes, Nix, Foster, & Jones, 2001). Although child outcomes were not directly measured, consistent and positive caregiving is clearly one factor that can promote children's prosocial behavior.

The amount of residential stability or turnover among neighborhood residents is another key factor. Sampson (1991) found that areas with high owner occupancy had lower crime rates. Higher owner occupancy has also been correlated with a lower probability of lead exposure in children (Sargent, Bailey, Simon, Blake, & Dalton, 1997). Additionally, high rates of residential mobility negatively influenced friendship networks in the neighborhoods and correlated with an increase in anonymity among neighbors (Sampson & Groves, 1989). These factors may also indirectly interact with parenting behaviors. Areas with greater mobility have been correlated with higher rates of child maltreatment, especially in less impoverished areas (Coulton, Korbin, Su, & Chow, 1995). Similarly, parents living in areas with greater residential stability demonstrated greater warmth toward their children and utilized more appropriate and consistent discipline (Pinderhughes et al., 2001).

The degree of racial similarity among neighborhood residents has been associated with mixed findings regarding cognitive and behavioral outcomes in children. Greater verbal ability and decreased internalizing behaviors in 5–6 year old boys has been associated with high racial similarity whereas decreased internalizing behaviors in children aged 3 and 4 have been associated with low racial similarity in a neighborhood (Chase-Lansdale & Gordon, 1996; Chase-Lansdale, 1997). In one study of the neighborhood effects on preschool and early school age children, greater ethnic diversity in a neighborhood was negatively associated with the intellectual functioning of Caucasian children, however, it had no association with the intellectual functioning of African American children (Chase-Lansdale,

Gordon, Brooks-Gunn, & Klebanov, 1997). In an examination of neighborhood effects on families, the presence of ethnically diverse neighbors was associated with less maternal warmth as well as lower-quality learning environments (Klebanov, Brooks-Gunn, Chase-Lansdale, & Gordon, 1997). The type of family structures in a neighborhood is also associated with child well being. Neighborhoods characterized by a high rate of births among unmarried mothers were a strong predictor of risk for poor developmental outcomes in children and adolescents (Coulton & Pandey, 1992).

In summary, characteristics of a neighborhood's residents relate to child development, above and beyond family characteristics. High socioeconomic status, residential stability, and racial homogeneity in a neighborhood are all positively associated with aspects of child well being both indirectly and directly. In contrast, low SES, high residential mobility, and racial heterogeneity are all conditions that have been linked with poor child outcomes. These characteristics are often associated with each other, multiplying the risk to children. For example, it has been shown that the combination of poverty, overcrowded housing, and rapid population turnover is the strongest predictor of rates of low birth weight babies (Struening, Wallace, & Moore, 1990; Wallace, 1990).

Characteristics of Physical Surroundings

Overcrowding within a neighborhood or within a home can negatively influence child development. Neighborhood crowding, defined as the concentration of people in an area as measured by census tracts, has been associated with lower verbal ability and higher rates of externalizing behaviors in children (Chase-Lansdale & Gordon, 1996). In a study of 36 month old children, those children classified as "resilient" were more likely to be living in a home with a lower population density (Bradley et al., 1994). In another study, children who lived in homes with high density reported that they felt angry more often than did children living in homes with lower density and were more likely to deal with their anger by acting out (Saegert, 1982).

Substandard and vacant housing have also been linked to indicators of child health and well being. Specifically, areas with high rates of substandard housing have been correlated with higher rates of infant mortality and infants born to teenage mothers (Coulton & Pandey, 1992). Children living in areas with a high rate of nonresidential buildings had higher levels of worry, fear, anger, and unhappiness and were more likely to describe themselves as lonely (Homel & Burns, 1989). The physical characteristics of the neighborhood are also associated with crime rates. Areas characterized by high rates of residential properties, few vacant areas, and few major streets had lower crime rates (Greenberg, Rohe, & Williams, 1982).

Notably, those areas characterized by low rates of residential housing and high rates of vacant houses were also more likely to be low SES neighborhoods (Greenberg et al., 1982). This is another example of the clustering of risk factors.

The degree of pollution can have a detrimental effect on child development. Young children are more sensitive to the ill effects of pollutants or toxic substances than adults because of their higher metabolism and higher rate of oxygen consumption relative to size (Bearer, 1995). For example, a 6 month old child exposed to radon will, over time, receive twice the exposure as an adult (World Health Organization,1986 as cited in Bearer, 1995). One pollutant that is common in the United States is lead, which is present in the paint of many old houses and in some sources of drinking water. Ingestion of lead is also more detrimental to children than adults because children up to the age of 2 absorb more of the lead into their system than adults (Rout & Holmes, 1991 as cited in Bearer, 1995). Exposure to lead in childhood can lead to an increase in destructive and withdrawn behavior (Wasserman, Staghezza-Jaramillo, Shrout, Popovac, & Graziano, 1998). In addition, a meta-analysis demonstrated that low-level lead exposure in childhood is associated with intellectual deficits (Needleman & Gatsonis, 1990). Increased chance of low-level lead exposure has been associated with higher amounts of vacant and old houses in a neighborhood (Sargent et al., 1997).

Noise is another common pollutant in crowded, urban settings or areas near major highways or train tracks. One study found that children in classrooms exposed to chronic train noise had decreased academic performance compared to their peers on the quieter side of the building (Bronzaft & McCarthy, 1975). Cohen, Glass, and Singer (1973) also found that the level of apartment noise accounted for a substantial proportion of variance in auditory discrimination. Additionally, auditory discrimination was found to be a major factor in reading achievement (Cohen et al., 1973). These findings suggest that children living in areas with high noise levels are more likely to have poor auditory discrimination, which can lead to a deficit in reading achievement. In summary, overcrowded conditions, substandard housing, high rates of vacant buildings, high rates of nonresidential buildings, and pollution have a negative impact on child well being. Unfortunately, few studies have been conducted that examine physical aspects of a neighborhood that exert positive influences on child well being.

Characteristics of Community Institutions

The availability and accessibility of high quality resources in local neighborhoods is a key issue for both parents and children. For example, the amount and quality of available child care resources in the community can be influential for the cognitive development of children. Participation in after school care has been associated with better grades as well as better teacher ratings on children's work habits, peer relations, and emotional adjustment (Posner & Vandell, 1994). In addition, when comparing children in formal after-school care to children in informal care, children in formal programs spent the greatest amount of time with adults and peers (Posner & Vandell, 1994). Attendance at adequate day care in the first three years of life is positively related to the development of math and reading skills (Caughy, DiPietro, & Strobino, 1994). One study even found that in the first two years of schooling, children from low SES backgrounds were comparable to high SES peers in terms of cognitive growth in the school year but fell behind in cognitive growth over the summer months (Entwisle, Alexander, & Olson, 1997). This suggests that children from low SES backgrounds are not being exposed, at home or in their neighborhood, to resources that facilitate cognitive growth. The success of high quality child care and early intervention programs in achieving long term effects on cognitive and socioemotional development indicate that access to resources is an important aspect of child well being (Leventhal & Brooks-Gunn, 2000). The importance of high quality, available resources should not be overlooked. Low quality child care is often characterized by higher child to adult ratios which leads to less supervision, increased tolerance of aggression, and increased child injuries (Entwisle et al., 1997; Hayes, Palmer, & Zaslow, 1990).

Access to resources also has a significant impact on child health. Individuals living in poor and middle class neighborhoods make more emergency room visits than individuals living in affluent neighborhoods (Brooks-Gunn, McCormick, Klebanov, & McCarton, 1998). Moreover, individuals living in middle class neighborhoods participate in more routine doctor visits as compared with individuals residing in either poor or affluent neighborhoods (Brooks-Gunn et al., 1998). This study suggests that the SES of a neighborhood may influence the types of services available to the residents, which in turn affects their health service utilization. For example, Lash and colleagues (1980) found that part of the variance in rates of infant mortality and child health is explained by the availability of services (as cited in Sampson, 1992). The authors note that the quality of health care and physician rates vary significantly by community; areas with low SES as well as areas with high rates of ethnic minorities and transient populations are associated with the poorest health care services. Again, the success of interventions to increase accessibility and quality of health care services in decreasing infant mortality suggest that access to high quality resources is an important aspect of child well being (Sampson, 1992).

The amount of resources in a neighborhood can influence parenting behaviors as well. In areas where there is less dissatisfaction with public services, parents have shown high warmth and more appropriate and consistent discipline as well as fewer harsh interactions with their children (Pinderhughes et al., 2001). When mothers perceive their neighborhood to afford more resources for their children, these children have reported less adult supervision (O'Neil, Parke, & McDowell, 2001). Neighborhoods with fewer resources have also been associated with higher rates of child loneliness (O'Neil et al., 2001). Access to resources is also important, even if resources are present in a neighborhood. One study found that in areas where mothers felt that their child's activities were compromised by the physical quality of the neighborhood, they were more likely to limit their child's participation in those activities (O'Neil et al., 2001). Resources can also have a positive impact on social support for parents. Ross (2000) found that adult participation in formal neighborhood organizations was associated with more informal ties with neighbors.

In summary, the availability of resources in an area can have a positive impact on child rearing strategies and child well being. The quality of available resources is also an important aspect of consideration, as is the accessibility of the resources. The quality of resources within low SES neighborhoods may be an important factor that explains patterns of utilization within the health care and other systems.

Intermediary Influences within Communities

In this section, we review literature that examines factors that characterize the interconnections among residents and institutions. Specifically, studies of exposure to community violence and neighborhood safety reveal conditions that are detrimental to child well being. In addition, literature on the formation and quality of social networks at the neighborhood level, or the social cohesion of a local community, informs our awareness of optimal conditions that favor child development.

Community Violence and Safety

The amount of crime and safety in a neighborhood has distinct influences on child well being. High rates of exposure to community violence have been linked to increased antisocial behavior, increased reported stress symptoms, decreased cognitive performance, less positive social interactions, and more negative social interactions in child populations (Farver, Ghosh, & Garcia, 2000; Ingoldsby & Shaw, 2002; Osofsky, Wewers, Hann, & Fick, 1993). One study found that children who were raised in impoverished and dangerous neighborhoods were more likely to describe themselves as lonely (O'Neil et al., 2001). In addition, it has been shown that children who say they feel unsafe in their neighborhoods have lower self-worth, lower scholastic competence, lower peer acceptance, and poor behavioral conduct (Farver et al., 2000).

Farver, Natera, & Frosch (1999) report data confirming a pathway of influence involving urban preschool children's exposure to chronic community violence. Their sample involved 64 mothers and children who attended a Head Start program servicing families from a high crime and low-income community. Using path analysis, these researchers showed that community violence exposure was associated with a reduction in children's positive peer interaction and cognitive performance. Further, children's distress symptoms fully mediated the effects of community violence on preschoolers' cognitive performance, and partially mediated the effects on positive peer interaction. The amount of distress that is created through exposure to violence negatively affects children's ability to learn. The researchers further surmise that other unmeasured factors, such as parental restriction of child interaction in an unsafe neighborhood, might account for unexplained variance in children's peer interaction. Taken together, these findings reveal that community violence has a significant impact on both cognitive and social functioning for children as young as preschool.

Certain aspects of a community may influence crime rates. Neighborhood disorder is defined as the lack of appearance of order and control in a neighborhood (Johnson, Jang, De Li, & Larson, 2000). It includes aspects such as vandalism, abandoned houses, and burglary. Neighborhoods that are characterized by a high rate of disorder have been shown to have higher rates of crime (Johnson et al., 2000). The amount of informal integration with neighbors and the amount of participation in organizations are both related to rates of neighborhood disorder, with higher rates of disorder correlated with lower rates of integration and participation (Ingoldsby & Shaw, 2002). Another study involving 150 African American caregivers of preschool children found that parents' reports of neighborhood disorder were negatively associated with social support from neighbors, community contacts and family members (Waanders & Mendez, 2002).

Adults who see a lot of disorder also have increased levels of fear and mistrust (Ross & Jang, 2000). This can influence the parenting practices of individuals living in unsafe neighborhoods. In neighborhoods where there is a high rate of crime and danger, mothers are more likely to place limitations on the activities of their children and are more likely to have harsh interactions with their children (O'Neil et al., 2001). Mothers who live in neighborhoods with less danger are more likely to exhibit warmth and appropriate and consistent discipline (Pinderhughes et al., 2001). Violence toward children is also intertwined with many neighborhood influences. The highest rates of child maltreatment are often found in neighborhoods that have a high degree of poverty, high unemployment, a high number of female-headed households, more racial segregation, more abandoned housing, and a high degree of population loss (Coulton et al., 1995).

Social Cohesion

Sampson (1992) proposes a theory that illustrates one mechanism through which neighborhood structures influence child development (Gephart, 1997; Sampson, 1992). In this theory, community-level structural features (the proximal characteristics discussed earlier) influence child development through community level processes such as social networks and social control in a neighborhood (Gephart, 1997; Sampson, 1992). This theory emphasizes the role of social cohesion within a neighborhood or community that may contribute to a sense of collective responsibility for promoting positive outcomes for children.

Few studies have examined directly the relationship between social cohesion and child development; however, studies have linked parenting practices to social organizational variables. Communities with high rates of social disorganization (defined as the extent to which the community has economic and business problems, poor schools, inadequate public and social services, and low morale and involvement) are associated with a lower quality of parenting (Simons, Johnson, Conger, & Lorenz, 1997). In communities where there are high levels of social integration, children report less adult supervision of neighborhood activities (O'Neil et al., 2001). Other studies suggest that increased amounts of informal social integration can buffer the effect of neighborhood disorder on adults' fear and mistrust (Ross & Jang, 2000). Based on an exhaustive review of the literature, Bronfenbrenner concluded that the existence of social networks connecting families with sources of material and social assistance played a major role in determining the accessibility of healthcare (Bronfenbrenner as cited in Sampson, 1992).

Collective efficacy is also a mechanism through which the neighborhood may influence the development of individual children through the behavior of adults. *Collective efficacy* is defined as "the linkage of mutual trust and the shared willingness to intervene for the common good" (Sampson, 2001, p. 10). When neighborhoods are characterized by connectedness of social networks among families and a common set of expectations and obligations among adults, there may be an increase in control and supervision of all children in a neighborhood (Coleman, 1990 as cited in Sampson, 1992). Parents in communities with dense social networks and high stability may be more likely to assume responsibility for supervision of all neighborhood youth (Coleman, 1990 as cited in Sampson, 1992; Sampson & Groves, 1989). Clearly, the nature of social cohesion within a neighborhood can affect the well being of both parents and children.

Certain neighborhood characteristics may influence the degree of social cohesion. For example, the amount of concentrated disadvantage and residential stability negatively influences the amount of collective efficacy in a neighborhood (Sampson, 2001). Sampson (1991) found that neighborhoods with high levels of poverty were also characterized by decreased social cohesion and a decrease in shared expectations for social control. In addition, he found that neighborhood stability was associated with higher acquaintanceship and less anonymity in that neighborhood (Sampson, 1991). *Acquaintanceship* is "the proportion of residents who said that most of the people in the area were friends or acquaintances" and *anonymity* is "the extent to which people in a neighborhood know each other" (Sampson, 1991, p. 49–51). High density of acquaintanceship networks and low levels of anonymity are associated with higher community social cohesion (Sampson, 1991). In contrast, high collective efficacy, high rates of neighbors helping one another, and emotional attachment to the neighborhood are associated with lower rates of violence and crime (Sampson, 1997; Greenberg et al., 1982; Sampson, 2001). Moreover, Sampson and Groves (1989) found that in areas with a higher density of local friendship networks, there were lower rates of robbery. Neighborhoods with high levels of social support have been correlated with decreased social disorganization (Simons et al., 1997).

In sum, the study of community and interpersonal violence suggests that unsafe conditions have both a direct (e.g., symptoms of distress) and indirect impact (e.g., parental restrictions and or increased parenting stress) on children. However, neighborhoods and communities with greater collective efficacy and social cohesion tend to share responsibility for promoting positive outcomes for young children.

Macro-level Community Characteristics

Here, we present literature that addresses the pervasive impact of broader community characteristics that have received some attention by researchers, namely poverty and cultural context. Recent substantive volumes that address the influence of neighborhood level variables on children from economically disadvantaged communities are available (e.g., Brooks-Gunn, Duncan, & Aber, 1997). Additionally, we highlight the issues involved in disentangling socioeconomic status of residents, communities, and the cultural background of residents. Although several studies have examined the ethnic diversity of particular neighborhoods, far less is known regarding how cultural practices of specific communities play a role in shaping the development of young children.

Impoverished Communities

In this country, income poverty has become increasingly urban, concentrated, and affiliated with other indicators of disadvantage (Gephart, 1997). This, in a sense, has given new meaning to the term "poverty" that goes above and beyond family income. For example, poverty has been associated with increased neighborhood violence as well as fewer and lower quality resources in neighborhoods (Taylor & Covington, 1988; Lash et al., 1980 as cited in Sampson, 1992). In some studies, neighborhood income level is used as a proxy variable for economic resources, social infrastructure and institutions, and the availability of positive role models and socializing agents (Chase-Lansdale & Gordon, 1996). These examples are an excellent illustration of the tendency of factors influencing child development to cluster together, often magnifying their influences.

Within urban communities, many children face increased challenges to development due to a lack of economic resources. Garbarino (1995) has described socially toxic environments as characterized by a constellation of negative factors that place children at-risk for poor school adaptation. Despite some improvements in national poverty rates, the number of vulnerable children living in poverty is still approximately one in five (National Center for Children in Poverty, 1999). In the research literature, membership in low-income families is associated repeatedly with poor developmental and educational outcomes (Brooks-Gunn, Duncan & Aber, 1997; Huston, McLoyd, & Garcia Coll, 1994), particularly for children from ethnic minority communities (McLoyd, 1990; 1998). Earls and Buka (2000) note that we have yet to establish the relative importance of deleterious conditions within impoverished neighborhoods and argue instead for the study of neighborhood characteristics across low, moderate, and high socioeconomic levels to more precisely identify beneficial aspects of neighborhoods.

The disproportionate impact of poverty on communities comprised of ethnic minority populations also remains a critical issue for study. To date, we have little systematic data that can tease apart influences of neighborhood socioeconomic status, family socioeconomic status, and cultural context for young children (McLoyd, 1998). This finding remains troubling when we examine national figures regarding neighborhood poverty. The 1996 Child Trends document (U.S. Department of Health and Human

Services, 1996a) reveals that African American children are most likely to live in very poor neighborhoods (18.6%) followed by Hispanic children (11.3%) with just 1.2% of white children living in highly impoverished neighborhoods. Of non-black children turning 18 between 1988–1990, three-fourths (73%) report never experiencing poverty. In contrast, almost half of black children (47%) report experiencing 6 or more years of poverty during childhood, 28% report 11 or more years, and 6% report living in poverty during all 17 years of their lives (U. S. Department of Health and Human Services, 1996a).

Culture and Context

More in-depth study of the cultural context of children, families, and neighborhoods would refine our knowledge base for many children at-risk for negative developmental outcomes.

> Culture refers to the way people live; the rules they set for themselves; the general ideas around which they organize their lives; the things they feel are good or bad, right or wrong, pleasurable or painful. Cultural norms or standards for behavior are learned from those around us: relatives, teachers, and friends (Rose, 1997, p. 9)

Through this description, we see that understanding of culture requires appreciating systems of shared meaning that are socially transmitted (Garcia Coll & Magnuson, 2000). Even though culture may be described as a shared phenomenon, it is variable and dynamic, rather than monolithic or static (Korbin, 2002). While there is variability among groups, there is also variability within groups. Additionally, culture cannot be viewed as having a uniform influence on all members who may identify with a given culture. Individuals each have different experiences as members of cultural groups. Such elaborations touch on culture's multi-contextual potential for influencing children's development.

Conceptualizing culture within the framework of a developmental niche is helpful in making connections between cultural influences and human development (Super & Harkness, 1994). A developmental niche accounts for three aspects that shape children's lives: 1) physical and social settings of everyday life, 2) customs of child care and child rearing, and 3) the psychology of the caretakers. Additionally, these aspects not only shape the child's development, but they are influenced by each other and the larger human ecology. These customs and settings that comprise each child's developmental niche mediate universal goals that all parents have for their children such as 1) physical survival and health, 2) development of the capacity for economic self-sufficiency, and 3) development of behavioral competencies (National Research Council Institute of Medicine, 2000). In spite of having shared, universal goals for their children, different cultural practices related to these goals typically result in varied developmental outcomes.

Specifically, research on early childhood development has included combinations of symbolic and behavioral inheritances. Symbolic inheritances may include parents' expectations, goals, and aspirations for their children; the values that govern differential approaches to discipline; gender roles; religious or spiritual values; and ideas and beliefs about health, illness, and disability. Consideration of behavioral inheritances are circumscribed in "scripts" that characterize everyday behavioral routines for such common activities as sleeping, feeding, and playing, among others, and the distinctive contexts that shape cognitive, linguistic, and social-emotional developmental and the specific skills or behaviors. The integration of these stances leads to the most comprehensive approach to manifestations of the influence of culture (National Research Council Institute of Medicine, 2000).

Examinations of the influence of culture may focus on a combination of the following: race, ethnicity, social class, religion, region, gender, or poverty, to name a few. Despite the wide breath of possibilities housed under the umbrella of culture, most studies have conceptualized cultural influences as race or ethnicity, thus limiting our understanding of culture. Initially, cross-cultural studies focusing on different peoples around the world set the stage for examining cultural variability within the United States. Impacts of membership in a cultural group can be studied during early childhood, as preschoolers' become aware of the enduring categorizational component to race (National Research Council Institute of Medicine, 2000). Yet, caution must be exercised when conducting and interpreting studies using a comparative framework. Too often, research has highlighted deficits of a given group and neglected the positive influences that culture offers (Garcia Coll & Magnuson, 2000). Additionally, some of these studies are based on stereotypes of different cultural groups. Such practices not only limit our understanding of different cultures and their influences on children's development, but they also affect the manner in which services are delivered to different groups.

One important aspect to studying culture is the level of acculturation of an individual, family, or community. The term *acculturation* "refers to the process of adapting, and in many cases adopting, to a different culture than the one in which you were enculturated," (Matsumoto, 1996, p. 105). Although it is difficult to assess the acculturation level of young children, we can look to the degree that parents resonate with particular cultural values and practices. In particular, child-rearing practices have been a prime vehicle for the transmission of cultural values (Keats, 1997). Parents' level of cultural identification affects their children via parenting beliefs, practices, and the values transmitted to their children. Moreover, the degree to which neighborhood institutions reflect the cultural beliefs of the residents may be an important, yet overlooked, aspect contributing to social cohesion within a community.

Cultural values have an overarching influence on parents' own values, even in light of individual family and personal circumstances. In a study involving Mexican American and Puerto Rican parents of disabled children under age five, it was found that parents construct their values from the models presented by their culture as well as their own personal and unique experiences (Arcia, Reyes-Blanes, & Vazquez-Montilla, 2000). For example, specific child characteristics such as presence of a disability influenced parents' views about their child. However, parents' views of their child were also subject to the influence of the predominant attitudes or values of the parents' cultural group.

Cultural influences on children's socioemotional development may arise via larger cultural schema ingrained in the parents. Both cultural and class differences on mothers' long-term socialization goals for their children's behavior were examined among middle- and lower-class Anglo, middle- and lower-class island Puerto Rican, and lower-class migrant Puerto Rican mothers of toddlers (Harwood, Schoelmerich, Ventura-Cook, Schulze, & Wilson, 1996). Broad-level cultural constructs influenced mothers' beliefs regarding long-term socialization goals and child behavior. While Anglo mothers were more likely to evaluate child behavior under the rubric of self-maximization, Puerto Rican mothers used the construct of proper demeanor in evaluating their children's behavior. Additionally, while social class effects were present, they were outweighed by the influence of the broad cultural schema. Holding to this schema as a reference has implications for mothers' subsequent reactions to children's behaviors.

Additionally, parents' personal experiences with acculturation have bearing on the family environment and the relationships therein. For example, negative effects from the stress of racial discrimination has been associated with African-American mothers' relationships with both their children as well as their intimate partners (Murry, Brown, Brody, Cutrona, & Simons, 2001). In this way, the cultural milieu that surrounds a parent or family, simultaneously affects personal relationships while transmitting information about the experience of membership in a particular ethnic group. The transaction between families and the surrounding cultural context may also have positive and negative influences on child outcomes.

In sum, findings from the acculturation literature sample the different approaches to understanding how broad, macro-level influences such as culture are translated into more immediate effects on the child. Currently, information on the mechanisms through which culture in combination with the effects of poverty influences children and families is limited. Disentangling these influences will require innovative research designs that involve culturally diverse groups of young children from a range of communities.

Going Beyond the Neighborhood: Community Considerations in State and National Policy to Promote Child Well Being

Attempts to recognize and modify the trajectories of young children are incomplete without considering the full array of contextual influences. Since the 1960s, policymakers have shown increasing awareness of the influence of communities on child well being. For example, the Johnson Administration's War on Poverty yielded targeted programs like Head Start as a mechanism for assisting economically disadvantaged families facing increased stress associated with child-rearing. More recently, Hillary Rodham Clinton's publicized efforts in "It Takes a Village" and George W. Bush's Leave No Child Behind Act reinvigorated the idea that investment in young children's well being is a community issue and not simply a family issue. Increasingly, state and national agencies are supporting programs aimed at promoting child development and growth within community settings. Changing attitudes regarding educational policy and the importance of early intervention are also guiding macrosystem beliefs that may translate into enhanced services for young children.

In an effort to illustrate how research on neighborhood and community environments has influenced policy, we conclude our review with an analysis of several state and national approaches to support children's school readiness. Throughout the 1990s, increased discussion and funding has been allocated to target the enhancement of young children's readiness to enter formal schooling. Although multiple examples exist, we focus our comments to school readiness initiatives that reflect an awareness of community context and ecological variables in their work with children, families, community residents and institutions. They include federally supported Head Start and Early Head Start Programs, and South Carolina's state-funded initiative, First Steps to School Readiness.

Head Start: A National School Readiness Initiative

Head Start was created in 1965 as an outgrowth of the Johnson Administration's War on Poverty (Zigler & Styfco, 1996). Nationally, Head Start serves 950,000 children between the ages of 3–5 years of age. To qualify for the program, family income level must fall below the federal guidelines for poverty. Additionally, federal regulations require that 10% of the children served within Head Start have special needs or a disability. The creation of Head Start was based on providing the following six components to young children and families: early childhood education, health screening and referral, mental health services, nutrition education and hot meals, social services for the child and family, and parent involvement. The more recent Performance standards for Head Start organize services according to five major categories: Health, Mental Health, Parent Involvement, Community Involvement, and Child Development and Education.

The Head Start program takes a broad approach in serving young children and their families. While Head Start programs receive 80% of their funding from the federal government, the remainder comes from local sources which are often in-kind-services. Additionally, although the program's funding source is federal, local agencies or school districts apply for program funds, thereby resulting in greater local control. Nonetheless, each agency participating in the Head Start program is responsible for adhering to the program's national performance standards. The program's multi-faceted approach includes serving children directly (i.e., in the classroom), children's families, and also working with the surrounding community. These stipulations reveal how the involvement of key stakeholders from the family, school, agency, and neighborhood context is conceptualized as necessary to promote early educational development for children from low-income communities.

In response to conflicting findings concerning the impact of Head Start, the Administration of Children and Families (ACF) undertook an examination of Head Start in the Family and Child Experiences Survey (FACES) in the 1990s. The goal of the FACES studies was to examine the quality and effects of Head Start. Beginning in the Spring of 1997, data were collected annually on a nationally representative sample of Head Start programs, classrooms, teachers, parents, and children. Comparisons with findings from six national research studies on other preschool programs reveal that Head Start classrooms have higher quality than most center-based early childhood programs. Children participating in Head Start experienced gains in language development and in social skills and relationships. Families reported positive experiences with Head Start and see it as a community resource that supports families in raising their children. Parents also reported active involvement in many areas of the Head Start program as well as in participating in a variety of activities at home with their children (ACF, 2000).

Early Head Start: Program Expansion and Study
of Community Infrastructure

The reauthorization of the Head Start program in 1994 brought the creation of a new program entitled Early Head Start. Evidence from research and practice illustrating the impact of high quality programs on young children's development and family goals was pivotal in Congress' backing of the program. Early Head Start provides comprehensive services to low-income families with infants and toddlers, as well as pregnant women. Early Head Start follows the same income guidelines as the Head Start program. This two-generation program currently serves around 55,000 children within 664 communities (ACF, 2002).

Early Head Start programs select from several different service delivery models to match services with the needs of families within their community. Programs with a center-based orientation provide all services through center-based child care and education. Additional services include parent education and at least two home visits per year for each family. Other Early Head Start programs utilize a home-based model, where families are served through weekly home visits and a minimum of two group socializations per month for each family. Still other programs provide a mixed approach, where some families receive center-based services, some families receive home-based services, or some families receive a combination of the two either at the same or different times (ACF, 2002).

The Early Head Start Impact study, a rigorous evaluation of 17 Early Head Start programs involving random assignment of families to either EHS or a control condition, showed that involvement in the program had significant and positive impacts for participating children and families (ACF, 2002). The study involved 3,000 children and families, half of whom received Early Head Start services. Assessments of parents and children were conducted when the children were 14, 24, and 36 months of age. Families answered questions about their use of services at 6, 15, and 36 months after enrollment and when exiting the program. Children participating in Early Head Start experienced positive outcomes in the areas of cognitive, language, and socioemotional development when compared with children who did not participate in the program. Program participants also experienced a wide range of favorable impacts with regard to parenting. Additionally, program effects were also found on parent participation in education and job training activities. Families participating in the mixed-design orientation experienced the strongest pattern of positive outcomes. These findings illustrate the multifaceted influences on young children's social and cognitive development, and how early intervention in multiple contexts can benefit children facing risks associated with growing up in poverty.

State-Level Initiatives: South Carolina First Steps to School Readiness

An example of a state-level initiative that incorporates an ecological perspective in the approach to promoting positive outcomes for young children is South Carolina's First Steps to School Readiness (First Steps, 1999). The initiative is built around developing collaborative relationships among agencies and organizations given the task of providing the full range of services in early childhood. These services include the health care system (and mental health care system), the child care system, the child welfare system, the disabilities and special needs system, the economic, housing, and employment assistance systems, early education programs, adult education programming, and family support programs. The First Steps statewide initiative builds on several premises including: many resources for early childhood development exist; the amount and type of resources vary from one community to another; certain gaps in resources exist; and each community needs a unique plan to fill its gaps by building on its resources. The primary goals of the initiative involve coordination of existing and new resources and mobilizing these resources for the benefit of children. The First Steps program is a collaborative initiative designed to promote coordination and mobilization of resources across these disparate systems and programs. Modeled after North Carolina's Smart Start initiative, First Steps attempts to create change in systems, service delivery, and, consequently, in child outcomes across the state.

The impetus for the development of South Carolina's statewide initiative was based upon low rates of school readiness (Boyer, 1993). School readiness, as defined by First Steps, encompasses multiple dimensions of learning and development including health and physical development, emotional well being and social competence, approaches to learning (e.g., curiosity, independence, cooperation, and attention), communication skills, cognition, and general knowledge. A set of critical determinants (Early Education, Childcare, Health, Parent Education, Family Strengthening, and Transportation) is hypothesized to exert both direct and indirect effects on the dimensions of readiness. First Steps enabling legislation is grounded in the assumption that improving school readiness is best achieved through collaborative strategies based on local needs targeting multiple determinant areas (Kubisch, Weiss, Schorr, & Connell, 1995). Counties form a partnership board composed of local groups and organizations with formal or informal ties to the dimensions or determinants of school readiness. These boards are initially charged with developing a collaborative effort, conducting a needs and resource assessment, identifying and prioritizing gaps in services, and initiating a strategic planning process. Based on these strategic plans, boards propose and receive funding to implement strategies that provide best practice services targeting specific needs of the community.

Through a two-staged process, all 46 counties in South Carolina applied for and were successful in obtaining an initial planning grant and subsequent implementation grant to support specific programs to promote school readiness. This application process involved a review of the county plans to ensure that resource duplication did not occur, and that the strategies proposed by each county were a documented best practice. Ultimately, a common framework at the state level allowed each county to determine the appropriate allocation of resources to meet the needs of their residents. While some counties focused on establishing high quality child care, others needed to address pressing health care access issues. In more rural locations in the state, communities often used First Steps funding to offer home visitation programs in order to overcome the lack of public transportation for residents. Finally, a state-wide media campaign was simultaneously launched in order to publicize the different First Steps interventions and create a macro-system level commitment to early intervention among residents of the state. The First Steps initiative reveals how state legislatures can target a specific issue during early childhood, namely school readiness, while simultaneously allowing for individualization of the initiative at the local community level.

Conclusions and Future Directions

This review provides evidence that neighborhood and community variables do influence child development. Unfortunately, we know far more about the negative outcomes associated with children's exposure to poor neighborhood environments. To date, quality research examining the mechanisms of influence regarding positive development outcomes and neighborhood features is lacking. Yet, evidence does show that neighborhood residents, institutions, and resources make a tremendous impact on the family caregiving environment, which likely relates to better childhood outcomes. The research on community violence, poverty, and social disorder suggests that these conditions must be ameliorated in order to actualize the full potential of young developing children. Some other observations are also offered as preliminary conclusions to foster further inquiry in this area.

First, many risk factors at the neighborhood level tend to cluster or co-occur. Therefore, investigations that consider multiple problems simultaneously may provide a clearer picture than studies that seek to study risk factors in isolation. Second, cumulative risk is likely more significant than the presence of any single risk factor. Considering that poor neighborhoods also tend to contain vacant or unsafe housing, high levels of noise, pollution, and lead, studies that examine variation in the total number of risk factors across both urban and rural settings would be informative. Third, studies of neighborhood residents should consider not only the racial heterogeneity of the residents but also the influence of the cultural milieu on the development of cultural beliefs and child rearing practices. These studies must extend beyond the study of acculturation of families to include measures of the level of acculturation among neighborhood residents and surrounding neighborhood organizations.

Literature on the positive impact of neighborhood enhancements and community development efforts tends to be limited to adolescents and adults (Klebanov et al., 1997). Replication or reexamination of the impact on young children and families would greatly inform public policy. Currently, we have no accepted benchmark for evaluating components of neighborhoods that are minimally necessary in order for optimal development to occur during the early childhood period. A number of interventions that create more caring communities (e.g., Hawkins & Catalano, 1992) suggest that social cohesion and the collective focus of communities can mitigate the impact of a range of risk factors. Such information can be translated to guide the development of interventions at the state and national level, where leaders appear increasingly responsive to efforts to individualize large-scale programs based upon local community needs. Ultimately, more research on the transaction between child characteristics, family context, and community characteristics over time will more precisely inform the mechanisms of influence.

References

Administration for Children and Families (ACF). (1999). *Early Head Start.* Retrieved on August 2, 2002 from http:www2.acf.dhhd.gov/programs/hsb/about/programs/ehs.htm.

Administration for Children and Families (ACF). (2000). FACES findings: New research on Head Start program quality and outcomes June 2000. Washington, DC: U.S. Department of Health and Human Services.

Administration for Children and Families. (2002). *Early Head Start benefits children and families.* Washington, DC: U.S. Department of Health and Human Services.

Arcia, E., Reyes-Blanes, M. E., & Vazquez-Montilla, E. (2000). Constructions and reconstructions: Latino parents' values for children. *Journal of Child and Family Studies, 9*(3), 333–350.

Bearer, C. (1995). Environmental health hazards: How children are different from adults. *The Future of Children*, 5(2), 11–26.

Belsky, J. (1980). Child maltreatment: An ecological integration. *American Psychologist, 35*, 320–335.

Boyer, E. L. (1993). *Ready to learn: A mandate for the nation.* Princeton, NJ: The Carnegie Foundation for the Advancement of Teaching.

Bradley, R. H., Whiteside, L., Mundfrom, D. J., Casey, P. H., Kelleher, K. J., & Pope, S. K. (1994). Early indications of resilience and their relation to experiences in the home environments of low birthweight, premature children living in poverty. *Child Development, 65*, 346–360.

Bronfenbrenner, U. (1999). Environments in developmental perspective: Theoretical and operational models. In S. L. Friedman & T. D. Wachs (Ed). *Measuring environments across the life span: Emerging methods and concepts* (p. 3–28). Washington, D.C.: APA.

Bronzaft, A. L., & McCarthy, D. P. (1975). The effect of elevated train noise on reading ability. *Environment and Behavior, 7*(4), 517–527.

Brooks-Gunn, J., Duncan, G. J., & Aber, J. L. (Eds.) (1997). *Neighborhood poverty: Context and consequences for children. Volume 1.* New York, Sage.

Brooks-Gunn, J., McCormick, M. C., Klebanov, P. K., & McCarton, C. (1998). Young children's health care use: Effects of family and neighborhood poverty. *Journal of Pediatrics, 132*, 971–975.

Caughy, M. O. B., DiPietro, J. A., & Strobino, D. M. (1994). Day-care participation as a protective factor in the cognitive development of low-income children. *Child Development, 65*, 457–471.

Chase-Lansdale, P. L., & Gordon, R. A. (1996). Economic hardship and the development of five- and six-year-olds: Neighborhood and regional perspectives. *Child Development, 67*, 3338–3367.

Chase-Lansdale, P. L., Gordon, R. A., Brooks-Gunn, J., & Klebanov, P. K. (1997). Neighborhood and family influences on the intellectual and behavioral competence of preschool and early school-age children. In J. Brooks-Gunn & G. J. Duncan & L. J. Aber (Eds.), *Neighborhood poverty: Context and consequences for children* (Vol. 1, pp. 79–118). New York: Russell Sage Foundation.

Cicchetti, D. & Lynch, M. L. (1993). Toward and ecological transactional model of community violence and child maltreatment: Consequences for children's development. *Psychiatry, 56*, 96–118.

Cohen, S., Glass, D. C., & Singer, J. E. (1973). Apartment noise, auditory discrimination, and reading ability in children. *Journal of Experimental Social Psychology, 9*(5), 407–422.

Coulton, C. J., Korbin, J. E., & Su, M. (1996). Measuring neighborhood context for young children in an urban area. *American Journal of Community Psychology, 24*(1), 5–32.

Coulton, C. J., Korbin, J. E., Su, M., & Chow, J. (1995). Community level factors and child maltreatment rates. *Child Development, 66*, 1262–1276.

Coulton, C. J., & Pandey, S. (1992). Geographic concentration of poverty and risk to children in urban neighborhoods. *American Behavioral Scientist, 35*(3), 238–257.

Crane, J. (1991). The epidemic theory of ghettos and neighborhood effects on dropping out and teenage childbearing. *American Journal of Sociology, 96*, 1126–1159.

Duncan, G. J., Brooks-Gunn, J., & Klebanov, P. K. (1994). Economic deprivation and early childhood development. *Child Development, 65*(296–318).

Durkin, M. S., Davidson, L. L., Kuhn, L., O'Conner, P. & Barlow, B. (1994). Low-income neighborhoods and the risk of severe pediatric injury: A small-area analysis in Northern Manhattan. *American Journal of Public Health, 84*, 587–592.

Earls, F. & Buka, S. (2000). Measurement of community characteristics. In J. P. Shonkoff &

S. J. Meisels (Eds.), *Handbook of early childhood intervention: 2nd edition* (pp. 309–324). New York, NY: Cambridge.

Entwisle, D. R., Alexander, K. L., & Olson, L. S. (1997). *Children, schools, and inequality*. Boulder: Westview Press.

Farver, J. A. M., Ghosh, C., & Garcia, C. (2000). Children's perceptions of their neighborhoods. *Journal of Applied Developmental Psychology, 21*(2), 139–163.

Farver, J. A., Natera, L. X., & Frosch, D. L. (1999). Effects of community violence on inner-city preschoolers and their families. *Journal of Applied Developmental Psychology, 20*(1), 143–158.

Federal Interagency Forum on Child and Family Statistics. (2002). America's Children: Key National Indicators of Well-Being, 2002. Washington, DC: U.S. Government Printing Office.

Garbarino, J. (1995). *Raising children in a socially toxic environment*. San Francisco: Jossey-Bass.

García Coll, C. & Magnuson, K. (2000). Cultural differences and sources of developmental vulnerabilities and resources. In J. P. Shonkoff and S. J. Meisels (Eds.), *Handbook of early childhood intervention*, 2nd edition (pp.94–114). Cambridge, MA: Cambridge University Press.

Gephart, M. (1997). Neighborhoods and communities as contexts for development. In J. Brooks-Gunn & G. J. Duncan & L. J. Aber (Eds.), *Neighborhood Poverty: Contexts and Consequences for Children* (Vol. 1, pp. 1–43). New York: Russell Sage Foundation.

Gilliam, W. S. & Zigler, E. F. (2000). A critical meta-analysis of all evaluations of state-funded preschool from 1977 to 1998: Implications for policy, service delivery and program evaluation. *Early Childhood Research Quarterly, 15*(4), 441–473.

Greenberg, S. W., Rohe, W. M., & Williams, J. R. (1982). Safety in urban neighborhoods: A comparison of physical characteristics and informal territorial control in high and low crime neighborhoods. *Population and Environment, 5*(3), 141–165.

Harwood, R. L., Schoelmerich, A., Ventura-Cook, E., Schulze, P. A., & Wilson, S. P. (1996). Culture and class influences on Anglo and Puerto Rican mothers' beliefs regarding long-term socialization goals and child behavior. *Child Development, 67*, 2446–2461.

Hawkins, J. D. & Catalano, R. F. (1992). Communities that care: Action for drug abuse prevention. San Francisco: Jossey-Bass.

Hayes, C. D., Palmer, J. L., & Zaslow, M. E. (1990). *Who Cares for America's Children? Child Care Policy for the 1990s*. Washington, DC: National Academy Press.

Holahan, C. J. & Wandersman, A. (1987). The community psychology perspective in environmental psychology. In D. Stokols & I. Altman (Eds.), *Handbook of environmental psychology* (pp. 827–861). New York: Wiley.

Homel, R., & Burns, A. (1989). Environmental quality and the wellbeing of children. *Social Indicators Research, 21*, 133–158.

Ingoldsby, E. M., & Shaw, D. S. (2002). Neighborhood contextual factors and early-starting antisocial pathways. *Clinical Child and Family Psychology Review, 5*(1), 21–55.

Jask, P. (n.d.). Universal preschool? Lightning rod for public and family responsibilities. An interview with Karen Hill-Scott, Kathleen Gooding, and Douglas Price. *Council on Foundations*. Retrieved on August 2nd from http: www.cof.org simulconference ac2000 ss preschool.htm.

Johnson, B. R., Jang, S. J., De Li, S., & Larson, D. (2000). The 'invisible institution' and black youth crime: The church as an agency of local social control. *Journal of Youth and Adolescence, 29*(4), 479–498.

Keats, D. (1997). *Culture and the child. A guide for professionals in child care and development*. New York: John Wiley & Sons.

Klebanov, P. K., Brooks-Gunn, J., Chase-Lansdale, P. L., & Gordon, R. A. (1997). Are neighborhood effects on young children mediated by features of the home environment? In

J. Brooks-Gunn & G. J. Duncan & L. J. Aber (Eds.), *Neighborhood Poverty: Context and Consequences for Children* (Vol. 1, pp. 119–145). New York: Russell Sage Foundation.

Klebanov, P. K., Brooks-Gunn, J., & Duncan, G. J. (1994). Does neighborhood and family poverty affect mothers' parenting, mental health, and social support? *Journal of Marriage and the Family, 56*(May), 441–455.

Korbin, J. E. (2002). Culture and child maltreatment: Cultural competence and beyond. *Child Abuse & Neglect, 26,* 637–644.

Kubisch, A. C., Weiss, C. H., Schorr, L. B., & Connell, J. P. (1995). Introduction. In J. P. Connell & A. C. Kubisch & L. B. Schorr & C. H. Weiss (Eds.), *New approaches to evaluating community initiatives* (Vol. 1). Washington, D.C.: The Aspen Institute.

Kupersmidt, J. B., Griesler, P. C., DeRosier, M. E., Patterson, C. J., & Davis, P. W. (1995). Childhood aggression and peer relations in the context of family and neighborhood factors. *Child Development, 66,* 360–375.

Leventhal, T., & Brooks-Gunn, J. (2000). The neighborhoods they live in: The effects of neighborhood residence on child and adolescent outcomes. *Psychological Bulletin, 126*(2), 309–337.

Lewis, M. (2000). Toward a development of psychopathology: Models, definitions, & prediction. In A.J. Sameroff, M.L. Lewis & S. Miller (Eds.), Handbook of developmental psychopathology: 2nd Edition (pp. 3–22). New York, NY: Kluwer.

Matsumoto, D. (1996). *Culture and psychology.* New York: Brooks Cole.

Murry, V. M., Brown, P. A., Brody, G. H., Cutrona, C. E., & Simons, R. L. (2001). Racial discrimination as a moderate of the links among stress, maternal psychological functioning, and family relationships. *Journal of Marriage and Family, 63,* 915–926.

National Research Council Institute of Medicine. (2000). *From neurons to neighborhoods.* Washington, DC: National Academy Press.

Needleman, H. L., & Gatsonis, C. A. (1990). Low-level lead exposure and the IQ of children. *Journal of the American Medical Association, 263*(5), 673–678.

O'Neil, R., Parke, R. D., & McDowell, D. J. (2001). Objective and subjective features of children's neighborhoods: Relations to parental regulatory strategies and children's social competence. *Applied Developmental Psychology, 22,* 135–155.

Osofsky, J. D., Wewers, S., Hann, D. M., & Fick, A. C. (1993). Chronic community violence: What is happening to our children? *Psychiatry, 56*(February), 36–45.

Pinderhughes, E. E., Nix, R., Foster, E. M., & Jones, D. (2001). Parenting in context: Impact of neighborhood poverty, residential stability, public services, social networks, and danger on parental behaviors. *Journal of Marriage and Family, 63,* 941–953.

Posner, J. K., & Vandell, D. L. (1994). Low-income children's after-school care: Are there beneficial effects of after-school programs? *Child Development, 65,* 440–456.

Project on Human Development in Chicago Neighborhoods. (n.d.). PHDCN general overview. Retrieved July 26, 2002, from *http://phdcn.harvard.edu/about/about.html*

Ross, C. E., & Jang, S. J. (2000). Neighborhood disorder, fear, and mistrust: The buffering role of social ties with neighbors. *American Journal of Community Psychology, 28*(4), 401–420.

Rose, P. I. (1997). *They and we. Racial and ethnic relations in the United States.* New York: McGraw-Hill.

Saegert, S. (1982). Environment and children's mental health: Residential density and low income children. In A. Baum & J. E. Singer (Eds.), *Handbook of Psychology and Health* (pp. 247–271). Hillsdale, NJ: Erlbaum.

Sameroff, A. (1975). Transactional models in early social relations. *Human Development, 18,* 65–79.

Sampson, R. J. (1991). Linking the micro-and macrolevel dimensions of community social organization. *Social Forces, 70*(1), 43–64.

Sampson, R. J. (1992). Family management and child development: Insights from social disorganization theory. In J. McCord (Ed.), Facts, Frameworks, Forecasts: Advances in Criminological Theory, Volume 3 (pp. 63–93). New Brunswick: Transaction Press.

Sampson, R. J. (2001). How do communities undergird or undermine human development? Relevant contexts and social mechanisms. In A. Booth & A. C. Crouter (Eds.), *Does It Take a Village? Community Effects on Children, Adolescents, and Families* (pp. 3–30). Mahwah: Lawrence Erlbaum Associates.

Sampson, Robert J. (1997). Neighborhoods and violent crime: A multilevel study of collective efficacy. *Science, 277*, 918–924.

Sampson, R. J., & Laub, J. H. (1994). Urban poverty and the family context of delinquency: A new look at structure and process in a classic study. *Child Development, 65*, 523–540.

Sampson, R. J., & Groves, W. B. (1989). Community structure and crime: Testing social-disorganization theory. *American Journal of Sociology, 94*(4), 774–802.

Sargent, J. D., Bailey, A., Simon, P., Blake, M., & Dalton, M. A. (1997). Census tract analysis of lead exposure in Rhode Island children. *Environmental Research, 74*, 159–168.

Simons, R. L., Johnson, C., Conger, R. D., & Lorenz, F. O. (1997). Linking community context to quality of parenting: A study of rural families. *Rural Sociology, 62*(2), 207–230.

Super, C. M. & Harkness, S. (1994). The developmental niche. In W. J. Lonner and R. S. Malpass (Eds.), *Psychology and culture* (pp. 95–99). Boston, MA: Allyn and Bacon.

Struening, E. L., Wallace, R., & Moore, R. (1990). Housing conditions and the quality of children at birth. *Bulletin of the New York Academy of Medicine, 66*(5), 463–478.

Taylor, R. B., & Covington, J. (1988). Neighborhood changes in ecology and violence. *Criminology, 26*(4), 553–589.

Tienda, M. (1991). Poor people and poor places. Deciphering neighborhood effects on poverty outcomes. In J. Huber (Ed.), Macro-micro linkages in sociology (pp. 244–262). Newbury Park, CA: Sage.

U. S. Department of Health and Human Services (1996a). Trends in the well being of America's children and youth: 1996. Office of the Assistant Secretary for Planning and Evaluation. Washington, D.C.

Wilson, W. J. (1987). *The truly disadvantaged: The inner city, the underclass, and public policy*. Chicago: The University of Chicago Press.

Wallace, R. (1990). Urban desertification, public health and public order: 'Planned shrinkage', violent death, substance abuse and AIDS in the Bronx. *Social Science and Medicine, 31*(7), 801–813.

Waanders, C. & Mendez, J. (2002). Neighborhood and family determinants of parent involvement during Head Start. Manuscript in preparation.

Wandersman, A. & Nation, M. (1998). Urban neighborhoods and mental health: Psychological contributions to understanding toxicity, resilience, and interventions. *American Psychologist, 53*(6), 647–656.

Wasserman, G. A., Staghezza-Jaramillo, B., Shrout, P., Popovac, D., & Graziano, J. (1998). The effect of lead exposure on behavior problems in preschool children. *American Journal of Public Health, 88*(3), 481–486.

Zigler, E. F. & Styfco, S. (1996). Head Start and early childhood intervention: The changing course of social sciences and social policy. In E. F. Zigler, S. L. Kagan, and Hall, N. W. (Eds.), *Children, families, and government. Preparing for the twenty-first century* (pp. 132–155). Cambridge, MA: Cambridge University Press.

Chapter 6

The Integration of Levels
of Research Findings

Martin Bloom and Thomas P. Gullotta

The various social and behavioral sciences remain relatively isolated, not because of some master plot by an evil genius, but because the natural dissimilarities among the several content areas makes it difficult to formulate and test their connections. (Or, to paraphrase Winston Churchill's remark about the conflicts between England and America, we are several social sciences separated by a common language.) Hence, we resort to metaphor as a heuristic to convey our sense of how to connect the multiple layers of research findings on the effective promotion of prosocial values in young children. To give the reader a hint about where we are going, think of this as a kind of systems or ecological theory (Bronfenbrenner, 1979; Germain & Bloom, 1999) in which natural or everyday subsystems and systems (such as families and children and teachers) are interrelated by means of their communications and transactions such that what happens in one system affects the other systems to some degree. We will also characterize the artificial connections such as between professional helping systems which insert themselves into the lives of their clients or consumers. The conceptual challenge is to estimate the effect of those intersystem communications so that we can generate practice strategies for achieving specific objectives.

Imagine four large plastic trays, set in a large metal frame so that one tray is at the bottom and the other trays situated above it, one on top of the other. These trays represent holding spaces for the relatively strong empirical findings about 1) individual, 2) small natural group including family, peers, and classroom; 3) larger natural groupings like neighborhood, school, and local businesses; and 4) still larger natural groupings such as the community, governments, large scale organizations, and the like. The frame in which these trays are set represent the legal system, the dominant culture and pertinent subcultures, and value systems, cutting across all trays, and applying to each of them. In short, we are positioning all of the actors in our integrative drama.

We modify this metaphor in one important way: we conceive of these four trays as an inverted pyramid (see Figure 1). The second (small group)

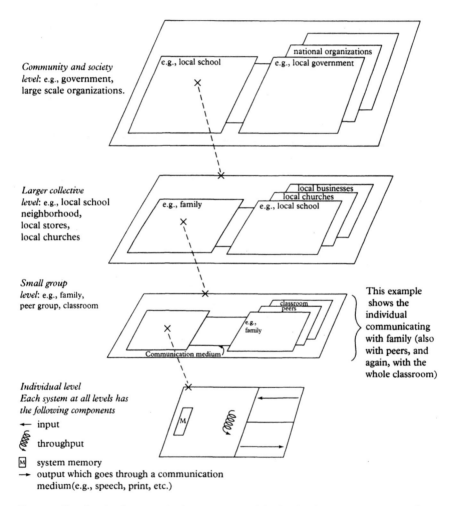

Figure 1. Four levels of communication systems, each higher level contains one system from the previous lower level, indicated by X- - - -X.

tray is conceived as simultaneously *containing* the first (individual) tray as members of the small groups. (This is represented by the string attached to two levels: X-----------X.) A child, from this perspective, would be viewed in the second tray as member of the family and of his or her peer group, and of the classroom, simultaneously. (The several types of small groups are represented by the sets of large boxes within the given diagram.) The particular membership roles becomes activated when an actor (individual or group) is in one physical setting or another. When a parent comes to the classroom and acts as a teacher's aide, there may be some momentary confusion because the children are not used to mixing family and school roles. Likewise, each of the higher trays contains the lower trays as members or potential members. By allowing one actor to be in more than one system at the same time is, of course, true to life, but also permits us to analyze each system separately.

To put this another way, we can begin to see both distinctive findings (in individual trays) and interactive ones (within a complex higher tray containing members from lower trays). We conceive of the interaction to be a communication process, where one portion of a system (say, the individual child) speaks to his mother (whose is both individual person and role holder involving the family system). The mother takes in the information, processes it in terms of past communications and future expectations, and responds. The child receives the response, processes it, and reacts in return. This communication cycle is a basic unit in describing interaction and the transmission of influence. As the child processes the mother's statement, it becomes entered in the child's memory, and acts in the future as part of the child's reservoir of information about dealing with the world. This includes learning of behaviors, expectations, values, and all of the matters of which socialization consists. Likewise, at different levels, the component subsystem (like a family) of a larger system (such as the school) takes in information, makes it part of its processing system, and responds accordingly. For instance, the "school" says (through it spokesperson) that the family must bring in a signed vaccination form for the school's records to permit the child to come to school. This cross-system communication influences what the parents do in terms of obtaining that certification. Such messages from larger systems to smaller ones become ways in which these macro systems influence and continue to influence the micro systems. However, it is also possible that micro systems can influence the macro ones, such as a child making a request for more stories and less "free" time at preschool.

We conceive of the substantive chapters of this book as fitting *primarily* in one or another of these trays. They summarize vast territories of information focused on social competency, and have summarized the empirical generalizations that they find especially useful in promoting these prosocial values in young children. Sometimes their findings need to be sorted out into these distinctive trays because they span traditional borders. Joe Durlak, for example in chapter 4, addresses research dealing with parenting practices, but also empirical evidence about neighborhoods, as influences of their component members. Each portion of information can be sorted into separate trays, but it is more likely that they will be centered in that level which does the originating of the communication. So, the school-originated vaccination request to families with school-aged children would be housed at the school level (third level) since this is where the request originates.

However, what our authors were not asked to do as such is to provide connective links between and among these findings in the four trays. We take this assignment as the task of the present integrative chapter. We will summarize very briefly the major principles of each tray as described in these chapters, and then we will attempt the difficult task of suggesting how these principles interact with each of the other principles.

Margaret O'Shea (Chapter 1) has filled the individual tray with important empirical principles, including the following: Experience makes long-lasting connections between sensations and the brain where this information is processed and stored for future use as cognitions, affective states, learning, and behavior. Socially positive experiences (such as good prenatal care, warm and loving attachment, positive age-appropriate stimulation—to be discussed in the second tray) create socially positive learnings. Unstimulating experiences slow down brain development. Infants come to trust caregivers by means of touch, voice tone and speech, comforting motions, feeding, and being kept warm and dry.

O'Shea continues with a discussion of toddlers (1- to 2-year range) who learn to walk, talk (including saying 'no' as showing their growing independence), and relate to others, which will soon bring us to the second tray. Toddlers learn to play (solitary at first, parallel with others later); they learn to express emotions such as jealousy, affection, pride, shame, fear—again, often in the context of others. Toddlers show intellectual developments through curiosity, naming things, and learning about simple cause/effect relationships; they show increasingly sophisticated motor skills.

O'Shea's discussion of preschoolers, aged 3 to 5, is the central concern of the Bingham project. She discusses the preschoolers' improved motor skills and self-sufficiency in dealing with immediate challenges, but also the possible frustration and crying behavior when unable to perform at a desired level. Increasingly, the development of preschoolers involves member interactions in family and school. Language skills involve engagement with peers and new adults (teachers), increasingly complex games, more exploring behaviors, more 'why?' questions. Preschoolers request repeated telling of the same stories (reinforcing neural pathways) and repeated games and activities (hence the various 'centers' in the preschool, to play with blocks, paints, foods, books, etc.) so as to gain greater mastery over these familiar tools, and explore new uses. Through all of these activities, O'Shea sees attachment of child to parents at 6 to 8 months as critical for the child's sense of security, self-esteem, self control, and social skills.

The stage is now set with these empirical findings of toddlers' behaviors to consider other chapters, other trays.

Susanne Denham and Roger Weissberg (Chapter 2) fill in a portion of the second tray (small group) and another aspect of the first tray (individual) with their discussion of social-emotional learning (SEL) in early childhood. SEL involves both the individual feelings and the interpersonal or member behaviors in small groups. SEL involves the expression of one's own feelings in relationship to the feelings of others in socially appropriate ways, an important lesson for toddlers. As Denham and Weissberg point out, it is adults (parents, teachers especially) who construct scaffolds for the child's social and emotional learning. Adults and children are together members of the second tray, the small group, with its dynamic of communication exchanges that get embedded as part of the processing and storage components of all member, as well as in this family's collective memory.

As described in the individual tray, children are growing in their emotions, cognitions, and behaviors, with emotional growth preceding the other two. This necessitates a transition period when emotions get expressed, but social norms are not necessarily honored in the process. Parents and teachers represent part of that transition, helping the child to master his or her feelings in relation to social others. When children can manage their emotional arousal within social interactions, they are not merely ready for school, but they are positioned to adjust successfully to the new demands, to thrive on new experiences, and to attain good grades. They are likely to have positive interactions with teachers and good relationships with their peers.

Denham and Weissberg offer a great deal of documentation for how the components of SEL—the skills of self-awareness, self-management, and emotional expressiveness—play their role in the development of the child. In our terms, children may learn (or may not be taught to learn) these social and emotional skills as members of peer, classroom, and family groups. When children are at high risk of not learning these skills, society has often deemed it necessary to provide some special training at a pre-school so as to enable these children to be ready for the educational experience in public school that will set a large portion of their life course.

Denham and Weissburg are concerned with children at risk, those who have specific SEL deficits such that their intense emotions are ill-expressed, making them likely to suffer difficulties in social interactions as they make their way through the public school phase, and beyond. They emphasize the literature on *thinking* about interpersonal interactions (social problem solving) so as to develop responsible decision making and the appropriate management of interpersonal relationships. These lessons may be facilitated by sensitive parents and teachers. For example, Denham and Weissberg, along with O'Shea, emphasize the importance of attachment with caring adults, who, in effect, are trusted to aid the child in thinking and feeling through a given situation so as to achieve a positive outcome. As members of the small group, this natural parental or teacher assistance gets incorporated into the processing and storage capacity of the child; it is also a natural part of the family's values and the school's teaching philosophy. Adults can teach about emotions and behavior; they can model appropriate behaviors and emotions; and they can give contingent reactions to children's expressed emotions and behaviors—more by encouraging the positive ones, than by discouraging the negative ones. Denham and Weissberg conclude with advice on where do we go from here—and on what specific programs are needed to institutionalize SEL to promote prosocial learning in youngsters.

We listened to this advice as we developed the Bingham program. From our search of the literature and consultations with the authors of the chapters discussed in this paper, we identified five key concepts that captured the essence of SEL—kindness, emotions, respect, cooperation, and self-control. That is, we recognize the need to introduce some planned interventions artificially so as to get the natural systems to work effectively. These artificial or planned interventions are efforts focused on specific topics, time-limited, and run parallel with the existing natural systems as an aid to get them to perform their functions more smoothly and more completely.

Alice Sterling Honig (in Chapter 3) contributes information to the small group tray in her extensive review of the literature and experiences on how teachers and caretakers of young children contribute to the development of prosocial behaviors. Honig also recognizes contributions to the third tray (formal organizations like schools), as the curriculum is constructed to achieve certain goals. She directs our attention to seemingly intrinsic altruism in the very young as a phenomenon worthy of further study, but spends most of her efforts on the learning of reciprocal helpfulness and social responsibility, especially in light of recent expositions on bullying and other forms of violence in schools. She, too, notes that attachment theory presents the foundations of prosocial behavior, particularly in terms of teachers' responses to securely attached (less response!) vs insecure children (more response). Thus, the classroom ambience and philosophy makes an important difference in the climate for prosocial interactions, Honig notes.

Honig characterizes the major dimensions of a class room that promotes prosocial behaviors. They are child-centered, but with teachers exhibiting a model of firm calmness. They use inductive reasoning in sorting out interpersonal problems. They emphasize cooperation rather than competition in school learning. They engage children in peaceful games and sports. They arrange classroom spaces to boost prosocial play.

Reading (being read to, but also looking at book pictures) is important to education, and teachers can select books that emphasize prosocial messages. Honig catalogues a set of such materials, a "prosocial library." However, evil exists in the world, and books may enable children to deal with worries and painful experiences.

Teachers can also introduce prosocial songs, group conversation times to discuss prosocial interactions ("magic circles") where children can feel safe talking about difficult issues of fear or anger. "Kindness jars" contain slips of paper where teachers record children's acts of kindness in class, which are read before lunch. Fairness may be discussed, including the extra generosity needed for someone with special needs. Everyone should get some special attention at some time at school and at home. Many ideas for concretizing the nature of prosocial actions and reinforcing its performance are presented.

Children, Honig points out, may be enlisted to pitch in and help with common needs, like setting up the art table materials, putting seed at the bird tray and feeding the gold fish (a totally exhilerating experience for MB as a kindergartner, remembered 60+ years later), cleaning up crumbs from lunch, and comforting a peer who appears to be in distress—all tasks that connect the child to the group and to the environment.

Like Denham and Weissberg, Honig supports the use of specific, active peacemaking techniques such as problem solving, although they use different words for the same general ideas (a common challenge for would-be integrators of literatures). Problem solving steps pull together some of the earlier themes, awareness of the difficulty, alternative solutions, thinking about consequences, all before any action is taken. This slowing down of impulsive action, and thinking about the situation uses the growing repertoire of an individual's processed and stored information, now in the service of a member of the group.

Honig rains down many ideas, such as special social ceremonies for solving social spats; the "helping coupon" in which children create a coupon to help at home, which parents and family members can draw on, like setting the table; a prosocial children's book lending library; puppet skits to illustrate emotions and problem solving; collective art projects expressing emotions and solutions (the collaborative effort itself); visits from "moral mentors"—people who serve at local soup kitchens, or volunteer tutors—and controlled use of TV and other media for prosocial purposes. All of these ideas surround the children, teacher, and parents in a supercharged environment that presents and supports prosocial behaviors and norms that children incorporate into themselves as they continue to process new information to be compared against these stored moral norms.

An important point emerges from Honig's discussion, the connecting of school to home, of working closely with parents to establish and reinforce prosocial behaviors, like the lending library or the "helping coupon." The Bingham TIPS for parents began as an outgrowth of this connecting idea. Beyond this, Honig discusses civic literacy training, becoming aware of, and getting involved in one's community for socially good projects. This is the shortest section in her chapter, suggesting that it may be the area in greatest need as we think about future directions for research and practice.

Joseph Durlak (Chapter 4) discusses how families promote optimal development in young children, employing the ecological and the risk/protective/promotive factor approaches. By ecology, he refers to Bronfenbrenner's theory that multiple systems should be viewed in conjunction with one another to understand the behavior of any one of them. So, looking at a preschooler's angry behavior means more than just an individual's emotional outburst. It also concerns the small group experience in frustration in "... my not being able to use a toy now when I want it." It may also involve the fact that this particular child comes from a deprived home and neighborhood where such toys and their exclusive use is a rarity. It also involves the more distant decisions by persons who know nothing of this particular child, but whose actions affect whether or not her parents have educational or employment opportunities that might enable them to make a better home for their family.

By the "risk/protective/promotive" approach, Durlak refers to a body of theory suggesting that multiple factors affecting individuals, small groups, larger communities may act to inhibit constructive growth and development (risk), or may act to protect existing states of healthy development (protective function), and even promote new or expanded development (promotive function). These three distinctions mark an important development over the "risk and protective" approach commonly found in the literature because it distinguishes the promotive function, which gives practitioners positive guidance for affecting desired change.

Within these frameworks, Durlak examines the literature in parenting, family systems, and factors outside families that influence positively or negatively children's prosocial development. The tables he constructs are models of reducing huge literatures into practice principles. So, for example, parenting involvement, responsiveness, acceptance/nurturance style, disciplinary style, communication patterns can have distinctive patterns that lead to risks for children, or to protective or promotive outcomes. A classic finding is that warm and supportive styles of acceptance/nurturing leads to protective and promotive outcomes, while rejecting and hostile parenting leads to risky outcomes for the children. These findings are clearly in the second tray, small group. However, parenting styles do not emerge out of the blue; rather, they frequently follow cultural and familial styles, as well as contemporary social forces and values, influences from the third and fourth trays in terms of our metaphor.

Durlak goes on to discuss findings that involve other aspects of the family situation, such as marital conflict, domestic violence, parental psychopathology, and economic strain, as related to risky behavior for their children, while parental well-being, supportive sibling relationships, and a structured, cohesive, and problem-solving family environment all lead to protective and promotive outcomes for the youngsters. Again, we presume that these kinds of family situations arise out of their own contexts, which can include the larger community pattern of discrimination by ethnicity, gender, and other bases. The limitation and stresses created in the macro ecological systems play out in the way group members experience these forms of oppression, that are embedded in their processing and storage of information about how the world operates—which they pass along to their children. Durlak documents this line of reasoning with his discussion of neighborhood and community influences. For example, supportive relatives and neighbors, supportive supervisors at work, and supportive social policies that assist the poor all lead to protective and possibly promotive outcomes on children, whereas role strain at work, and poor quality or difficult to access services from the community lead to risks for the children in the family.

Julia Mendez, Lindsey Stillman, Doré LaForett, Abraham Wandersman, and Paul Flaspohler (Chapter 5) expand on the themes of neighborhood and community influences favoring growth and development in young children, using an ecological orientation (as did Durlak) in order to emphasize the bidirectional nature of these contextual influences. They emphasize that child development is strongly influenced by the family context. Next are the proximal influences of the neighborhood and the immediate physical surrounds. These include characteristics of residents (such as socioeconomic standing, residential stability, and racial heterogenity), characteristics of physical surroundings (like overcrowding, substandard housing, degree of pollution), and characteristics of community institutions (including availability and quality). All of these factors have important influences on child well being, let alone mortality.

In the next context labeled intermediary, Mendez and colleagues look at factors of community social cohesion as well as the rates of crime and violence. For example, certain aspects of a community may influence crime rates, such as neighborhood disorder, abandoned houses, vandalism. These crime rates influence levels of fear and mistrust among residents, which in turn may influence parenting practices, such as setting limits on what activities children are allowed to engage in. However, the levels of informal integration with neighbors also affects rates of neighborhood disorder, illustrating the bidirectional nature of social influences.

With regard to the largest context, culture and macro-level community characteristics, Mendez and her colleagues point to poverty in its protean forms as having negative influences on the growth and development of youngsters (and, of course, the lives of adults living under these conditions). These authors point to the disproportionate burden that ethnic minorities carry in this regard.

Further, with cultural influences, singly or in combination with ethnicity, social class, religion, gender and so forth, presents another set of influences on the well being of children as mediated by their parents. (The authors note that such cultural influences are not necessarily uniform for all members of that cultural group.) Parents use their cultural values as they choose to do or not do certain parenting practices, which may or may not be in conformity with the dominant culture's views of such practices. Being out of step with the dominant culture adds another layer of stress to such families, and plays out in parents' expectations for their children's long-term socialization goals. Thus, we are looking at a three or four tray interconnection of macro, mezzo, and micro group factors affecting the well being of individual children. If we add the national level, such as Mendez' and colleagues' discussion of national policy initiatives such as Head Start, or their discussion of a state level initiative, the South Carolina First Steps to School Readiness project, then we are connecting an enormous range of systems and subsystems, their strengths (protective and promotive factors) as well as their limitations (the multiplicity of risk factors).

Awareness of the strengths of involved peoples as well as their limitations, and awareness of the risk and protective/promotive factors at each of these levels, means that we can try to establish such rules and practices that reduce the risks and increase the protective/promotive factors through specific actions. For example, Head Start initially set requirements for the program as involving family income below the level of poverty. Moreover, 10% of the children admitted were to have special needs or disabilities. Recognizing that this preschool initiative set children in a family context as well as school context meant providing a variety of family-oriented health and employment services. Research showed that there were positive results, not only for children's gains in language development (compared to non-Head Start programs), but also parents were more involved at home with their children. These results led to other developments in Head Start, such as the Early Head Start program expansion into earlier years. Again, evidence supported these ventures in both very young children and their families. Thus, we have good reason to consider multi-level initiatives where one level is designed to influence other levels, and be influenced by them. And this takes us back to our original question, on integrating findings across levels.

In this final section of the chapter, we turn to the difficult issue of offering suggestions for how an artificial and specially planned educational component (the pre-school in our experimental situation) can be conceptualized within the ordinary flow of natural system communications. We view this special pre-school as artificial in the sense that it is not an ordinary part of social life in the way public school education is, or the way families ordinarily function. We can make choices about how to arrange the curriculum and have teachers act toward children that may facilitate at-risk children (or more correctly, children with potential) in fulfilling their potential. It is time-limited and focuses on specific lessons conceived to enhance similar teachings at home, or to supplement when such teachings are not as strongly present.

Fortunately, the communication model offers one solution, where some artifical or special subsystem level sends a message received by another actor at a different system level, and stores the information as needed. Instead of looking at horizontal trays, we now ask the reader to imagine diagonals connecting the several levels. (See Figure 2.) These diagonals represent any *planned interventions* in social situations that may be needed when the ordinary communication patterns may be lacking or deficient, or when the presence of this intervention might make a desired communication pattern more likely in the future. So, if harried parents are not able to supply adequate or sufficient caring messages, then it may be possible for other group members (such as trained teachers) to supply some of these messages. In the Bingham project, we were intentionally supplying teachers with caring messages and reinforcement for prosocial behaviors, beyond those provided by conventional teacher training and experience. Therefore, by having an experimental and control group design, we should be able to see the general development of children in ordinary pre-schools (control groups) as compared to the stronger pro-social development of children in planned (experimental) programs.

How many diagonals are needed to connect services to predictable risks or possible promotive factors is a matter of on-the-ground investigation. In the Bingham study, for example, we recognized the demographics

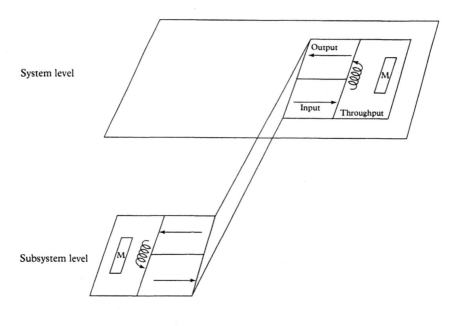

Note: |M| = system memory

Figure 2. Inter level communications.

of our participants, and the predictable risks their children faced. While not true in all cases, in many situations, the preschool teachers were able to complement or compensate for what parents were able and willing to deliver to their children. By planned training, we were able to emphasize how teachers might be able to address gaps in children's learning experiences. Moreover, by being sensitive to the limitations these parents faced, as well as the high turnover among preschool instructors, we were able to reduce the information pressures we were making on parents. By emphasizing the positives—learning kindness, cooperation, etc.—we were not only enabling the children at preschool to profit from this experience, but we were, in principle, making it easier on the parent at home. Reinforcing these kinds of learning at home may be a source of pleasure for parents, which acts synergistically with the preschool education to promote prosocial developments in young children.

In one sense, the Bingham curriculum (see Chapter 7) is our attempt to state (or to operationalize) the essential principles for influencing prosocial behavior at different levels, primarily from the preschool teacher to the child in this first phase of our studies. Therefore, for each of the learning principles mentioned above, which involves horizontal communications among members of a natural social system (like a family or an ordinary school setting), it may be possible to plan interventions to complement or to compensate when these natural positive communications are limited. We have to recognize that these artificial diagonals are never as strong in intensity or frequency as horizontal communications. However, the strength of the diagonal communications is that they can be focused on particular topics (like "kindness," "cooperation," etc). for planned periods of time sufficient to measure their effect. These artificial social systems also can be completely removed to enable the natural systems to take over with more vigor and resources. However, they may also involve the use of "booster shots" in cases where the first dose does not seem to be sustained over time; booster shots are also artificial, until the child incorporates this special medicine and no longer needs the artificial stimulus.

This diagonal approach is useful both in situations where positive family and neighborhood communications may be deficient, and where these positive life lessons are present so as to be further enhanced. We take a strengths position on enhancing positive capacities in children, while we also recognize that there are deficient social situations that requires reduction of risks and protection of existing strengths. Fine tuning these planned interventions to engage in both risk reduction and the enhancement of both protective and promotive factors is our task for the future.

For the present, we can summarize the classroom practice principles emerging from the Bingham Project: First, in terms of teaching all-too-busy teachers, the fewer the concepts to be learned and practiced until perfected, the more likely that success will occur. Thus, we limited the multitude of variables to our five key concepts, and introduced each, one at a time over several weeks, in the classroom.

Second, practice makes permanent. We encouraged child care teachers to design their own interventions (songs, poems, games, and other exercises) that promoted the five key concepts. Activities in the curriculum guide were presented as examples of what might be done, not as absolutes to be followed. By encouraging teachers' imagination and creativity, we strengthened their connection to the curriculum.

Third, unlike other interventions that rely on out-of-classroom instructional methods, the addition of an on-site coach strengthens the likelihood of program fidelity. Notice, also, the intentional use of the word "coach." Unlike a consultant, we expect the coach not only to model prosocial behaviors, but to gently correct teaching actions that discourage the emergence of a child's prosocial behavior.

Fourth, parents are important partners in solidifying classroom prosocial instruction. Our approach respected the hectic and frazzled world in which many parents reside. Rather than add to their stress by requiring parenting education—often offered at the end of a workday when all a parent wants is to go home and collapse—we chose to use a series of brief "Tips" for parenting. These educational notes were accompanied by a teacher's personal note to the parents about their child demonstrating a particular desired behavior, and often found their way to the refrigerator door as continual reminder of rewarding desired behavior.

Finally, we learned that there is an enormous value to ongoing independent classroom observation. Often, a research assistant, whose wallpaper-like behavior recording live data, is thought of as a temporary "add on" to a program. Our experiences challenge this perspective. Without ongoing feedback, progress in developing teaching skills that are maintained after the departure of the coach is absent. Without classroom observation, the contrast between verbal commitment and actual classroom practices would not have been revealed.

In the next chapter, we present the Bingham curriculum.

References

Bronfenbrenner, U. (1979). Ecology of human development: Experiments by nature and design. Cambridge, Mass.: Harvard University Press.

Denham, S., & Weissberg, R. P. (2004). Social-Emotional Learning in Early Childhood: What we know and where to go from here. (Chapter 2). In E. Chesebrough, P. King, M. Bloom & T. P. Gullotta (Eds.). A blueprint for prosocial behavior in early childhood. New York: Kluwer Academic/Plenum Publishers.

Durlak, J. (2004). How to help families promote optimal development in young children. (Chapter 4) In E. Chesebrough, P. King, M. Bloom & T. P. Gullotta (Eds.). A blueprint for prosocial behavior in early childhood. New York: Kluwer Academic/Plenum Publishers.

Germain, C. B. & Bloom, M. (1999). Human Behavior in the Social Environment: An Ecological Approach (2nd ed.). New York: Columbia University Press.

Honig, A. S. (2004). How teachers and caregivers of young children can help them become more prosocial. (Chapter 3) In E. Chesebrough, P. King, M. Bloom & T. P. Gullotta (Eds.). A blueprint for prosocial behavior in early childhood. New York: Kluwer Academic/Plenum Publishers.

Mendez, J. L., Stillman, L., LaForett, D. R., Wandersman, A., & Flaspohler, P. (2004). Neighborhood and community influences favoring the growth and development of young children. (Chapter 5). In E. Chesebrough, P. King, M. Bloom & T. P. Gullotta (Eds.). A blueprint for prosocial behavior in early childhood. New York: Kluwer Academic/Plenum Publishers.

O'Shea, P. (2004). What do we know about how children learn? The social, intellectual, and cognitive development of children: A guide to the first five years. (Chapter 1). In E. Chesebrough, P. King, M. Bloom & T. P. Gullotta (Eds.). A blueprint for prosocial behavior in early childhood. New York: Kluwer Academic/Plenum Publishers.

Chapter 7

Bingham Early Childhood Prosocial Behavior Program*

Elda Chesebrough and Patricia King

CONTENTS

---

*For a very few readers, this curriculum may be all that is needed to enable a program to work toward this noble and necessary goal of promoting prosocial behavior in early childhood. For most of us, however, coaching is both needed and necessary if real classroom change is to occur. We would remind readers that even the most talented individuals among us are coached. That is, writers have editors; sports stars have coaches; actors have directors. For a reader to believe that without coaching feedback he or she can implement this program, while not unimaginable, would be most challenging. Because we firmly believe in the value of coaching to improve skills, we have worked with the Child Welfare League of America to provide this service to interested readers. The Child Welfare League is America's oldest and most respected member organization focused on the needs of children in the United States. They can be reached at (617) 770-3008 or check Child and Family's website at www.cfapress.org.

INTRODUCTION

The Bingham Early Childhood Prosocial Behavior Program has a simple purpose. By training and on-going coaching of the teaching staff at an early childhood program, the children attending that program will learn to respect themselves and others. This effort does not replace an existing cognitive curriculum. Rather, it enriches and gives purposeful meaning to teachers' efforts to fully develop the social and emotional intelligence of the children in their care.

Work on this project began in the mid 1990's with funding from the Federal government, but slowed to a crawl when support ended due to the budget recession act. Tragic events, across the nation, involving school violence in the late 1990's, led the Bingham Foundation to approach Child and Family Agency to continue development of the project, to implement the program in real world not laboratory settings, evaluate the results, and, if successful, disseminate the curriculum. A respected team of national advisors interested in early childhood and social development provided insight, guidance, and encouragement as the effort advanced.

This program focuses on five key skills children need to have for successful social interactions: kindness, emotions (understanding and expressing), respect, cooperation, and self-control. The ultimate goal is to increase the social and emotional abilities of children so they can get along well with others as the basic foundation for their development in later years.

This Program is based on the premise that aggression is a generally stable type of behavior beginning early in life (Loeber, 1991; Olweus, 1979), with children as young as three-years-old sometimes exhibiting aggressive and disruptive tendencies, which, if left unmodified, leave them significantly at risk for conduct disorders, school failure and substance abuse during their adolescent years (Patterson, 1982). These aggressive unsocial acts are primarily learned behaviors (APA, 1994) that, if attended to early enough, can be changed. Through the use of appropriate consistent modeling and sound educational principles, the preschool child can be taught prosocial skills before less desirable patterns of behavior are established.

This program is especially responsive to the needs of teachers who report that their single most difficult challenge is aggressive and disruptive behavior (Connecticut Head Start State Collaboration Office, 2000). With use of this resource, a six-hour initial training, follow-up workshops, and on-site observation and technical assistance from an early childhood coach, each preschool teacher receives the tools to address problem behavior and encourage prosocial skills.

The concept of coach is a direct result of the real-world needs of early childhood programs. Staff turnover in early childhood programs can be as high as 70% a year with a national average exceeding 50%. A curriculum that requires intensive teacher training is good only as long as the teacher is employed in the program.

In addition, staff training is an evolving process. A one-time event, no matter how intense, is not as effective as training in which the staff member is actively involved and supported at all phases. When training is an ongoing process with opportunities for supported active experimentation, teachers are more likely to practice the newly learned skills and find ways to include the activities in their program (King, 1990).

The Bingham Program uses a coach to teach staff how to set up a classroom, interact with children and families, provide activities to help children develop prosocial skills, and then how to bring this information into the reality of the classroom. When new staff are hired into the center, the coach provides individualized training to bring her knowledge up to the level of the other classroom staff. The coach is able to model methods of teaching prosocial skills and help the staff become more effective in helping children work and play well together and decrease aggressive and anti-social behavior.

Finally, the Bingham Program supports enhanced parent and teacher collaboration to improve childrens' prosocial skills. Positive parent involvement and consistent reinforcement of targeted behavior significantly increases the child's successful acquisition of new social skills. This is accomplished through a series of *Tips for Parents*, written communication from teachers to each parent, with concrete examples of their child's prosocial interaction and ideas to promote prosocial skills at home. For example, the *Tips* on "Raising a Kinder, Gentler Child" suggests ways that parents might be aware of and further encourage kind behaviors. These *Tips for Parents* parallel the themes presented in the classroom.

We believe that the Bingham Program is suitable for a broad range of early childhood education settings, and that it meets the diverse needs and expertise of childcare teachers. Using the Bingham curriculum within the context of a coaching model sets the program apart from other prosocial programs. Teachers who participated in the pilot programs feel that the material is responsive to their needs and that the coaching and hands-on training is there to help them advance the prosocial skills of their children.

References

American Psychological Association, Commission on Violence and Youth. (1994). *Violence and Youth: Psychology's Response (Vol. 1).* Washington, D. C.: American Psychological Association.

Connecticut Head Start State Collaboration Office. (2000). Collaboration for Young Children with special needs workshop group: Summary of survey results. January 2000. Unpublished report.

King, P. (1990), A Comparative Study of Lecture/Discussion and Experiential Learning Methods When Training Child Care Providers in Whole Language Curriculum. Masters thesis, University of Connecticut.

Loeber, R. (May, 1991). Antisocial behavior: More enduring than changeable? *Journal of the American Academy of Child and Adolescent Psychiatry, 30,*(3) 393–397.

Patterson, G. R. (1992). Age effects in parent training outcome. *Behavior Therapy, 23,* 719–729.

Olweus, D. (1979). Stability of aggressive reaction patterns in males: A review. *Psychological Bulletin, 86,* 852–875.

LESSON 1: THE DEVELOPMENTAL WORLD OF PRESCHOOL CHILDREN

This lesson provides an overview of the physical, cognitive, language, social, and emotional domains of child development. There are suggestions for classroom experiences to encourage development in each domain. There is a greater detailed discussion on the social and emotional domains including the roots of attachment, the role of the parent or caregiver, the relationship among children's temperament, behavioral characteristics, and the role of the teacher; the definition of prosocial behavior, and teaching strategies to facilitate positive social interactions and social competence. At the end of this lesson is a list of references used in the development of this lesson.

Following the references are a pre-test/post-test and opportunities for teachers to apply the information in their daily work with young children. We suggest completing the pre-test before doing the reading and participating in the training. Once the reading, the training, and the *Practice Makes Permanent* pages have been completed, cover up the pre-test answers and answer the questions again. Compare the pre-test to the post-test to see what has been learned.

Child Development

Few preschool teachers would continue in their chosen profession if they did not love young children. There is something wonderful about the tentative efforts of a three year old to master a rapidly expanding world and the attempts of a four year old to communicate fantasies, game plans, and proud new discoveries! No matter what the plan for the day might be, children manage to create their own special humor, questions, insights and challenges—within themselves, with their peers, and with their total world. Teachers, like parents, have the privilege of sharing in their youngsters' triumphs and disappointments. However, along with this privilege, comes the responsibility of gently guiding children.

Unlike parents, however, most teachers do not know their children from the time they are born. When preschool children enter a classroom, they have already had at least three years of experience under the care of others: parents, grandparents, guardians, and teachers. They have already begun to sample life in this world and they come with their own personality, experiences and needs. When teachers understand their children are unique individuals, teachers can then create an environment that is responsive to the their need for safety, nurturing and growth.

Similarly, with a basic understanding of child development, teachers are able to plan activities to challenge children without frustrating them. When expectations are too high or too low, children become frustrated, bored, and disappointed, which affects their self-esteem. These feelings may also lead to uncooperative behavior and demonstrations of violence and aggression from children who are under- or over-challenged. With this knowledge of basic child development, teachers are able to plan a program to foster the prosocial skills of kindness, self-control, cooperation, respect for self and others, and identifying emotions.

Domains of Child Development

Child development has been studied for generations. It has been established through research that child growth and development comes in predictable patterns. The well-known psychologist, Erik Erikson (1968) believed that development occurs in eight stages, starting with infancy and progressing through adulthood and old age. Another viewpoint, held by Stanley Greenspan & Nancy Greenspan (1989), is that children develop emotionally in six stages from birth through about age four. There are many theories on how and when certain events take place in a child's development, but most emphasize that development occurs in a predictable manner, and not by random maturation.

There are five major domains of development: physical, cognitive, language, social, and emotional. While much of the material for this program deals with the social and emotional development and strategies that can enhance a child's growth in these areas, it is very important that each teacher has a well-rounded knowledge of the development of the whole child. All aspects of development are interrelated. For example, riding a tricycle is a physical activity. However, riding a tricycle may also involve learning to share and wait for a turn. A social and emotional perspective exists for skill development in each area.

The following tables outline developmental skills in each domain at ages three-, four-, and five-years. Social and emotional development are presented together because these domains are so interrelated that it is unproductive to separate them.

It is important to remember that children grow and develop at their own pace. Skill development for some children is a little ahead of or a little behind others of the same age.

PHYSICAL DEVELOPMENT. Physical development is the maturation of both large and small muscles. Large muscles (balance, gross body coordination, and flexibility) develop before small muscles (finger speed, arm steadiness, eye-hand coordination, and finger and hand dexterity): a child is able to walk and run before he is able to make meaningful marks with a pencil on a paper or tie his shoes.

Age	Characteristics	Classroom Experiences to Encourage Physical Development
3 Years	✓ Walks backwards ✓ Runs with swinging arms ✓ Balances on one foot ✓ Climbs stairs with alternating feet ✓ Throws objects overhand ✓ Jumps **off** low objects ✓ Has difficulty jumping **over** objects ✓ Rides a tricycle, turns and stops well ✓ Plays hard and tires easily ✓ Become irritable if overtired ✓ Cuts a straight line with scissors ✓ Colors with pencils, markers, crayons ✓ Draws lines and circles ✓ Pours juice ✓ Uses fork and spoon skillfully ✓ Dresses and undresses self ✓ Brushes teeth and hair ✓ Washes hands ✓ Usually has control of bladder and bowels but may still have occasional accidents	✓ Provide a variety of outdoor and indoor gross motor equipment such as balls, hoops, balance beams, riding toys with pedals, and climbing apparatus ✓ Play creative movement recordings during free choice and group times ✓ Provide bean bags and large targets such as laundry baskets ✓ Create indoor and outdoor obstacle courses that gently challenge agility, balance, coordination and jumping skills ✓ Provide a variety of dress-up clothes. ✓ Provide crayons, large pencils, makers and paint brushes ✓ Provide paper of varying sizes from 3″ × 5″ index cards to large murals ✓ Provide scissors and pattern cards ✓ Provide activities that require small muscle coordination (such as sorting/matching buttons, nuts and bolts) ✓ Provide clay and play dough with rollers, cutters, and pounding tools ✓ Provide daily opportunities for children to serve their own meals using child sized pitchers, glasses, bowls, and utensils.

(Continued)

Age	Characteristics	Classroom Experiences to Encourage Physical Development
4 Years	✓ Runs and jumps with skill ✓ Hops on one foot ✓ Gallops ✓ Pumps self on swings ✓ Bounces and catches a ball ✓ Walks heel to toe ✓ Skips unevenly ✓ Walks down stairs with alternating feet ✓ Jumps rope and plays action games such as tag ✓ Has increased endurance with high energy levels ✓ Prints name and draws simple objects ✓ Buttons, snaps, zips, buckles, and laces ✓ May become overexcited and less inhibited in group activities	In addition to those activities listed above, offer the following: ✓ Outdoor and indoor gross motor activities to build and test endurance and listening skills (such as freeze tag, low competition running) ✓ Hopping, galloping, skipping games ✓ Throwing and catching games ✓ Jump rope games ✓ Jumping games that involve distances or targets ✓ Add stencils and tracing activities to writing center ✓ Lacing cards and weaving activities. ✓ Dress up clothes including lace up shoes
5 Years	✓ Hops; skips; kicks; gallops ✓ Walks backward quickly ✓ Skips and runs with agility and speed ✓ Throws accurately ✓ Jumps over objects ✓ Navigates a 2" wide balance beam ✓ Jumps down several steps at a time ✓ Climbs objects with confidence ✓ Rides a 2 wheel bicycle ✓ High energy/rarely shows fatigue ✓ Seeks active games and environments ✓ Writes name and can copy simple shapes freehand	In addition to those activities listed above, offer the following: ✓ Offer a variety of physical challenges using balls, hoops, cones, balance beams, hopping and jumping targets, and climbing structures ✓ Introduce competitive games such as relay races ✓ Use progressively smaller balls and targets as levels of mastery are achieved ✓ Offer regular size pencils, markers, and crayons and stencils ✓ Offer shapes to cut out ✓ Provide a writing center with materials for journal writing, and tracing

(Continued)

Age	Characteristics	Classroom Experiences to Encourage Physical Development
	✓ Develops dominance between the right or left hand ✓ Draws recognizable figures ✓ Cuts circles and squares ✓ Sews and laces well ✓ Ties shoes	✓ Provide a variety of clothing, shoes, and boots for dressing and lacing practice

COGNITIVE DEVELOPMENT.   Growth in cognition is the development of more complex thought patterns. Measuring the development of thinking skills can be challenging. Unless a child decided to share his newly acquired thought patterns, it is difficult to measure. A child's understanding of number and letter concepts is less observable than the child's ability to jump over an object or speak in a complex sentence. While the chart below outlines abilities at ages three, four and five years, some characteristics are relevant throughout the preschool years.

- Children's thinking becomes more complex and they can begin to plan.
- Children learn to use language to express their ideas—not just to label things or have their needs met.
- Children can recall memories and relate them to the future (such as remembering the story a volunteer read and looking forward to having the volunteer read again).
- Children believe in causal relationships for two events that are linked closely in time. (For example, when a child falls off the rocking chair and the fire alarm is heard 30 seconds later, the child may believe her fall off the rocker caused the fire alarm.)
- Children apply animation (give human characteristics) to objects, such as the teapot in Disney's *Beauty and the Beast*.
- Children believe in magic (the Easter Bunny).
- Children describe objects by appearance and actions. (For example, "the teacher with the eyeglasses" or "the teacher who sings songs.")
- Concepts which cannot be manipulated, such as "time, space and age" are very difficult to understand.
- Children have an increased interest in letters/reading and numbers/counting.

Age	Characteristics	Classroom Experiences to Encourage Cognitive Development
3 Years	✓ Curious about the world around them ✓ Recognizes and names basic colors ✓ Recognizes their own name in print ✓ Counts to at least 10 ✓ Compares objects by size, shape and color ✓ Recognizes that shapes, letters, and numbers are different ✓ Attention span begins to increase ✓ Sits for 5–10 minutes at a time for a story or an activity ✓ Begins to recognize logos for favorite commercial items such as fast food chains	✓ Play color, matching, counting, and sorting games ✓ Use manipulative (i.e., colored blocks, or counting bears) for sorting and sequencing activities ✓ Label cubbies and shelves with pictures and words ✓ During group times, include information about the local environment and relevant current events such as newspaper photos of beached whales and forest fires ✓ Plan opportunities for the children to share their family traditions and cultures with the group ✓ Provide many hands-on experiences with letters, numbers, shapes, and colors (such as plastic letters in play dough, a print-rich environment, counting games) ✓ Share excitement about learning and coming to preschool
4 Years	✓ Continues to be very interested in others and the world around them ✓ Makes simple sets of objects ✓ Identifies and labels shapes and colors ✓ Begins to recognize letters and numerals in the world around them (such as: discovering a sign has letters which are same as one or more letters in the child's name ✓ Stays involved in a task for a longer period of time (12–20 minutes)	In addition to those activities listed above, offer the following: ✓ More frequent and slightly longer group activities ✓ Invite guests such as parents and professionals to share stories of their heritage, culture, and life experiences ✓ Go on brief field trips ✓ Provide specific opportunities to work with math manipulatives for sorting, sequencing and creating sets and subsets ✓ Plan games and sensory activities with letters and sounds ✓ Provide opportunities to identify and match objects, shapes, letters and numbers

(Continued)

Age	Characteristics	Classroom Experiences to Encourage Cognitive Development
5 Years	✓ Identifies from memory important letters and sounds such as letters in her name ✓ Matches numerals and sets of objects (1–10) ✓ By memory counts to at least 20 ✓ Understands most prepositions ✓ Understands concepts such as opposite, same, different, longer, shorter, etc. ✓ Attention span is lengthened and he may be able to attend to an activity for 20 to 30 minutes ✓ Understands the consequences for their behavior	In addition to those activities listed above, offer the following: ✓ Play letter and number games (such as bingo and letter lotto) ✓ Provide manipulatives with specific activities to teach concepts of sets and counting ✓ Include opportunities in routine activities for children to practice skills in preposition, color, shape, counting, and letter recognition (such as: finding specific colors, shapes, letters or words in magazines and catalogs)

LANGUAGE DEVELOPMENT. Language is both receptive (understanding) and expressive (communicating). Children are able to understand spoken language before they are able to use words to communicate with others.

Age	Characteristics	Classroom Experiences to Encourage Language Development
3 Years	✓ Vocabulary is about 2000–4000 words ✓ Language is clear and easily understood ✓ Speaks in simple, intelligible sentences of three or four words ✓ Uses words to express feelings ✓ Follows simple directions	✓ Offer the children opportunities to listen and participate in storytelling; singing songs, and reciting rhymes and finger plays ✓ Use active and concrete figures in stories, such as puppets and flannel board objects ✓ Use props such as tape recorders and big books to keep attention focused

(Continued)

Age	Characteristics	Classroom Experiences to Encourage Language Development
	✓ Enjoys simple finger plays and rhymes ✓ Has difficulty engaging in any activity while talking ✓ Speaks while others are speaking ✓ Topics of conversations change quickly and often ✓ Often mistakes one word for another ✓ Enjoys songs with a lot of repetition ✓ Frequently asks "who, what, where, why" questions ✓ Shows confusion when asked "why, how, when" ✓ Overuses "But, because, when" in conversation ✓ Does not understand time sequences like "before, until, after" ✓ Does not understand prepositions such as "through, between, around" ✓ In a story, they are likely to focus on their favorite parts, instead of the point or object	✓ Encourage speech and conversation during dramatic play by modeling and asking questions ✓ Use simple one or two-step directions when you want the children to do something: such as "Put your boots in your cubby and come sit with me." ✓ Provide appropriate words when children struggle to communicate an idea. ✓ Model problem solving and the use of words to communicate: such as "Please may I. . . . .," "Tell her you are playing with it now and she can have it when you are done with it." "What can you do to make him feel better?" etc.
4 Years	✓ 4000–6000 word vocabulary ✓ Speaks in five or six word sentences ✓ Likes simple songs ✓ Learns many rhymes and finger plays and enjoys reciting them ✓ Hesitates when speaking in front of a group ✓ Enjoys telling others about their families and themselves ✓ Begins to tease others	In addition to those activities listed above, offer the following: ✓ Tell silly jokes and read humorous books ✓ Answer questions simply, but honestly, with minimal detail ✓ When asked a question, rephrase and redirect it to the child: such as "tell me what you think will happen if. . . . ."

(*Continued*)

Age	Characteristics	Classroom Experiences to Encourage Language Development
	✓ Uses verbal commands to lay claim to things: such as "after rest time I want to use the magnifying glasses" ✓ Uses facial gestures to express emotions; reads others' body cues copies behaviors of other children and adults ✓ If reminded, controls their vocal pitch and volume for prolonged periods ✓ Begins to use advanced and complex sentence structures ✓ Learns new vocabulary if the words are connected to life experiences. For example, child may use the word "whale" in conversation; after visiting the aquarium she may distinguish beluga whales from humpback whales. ✓ Repeats a four or five step directive or the sequence in a story ✓ Can be silly ✓ Is interested in language. For example when exposed to Spanish an English speaking child may be fascinated with the language. ✓ Engages in continuous chatter	✓ Use an audio or video recorder to capture children's creativity when making up creative stories and jokes ✓ Help children act out their favorite stories or their own creative stories ✓ Encourage the children to "read" a story from the pictures in a book ✓ Provide alphabet letters and numerals in a variety of forms: magnets, felt, wood, sandpaper, etc. ✓ When children are faced with challenges, help them verbalize their feelings, actions, and plans
5 Years	✓ 6000–8000 word vocabulary ✓ Communicates effectively, using correct tense and speech patterns ✓ Recites his complete name, address, phone number, and birthday ✓ Enjoys looking at books ✓ Accurately retells a story in sequence	In addition to those activities listed above, offer the following: ✓ Allow ample time for dramatic play and storytelling. ✓ Encourage the children to act out stories and make up plays. ✓ Provide sequencing cards and encourage children to tell a story. ✓ Help children practice reciting their name and personal information.

(Continued)

Age	Characteristics	Classroom Experiences to Encourage Language Development
	✓ Uses complete and complex sentence structures ✓ Enjoys jokes and plays on words. ✓ Interrupts others less ✓ Takes turns when speaking ✓ Shares experiences verbally ✓ Memorizes words to songs including those from the pop culture ✓ Shows off mastery of language in front of a group; may become extremely shy if unsure of themselves ✓ Remembers and recites simple poems ✓ Repeats full sentences and expressions ✓ Uses pitch and inflection when speaking ✓ Uses non-verbal gestures and facial expressions when teasing peers ✓ Enjoys acting out plays and stories	✓ Listen to the children when they speak and engage them in meaningful conversation. ✓ Ask open-ended questions when they are speaking, and probe for further information: such as "Tell me about your trip to the mall." ✓ Use concrete manipulative materials for letter recognition ✓ Practice sounding out letter combinations. ✓ Expose the children to a wide variety of literature from many sources and cultures. ✓ Link varied reading materials to concrete activities in the classroom (such as after reading a book about a child from another country, have a cooking or art project that connects the book; provide fishing magazines after a trip to the aquarium).

SOCIAL AND EMOTIONAL DEVELOPMENT. Social and emotional development in children is the basis for both violent and aggressive behaviors, as well as appropriate and kind behaviors. The **Bingham Early Childhood Prosocial Behavior Program** focuses on the social and emotional development of the preschool child and on activities that promote healthy prosocial skill development.

Age	Characteristics	Classroom Experiences to Encourage Social and Emotional Development
3 Years	✓ Begins to enjoy playing with peers ✓ Begins to share toys and take turns	✓ Be specific and reinforce appropriate play and social interactions (such as; "I like the way you gave Keith a turn on the trike!")

(Continued)

Age	Characteristics	Classroom Experiences to Encourage Social and Emotional Development
	✓ Usually wants to help and to please others (especially adults) ✓ Enjoys dramatic role playing activities, or "playing dress up" ✓ Often needs help to resolve a social conflict or problem ✓ Plays well with others if there are enough materials and ample space for activities ✓ May regress to whining and temper tantrums if unhappy ✓ Demonstrates intense feelings, such as fear or affection ✓ Self confidence increases	✓ Establish clear expectations that the children can understand and follow (such as "Keep your feet on the floor"). ✓ Provide materials and experiences where children can be challenged yet successful (500 piece puzzles are too challenging; 4 piece puzzles may be too simple). ✓ Provide opportunities for children to help with classroom duties (such as watering the plants and feeding the pets). ✓ Provide daily opportunities for activities that promote socio-dramatic play (such as dress up, doll houses, and block play). ✓ Consistently reinforce appropriate interactions between children. ✓ Provide opportunities for children to talk and share their personal experiences in small groups such as meal and snack times, in large groups, and one to one. ✓ Assist in negotiation efforts by guiding the children toward their own solutions.
4 Years	✓ Begins to enjoy playing cooperatively with peers ✓ Begins to build friendships with peers and complements their clothing, appearance or actions ✓ Begins to understand the concept of taking turns when playing games	In addition to those activities listed above, offer the following: ✓ Set clear limits and follow through on consequences. ✓ Set up a "peace" or negotiation table to talk over problems. ✓ When a conflict arise facilitate role playing with puppets or stuffed animals. *(Continued)*

Age	Characteristics	Classroom Experiences to Encourage Social and Emotional Development
	✓ Wants to resolve negative conflicts, but still needs help with negotiation ✓ Angers easily if she can't have her own way ✓ Shows empathy and concern towards others ✓ Understands that inappropriate behavior has consequences ✓ Justifies aggressive act ("I hit her because she was looking at my doll") ✓ Struggles to complete tasks that require more than 7–10 minutes ✓ Easily distracted ✓ Waiting for anything is challenging ✓ Demonstrates an ability to control intense feelings, but may still need adult support ✓ Independence increases as self help skills improve ✓ Demonstrates emotional extremes ("I love you!" / "I hate you!") ✓ May show fear of specific objects or situations such as witches or getting lost. ✓ Is bold and adventurous and may engage in unsafe behaviors such as climbing fences and jumping off tables. ✓ Demonstrates self confidence ("I can do that!")	✓ Encourage the children often by acknowledging and reinforcing positive behaviors. ✓ Include opportunities for free choice activity and dramatic play. ✓ Encourage creative dramatics and storytelling. ✓ Encourage the children to care for others who are hurt or upset. ✓ Talk with the children about how their behavior affects others. ✓ Plan small group activities for up to four children at a time. ✓ Plan a program that is balanced with active and quiet activities. ✓ Plan transitions that are short and ease small groups of children into the next activity. ✓ Partner children with good social and problem solving skills with children who are less mature. ✓ Offer projects to encourage awareness of diversity (for example: skin-color paints, crayons, and markers; multi-cultural dolls; display pictures representing a variety of family compositions, men and women in nontraditional roles; etc.).
5 Years	✓ Usually conforms to the group and follows rules ✓ Eager to please adults	In addition to those activities listed above, offer the following: ✓ Look for positive behaviors and reinforce them. *(Continued)*

Age	Characteristics	Classroom Experiences to Encourage Social and Emotional Development
	✓ Shows pride in her work ✓ Is affectionate: wants to hug and be hugged ✓ Becomes angry when frustrated when unable to complete a task ✓ Engages in dramatic play which becomes more elaborate and complex ✓ Generally cooperates ✓ Forms close friendships and excludes some peers ✓ Becomes "bossy" ✓ Uses threats to get what they want ("I'll tell," "I won't be your friend," 'You can't come to my party.") ✓ Jokes and teases to get attention ✓ May use verbal insults ("You're ugly!) or threaten to hit another child if frustrated or angry, however, there is less actual physical aggression at this age ✓ Enjoys being with others and can be warm and empathetic	✓ Sit down with the children and develop classroom rules (limits) and the consequences for not following them. ✓ Teach negotiation skills. ✓ Discuss diversity including strengths of others. ✓ Plan activities to build empathy skills: talk about feelings, send cards to sick children and staff, make a gift for a new baby, partner newly enrolled children with children who have been enrolled and know the routine.

The Social and Emotional World of the Preschool Child

Roots of Attachment

A child develops a sense of the world from their parents and the relationship established with their parents. Parents who are loving, attentive, and responsive to the baby let her know that she is safe and loved. Parents and caregivers that are sensitive to what a baby is feeling, what a baby needs, or what might be upsetting a baby, allow her to experience a world that is warm and comforting and safe to explore.

According to Erik Erikson (1968), the crucial social emotional task for babies in the first year or two of life, is to develop a sense of trust in the world and in her parents. This relationship between the baby and the parents is dependent on:

1. The ability of the parents to recognize the baby's needs and respond sensitively to them: providing nourishment, keeping the baby clean, and comforting her.
2. The characteristics and temperament of the infant:
   - easy and mellow
   - sensitive to internal and external changes
   - easily irritated or upset
   - harder to comfort

Infants vary in terms of activity level, intensity of reaction, adaptability, general quality of mood, distractibility, and attention span. Three temperamental characteristics are identified in the first months of life and remain stable throughout childhood and into adulthood:

- activity level
- shyness or sociability
- emotionality

The Role of the Parent/Caregiver

Through the daily interactions of feeding, diapering, bathing, and playing, babies become attached to their parents. Most parents do not know what their infant wants or needs. Each parent's personality and ideas about child rearing contribute to how that parent interprets what his baby is communicating. Personal and cultural beliefs and values also affect how a parent decides to respond. Some parents are highly protective of their children, unwilling to leave them with a sitter or relative for even short periods of time. These same parents may carefully control everything in the child's world (such as: diet, television, and playmates). Other parents want their children to get used to many different situations and be challenged in many ways (such as trying new foods and experiencing many different people). Some parents spend a lot of time talking and playing with their babies, while other parents tend to be quieter and less interactive. No matter what approach a parent takes, if the relationship is consistent and loving, then the child can develop a sense of security and trust in the world around her.

A growing child gradually learns to trust others in her environment, to trust herself as she explores new things, to trust other parts of her world as she continues to make discoveries. As the baby becomes a toddler with a new sense of self-awareness, that trust is vitally important. The toddler's favorite word, "No!" is really just an effort to let others know that she has her own ideas about things and isn't afraid to try those ideas. When adults support toddlers by offering simple, reasonable choices and assistance when necessary, toddlers develop autonomy and independence. For example, a child may be offered a choice of sitting on the floor or in a chair to put on his shoes rather than asking "Are you ready to put on your shoes?" Adults may let him try to put on and button his own coat, but be nearby to help if he has trouble.

The Preschool Child

The preschooler's social world is centered on her emerging aware-ness of herself. She continues to try new things, experiment, imagine, and fantasize in an effort to define herself and to master new skills and under-standings. A preschool child continues to find out what she can do, what she likes, and what brings reward by:

Behavior	Example
Playing different roles	Such as: mommy, daddy, sister, brother, firefighter, etc.
Testing new situations	Such as: going to preschool and experimenting with giving up naps
Experimenting with new interactions and behaviors	Such as: "If I push her off the bike, then I can ride it!"

The adult responses to children's behavior results

1. in children's feelings of guilt for having tried something new and being unsuccessful.
   OR
2. with the child and the adult working together to find alternative ways to accomplish the same goal safely and successfully.

A child's ability to take risks is a very positive developmental step. When children are confident and trusting enough to take initiative, they most likely have been encouraged and have had lots of emotional support. Careful, positive, guidance assists children in strengthening the emerg-ing sense of self-confidence and self-worth that they need to successfully navigate through early childhood.

The Preschool Child in Child Care

Each child has a unique temperament; her own manner of thinking, behaving and reacting. Temperament can be affected by experiences and relationships that influence how well children connect with others and makes adults aware of their styles, strengths, and needs.

Temperament	Behavioral Characteristics	Role of the Teacher
Confident and trusting in approach to others and establishment of new relationships	Positive, upbeat, willing to try new experiences	Provide a variety of new experiences and challenges; ask thoughtful questions.
Lacks confidence, is not trusting of others and is slow to establish new relationships	Challenges adults and children and tests limits	Be firm and consistent; remind children of the rules with positive statements; model appropriate interactions with others
Cautious, shy, and tentative in approaching others and establishing new relationships	Tries new experiences but needs support from adults and peers	Model appropriate interactions; gently encourage new experiences; reinforce attempts at new relationships

When assessing a child's temperament, ask the following questions:

- How readily does he approach me and other children?
- Does she seem to expect others to like her?
- Does he go to a teacher when upset or confused?
- How does she cope with frustration or disappointment?
- Does he tend to seek out friends for play, or prefer to play alone?
- Does she seem basically happy and interested in the preschool center?

As children enter the classroom each morning, their individuality is easily observed. No matter how he handles his arrival into the center, a greeting from a teacher welcomes the child and helps ease that transition. Here are three possible arrival behaviors and implications for the teacher.

Children Enter the Center	The Teacher
Eager to begin the day	Gives him a hearty greeting
• Runs in ahead of parents	• Listens to his stories and ideas
• Chatters with a full agenda of ideas	• Points out activities in the room
• Happily waves goodbye to parents	• Says goodbye to the parent
Needing time to settle in and warm up	Gives her a quiet, soothing greeting
• Walks in holding tightly to her parent's hand	• Offers her a hand to hold or lap to sit in
• Quietly, shyly and tentatively speaks to others only when her parent insists	• Quietly shares the agenda of the day and provides a quiet activity
• Allows her parent to leave once she is involved with an activity	• Stays with her while her parent leaves and helps her begin an activity
Unsure, afraid, even angry.	Gives him a quiet, soothing greeting
• Clings to parent and may be carried in	• Gently touches hand or back while parent continues to hold him
• Cries, screams, or yells to go home	• Holds him while parent leaves
• Blocks the door so the parent cannot leave	• Gets him involved in a quiet activity

What Is Prosocial Behavior?

Parents and teachers of children of all ages want to find ways to encourage children to be kind, considerate, and socially responsible people. As a nation, we hear daily of the widespread effects of violence on children, and increasingly, about the violent behaviors more and more young children are showing towards others. We know that children learn behavior and values from others. We also know that very young children need to learn how to manage many intense emotions and impulses as part of the normal process of growing up.

By prosocial behavior, we mean a repertoire of skills that facilitate social interaction and social competence. These include kindness, identifying and expressing emotions, respect for self and others, cooperation, and self-control. We want children to:

✓ Learn to be kind and accept kindness from others. They should be able to give and receive attention, approval, affection and support. We want them to demonstrate altruistic behaviors, such as helping others and sharing.

✓ Understand and express feelings, to empathize with others. Empathy is the ability to see a situation from another's perspective. We want children to be sensitive to the distress of others.

✓ Respect themselves and others, to treat others respectfully, to value people for who they are, to value diversity. This includes manners and behaving in a socially appropriate fashion. For example, if someone says hello, it is cordial to return a greeting (excluding strangers). If you are in church, it is respectful to be quiet.

✓ Cooperate with others; to share with others, negotiate and behave in a fair and just manner; work and play with others toward a common goal.

✓ Develop self control; learn to regulate emotions, solve problems peacefully and manage anger without aggression.

Martha Bronson (2000) has described the emotional and social behaviors which young children are able to learn to manage. She also describes the adult behaviors that help children learn to control certain behaviors and to express themselves in prosocial ways. She notes that preschoolers:

✓ Are able to develop more control over their own negative emotions and behaviors because they have greater use of language, and a greater understanding of the rules and expectations.

✓ Have the mental ability to remember, think, and believe.

✓ Are able to consider what another person might be thinking or feeling.

✓ Have the ability to try out different roles and perspectives through their dramatic play.

✓ Are able to interact cooperatively with peers and with adults.

✓ Have the ability to know what is expected of them and act according to prosocial rules of behavior.

Bronson (2000) discusses six (6) specific strategies teachers can use to support prosocial behavior of preschoolers:

Teaching Strategy	This Means
Use "stage setting" and "coaching" of appropriate peer interactions.	Talk children through the process of working out a problem (such as: having children describe the problem, brainstorm possible solutions and then pick a solution to try).

(Continued)

Teaching Strategy	This Means
Model and communicate caring actions and values.	Show children what it means to be kind and considerate (saying please and thank you, waiting for a turn, etc.); making a picture for someone who is ill or feeling sad, etc.
Use prosocial reasoning to guide children's behaviors, and emphasize the effect of their behavior on others.	"If you take all the animals, then Tasha will not have any. She will be sad because she was enjoying playing zoo with you."
Never use physical punishment and avoid criticism and that demeans a child.	Use kind, gentle words and soothing actions. For example, when one child hurts another, talk about what happened and how to repair the damage while gently touching the child.
Attribute positive prosocial qualities to the child.	Use words such as "kind" and "thoughtful." For example, "You were kind to share the playdough with her;" "Making a picture for Jaman's sick sister is very thoughtful."
Give the children age and skill appropriate responsibilities.	Such as cleaning the table (three-year-olds) and sweeping the floor (five-year-olds).

Summary

With an understanding of basic child development, teachers can plan activities to encourage the development of physical, language, cognitive, social, and emotional skills. All of these domains are interrelated and a social and emotional perspective exists for skill development in each domain. The research of Erik Erikson (1968) provides an understanding of psychosocial development and the research of Martha Bronson outlines the social skills preschool children can manage and how teachers can support prosocial behavior. With knowledge of how children learn and develop, teachers can plan general and specific teaching strategies:

    ✓ to enhance children's ability to understand emotions and express their feelings appropriately.
    ✓ to develop problem solving and conflict resolution skills.
    ✓ to value respect for self and others.

✓ to develop self control thereby managing emotions and using problem solving skills.

✓ to develop social skills to increase positive interactions with peers.

The next lesson, discusses how violence and stress affects preschool children and offers classroom strategies for preschool teachers.

References

Bronson, M. B. (2000). *Self Regulation in Early Childhood*. New York: Guilford.

Erikson, E. H. (1968). *Identity: Youth and Crisis*. New York: Norton. Greenspan, S. & Greenspan, N. T. (1989). *First Feelings: Milestones in Emotional Development of Your Baby and Child*. New York: Penguin.

	Pretest			*Posttest*	
1.	T	F	There are three domains of development: physical, cognitive, social.	T	F
2.	T	F	All domains of development are related.	T	F
3.	T	F	The first social emotional task for babies is to smile.	T	F
4.	T	F	The social world of the preschool child is developed as children role play, test, and experiment.	T	F
5.	T	F	Temperament is how children think, behave and react.	T	F
6.	T	F	All preschool children are cautious, shy and tentative in approaching others and in establishing new relationships.	T	F
7.	T	F	When children enter a classroom unsure, afraid, or angry, the child will adjust best if left to explore the room independently.	T	F
8.	T	F	Prosocial behavior is simply being kind to others.	T	F
9.	T	F	A child who is empathetic will never have a problem getting along with others.	T	F
10.	T	F	One thing teachers can do to support prosocial behavior in preschool children is to give the children age and skill appropriate responsibilities such as cleaning the table and sweeping the floor.	T	F

PRACTICE MAKES PERMANENT

For your own review and to better understand the information in this lesson, respond to the following questions. This is for your own use and may be discussed in training.

1. The five domains of development are:

    a.   b.

    c.   d.

    e.

2. Identify a child in your group and list three skills he or she has developed in each of the following areas:

Child	1	2	3
Physical			
Cognitive			
Language			
Social/Emotional			

3. How might the domains of physical, cognitive, and language be related to social and emotional development? For example, how might the ability to use a scissors to cut out a circle be related to social and emotional development?

4. Three temperamental characteristics which are identifiable in the first months of life are:

    a.

    b.

    c.

5. Preschool children experiment with new things, by role-playing, testing new situations, and experimenting with new interactions and behaviors. Give specific examples of how you have observed this in children enrolled in your classroom.

Behavior	*Child*	*Example*
Role-playing		
Testing		

6. Temperament, behavioral characteristics, and the role of the teacher are discussed in this lesson. For each temperament, identify a child in your group and complete the following with specific teacher behaviors to support the children.

Temperament	Child	Teacher Behavior
Confident and trusting		
Lacks confidence, is not trusting		
Cautious, shy, tentative		

7. This lesson identifies three possible arrival behaviors. For three children in your group, outline what teachers can do to support these children.

Child	Enters the Center	The Teacher
	Eager to begin the day.	
	Needing time to settle in and warm up.	
	Unsure, afraid, even angry.	

8. The five specific prosocial behaviors of this program are:

    a.   d.

    b.   e.

    c.

9. Martha Bronson (2000) outlined 6 specific strategies teachers can use to support prosocial behavior of preschool children. For each strategy outlined below, describe specific behaviors you will try for specific children.

Teaching strategy	Child	I Will Try This
Use "stage setting" and "coaching" of appropriate peer interactions		

Teaching strategy	*Child*	*I Will Try This*
Model and communicate caring actions and values.		
Use prosocial reasoning to guide children's behaviors, and emphasize the effect of their behavior on others.		
Never use physical punishment and avoid criticism that demeans a child.		
Attribute positive prosocial qualities to the child.		
Give the children age and skill appropriate responsibilities.		

LESSON 2: THE EFFECTS OF STRESS AND VIOLENCE ON THE PRESCHOOL CHILD

This lesson provides an overview of the effects of violence and the impact of stress on young children. The reader is guided through strategies for calming a child in extreme stress and recognizing the signs of a child in chronic stress. Communication is defined and guidelines for effective communication are outlined. Anger management, impulse control, and the development of empathy skills are discussed. At the end of this lesson is the list of references used in the development of this lesson.

Following the references are strategies for anger and impulse management and the teaching of empathy skills. When teachers use these strategies in their daily interactions with young children, children will begin to learn how to control their anger and impulses and how to be empathic toward others.

Following the strategies are a pre-test / post-test and opportunities for teachers to apply the information in their daily work with young children. We suggest completing the pre-test before doing the reading and participating in the training. Once the reading, the training, and the *Practice Makes Permanent* pages have been completed, cover up the pre-test answers and answer the questions again. Compare the pre-test to the post-test to see what has been learned.

The Preschool Child in Society

In our society great demands are placed on parents and children:

- To allow both parents to work outside the home, more children are enrolled in childcare programs from shortly after birth.
- When opportunities for employment and improved quality of life are in different parts of the country or the world, families are separated.
- Because they are working or live too far away, grandparents, aunts, uncles, and cousins are not able to support young families.
- Children are the most overweight and under-active in history.
- Children are spending more time (on average four hours per day) in front of a television or computer.
- Some children use computer software and watch television programs with inappropriate content (violence, language, and explicit sexuality).

- Psychologists and educators are concerned that children no longer have the opportunity to experience childhood innocence, as they are faced with harsh images and messages.

Children who live in families that experience poor medical care, poor nutrition, and inconsistent housing face obstacles to healthy growth and development. Just as important is the strain on the parents of these children. When parents struggle to provide food, shelter, and medical care for their children, when parents are worried about finances, when parents lack fulfilling personal relationships, they are further challenged to teach their children more than survival skills.

Not all children face these challenges. Some families are able to provide a comfortable home, healthy meals, and preventive health care. There are enough children at risk to take a hard look at how we are raising tomorrow's leaders. While there is still much work to be done, educators and childhood advocates are promoting social policies to support the needs of children. For example:

- Childcare regulations, though still weak in many areas, are being strengthened.
- Money is being allocated to children's support programs such as child care subsidies and universal health insurance.
- Colleges and universities are increasing their programming in early childhood fields such as education, special needs, and mental health.

The Impact of Violence and Stress on Young Children

The Effects of Violence on Young Children

At some point, almost every child is affected by violent or impulsive behavior. Violence experienced by young children is influenced by many factors. For example:

- Poverty limits choices and families may live in neighborhoods with a high rate of crime.
- Adults who abuse substances often neglect their children as they gratify their own needs.
- Physical abuse may result when parenting skills are weak.
- Use of handguns is common in some neighborhoods, some homes, and in many television programs.
- Children's television programming often features inappropriate use of martial arts, use of weapons, and poor examples of social skills.

- Popular children's toys include war toys and action heroes who reflect television characters.
- Children's clothing and home accessories such as toothbrushes, bed sheets and beach towels feature violent television characters.

In addition to "fantasy-based" characters, children increasingly view violent acts on the evening news, in the paper, and sometimes in their own neighborhood. Children's viewing of violent television programming has measurable effects including:

✓ shorter attention span
✓ lack of respect for others
✓ attempting to settle disputes with violence, such as hitting, karate chops, and kicks

Among industrialized countries throughout the world, the United States ranks *last* in protecting children from gun violence: (Children's Defense Fund, 2001)

- 10 children die each day from gunfire in the U. S.
- In 1998, 3,761 children were killed by gunfire.
  ○ 609 never reached high school
  ○ 179 never reached age 10
  ○ 83 children never celebrated their 5th birthday
- It is estimated that millions of children experience violence in the home and come to see violence as acceptable behavior.
- 22% of violent crime victims in the U. S. are under age 18 years.
- In 1999, 16% of those arrested for serious violent crimes were juvenile offenders.
- The majority of serious, violent juvenile offenders are boys who display behavior problems as early as age 7.

Compared to the number of children who are traumatized by witnessing violence, few children experience serious physical injuries from direct violent behavior. However, in both cases the psychological result of exposure to violence is very real. Children who live with violence respond in different ways, according to their

✓ age
✓ gender and
✓ role in the family

Children exposed to violent situations learn

✓ that violence is an acceptable part of life.
✓ that people who love you also hurt you.

✓ how to get what they want through aggressive behavior.
✓ people are not to be trusted.
✓ not to communicate about feelings.

Listed below are a number of *possible* emotional and developmental consequences for children who have experienced or witnessed domestic violence, as described in *Children of Battered Women* (Jaffee, 1995).

✓ limited tolerance for frustration and anger
✓ poor impulse control
✓ sadness, depression, stress disorders, psychosomatic complaints
✓ sexual acting out
✓ loneliness, fear, running away
✓ low self-esteem, sees few options to succeed
✓ increased social isolation
✓ poor social skills
✓ feelings of powerlessness
✓ constant fear and terror
✓ confusion and insecurity
✓ lying, stealing, cheating
✓ poor understanding of personal boundaries
✓ an assumption that violence is normal
✓ self-blame for conflict and violence
✓ use of violence to solve problems

Exposure to violence has a devastatingly harmful impact on children's ability to feel good about themselves and their world, to develop caring relationships and friendships, to learn how to get along with others, to be respectful and responsible, to develop self awareness and control. All of these factors affect the ability of preschoolers to adapt to a childcare setting with positive outcomes.

The Impact of Stress on Young Children

Children are vulnerable to the harmful effects of stress as they feel ongoing pressure, are uncertain about the future, and are exposed to violent behavior. Exposure to domestic violence, through the media or by personal experience, contribute to a stressful living environment for children.

Not surprisingly, many preschoolers have developed a number of fears. They may worry that

• their parents will not come home.
• their parents will be upset or angry when they come home.
• their neighbors will hurt them in some way.
• loud voices and noises are the beginning of violent behavior.

In addition,

- as their parents move or change jobs children may experience frequent change in childcare arrangements, friendships, routines, and home dwelling.
- children may experience changes in their childcare center when there is staff turnover.

It is fairly easy to recognize when a child is in an extreme state of stress. For example, a child might react strongly to an experience that is generally non-threatening (perhaps an insect or animal terrifies them, the sight of a person scares them, or a playmate about to fall off of a piece of play equipment causes alarm). In such a situation, the role of the teacher is to determine what is causing the strong reaction and provide support. For example,

- Calmly kneel by the child.
- Ask what it is that is causing the reaction (i.e., "why are you crying/screaming/scared, etc").
- Visually scan the area to see if you can determine the cause.
- If the danger is apparent, take action to help her feel safe, (i.e. move away from the spider).
- If the danger is not apparent (i.e., a memory of an unpleasant experience brought to mind by a classroom activity)
  ○ reassure him in a calm, soothing voice.
  ○ tell him you can see that he is frightened or scared.
  ○ gently ask if he can talk about what is he is feeling or remembering.
  ○ redirect him to another activity.
  ○ document the incident.
  ○ discuss the incident with a program supervisor.

It is harder to recognize when children are dealing with chronic stress. There is no single situation that triggers an emergency stress response, but rather a series of constant little stresses. If these little stresses, fears, and worries don't settle down, the body doesn't have time to relax and the child is in a constant state of alert.

The child may be unable to	The teacher may notice
concentrate and respond to questions.	she may not make eye contact because she is looking around the room to detect threats.
settle into an activity or engage in complex play.	he plays alone and is involved in an activity for only a few minutes.

(Continued)

The child may be unable to	The teacher may notice
be open to learning new ideas and skills.	she does not seem to process discussions: she appears to tune out.
rest or sit quietly at group time, meal time, or rest time.	he pays no attention to group stories or discussions, does not talk with others at meals, has trouble settling for rest time.

When dealing with chronic stress, it is nearly impossible for children to verbalize what they are anxious about. First, she has limited language skills. However, most of the time she does not know specifically what keeps her on guard because it is a general fear of something bad, dangerous or upsetting that has been created from all the little hurts and events that she has witnessed or experienced. Because chronic stress is not related to a specific fear, it is even harder to help her cope with the fear and to put it behind her.

Common behaviors of preschool children who are reacting to either acute or chronic stress include:

- loss of appetite or changes in eating patterns
- sleep disturbances or changes in rest patterns
- increased violent or aggressive behavior
- temper tantrums
- withdrawal, unusual shyness
- over-sensitivity
- stealing
- irregularity or diarrhea
- general irritability
- developmental regression (thumb sucking, bed wetting, etc)
- new fears (being alone in the dark, etc)
- verbal abuse and increased talking back
- regression in play to simpler forms
- whining
- testing and pushing limits
- lying
- unusual clinging to a parent or teacher

It is important to remember that all children experience some stress as part of growing up. All have "off" days, when they are tired, bored, not feeling well, or simply wishing they were elsewhere. Children also experience specific changes and events which produce temporary stress. For example:

- a trip to the hospital to visit a sick relative or friend.
- a parent leaving home for military duty.
- death of a relative, friend, or pet.
- anticipation of a special birthday party or trip.

Other transitions create stress which may take longer to resolve. For example:

- the birth or adoption of a sibling.
- moving to a new neighborhood.
- adult employment changes such as loss of a job or working extra hours.
- family restructuring such as a grandparent moving in, a parent marrying or changing partners, families blending and children gaining step- or half-siblings.

Patience, kindness, and understanding go a long way toward helping children work through their reactions to major changes.

Counteracting the Effects of Stress or Violence for Preschool Children

Typically, children under stress or that have been exposed to violence exhibit predictable behavior patterns. These behaviors range from being quiet and withdrawn to overtly aggressive and hostile. With such a wide range of possibilities in the classroom, a teacher will have to keep a wide variety of skills and tactics for not only maintaining order but also enriching the experience of each child.

Preschool teachers are able to:

✓ offer children help, reassurance, and comfort.
✓ help children learn how to handle their fears and stress.
✓ provide a preschool experience that lets the children know they are safe, loved, and protected.
✓ develop a relationship with each individual child in ways that give hope, acceptance, and security.

Effective strategies for dealing with children under stress include:

Teacher Behavior	Such as
Communicate openly and honestly with children and parents.	"Yes, your Dad moved away. I know that is hard for you."
Demonstrate respect for feelings of each child.	Ask him to help you understand what he is feeling.
State expectations simply and directly in a positive way.	"When we are in the hallway we must walk and use quiet voices."

(Continued)

Teacher Behavior	Such as
Remain positive about each child: Value each child for who he is.	Reinforce the positives and make it clear that it is the behavior, not the child that is unacceptable.
Encourage impulse control, empathy, problem solving skills, and anger management by facilitating.	Teach children to think before they act. Point out how behaviors make others feels. Help children control anger by teaching them to count before they act, take deep breaths, make other choices.
Model appropriate behaviors.	Behave as you want children to behave; abide by classroom rules; use good manners.
Offer alternatives to aggressive or other inappropriate behavior.	Offer opportunities for pounding playdough or running and screaming outside.
Involve the parents in the decisions at school.	Parent Advisory group, focus groups, or surveys to get the opinions of parents.
Accommodate individual differences.	Allow children who are slow eaters to start lunch earlier; allow them the time to finish their meal.
Help children understand and cope with diversity.	Talk about differences often; appearance, lifestyles, family composition, country of origin, traditions, etc.

The Importance of Communication

Communication is the act of passing on ideas. Communication is most effective when it includes feedback from each partner that his or her message was received and understood. Appropriate, positive communication with children is critical to the implementation for a successful prosocial program.

- ✓ When teachers provide meaningful feedback, children's appropriate behavior is validated.
- ✓ Children are more likely to engage in appropriate, prosocial behavior to reach their objective when communication is positive, respectful, and clear.

✓ When teacher communication is respectful, clear, positive, and frequent children are more likely to demonstrate appropriate behavior.

✓ When teachers are able to identify and communicate the desired appropriate behavior, children are more likely to learn what is expected and desired.

Two-way communication occurs when both individuals have opportunities to send their messages and respectfully listen to the messages sent to them. Two-way communication between teachers and children is more effective than directives. When a message is sent to a child and she responds to the teacher, two-way communication is at work.

Feedback is a response to communication or behavior and can be verbal or non-verbal, positive or negative. A hug, a smile, a gentle touch or making eye contact offers positive feedback and lets children know that they are on target with desired behavior. A frown, a stern look or ignoring undesirable behavior lets them know that the behavior is not acceptable. Non-verbal feedback is especially effective when teachers want to reinforce or discourage behavior without interrupting a child's play.

When a child throws toys, or climbs cubbies, or runs around the room, or engages in other inappropriate behavior:

This teacher behavior	Is an example of	Results in
Yelling across the room to her, "Stop that right now!"	A directive: one-way communication	No learning takes place. She may not know what is unacceptable. She knows how to grab the teachers' attention.
Go to him, make eye-contact and say: "If you push Heather, she might get hurt. How else can you tell her you are still playing with the clay?	Two-way communication	He learns to solve problems using words rather than aggression.

Meaningful feedback is more effective than non-specific feedback. Unless safety is an issue, positive statements are more effective than negative statements. Clear and specific communication helps children understand what is appropriate. For every unacceptable behavior, there is an acceptable and appropriate behavior.

	Meaningful	Non-specific
When teachers provide positive, *meaningful feedback*, children know they are respected and their ideas and opinions count, therefore they recognize and repeat appropriate behavior.	"I noticed that you put all the pegs back in the bucket. Thank you." "You were very gentle with Keith's baby sister." "Thank you for helping pick up the blocks so we could all go outdoors." "You remembered to walk to the door today."	"Good job!" "Good for you!" "Way to go!" "You're the man!"
	Positive statements	*Negative*
Unless safety is an issue, *Positive statements* are more effective than negative statements and children are supported as they explore and experiment with behaviors.	"Keep your feet on the floor." "Use a quiet voice," or "Save loud voices for outdoors." "Put the paper towel in the trash can." "What can you do to clean up the spill?" or "Get some paper towels to clean up the spill."	"Get off the cubbies," or "Don't climb the cubbies." "Stop yelling!" "Don't throw that at your friends!" "Can't you ever pour juice without spilling it?" or "I'll pour your juice from now on."
	Clear and Specific	*Unclear and Non-specific*
When communication is *Clear and Specific* children understand what is expected.	"Tell Sashi she can feed the baby when you are done feeding her." "Put all the cubes in this bucket and the pegs in this bucket." "You may paint at the easel or build in the block corner."	"Use your words." "Clean up the toys." "Find something to do," or "Go play with something else."

In addition to providing meaningful feedback, making positive statements, and being clear and specific in her communication, the role of the teacher is to help children understand the differences between appropriate and inappropriate behavior. When children demonstrate inappropriate behavior, they may not know what behavior is acceptable. Remember, for each and every unacceptable behavior, there is an acceptable and appropriate behavior. The teacher helps the children learn the difference by modeling and direct instruction.

This requires that teachers	Which means
learn to quickly identify the opposite of the inappropriate behavior.	You want children to walk instead of run. You want the screamer to speak in a quieter voice. You want the child standing on the table to keep his feet on the floor.
state the desired behaviors in positive language.	"Please walk in the classroom and hallway," or "You can run on the playground." "Please tell me the problem in a quiet voice." "Keep your feet on the floor," or "You can stand on this platform."
be alert to demonstrations of appropriate and acceptable behavior and reinforce it.	"You remembered to walk down the hall!" "I heard you talking softly to your friend." "I noticed that you remembered to keep your feet on the floor all morning."

Anger Management and Impulse Control

Two of the most difficult behaviors to manage in a classroom are (1) sudden, unpredictable bursts of anger and (2) children who act impulsively, moving from one activity to another with no regard for consequences or for other children. These two behaviors can create havoc in an otherwise peaceful classroom, even if only one child is demonstrating the behaviors. If left unchecked, this conduct may lead to a variety of inappropriate behaviors from many of the children. Children demonstrating these behaviors require a good deal of the teachers' time. The child needs the guidance of the teachers to help her recognize cues and triggers for her sudden behavioral outbursts. Once she recognizes the signs of an impending outburst, she can learn to control it. With teacher support, once she understands what triggers her behavior, she can begin several specific activities, some as simple as taking deep breathes before acting. Teaching her to "think before you act" is key to helping her change this behavior. The role of the teacher is to help her break the connection between the stimulus and the response, focusing attention away from what caused the behavior to a more positive behavior or activity. Teachers:

- ✓ model appropriate behavior.
- ✓ consistently and patiently repeat class rules or limits using positive language.
- ✓ reinforce attempts at self control.
- ✓ remember to prioritize and keep perspective of what is important (not over-react to small situations.

Two common approaches for teaching children to control their impulses include cognitive problem solving and behavioral skills training.

Cognitive problem solving	The teacher and the child identify the problem, identify solutions, identify consequences, select a solution, and make a conscientious plan to change the behavior. The child is an active participant helping to identify and planning to change her behavior. The teacher is non-judgmental and communicates openly and honestly with her.
Behavioral skills training	Teaches children the skills needed to be successful in the classroom. Teachers plan and coach children through activities designed to teach skills such as sharing, trading toys, and taking turns. These cooperative skills can be taught through games, songs, finger plays, and dramatic play.

Teacher strategies to help children develop anger management and impulse control are found at the end of this lesson. *Specific activities* to teach anger management and impulse control are found in the Appendix.

Developing Empathy Skills

Empathy is the ability to recognize and understand the feelings of another person. Children learn empathy through the display and role modeling of empathy by their parents, teachers, peers, and other role models. The role of the teacher is to help children understand that the things they do and say affect others in both positive and negative ways. The roots of empathy begin in two-year-olds and 3-year-olds continue to develop it.

However, it is not until age four that children can understand the thoughts, feelings, and perspective of others.

Empathy is critical to developing prosocial skills. The child needs guidance and support to learn how to look at things with the same perspective as others. The teacher may find it useful to role play a variety of feelings so the child can experience what others feel and understand the perspective of others. Teachers can use stories and songs to convey information and puppets and dramatic play activities to promote conversation about empathy and feelings. Since empathy for others involves the discovery of feelings, and since feelings are abstract and cannot be touched or handled, empathy is difficult concept for young children to understand.

Teacher strategies to help children develop empathy are found at the end of this lesson. *Specific activities* to teach empathy are found in the Appendix.

Summary

Decision making is a learned skill requiring children to weigh their choices and consequences of their behavior and anticipate the outcomes. While the lives of many children are affected by violence and stress, with consistent routines and limits, positive reinforcement, and the freedom to appropriately express their emotions and feelings in a safe environment, children learn socially appropriate behaviors.

Children learn prosocial behaviors through modeling, practice, and the reinforcement of appropriate behavior. Teacher behavior is key in

- Demonstrating appropriate behaviors.
- Identifying and reinforcing appropriate classroom behaviors.
- Planning specific activities to promote the development of prosocial skills.
- Coaching students as they develop these skills.

The next lesson discusses the role of the environment on the development of prosocial behavior.

References

Children's Defense Fund. (2001). *2001, The State of America's Children.* Washington, D.C.: Beacon Press.

Erikson, E. H. (1968). *Identity: Youth and Crisis.* New York: Norton.

Jaffee, P. G. (1995). *Children of Battered Women.* Thousand Oaks, CA: Sage.

Strategies for Anger and Impulse Management

Teacher Behavior	*Use group time to discuss classroom issues*
For Example	As classroom issues are identified, bring them to group times for discussion and problem solving. Issues might include:

✓ A discussion to modify playground rules in response to balls being intentionally thrown into the street.

✓ A discussion about privacy when children's personal belongings are taken from their cubbies by others.

✓ A discussion about clean up time when children begin to run around the room instead of cleaning up.

Because	Large and small group times are prime opportunities for discussing classroom issues including those dealing with anger and impulse management.

Teacher Behavior	*Install a "peace table"*
For Example	This method is most effective with children four years old and older, as their negotiation skills have developed.

✓ Identify an area in the classroom where two children can engage in peaceful negotiation and a discussion of feelings when a dispute arises. This area should be off in a corner, separated from the general flow of movement.

✓ Equip the area with paper, pencils and crayons, puppets, and "feeling word" cards to help the children engage in constructive dialogues.

✓ When children are observed to be in a dispute, the intervening teacher invites them over to the peace table for a discussion. If the dispute involves a small object (such as a telephone, camera, or puzzle), bring it to the peace table.

✓ Begin a discussion with the children giving each a chance to share their perspective. "John, tell me what happened." "Maxie, tell me what happened." Summarize their comments and write it down. Help the children negotiate their way through to a resolution.

✓ After several months the children may become experienced and skilled at negotiation at the peace table. The teacher can then send the children to the peace table to negotiate a solution and have them report back when done.

Because	A peace table provides a structure and safe place for resolving conflicts.

Teacher Behavior	*Catch them being good*
For Example	✓ Throughout the day, as teachers are engaged in activities and observing the children at play, *be alert* to appropriate and positive interactions between children. For example: James and Juan are coloring at the same table. James has been using many colors and Juan has only used a single blue crayon. James states that he can't find a blue crayon and Juan gives James the blue crayon he has been using.
	✓ *Acknowledge* the appropriate interaction. For example: "Juan, how kind of you to share your blue crayon with James."
Because	This strategy reinforces appropriate behavior. When teachers frequently intervene to end inappropriate behavior or prevent a behavior from causing a disruption, appropriate behavior may not be seen.

Teacher Behavior	*Provide redirection*
For Example	This strategy requires the teacher to recognize inappropriate behavior before it gets out of control and then provide an appropriate alternate activity.
	✓ The teacher becomes aware that a child's behavior is inappropriate but the situation is not yet out of control. For example, three children have built a structure of blocks, and they begin to throw blocks at it in an effort to topple it.
	✓ The teacher intervenes and helps the children identify the problem. In this example, someone could get hurt by a block that is thrown or from the toppling tower.
	✓ The teacher then provides a similar activity that is acceptable. In this example it might be tossing bean bags and foam blocks.
Because	By recognizing inappropriate behavior before it occurs, and redirecting to a more appropriate behavior, children begin to understand the differences between inappropriate and appropriate behaviors, how circumstances may change what is acceptable. This is also a teacher demonstration of problem solving.

Teacher Behavior	*Think out loud*
For Example	✓ Identify a behavior that has the potential to cause disruption. As children learn to think about the consequences of their behavior, they can often be heard "thinking out loud" as they try to figure out how to accomplish a task. For example: Juan, Maria, and John are sitting on the floor in the library area listening to a teacher read a story. Marquis has decided

to get a book off the shelf and it appears that he intends to climb over everyone sitting on the floor.
- ✓ The teacher asks Marquis what he is going to do.
- ✓ After listening to Marquis' response, the teacher asks a series of questions designed to help him think through the consequences of his behavior.

TEACHER: "What are you going to do?"
MARQUIS: "I want to get a book."
TEACHER: "Which book do you want?"
MARQUIS: "That one right there with dinosaurs on the outside"
TEACHER: "How can you get that book without stepping on Juan"
MARQUIS: "Say, 'Excuse me?'"
TEACHER: "What will Juan do if you say 'Excuse me?'"
MARQUIS: "He will move out of the way"
TEACHER: "Go ahead and talk to Juan."

OR

TEACHER: "What are you going to do?"
MARQUIS: "I want to get a book."
TEACHER: "Which book do you want."
MARQUIS: "That one right there with dinosaurs on the outside."
TEACHER: "What will happen if you walk over Juan to get the book."
MARQUIS: "Maybe I will step on his leg?"
TEACHER: "And what will happen if you step on his leg?"
MARQUIS: "His leg will hurt."
TEACHER: "And what will happen if his leg hurts."
MARQUIS: "He will cry and maybe his leg will be broken."
TEACHER: "Do you want Juan to get hurt?"
MARQUIS: "No, I just want the dinosaur book."
TEACHER: "How can you get the dinosaur book without stepping on Juan?"
MARQUIS: "Maybe I can go that way (pointing to a path around the children)."
TEACHER: "I think that will work. Give it a try. Remember to stop and think and you can find a way to get something without hurting someone."

Because This strategy requires that teachers quickly intervene when they anticipate behavior that could become disruptive. While this strategy will interrupt the activity of the teacher, it becomes a "teachable moment" for the children and the group will not be disrupted.

Teacher Behavior	*Self-Directed "time out"*
For Example	This technique only works for children who can recognize when they are getting angry.

- ✓ Have individual private discussions with children who can recognize when they are getting angry. To be most effective, these discussions should occur when the child is calm and not involved in an activity which has the potential to lead to an outburst of anger.
- ✓ Ask him to identify what makes him angry and make a list.
- ✓ Ask him how he knows when he is getting angry and write it down.
- ✓ Ask him what he can do to calm himself when he is angry. If he cannot think of anything, offer suggestions such as moving away from the group, sitting in a chair with a special stuffed animal or doll, sitting in a cozy nook by himself.
- ✓ Help him develop a concrete plan with specific activities he can engage in when he identifies the triggers.

Because	This process helps him identify what triggers his behavior and how to redirect himself when he begins to know he is angry. This is also a focused lesson in problem solving.

Strategies to Teach Empathy Skills

Teacher Behavior	*Meal time discussions*

For Example

- ✓ Use lunch and snack times to talk about how children feel on a variety of topics such as food they like/dislike; favorite colors, activities, and books; weekend activities; and upcoming events.
- ✓ Ask open ended questions such as:
  "What is your favorite food?"
  "When do you eat it?'
  "Why is it your favorite food?"

Because	Often, the conversation will become animated about the strong feelings children have for the topic. This can lead to a discussion on food differences, cultural differences and respecting each other's uniqueness.

Teacher Behavior	*Sharing time*
For Example	✓ Plan a time each day to encourage the children to share their activities outside of the center. For some children this might be at arrival or early in the morning. For others it might be at snack time, at nap time, or late in the afternoon. ✓ Plan for group sharing and for individual dialogue. ✓ When ever possible, write group or individual experience stories and post them or keep them in a portfolio. ✓ Keep themes of friendship, empathy, kindness, cooperation, etc. in mind and as the children share their stories, ask questions related to these topics.
Because	This is an opportunity for children to share personal experiences and begin to understand the experiences and perspectives of others. Sharing can lead to discussions on food differences, cultural differences and respecting each other's uniqueness.

Teacher Behavior	*Community service*
For Example	✓ With the children choose a community service project such as collecting canned goods for a food drive, toys for a local shelter, planting a community garden, and collecting labels and box tops. ✓ As the project is planned and implemented, discuss with the children how the themes of kindness, friendship, cooperation, sharing, and empathy are related to what they are doing.
Because	Children are part of a larger community and these activities will help them gain an understanding of how their own personal behavior can help others.

Teacher Behavior	*Promote friendships*
For Example	✓ Encourage children to draw pictures of themselves with a friend, label and post them in the room and present them at a group time. ✓ Create friendship books for children as they exit the program and discuss their feelings when moving away or starting a new school.
Because	Children will begin to understand how their behavior affects relationships with others.

Teacher Behavior	*Acknowledge physical diversity*
For Example	✓ Invite persons with special needs into the classroom to discuss their life, work, etc and to lead an activity.

	✓ Open the conversation with everyday discussion about their work, etc. before exploring their special needs.
Because	Children will begin to understand how others are affected by challenges.

Teacher Behavior	*Take care of each other*
For Example	When a significant event occurs in the life of a child, recognize and celebrate it as appropriate. ✓ If a child is ill and out of school for several days, make a group card and send it to the child. ✓ When a parent marries and the child's family structure changes, talk about it. ✓ When a relative is ill or dies, make a group card. ✓ When a new sibling is born, make a group gift, card, and/or book.
Because	Children will begin to understand how their own behavior affects others.

Teacher Behavior	*Be aware of his arrival*
For Example	As he arrives, take the time to greet him. When he is observed to be unusually tired, clingy, or irritable, make a special effort to connect with him: ✓ Ask about his morning. ✓ Comment on his feelings—that he seems unhappy. ✓ Provide an arm over the shoulder or hug if he'll allow that. ✓ Ask him what would feel best for him to do first this morning and be prepared to make some suggestions of activities which don't require a lot of concentration or interaction with other children (listening to music tapes, art activities, solitary play with farm animals, etc.). ✓ Reassure him that everybody has quiet days or days when they don't feel their best and that you will be there to talk to or help him figure out what activities might work well today.
Because	There are clues—that his routine might have been disrupted (gone to bed late, had his sleep interrupted, or awoke early), that he might have spent time with a special person, that he anticipates an unpleasant experience—that can predict a challenging day for him. When a teacher is aware of these clues, she can plan to provide him with extra guidance and support.

Teacher Behavior	*Remain closely observant of the children identified to need extra support.*
For Example	Encourage him to participate in planned and routine activities, but if he seems unable to participate in a positive way, take him aside and ask him if he would like to read a book in the quiet corner or do something alone for a while. Be sympathetic to his feelings and supportive. For example: "When you push Juan away from you, I can see that you want to play alone today. It is okay to play alone. But tell Juan that you would . . . . . .
Because	This child is likely to need the extra support all day and possibly for several days.

Teacher Behavior	*Keep demands on the child to a minimum and modify plans to allow for a slower pace.*
For Example	While maintaining the general class routine, allow the child identified to need extra support to select quieter activities when she cannot cope with energy from the other children. Provide alternatives to group activities such as sitting quietly in the book corner. Occasionally, she might even need to nap during otherwise active periods.
Because	Teachers need to be aware of and prepared for each individual child and his or her needs.

Teacher Behavior	*Provide art activities such as easel painting and coloring.*
For Example	As she paints or colors, check in with her and ask her to tell you about her work. If she begins to describe an event, dream, or feeling, listen carefully and offer feedback such as, "And then what?" "I see," or "Hmmm." Give her an opportunity to talk about what is on her mind without asking too many questions. If she's describing an entire event or story, ask if she'd like you to write down her words.
Because	This allows the children to express and process their emotions and concerns in a very concrete manner.

Teacher Behavior	*Determine if she needs a transition object to help her feel connected to those she loves.*
For Example	✓ Laminate a photograph of the parent(s) or the whole family. Tape it inside her cubby or lunch box, post it on the bulletin board, or have her carry it around in her pocket. ✓ A stuffed animal from home is often soothing at naptime or during difficult transitions.

     ✓ A special memento of a family experience such as a photograph or postcard
     ✓ Small objects can remain in her pocket. Larger objects such as books or stuffed animals can be kept in her cubby until she needs it.
     ✓ Suggest she paint or draw a picture for her parent.
     ✓ Comment throughout the day that her parent would be proud of
     ✓ How quickly she picked up the blocks
     ✓ How well she brushed her teeth
     ✓ How well she shared the playdough, etc.

Because	This creates a home to school connection that will help her adjust to the new situation.
Teacher Behavior	*When possible, offer her a chance to take a "walkabout."*
For Example	When staffing permits, one teacher takes a child on a 5 to 10 minute walk through the building or on the grounds.
Because	This is an opportunity for her to be away from the stimulation of the group, to calm down, clear her head and, return to the classroom feeling more settled and comfortable.
Teacher Behavior	*Lead him or a small group of children through a physical relaxation exercise.*
For Example	Three specific activities are in the Appendix. ✓ Rag Doll ✓ Puppet ✓ Wiggle Body
Because	When the body is physically relaxed, the whole child becomes more relaxed.
Teacher Behavior	*Teach the children balloon breathing.*
For Example	Ask him to sit quietly, with his legs crossed and his back straight. Ask him to place his hands on his abdomen (stomach) and slowly take in a deep breath (through his nose). Point out how his abdomen swells like a balloon. Tell him to hold the breath a few seconds, and then slowly let the air out through his mouth. Have him close his eyes and picture floating high above the ground when his balloon belly is full, then gently coming down for a landing as he lets out all the air. Use a gentle voice as you lead him through this exercise.
Because	This activity will encourage tension reduction and emotional calming. Repeated often, he may learn to use his internal images to calm himself.

	Pretest			*Posttest*	
1.	T	F	Preschool children do not experience stress.	T	F
2.	T	F	Children's television programming often features violence and has measurable effects on children including shorter attention spans, lack of respect for others, and use of violence to settle differences.	T	F
3.	T	F	Stress may be demonstrated as aggressive and hostile behavior as well as quiet and withdrawn behavior.	T	F
4.	T	F	One thing a teacher can do to help children deal with their stress is to ignore it. This will help the child to minimize the situation and "get over it."	T	F
5.	T	F	When teachers help children understand the difference between appropriate and inappropriate behavior, children develop respect for the feelings of others.	T	F
6.	T	F	When communication is respectful, clear, positive, and frequent, children are more likely to engage in inappropriate, anti-social behavior to test the teacher.	T	F
7.	T	F	For each and every unacceptable behavior, there is an acceptable and appropriate behavior.	T	F
8.	T	F	Two common strategies for teaching children to control their impulses include time out and reporting to parents.	T	F
9.	T	F	Teacher behavior is key in planning specific activities to promote the development of prosocial skills.	T	F
10.	T	F	Preschoolers are too young to learn to think before they act, especially when they are angry.	T	F

PRACTICE MAKES PERMANENT

1. How has violent television programming affected the preschool children in your group?

2. Looking at the following list of characteristics, check those you observe in the children in your group.

- ☐ Poor impulse control
- ☐ Sexual acting out
- ☐ Increased social isolation
- ☐ Feelings of powerlessness
- ☐ Constant fear and terror
- ☐ Confusion and insecurity
- ☐ Limited tolerance for frustration and anger
- ☐ Poor understanding of personal boundaries
- ☐ Sadness, depression, stress disorders, psychosomatic complaints
- ☐ Poor social skills
- ☐ Loneliness, fear, running away
- ☐ Lying, stealing, cheating
- ☐ Assumption that violence is normal
- ☐ Use of violence to solve problems
- ☐ Self-blame for conflict and violence
- ☐ Low self-esteem, sees few options to succeed

3. What stress-inducing changes, events, or transitions might the children in your group be experiencing?

Chronic Stress

- ☐ Victim of trauma induced by event of nature like hurricane, blizzard, fire
- ☐ Witnessing traumatic event in person or vicariously through media
- ☐ Parents working multiple jobs
- ☐ Victim of trauma such as abuse
- ☐ Child's chronic medical illness
- ☐ Chronic medical illness of family member.
- ☐ Lack of quality time with parents because parents are too busy

Situational Stress

- ☐ A trip to the hospital to visit a sick relative or friend
- ☐ Anticipation of a special birthday party or trip
- ☐ Death of a relative, friend, or pet
- ☐ The birth or adoption of a sibling
- ☐ Moving to a new neighborhood
- ☐ Adult employment changes such as loss of a job or working extra hours
- ☐ A parent leaving home for military duty

☐ Poverty and resulting effects such as poor nutrition, poor health care, inconsistent child care

☐ Family restructuring such as a grandparent moving in, a parent marrying or changing partners, families blending and children gaining step- or half-siblings

4. What behaviors have you seen in the children in your group that tell you they are under stress.

☐ Loss of appetite or changes in eating patterns

☐ Sleep disturbances or changes in rest patterns

☐ General irritability

☐ Increased violent or aggressive behavior

☐ Temper tantrums

☐ Withdrawal, unusual shyness

☐ Over-sensitivity

☐ Stealing

☐ Unusual clinging to a parent or teacher

☐ Developmental regression (thumb sucking, bed wetting, etc)

☐ New fears (being alone in the dark, etc)

☐ Verbal abuse and increased talking back

☐ Regression in play to simpler forms

☐ Whining

☐ Testing and pushing limits

☐ Lying

☐ Irregularity or diarrhea

5. Complete the item below identifying what teachers can do to support a child experiencing stress.

Cues a child is experiencing stress	*Teacher support*
No eye contact, scans the room to detect possible threats	
Plays alone and is involved in an activity for only a few minutes.	
Seems to "zone out" and does not seem to process discussions (such as group meetings about a special event or learning activity).	
Pays no attention to group stories or discussions, does not talk with others at meals, has trouble settling for rest time.	

6. When communication is respectful, clear, positive, and frequent, children are more likely to demonstrate appropriate behavior. How would you handle the following situations?

At least three times a day Jovan insists on climbing the cubbies to get the Legos stored on top.

Maria has just hit Jovan in the stomach with the broom because Jovan tried to take the broom from Maria to clean up flour under the sensory table.

Maria does not sleep at nap time and she makes noise, usually waking the rest of the group about one hour before their natural wake-up time.

7. Rephrase the following into positive statements.
   "Don't sit on the table."

   "Can't you ever be kind to anyone?"

8. Identify one anger and impulse management strategy you will try. Why did you choose this activity?

9. Identify one strategy you will use to teach empathy skills:

LESSON 3: THE ROLE OF THE ENVIRONMENT ON THE DEVELOPMENT OF PROSOCIAL BEHAVIOR

This lesson discusses how the preschool environment influences the development of prosocial behavior in young children. Concrete guidelines outline practical approaches to structure indoor space so as to reduce confusion and conflict. The playground is discussed with a challenge to think "outside the box" when planning outdoor activities. Classroom management sets the tone for the emotional environment of the program and guidelines are offered in regard to interpersonal interactions as well as limit setting, routines, and transitions. Teachers are further challenged to provide an environment of sensory experiences for the children. The S.C.O.R.E. C.A.R.D, a tool to help assess areas of strength and areas which need to be reevaluated and modified, is introduced. At the end of this lesson is the list of references used in the development of this material.

Following the references are strategies for making transitions to new activities. When teachers use these strategies in their daily interactions with young children, they will find transitions easier to manage.

Following the strategies are a pre-test/post-test, the S.C.O.R.E. C.A.R.D. and opportunities for teachers to apply the information in their daily work with young children. We suggest completing the pre-test before doing the reading and participating in the training. The S.C.O.R.E. C.A.R.D. can also be used in the same way. Once the reading, the training, and the *Practice Makes Permanent* pages have been completed, cover up the pre-test answers and answer the questions again. Compare the pre-test to the post-test to see what has been learned.

The Learning Environment

Classroom environment sets the tone for a **prosocial** preschool program. When children enjoy where they go each day, they feel comfortable and they have stability in their lives. Enjoyment, comfort, and stability contribute to children's sense of safety and security, their openness to intellectual stimulation, and their ability to work and play cooperatively. When children feel comfortable enough to explore, discover, and challenge themselves, they will learn by interacting with their environment. Children are happier, more socially and cognitively competent, work longer, use more social skills, and engage in more cooperative play in environments that are appropriately designed.

A Well Planned Classroom	*A Poorly Planned Classroom*
Stimulates the children's learning.	Distracts children and inhibits concentration.
Helps children develop a sense of responsibility.	Bores and frustrates children.
Promotes positive self-esteem.	Encourages inappropriate behavior.

The Physical Indoor Space

THE IMPACT OF ROOM SIZE ON CHILDREN'S PERFORMANCE.   The size of the classroom is extremely important when determining the activity centers to be arranged, and the materials that should be placed in the classroom. It is also an important factor when considering how to appropriately decorate the space.

When Setting Up Activity Centers in a Small Space:

Try This	Because	For Example
Plan fewer centers or combine similar areas.	To avoid overcrowding: If too many centers are planned, the room will tend to have a cluttered appearance, and that can result in some children being overstimulated.	✓ Place the writing area, the library, quiet listening and computer areas in the same space—they all involve concentration and quiet work. ✓ Place the blocks, small manipulatives, and the math and science areas together,—they are more interactive and busier centers.
Keep materials off tops of shelves.	✓ It contributes to a "messy" appearance. ✓ It is a safety hazard: children will climb shelves to get to the materials stored on top of them.	Store art materials on child accessible shelves.
Paint the walls in light colors.	It will make the room appear to be more open and roomy.	Use soft white or pastels like pale mint green.

When Setting Up Activity Centers in a Large Space

Try This	Because	For Example
Use furniture to define interest centers.	The classroom will have a warm, comfortable feeling and running paths will be eliminated.	Use flannel boards, chalk boards, toy shelves and dramatic play equipment to confine activities to a specific part of the room.
Reduce the visual height of the ceiling.	High ceilings can make the room appear even larger than it is and noise will echo throughout the room.	Stencil or hang a wallpaper border at normal ceiling height; hang mobiles, children's 3-dimensional artwork, parachutes, and signs from the ceiling.*
Paint the walls in darker colors.	It will make the room appear warm and cozy.	Paint one or two walls in white or pastel colors and the other walls in darker, contrasting colors.

*Check with fire code first.
In addition, put all "junk art" materials out of site in storage bins, and labeled for future use.

APPROPRIATELY DESIGNED CENTERS REDUCES CONFUSION AND CONFLICT. Quality childcare classrooms are arranged in learning centers. Center-based activities allow children to make choices and work and play independently and in small groups. As they play and interact with each other in the learning centers, children develop social and interpersonal communication skills. Design classrooms to offer children the chance to develop their creativity, as well as to explore their curiosity through experimentation and problem solving.

Placement of the centers throughout a room can dramatically reduce the potential for conflict between the children. While deciding on the layout of the room:

Consider	This Will
using low dividers.	make it easier to supervise the children.
using classroom furniture such as toy storage shelves to clearly define each area.	limit the area to a few children in each area at a time and contain the activities so they do not spill over into the play of other children.

(Continued)

Consider	This Will
keeping activities requiring water, such as art, sensory table, and cooking near the sink.	make it easier for the children to set up and cleanup their activities.
having enough materials in each center for two or three children to engage in the same activity.	eliminate waiting and opportunities for conflict.
posting children's artwork at their eye level.	promote self-esteem.
keeping quiet activities, such as the book corner and writing center, together and away from noisy activities, such as block building and dramatic play.	keep disruption of quiet activity to a minimum and provide opportunities for children to have privacy when they want to be alone.
keeping cubbies near the entrance.	help children enter and exit the classroom with minimal disruption to the group.
placing trash cans near art and eating areas.	facilitate cleanup.
placing cots or sleeping mats into a corner.	avoid the temptation of climbing on them.
providing enough space in the block and gross motor areas.	reduce opportunities for children to get in each other's way.
providing clear pathways between interest areas.	avoid disruption of activities.
provide an area for large group meetings with enough space for children to sit comfortably.	reduce pushing and shoving.

Try sketching out a number of room arrangements on paper before deciding on which way to set up the centers. Then, rearrange the room periodically to offer some excitement and change for the children who have attended for a long period of time. Consider the following list of centers and their activity levels as you design the room:

QUIET: Language Arts; writing; library; quiet activity (puzzles)
SEMIACTIVE: Art Science and math; sensory tables; computer, small manipulatives
ACTIVE: Music; dramatic play; blocks
VERY ACTIVE: Large motor play; out door play

Finally, when the room is arranged the way you think you might want it, sit down on the floor at the doorway to see how it "feels" from a child's perspective.

- Is the room warm and inviting, or cold and sterile?
- Are the materials easily accessible, and are they challenging enough for all the developmental levels of the group?
- Is the room laid out conveniently and safely? Is it a place that a child will want to spend 6–10 hours of his or her day?

MATERIALS AND EQUIPMENT: SELECTION, DISPLAY, AND QUANTITY.   Once the classroom is set up in interest areas, consideration is given to the materials and equipment in the areas. Selection, display and quantity need to be considered.

Do This	Because	Example
Selection		
✓ Choose age appropriate materials that are safe, durable, and interesting to the children.	✓ Children always need materials they have mastered as well as materials that are challenging.	✓ For a classroom of 3- to 5- year-old children, provide materials for children age 2-1/2 to 6-years: 6 to 50 piece puzzles, Duplos and Legos, baby dolls and doll houses.
✓ Provide enough on shelves to stimulate children's interests, but not so much that they are over-whelmed or the area appears cluttered.	✓ Overstimulation and disorganization can make children feel overwhelmed and out of control thereby inhibiting the development of prosocial skills.	✓ Have several puzzles for each skill level. Display them on a puzzle rack with all the pieces in place.
Display		
✓ Label toy shelves with pictures and with words to identify where the materials belong.	✓ This is important to allow the children to start learning responsibility as they put away and care for their equipment. As a	✓ In the block area, laminate exact size outlines of the blocks onto the shelves. ✓ In the manipulatives center, laminate *(Continued)*

	bonus, labels of words and pictures provide a print-rich environment, which helps children develop pre-literacy skills.	photographs or pictures cut from catalogs onto the shelves, allowing room for storage and display.
✓ Store teacher supplies away from children's materials.	✓ Children will use materials they can reach.	✓ Keep cleaning supplies, teacher scissors and special books out of reach and out of sight.
✓ Keep tops of shelves and storage units clutter free.	✓ To prevent children from climbing to retrieve something they find interesting.	✓ Each day put everything away where it belongs.

Quantity		
✓ Provide at least 50% more activities than there are children enrolled in the class.	✓ To avoid conflict among the children	✓ If there are 20 children enrolled, there should be a minimum of 30 activities (activities, not pieces of equipment)
✓ Provide duplicates of some types of activities.	✓ To avoid conflict among the children	✓ Provide 2 or 3 exact copies of the favorite book, puppet or doll.
✓ Rotate materials on a regular basis.	✓ To keep children excited and their interest fresh	✓ Art and writing materials daily; books, small and large motor equipment and imaginary play and block accessories rotated weekly.

In addition, provide a variety of hard materials (tables, chairs, dividers, etc) and soft materials (pillows, cushions, curtains, soft play mats, etc). Some centers can be arranged in the sequence they will be used. For example, the art area can be arranged in the manner in which the children need to use the materials:

  ✓ Aprons, paper or trays on the first shelf.
  ✓ Crayons, paint and pencils on the second shelf.
  ✓ Materials to enhance their projects such as buttons and feathers on the third shelf.

The art center also needs quick and easy access to clean-up materials such as child-size brooms, dust pans, and sponges so the children can make the area ready for the next child.

Periodically rotate the materials in the sensory table and enhance play with a variety of supporting objects. For example:

Substance	Additional Materials
Water	Food coloring, bars of soap, dolls and washcloths, pumps, hoses, water wheels, measuring cups, clear plastic containers, boats, corks
Sand	Water, shovels, sand wheel, scoops, small plastic containers, small vehicles, small people
Styrofoam pieces	Plastic containers, scoops
Goop	Spoons, measuring spoons, scoops, small containers
Cornmeal	Same as for sand

ROOM DECORATIONS AND CHILDREN'S ART. Early childhood classrooms are decorated with either commercial materials or artwork from the children enrolled in that class. While it is wonderful to see artwork posted, too much of it can be distracting and affect the overall effectiveness of the classroom. Commercial materials such as pre-fabricated bulletin board displays should be kept to a minimum. The majority of any designated posting space within a classroom should be for attractive displays of children's work. In addition, every classroom should have space available to post parent notices or other parent communication pieces. Children's work should be hung at a child height so the children can see the display. Displays should reflect the work of the children: each project in the display should be unique, reflecting the varying fine motor and perceptual abilities of the children.

To promote pre-literacy skills of beginning letter and word recognition, items in a classroom should be labeled. When labeling, use appropriate lower or upper case letters. Along with the words, post laminated pictures (a drawing, photograph, or picture from a catalogue) of each item. A picture is not necessary if you are labeling a physical object, such as a chair, table, window, door, etc. In this way the children can start to identify letters and words with "things." When possible, label objects in English and another language relevant to population of children in the classroom. This is an easy and natural way to teach simple words and phrases to children.

CLEAN AND ORGANIZED CLASSROOMS. As stated earlier, a classroom that is cluttered or messy is distracting, causes children to be overstimulated, and can cause confusion and frustration for some children. Toys with many small pieces can be kept in small bins, buckets or zipper top plastic bags. Most materials can be stored on child accessible shelves in plastic containers such as shoeboxes and dishpans or on serving trays. This makes it easier for the children to choose their activity, remove it from the shelf, and return it when done. Materials that require teacher supervision must be stored where children cannot reach them.

The classrooms need to be cleaned on a regular basis. Routinely clean chairs and tables of crayon marks, chalk, clay and other damaging stains. In an effort to develop a sense of responsibility for their environment, the children can help in this process. Each class or group can be assigned a center or an area, and one day each week it is their responsibility to clean that area and make any necessary repairs. In this way, the children develop a sense of ownership for the materials. When the staff shows that cleanliness and organization are important, the children learn that their environment has value and they will take better care of their surroundings and the materials.

The Outdoor Space

SUFFICIENT OUTDOOR SPACE IS IMPORTANT. The outdoor play space for the children is important in relation to behavior and the development of prosocial skills. If the outdoor area is too small, overcrowding occurs and children become frustrated and irritated. If the children need to wait more than a few minutes to use a piece of equipment or if there is not enough room for running, children become frustrated. Unhappy and frustrated children find it difficult to follow rules and be nice to their friends.

The playground should be free of hazards and obstructions other than play equipment. If there are blind spots where the children cannot be seen, staff should develop a plan of supervision to be sure children do not hide or become lost in those spaces. Shock absorbing material should surround climbing equipment. The playground also needs to have shade and drinking water so the children do not become overheated and irritable in the warm weather. Finally, children should feel safe on their playground. Be sure the area is appropriately fenced and gates are secured.

APPROPRIATE AND AMPLE EQUIPMENT IS IMPORTANT FOR PLAY AND SAFETY. Usually, playgrounds have one or two pieces of large climbing equipment and several smaller pieces of portable equipment. When looking at your playground, try to imagine if there is enough equipment to avoid clusters of children waiting for turns. Look to see if the equipment is recommended for your preschool population. If the equipment offers activities that are too easy or too hard, the children will become frustrated and negative behaviors are likely to develop as children look for other things to keep them busy. In addition to the climbing structures, there should be an assortment of equipment that can be rotated on the playground to provide new and different activities for gross motor, fine motor, and sensorial development. Teachers should bring out at least two different activities each day to vary the routine for the children. The idea of supplemental activities is simple: When the children are happy and engaged with new and different activities, interpersonal conflicts will be reduced.

THINK "OUTSIDE OF THE BOX" FOR OUTDOOR ACTIVITIES.   Not only do children enjoy large, gross motor, activities on the playground, but they also enjoy activities that are traditionally held indoors. When possible, bring indoor activities out to the playground. Group time, easel painting, story-time, science and math, and art activities can all be adapted for use on the playground.

In the warm weather months, it is appropriate to offer a variety of water play activities with hoses, sprinklers, and sensory tables. Water play is a soothing activity for children. Small groups are most successful; plan water play activities for a few children, such as dishpans and containers for pouring and pails or cans with water and paint brushes to "paint" the building or fence.

Classroom Management: Components for Success

Classroom management is directly linked to the success of a positive and prosocial classroom environment. The goals of classroom management are

- ✓ To help the children learn self-control and responsibility.
- ✓ To promote kindness, respect and positive self-esteem.
- ✓ To promote cooperation and sharing and teach negotiation skills.
- ✓ To provide for a safe, stable, secure learning environment.

These goals are accomplished by

- ✓ Positive staff/child and child/child interactions.
- ✓ Setting limits.
- ✓ Planning a meaningful daily routine.
- ✓ Planning transitions.

POSITIVE STAFF/CHILD AND CHILD/CHILD INTERACTIONS.   All interactions between staff and children are a form of communication. These communications may be through spoken and written words, touch, or eye contact. While children may not always communicate in a way that is acceptable (such as yelling, pushing, making faces, or using gestures) teachers are their role models and teacher behavior should reflect what is expected from the children. If teachers behave inappropriately by throwing children's shoes across the room, yelling or calling across the room, or making faces at children, expect the children to do the same.

Here are some ideas for teachers to remember:

- ✓ Speak in a quiet, calm voice.
- ✓ Speak at the child's eye level.
- ✓ Use loud voices and call across the room only when safety is an issue.
- ✓ Use developmentally appropriate language.
- ✓ Use simple positively phrased one, two or three step directions (such as "Put your coat in your cubby and come sit on the carpet").
- ✓ Keep tone of voice consistent with the message. If absolutely necessary, the teacher can use a firm voice, but not one that is loud, antagonistic, or mean spirited.
- ✓ Address WHAT is happening and the child's behavior, NOT the personality of the child or the child's background. (Such as "You are angry and you pushed Jamal off the bike." NOT "Good boys don't push.").
- ✓ Written communication should be in the form of pictures and words to help the children understand.

Nonverbal communication can be very effective. A well-timed smile, hug, or raised eye-brow will let the children know exactly what the teacher feels about their activities.

SETTING LIMITS.   Together the teachers and children should establish classroom rules and limits and stick to them. There should be few rules. The rules may address safety issues, interactions with others, and taking care of the environment. Finally, state the rules in positive language. For example:

"We need to walk in the hall."   instead of   "Don't Run."
"Keep your feet on the floor."   instead of   "Don't climb on the cots."
"Use a quiet voice."   instead of   "Don't yell."
"Clean up your spills."   instead of   "Don't make a mess."

Setting limits is more than establishing basic rules. This includes determining how many children can be working and playing in an interest center at the same time. We know that

✓ Children are active learners—they learn by doing.
✓ Children are social—they like being with other people some of the time.
✓ Children like to have control over their activities.

We also know:

✓ Too many choices can be overwhelming for children.
✓ Sometimes children want to be alone and sometimes they want to be with their friends.
✓ More than 4 children at an activity center designed to accommodate 4 children is a recipe for hurt feelings, negative interactions between children, and misuse of the materials.

Teachers will find it helpful to limit the number of children allowed at one time in an interest center. When deciding the maximum number of children at an interest center consider the following:

✓ Children work best in groups of 2 to 4.
✓ The space in a center dictates the maximum number of children. (A book corner with 2 cushions or pillows has space for 2 children at a time).
✓ Some activities require more room than others. (Meaningful block building activities require room to move and build without knocking down the structure.)
✓ The quantity of materials limits the number of children who can use them. (A ball of playdough can only be divided two or three times before it is too small to provide a satisfactory experience.)

Once a decision is made about how many children can use an interest center at one time, children need to know what the limits are. Since children think in very concrete terms, the limits need to be shared with the children in a concrete manner. For example:

A four year-old wanted to join in the play in the housekeeping area. There was a limit of 4 children in that center and there were already 4 children there. The teacher told her there was no room for her and as she climbed into the doll cradle, the child responded, "I can fit right here!"

Children need something more concrete than words. A variety of cues can be used to help children better understand the limits:

✓ "Gingerbread people" cutouts laminated onto the table or posted on the wall provide a one-to-one correspondence: the number of children is limited to the number of cutouts.

✓ One central choice board has pictures of all the interest centers and pockets for the number of children permitted in each center. Children put a card with their name on it in the pocket of their choice.

✓ Children attach a clothespin with their name on it to a chart or sign posted in each center: the chart identifies how many children can use the center at once.

✓ Children hang their personal necklace or key chain on a hook in the interest center of their choice; provide one hook for each space.

DAILY ROUTINES.   For children to feel secure and stable, a consistent daily routine is important. When planning the daily schedule, every classroom must establish a routine that allows the day to flow smoothly from activity to activity. In a full-day program, the daily schedule includes:

Snack and lunch	Large groups	Indoor/outdoor
Free choice	Small groups	Active/quiet
Structured activity	Arrival and departure	Rest

The length of time for each activity might vary depending on how involved the children are as well as environmental changes and special events. For example:

✓ More time will be spent outdoors in fair weather and less in extreme cold or heat.

✓ It is time to go outdoors, but the children are actively involved in making playdough, so outdoor time is delayed until the activity is completed.

✓ Children are eager to celebrate a birthday after rest time and they are ready for lunch 15 minutes earlier than usual.

While outdoor time may not begin at exactly the same time each day, the children will know that outdoor time comes after group time and before lunch; nap happens after lunch, etc. When planning, allow for transition time to move smoothly from one activity to another. A predictable routine is important when trying to develop independence skills, teach responsibility, and assure children that their environment is stable. A sample daily schedule can be found in the Appendix.

TRANSITIONS.   For children, transitions occur throughout the day as they end one activity and begin another. Transitions are as simple as finishing a puzzle and moving on to block building and as complex as eating lunch and moving through cleaning up their space, brushing their teeth, toileting, listening to a story, and going to cots for rest time.

Transition time can cause stress for children.

- ✓ They may not be *ready* to change an activity.
- ✓ They want to control *when* they change.
- ✓ They may not understand *how* to accomplish the transition.

Large group transitions, when all children are moving from one activity to another (such as indoors to outdoors and lunch to rest) are often the most volatile times of the day. Frequently teachers ask children to "line up" to move from one activity to another. Developmentally, children are active and concrete learners. For those that understand what a line is, they cannot see the line if they are in it; therefore there is no line.

Because of their developmental stage, asking children to "line up" poses several issues:

- ✓ Most children want to be the "line leader" and many will push and shove their way to the front of the line, whining and crying when they cannot be the "line leader."
- ✓ Children become impatient waiting for the others and begin to wander away from the line.
- ✓ Children are active: standing in a line without bumping into someone else is challenging for most and impossible for others.

Since it is not appropriate to expect the children to walk in a straight and quiet line, be creative in your strategy to have groups move from one location to another. The possibilities are endless:

- ✓ Hop like a bunny.
- ✓ Move like a snake.
- ✓ Make a bus or a train.
- ✓ Sound like a tug boat.
- ✓ Move like a cloud.
- ✓ Walk on tip toes.
- ✓ Float like a balloon.

Rest time is another challenging time of day. It is important to keep lights dim, the room temperature comfortable, and some soft music playing. It is also important for the routine leading to nap to be followed each day. Activities to relax and calm children include:

- ✓ Blow up like a big balloon and very slowly let the air out.
- ✓ Wiggle the sillies out before they get on their mat/cot.
- ✓ Quietly lay with eyes closed and with a soft voice, talk the children through an activity of putting each body part to sleep, starting with toes.

✓ Suggest the children think of a happy or relaxing place and imagine that's where they are.
✓ Quietly read a book aloud.
✓ Gently rub the backs of the children.
✓ Gently rock the cots.

Allow children who do not sleep to do quiet activities on their cots after a rest of about 45 minutes.

As the children begin to wake up, they can quietly read books, do puzzles on their cot/mat, or quietly draw or color. Develop a signal to let the children know it is time to get up and begin the after-rest routines of putting away their personal belongings, tending to toileting needs, and moving on to the next activity. Appropriate signals include

✓ turning the lights on.
✓ turning the music off.
✓ playing active music.
✓ clapping hands in a certain pattern, etc.

Children thrive on consistency of routine. They feel secure when they know what will happen next. When children are not sure of what to expect, they feel insecure and this is often displayed in inappropriate behavior. Providing smooth, developmentally appropriate transitions helps children learn how to move from one activity to another without frustration.

At the end of this lesson are several strategies to make the transition easier for the children, and for the teachers.

Basic Classroom Management Rules for Success

The following are some basic things to remember when planning for classroom management.

✓ Preschool children are active learners, on the go every minute: it is hard to sit still.
✓ Preschool children learn through hands on, concrete manipulation.
✓ Preschool children have an amazingly short attention span.
✓ Children work better in small groups of 2–4 participants.
✓ Children pay attention when they are interested. (Just because it interests you, doesn't mean they'll like it!)
✓ Each child is unique and different with varying interests and skills.
✓ Children LOVE to laugh.

A Sensory Experience

Children are concrete learners: they learn through their senses. The following summarizes in terms of the senses of sight, sound, touch and smell, the components of a preschool environment that fosters safety, security, and independence:

Sight: How does the room look?
  ✓ Keep the room "clutter free"—label shelves and have two or three activities ready for use on each shelf. Children are less likely to become overwhelmed.
  ✓ Arrange the activities in a somewhat symmetrical pattern so the room has a "balanced" appearance.
  ✓ Post children's artwork attractively (but not on every inch of wall space).

Smell: Does the room smell inviting?
  ✓ Infuse the room with smells like cinnamon and cloves or vanilla to give it a warm and inviting feeling.
  ✓ Baking cookies or muffins produces a wonderful aroma.
  ✓ Strong cleaning agents, without a pleasant deodorizer, give a room a very sterile and "hospital-like" smell that can be uncomfortable for children. Even deodorizers with mint, bubblegum, or other fruity smells (strawberry, cherry) can sometimes leave unpleasant odors in the air.

Sound: Is the room a happy place to be?
  ✓ Play a variety of background music including classical, jazz, and rock and roll during free choice activities.
  ✓ During nap play children's lullabies or other soothing music.
  ✓ Keep the level of the music loud enough for the children to hear the words and melodies, but not so loud it drowns out conversations in the room.
  ✓ If the noise level in the room becomes too loud, use a signal to get the attention of the children, then whisper your directions. Whispering to children lowers the noise level!

Touch: Are there opportunities for sensory stimulation?
  ✓ Provide activities, such as shaving cream or another soft medium.
  ✓ Provide sand or water play.
  ✓ Clay and play dough should always be available on the shelves in containers, or on the discovery table.
  ✓ Put shaving cream, or pudding into zipper lock bags and the children can squeeze and squish them whenever they like.

✓ Include a soft, quiet, and cozy area equipped with puppets, dolls, and stuffed animals.

The S.C.O.R.E. C.A.R.D. System

Early childhood centers where children thrive are notable for their sense of caring, safety, and positive activity. Creating these special places is no accident! Step back and try to explore your classroom environment with a fresh eye. The S.C.O.R.E. C.A.R.D. provides a useful tool to help assess areas of strength and areas which need to be re-evaluated and modified. Please take some time to read through the different criteria of the S.C.O.R.E. C.A.R.D and evaluate your classroom for its strengths and weaknesses.

S—Safety	C—Classroom
C—Caring	A—Atmosphere
O—Organization	R—Rating
R—Respect	D—Dimension
E—Enrichment	

There are 29 items on the SCORE CARD. Think about each item and answer it honestly. The letter following each statement identifies components of the environment in terms of Safety (S), Caring (C), Organization (O), Respect (R) and Enrichment (E). Once the assessment is completed, use it for discussion with co-workers and develop an action plan to improve the weak areas.

Summary

This lesson discussed how the classroom environment sets the tone for a prosocial preschool program. When children are comfortable, happy, and feel safe they are more open to new ideas and more willing to work out difficulties with others. Factors that affect the classroom environment include the physical appearance of the room and the tone set by the teaching staff. The physical appearance of the room is affected by cleanliness, organization, arrangement of the furniture, the selection and quantity of materials and equipment. Teaching staff set the tone by setting appropriate limits, sending positive messages to the children, providing a daily routine, and managing transitions.

The next lesson examines the importance of fostering positive interactions and provides strategies for teachers to set the tone, develop emotional understanding, help children manage impulsive outbursts and angry emotions, develop conflict resolution skills, and create respectful environments.

Strategies to Ease Transitions

Teacher Behavior	Gaining Control of the Group
For Example	✓ Ring a distinctive bell or chime. ✓ Turn the lights on and off. ✓ Give directions in sign. ✓ Whisper directions. ✓ Count backwards from 10. ✓ Use a music box or musical instrument, or sing a few bars of a melody. ✓ Use a puppet to give directions. ✓ Say "1-2-3 eyes on me. 3-2-1 talking's done." ✓ Clap your hands in a specific pattern. ✓ Ask a child to make a sound or clap their hands. ✓ Use a specific song, finger-play or rhyme to announce that you need their attention.
Because	When it is time to clean-up, transition, or make an announcement, these strategies will help to gain the group's attention. The key to success is repetition, reminders, and when all else fails, do something unexpected.
Teacher Behavior	Clean-Up Time
For Example	✓ Sing a clean up song. ✓ Give the children a 5 minute warning that it will soon be time to clean up. ✓ Acknowledge the children that start the process, and gently guide those that are having difficulty. ✓ As each child finishes cleaning their area, have them attach a clothespin with their name on it to the "Ready, Set, Go" bin.
Because	No one wants to cleanup. These ideas may make it fun!
Teacher Behavior	Moving from one location to another
For Example	✓ Call children one by one according to a color or type of clothing they are wearing (such as blue sneakers, red sweaters, or long pants with belts). ✓ Whisper directions into the ear of each child. ✓ Ask each child a simple question (such as "How old are you?" or "How many legs does a bird have?" and send them to the next activity when they have answered. ✓ Use hair or eye colors (such as "All children with blue eyes").
Because	Children can move as a group in an orderly fashion, but the challenge is for them to gather at one place without all running at once to that spot and hurting each other.

S. C. O. R. E. C. A. R. D.

Safety	Classroom
Caring	Atmosphere
Organization	Rating
Respect	Dimension
Enrichment	

Directions: Check how often each item is incorporated into your classroom planning and activities.

Code: R = rarely   **O** = occasionally   **M** = most of the time   **A** = always

		R	O	M	A
1.	Classroom furniture is placed to create large open spaces for group activities such as story circle and movement to music. **(S, E)**				
2.	Classroom furniture is placed to create several distinct activity areas (dramatic play, science center, building blocks, painting, etc. **(O, E)**				
3.	Classroom furniture is placed in ways which minimize running indoors; for example, there is not a straight hallway down the center of the room with activity areas to either side. **(S)**				
4.	Classroom is arranged to provide each child with her own place to store special belongings. **(C, R)**				
5.	Classroom is arranged to provide places for quiet play away from high-energy activity. **(S)**				
6.	There are comfort corners in each classroom—large soft pillows piled on a rug with storybooks within easy reach. **(S, C)**				
7.	Children's artwork and special creations are regularly displayed in classroom–on walls, shelves, bulletin boards, in scrapbooks. **(C, R)**				
8.	Children's names and photographs are incorporated into changing classroom displays and themes. **(C, R)**				
9.	A daily schedule, with simple words and pictures, is posted so that children can anticipate upcoming activities and develop a sense of control over their daily routine. **(S, R, O)**				
10.	Basic classroom rules are posted, with accompanying pictures, to remind children of essential behaviors. **(S, R)**				
11.	There is a well-defined area for daily parent-school communications next to sign-in sheets. **(S, O, R, C)**				

12.	There is a colorful parents' corner or bulletin board with important information of childcare center events, as well as more general information on parenting, community resources and opportunities. **(C, E, O)**			
13.	Special projects and weekly themes are highlighted and displayed in an area which is easy for parents and children to view each day. **(O, E)**			
14.	Classroom contains several small group activity areas which enhances socialization among a few children at a time. **(S, E, O)**			
15.	There are a variety of developmentally appropriate games, puzzles, toys, dramatic props, and books which are rotated in and out of daily use. **(E, O)**			
16.	There are a variety of storybooks, posters and displays which focus on feelings. **(E)**			
17.	There are a variety of puppets, animals, and make-believe characters which are available for free play socialization, dramatic play, and as supportive props for group socialization activities. **(E)**			
18.	Classroom utilizes music to provide soothing and restful moments, to foster singing and dancing, to give expression to different types of feelings. **(C, E)**			
19.	Classroom schedules provide a balance of gross motor and fine motor activities, of indoor and outdoor recreation, of large group and small group play, of structured and unstructured time, of required activities and free choice options. **(E, O)**			
20.	Classroom furniture is placed in ways which facilitate teachers' ability to supervise children and to communicate with each other throughout the day. **(S, O)**			
21.	Classroom toys and art materials have clearly marked containers and storage places. **(O)**			
22.	In areas of high interest (such as the computer), there are clearly defined rules regarding time limits and number of children who may occupy area at one time. **(S, O, R)**			
23.	Transition cues—such as five minute warnings, lights flicked off and on, timers, specific music—are consistently used to prepare and support children in transitioning from one activity to another. **(R, O, S)**			
24.	Transition periods provide sufficient time for children to complete their previous involvements and prepare for the next activity; transitions are neither pressured nor haphazard but are gently paced with a clear focus. **(O, R, S)**			

25.	The noise level within the classroom is maintained at a comfortable range through careful monitoring, conscious use of moderate voices, reminders to children (and staff, if necessary), use of a variety of quiet, nonverbal checks (lights out, finger pointed high in the air, finger on lips, etc). (S, C, R, O)			
26.	Child care staff meets daily to review planned activities and share ideas and concerns. (O)			
27.	Teachers incorporate a few words or phrases in the native language of students who do not speak English as their primary language. (C, R)			
28.	Parents are welcome to visit and participate at any time in the center, and are invited to share their special interests and talents. (C, R, E)			
29.	Regular family events are scheduled at the child care site to facilitate parent-child interaction, parent-parent and parent-school relationships. (C, R, E, O)			

	Pretest			*Posttest*	
1.	T	F	In order to encourage the children to enter the room, it is usually best to place children's cubbies as far from the entrance of the classroom as possible.	T	F
2.	T	F	To discourage too many children from being in the block corner and using the blocks for weapons, the block area should be the smallest area of the room.	T	F
3.	T	F	When labeling shelves and areas of the room, only upper case letters should be used.	T	F
4.	T	F	Routine cleaning of the classroom is the responsibility of the teaching and maintenance staff therefore the children should not help clean up.	T	F
5.	T	F	The easiest way to help transition from indoor to outdoor activities is to have the children line up and walk in a straight line.	T	F
6.	T	F	Radio stations should not be played in the classrooms when children are present.	T	F
7.	T	F	Bulletin Board or "posting" space should be attractively displayed and not cluttered and include display of children's artwork and parent notices.	T	F
8.	T	F	To encourage prosocial behavior, when planning the daily schedule it is important to change the schedule each day to maximize the children's interest and decrease opportunities for unacceptable behavior.	T	F
9.	T	F	When posting classroom limits make short statements such as *"Do Not Run."*	T	F
10.	T	F	The final transition of the day should occur after rest time to discuss inappropriate behavior that occurred throughout the day.	T	F

PRACTICE MAKES PERMANENT

1. Name at least two interest centers that are:
   Quiet   Semi-active   Active/Very Active

   a.

   b.

2. Identify 3 specific ways you can provide the appropriate selection, display and quantity of supplies for the children.

   a.

   b.

   c.

3. Identify 3 characteristics of a well-organized classroom.

   a.

   b.

   c.

4. What kinds of activities, or equipment will you bring outdoors to enhance outdoor play?

   a.

   b.

   c.

5. Identify 3 positive statements asking children to stop an inappropriate behavior.

   a.

   b.

   c.

6. State 3 rules with positive language.

   a.

   b.

   c.

7. Outline 3 transitions that allow activities to flow smoothly.
   a.

   b.

   c.

8. List ideas for classroom organization that you will try in your class-room.
   a.

   b.

   c.

9. List ideas for transition activities that you will try in your classroom.
   a.

   b.

   c.

10. What is the most effective way you have found to get the attention of your group?

11. List two problems you currently have in your classroom and discuss some techniques using classroom management that can help alleviate those problems.

12. Using the S.C.O.R.E. criteria, evaluate your classroom and program. What areas need some improvement and how can you CHANGE them? What areas are you doing well in and why?

    Needs Improvement   *What's working?*

13. Using separate paper, draw a diagram of how you would like to rear-range your classroom. Include the layout of the shelves and learning centers (use separate paper).

LESSON 4: FOSTERING POSITIVE INTERACTIONS

This lesson discusses the importance of fostering positive interactions between children and between children and adults. The A–B–C–D–E approach to conflict resolution is introduced as a method of teaching children how to negotiate interpersonal differences. For children to communicate to work out their differences they must have a common vocabulary. Concrete activities are outlined to help children develop abstract concepts and vocabulary. This lesson further discusses the teacher's role in promoting respect and personal responsibility. At the end of this lesson is the list of references used in the development of this lesson.

Following the references are strategies for setting the tone in a prosocial classroom, developing emotional understanding, helping children manage impulsive outbursts and angry emotions, developing conflict resolution skills, and creating respectful environments. When teachers use these strategies in their daily interactions with young children, they are fostering positive interactions.

Following the strategies are a pre-test/post-test and opportunities for teachers to apply the information in their daily work with young children. We suggest completing the pre-test before doing the reading and participating in the training. Once the reading, the training, and the *Practice Makes Permanent* pages have been completed, cover up the pre-test answers and answer the questions again. Compare the pre-test to the post-test to see what has been learned.

The Importance of Fostering Positive Interactions

Each day early childhood teachers are faced with the challenge of enhancing the ability of young children to play, work, and communicate with others in ways that are considerate, socially appropriate and respectful. Early childhood classrooms may feel like battlefields of constant little skirmishes if children do not have the skills to get along with other children or the capacity to trust and learn from the adults caring for them. Moments of conflict and disagreement are normal for young children, just as they are in adult relationships. However, it is not necessary to let conflict and disagreement set the overall tone in childcare settings. To have successful social interactions, young children need to acquire skills such as the ability

  ✓ to recognize their own feelings and needs and those of others.
  ✓ to communicate their feelings and needs to others.

✓ to be a member of large and small groups.

✓ to engage in simple problem solving (i.e., how to meet their own needs while respecting others).

Helping children acquire these skills is an important role of preschool teachers. Increasingly, preschool teachers find they must devote considerable attention to helping young children figure out how to be safe, how to manage their strong emotions, and how to be caring friends. With these social skills children have the basic tools necessary to develop other cognitive skills and interests.

This lesson provides specific encouragement, guidelines, interaction strategies and classroom activities to foster the most basic social and emotional competencies of young children. Included are some teaching strategies that teachers can implement immediately. This program is designed to provide a framework to help teachers focus on the social dimensions of kindness, emotions, respect, cooperation and self-control. When teachers have identified the specific needs of their group, they can implement the strategies that will help teach children prosocial skills and improve the social environment of the classroom. Once these strategies are implemented, classroom behavior will begin a gradual improvement. The results will be unique, depending on the needs of the children and the possibilities and limitations of the teaching environment.

Setting the Tone

In Lesson 3, we learned how the classroom environment could be managed to foster a sense of safety, security, caring and respect. However, the *teacher* is the most important part of the child's learning environment. Teachers influence childrens' understanding of events. Teachers set the tone of the room; they teach caring and respect by being good role models for the children and their parents. When teachers are caring, respectful, and responsive to the children, the children feel loved, safe and secure in their early learning environment and they learn these values.

When teachers consistently provide opportunities for children to engage in specific activities, to practice the skills, and model the actions and behavior of adults, the loving and compassionate tone of the program will support children's attempts to imitate, understand, and internalize prosocial behavior.

We know that children learn through	The role of the teacher is to	For example
✓ specific instruction.	✓ plan developmentally appropriate, concrete, and meaningful activities to teach specific skills such as kindness, empathy, cooperation, sharing, and respect.	✓ see the appendix which outlines very specific activities.
✓ personal and active attempts to master new challenges.	✓ provide activities throughout the curriculum with multiple opportunities for children to use the skills. ✓ point out the connection between the child's actions and the prosocial skills demonstrated.	✓ when children are engaged in activities they will learn these skills: listening to stories is not as effective as performing physical tasks. ✓ tell him when he is being kind, cooperative, respectful, and demonstrating empathy.
✓ imitating adult behavior.	✓ consistently demonstrate kindness, empathy, cooperation, sharing and respect in interactions with children and adults (coworkers, parents, visitors).	✓ use manners such as "please," "thank you," "may I," and other polite words while talking to others, including the children. ✓ each day provide multiple examples of kind, empathic, cooperative, and respectful behavior.

Teachers are most effective when they are available to the children during free playtime and when they enter into the children's play on the floor, at the game table or in the science corner. Every interaction is an opportunity to

  ✓ show interest and appreciation for individual children and their efforts.

✓ encourage their language, imagination, curiosity, and self-expression.

✓ build childrens' self-confidence and develop their skills in negotiating and relating with others.

At the end of this lesson are strategies for setting the tone for a prosocial classroom.

Developing Emotional Understanding

A fundamental challenge for any preschool child is learning about her emotions and then understanding how to express her emotions in healthy ways. Typically, three- and four-year-olds act on impulse, tend to be reactive, and have emotions that change rapidly from one minute to the next. They need to be reassured that they are loved, needed, important, accepted and safe. The role of the teacher is to support the child's social and emotional development. When she feels safe, secure, and valued, she is able to satisfy her natural curiosity and explore her world. However, if she is insecure and has learned through experience that others will not respond to her with interest and consideration, she will lack self-confidence to explore her world and learn new skills.

It is normal for a preschool child to express emotions with his body: jumping up and down when excited, climbing into the lap of an adult when a hug is needed, and throwing or kicking toys when disappointed or frustrated. Each of these behaviors is a physical display of emotion. While every behavior has its extreme, jumping up and down and hugs are generally accepted and encouraged. However, throwing and kicking toys can be dangerous and is not tolerated.

Many of the behavior issues in a preschool classroom are the result of the child's inability to manage her emotions in a positive manner. The role of the teacher is to support her social and emotional development and help her learn appropriate ways to manage her emotions.

In order to manage his emotions, the child must first learn how to recognize and identify them. The teacher's role in recognizing the motivation for an unacceptable behavior is critical. The teacher will then be able to help him identify the emotion and develop a strategy to deal with it in a prosocial manner. For example, when he throws a crayon across the room he may be demonstrating frustration over the outcome of his drawing. The intuitive teacher knows him and knows the difference between frustration and intentional aggression. The teacher will ask him to pick up the crayon AND will talk with him about what he is feeling and help him problem-solve more appropriate ways to deal with his frustration.

Preschool children do not have the cognitive ability to ponder their disappointments: they do not have the ability to rationalize what happened, why it happened and why she behaved the way she did.

At the end of this lesson are several strategies for developing emotional understanding. When incorporated into the daily routine and adult / child interactions, a prosocial environment is nurtured.

Increasing Children's Emotional Self-Control

All children have moments when they are completely caught up in an emotion: dancing with great joy, shaking or shouting with fury, withdrawing from classroom activity, being overcome with sadness or fatigue. The changeable moods and emotions of young children can be challenging for teachers. As discussed in Lesson 2, a child's temperament and personal experience determines how she will respond to a variety of stimuli. She may be easily provoked, insulted, or upset. Or she may have the ability to ignore a lot of environmental stress, keep focused on what she is doing, and respond to intense situations as unfortunate episodes which do not necessarily affect her. While children's innate temperament cannot be altered, a supportive environment and understanding teachers help children cope with strong feelings.

Managing Stress and Fear

As discussed earlier, stress, pressure, and uncertainty affect children. This may include

- ✓ concerns about safety at home and in the neighborhood.
- ✓ memories of frightening events or of stories overheard about violent incidents.
- ✓ important people entering and exiting their lives.
- ✓ parents working long hours.
- ✓ parents dealing with their own mental health problems.
- ✓ economic life style changes due to moving or loss of income.

Even to children who live in secure homes with parents who are able to provide love and stability, the outside world may seem to be a scary place:

- ✓ Newspapers, television, and video games present multiple images of disaster, death, and inappropriate behavior.

✓ Children are aware when older siblings or adults are angry, upset, or worried.

Teachers of young children are able to recognize when children are overwhelmed, overstressed, or feeling afraid. They can provide children with opportunities to express that fear, to be comforted and reassured.

At the end of this lesson are several strategies that may be helpful for the child who is feeling vulnerable, anxious, stressed, or fearful.

Managing Anger

Helping children manage angry, volatile emotions is one of the most challenging tasks for preschool teachers. Not only may her personal safety be a concern, but her actions may affect the safety of others. Many disruptive outbursts actually reflect an impulsivity and lack of self-control, which doesn't necessarily imply anger, even though the behaviors are just as dangerous. Sometimes outbursts stem from other strong emotions, which then lead to disruptive behavior: frustration, deep disappointment, a sense of failure, and a fear that someone else will disapprove or reject her. There are also times when she is truly angry and her behavior is hostile and may be directed at others.

At the end of this lesson are strategies designed to help children manage impulsive and potentially harmful outbursts and angry emotions.

Promoting Problem-Solving and Conflict Resolution Skills

Preschool age children are in a period of tremendous self-discovery and growth. They are exploring new activities and worlds of knowledge and becoming more aware of other children and adults and of social expectations. Each day children are presented with many opportunities to learn how to get along with others and to be part of a learning community. The path to new understanding and skill development can be full of challenges. Providing encouragement, guidance, understanding, patience, and support will help children to grow beyond an egocentric understanding that "I am the focus of the world" to an understanding of "I am a member of this community."

Conflicts, whether between two children, between a child and an adult, or between two competing desires within the child herself, are an inevitable part of development. The preschool child often feels opposite pulls within her own heart. For example:

Independence	vs.	Security
Taking a risk and trying something new	vs.	Repeating a skill which has been mastered and risk being bored

Sometimes the internal conflict is a matter of having to choose between two attractive options, such as completing her solitary fantasy story with dolls or responding to a friend's invitation to play with her.

Sometimes the internal conflict has a moral dimension. For example: deciding whether or not to tell the teacher when he notices another child pushing someone away from the sand table. Often the internal conflict is knowing what one "should" do vs. wanting to act out the anger or impulse. Working out these internal conflicts is an important part of leaning to be a socially competent person—someone who

✓ has self-respect.
✓ respect for others.
✓ demonstrates self-control and makes wise choices.

Along with the internal conflicts experienced by children are the external conflicts which arise when playing and working with others, such as

✓ wanting a toy another child is using.
✓ wanting the undivided attention of the teacher.

Learning how to negotiate interpersonal conflicts is key to the development of overall social competence.

Below is an approach to conflict resolution which works well for handling both internal and external conflicts.

A–B–C–D–E Conflict Resolution

   The A–B–C–D–E approach to conflict resolution lists the five essential steps to effective problem solving. Even young children can be taught to use these thinking tools.

   A–Ask what the problem is.
   B–Brainstorm possible solutions.
   C–Consider emotional consequences.
   D–Decide on an option to try.
   E–Evaluate the effectiveness of the solution.

A. **Ask what the problem is.** Before children can consider other ways to handle a challenging situation, they must first be able to recognize what the real issue is. Therefore, the first step is to define the real problem.
   - ✓ Allow each child to state his own view of the conflict.
   - ✓ Listen non-judgmentally.
   - ✓ Repeat what each child said back to him or paraphrase his description of the problem.
   - ✓ Once each child has had the chance to express his own view, you can then acknowledge their different opinions, agreeing "they have a problem."
   - ✓ Do not take sides.

B. **Brainstorm ways to resolve the conflict.**
   - ✓ Encourage each child to think of all the different ways she could solve the problem.
   - ✓ Respond neutrally, encouraging all responses, no matter how far-fetched or inappropriate. The key here is to facilitate as much creative alternative thinking as possible.
   - ✓ Give each child time to suggest her own ideas.

C. **Consider aloud the feelings of each child involved and the likely emotional consequences of each option.**
   - ✓ Help each child state his own feelings clearly.
   - ✓ Accurately reflect back the emotions they described.
   - ✓ Acknowledge how each child feels up to this point.
   - ✓ Help each recognize the feelings of the other child.

D. **Decide on an option to try.**
   - ✓ Ask what each child thinks is the best choice.
   - ✓ Help them think about the realistic outcome of any option.
   - ✓ Help them consider what the likely emotional outcome will be for everyone involved.
   - ✓ Continue to facilitate their decision-making until both children agree to try one particular option.

E. **Evaluate the effectiveness of the solution tried.** This can de done formally or informally.
   - ✓ If needed, help the children put their plan in action.
   - ✓ Give them several minutes to work at playing cooperatively while observing the outcome of the attempt.
   - ✓ Approach the children and ask how they think their solution is working.
   - ✓ After they have determined that their solution is working, and if you agree that their solution has been successful, smile and acknowledge their good problem-solving. If you do not think it is working, point out why and begin ABCDE again.
   - ✓ It is also possible to catch each child's eye later during play and give a thumbs-up and nod of the head if it is clear both children are happily involved in their resolution of the conflict and it would be detrimental to interrupt their play.
   - ✓ When it appears that the option chosen is not working well, calmly approach both children and ask them how they feel their solution is working.
   - ✓ Reinforce their efforts.
   - ✓ Repeat back to them their opinion that the first solution doesn't seem to have solved the problem.
   - ✓ Return to the first step and have them again define the problem and consider other options.

Example of A-B-C-D-E Conflict Resolution

Situation: Maria and Amanda have been playing together in the housekeeping corner. They have been involved in preparing an elaborate meal, complete with lots of pretend foods and dishes set on the table. Maria folds a piece of drawing paper to use as an order pad, picks up a crayon, and tells Amanda to sit at the table so she can take her order. Amanda seems surprised, and then loudly states that she, Amanda, should be the waitress.

Both girls begin defending their choice to be the waitress, describing all the work they have done to get the food and the table ready. Their voices are getting quite loud and they sound increasingly angry at each other.

> TEACHER: (*Comes over to the girls, kneels down between the two of them.*) 'My, I can hear both of your voices all across the room. You sound really upset.'
>
> MARIA AND AMANDA both start describing the situation, starting with "She thinks...," and "She won't let me..."

TEACHER: (*calmly*) "I guess we do have a problem here. Can you each tell me what the problem is?"

AMANDA: "She won't let me be the waitress, too."

MARIA: " I got the paper to be the waitress, so she has to be the customer."

TEACHER: "It sounds like both of you want to be the waitress right now."

MARIA: "But it's not fair because only one person can be the waitress and I was first."

AMANDA: "But I set the table and got the dinner ready, too."

TEACHER: "Oh I see. Both of you were getting everything ready for the dinner? (*Maria and Amanda nod*). And both of you want to serve it?"

MARIA: "Someone has to eat it."

TEACHER: "So both of you were doing all this work to get the meal ready but then you needed someone to come and eat it? (*Girls nod.*) And Maria, you were hoping Amanda could be the customer?"

MARIA: "Yes cause I got the idea and got the writing pad. Then she said she has to be a waitress, too. But it was my idea."

AMANDA: (*upset*) "But we both did all the cooking!"

TEACHER: "I think I understand. Both of you worked very hard to get all the food ready and set this lovely table. Then Maria, you got the paper and pencil to be the waitress. But Amanda didn't want to be the customer. So Amanda decided to be a waitress too. But then you didn't have a customer, right? (*Girls nod.*) So I guess we do have a problem about who will be the customer to eat this good meal. Can you think of some ways you might be able to solve this problem?"

MARIA: "I can be the waitress and she can be the customer first."

AMANDA: "Maybe no one will be the waitress because it's not fair."

MARIA: "Maybe we can both be the waitress."

AMANDA: "But who will eat the food?"

MARIA: "We could take turns."

AMANDA: "Maybe Juan and Robbie will be the customers and we can both be waitresses!"

MARIA: "Yeah—but we'll have to get another plate."

TEACHER: "Those are a lot of good ideas. Amanda, when you told me what this problem was, you seemed hurt that you couldn't serve the food you and Maria both prepared. And Maria, you seemed upset that you couldn't serve the food because there wasn't anyone to be the customer if Amanda didn't play that role. Can you both think of a solution that would feel good to both of you?

AMANDA: "We both want to be waitress so we have to get someone else to be the customer."

MARIA: "Yeah—let's ask Juan."

TEACHER: "That sounds like a plan. Let me know how it works out."

Several minutes later, the teacher observes that both Maria and Amanda have seated two of their classmates at the table and are busily involved with taking orders, serving food, and finding more food to offer. The teacher walks over to the "restaurant" and comments, "What a busy restaurant this is!" One of the 'diners' exclaims, "This food is good!" The teacher smiles and adds, "We're lucky to have such good waitresses to feed all these hungry people!"

The Vocabulary of Conflict Resolution

Children need the vocabulary necessary to engage in effective problem solving. In *Raising a Thinking Child*, Shure and DiGeronimo (1994) provide the "I Can Problem Solve (ICPS)" process which begins to teach children words they need to solve problems and resolve conflicts. They suggests games to use with young children to teach word pairs that will help them make comparisons and understand consequences.

is/is not	and/or	some/all
before/after	now/later	same/different
why/because	if/then	fair/not fair

These concepts are not concrete. Children cannot not touch them or see them as they can touch a new food or see a bird. Shure and DiGeronimo suggest these concepts be taught through word games. Begin by playing games to illustrate obvious comparatives. For example,

Let's play a word game. We are going to use the words
is/is not and *are/are not*.

Alice *is* a girl.	This *is* a table.	She is a *woman*.	You *are* drinking milk.
She *is not* a goat.	It *is not* a chair.	She is not a *man*.	You *are not* drinking juice.

Making it silly will spark children's interest and make it fun. Use stories, puppets, and games to illustrate the meaning of words pairs. Children must understand what words mean before they can solve problems with words.

Continue with other word games to teach kids to understand word pairs.	✓ "Should we read a story *or* sing a song?"
	✓ "We can read a story *and* sing a song!"
	✓ "You may have *some* goldfish."
	✓ "You may not have *all* the goldfish."

Use if/then games to help children gain an understanding of consequences.	✓ "*If* I pour water on your head, *then* you will be wet." ✓ "*If* you want to paint, *then* you will need to put on a smock."
Later introduce consequences such as	"If you hit Michael, *then* he will not want to play with you."
Games, stories, and puppets are helpful when teaching children to understand feeling words.	"This girl is smiling. Do you think she is *happy* or *sad*?"
Expand with additional feeling words to help children understand emotions. Use story time, drawing, role-playing and puppet play to introduce feeling words.	"This child was building a tower, but the tower fell down. How do you think she feels? When you really want to build and you try and try but the building keeps falling you might feel angry, sad, or frustrated."
Children will begin to understand consequences and possible solutions by playing games using the following word pairs:	good time/bad time might/maybe fair/not fair why/because
Begin with non-problem situations.	✓ "This boy is playing in the water table. He is smiling. Is he having a *good time or is he having a bad time*?" ✓ "This child's block building fell down and she is crying. Is she having a *good time or is she having a bad time?*"
Then introduce options and consequences.	"If you throw the ball outside the fence, will I be happy, or will I be mad?"
Introduce the concept of fair/not fair in small group experiences.	"We are having oatmeal cookies for snack. We have four children here and we have four cookies. If I give you each one cookie is that fair or is it not fair? What if I give Maria all the cookies and give none to the others? Is that *fair* or *not fair?*"

Once children understand the words and have some practice using them, the role of the teacher is to help them understand how they might use words to solve problems. For example:

JUAN: "Miss Jen, come and play trucks with me!"
TEACHER: "I am reading a book to Robbie now. Do you think I can play with you *some* of the time or *all* of the time?"

JUAN: "All!"

TEACHER: "Can I read books and play trucks at the *same* time?"

JUAN: "I guess not."

TEACHER "If I leave Robbie in the middle of the story, will he feel *happy or sad?*"

JUAN: "Sad, I guess."

TEACHER: "Can you think of something *different* you can do right now?"

JUAN: "I can play trucks with Drew!"

TEACHER: "Good. I will play trucks with you and Drew *later, after* I finish the story."

For more examples of word games and more about the "*I Can Problem Solve*" approach, refer to Shure and DiGeronimo *Raising a Thinking Child*.

Most of what teachers say to children is fine, it works to solve the immediate problem and move things along peaceably. But other times teachers can respond differently to the same event, thereby moving children to a higher level of thinking – what we are calling prosocial or socially competent behavior. Working with children to help them learn how to think through conflicts and problems takes patience and understanding. It is much quicker to simply tell the children what to do, remind them of a classroom rule, or tell them not to fight. But every time an answer is provided for them, when children do not have the chance to think through the situation, a teachable moment is lost. When children are involved in defining the problem and thinking about the possible solutions and consequences, then they feel more responsible for their choices. If the situation presents an immediate safety concern, intervene first. Once the safety concern is resolved, look for the opportunity to talk through the problem with the children involved. **Strategies for developing conflict resolution skills are at the end of this lesson.**

Promoting Respect and Personal Responsibility

Helping the children learn to value themselves and to appreciate and respect others is important in teaching prosocial skills. For the purposes of this program:

✓ *Respect* is defined in the most universal sense: honoring and considering others, holding others in high regard, or having high regard for oneself.

✓ *Respect* grows from an appreciation of the care, concern, and effort others extend, not from blind obedience because "I told you so."

✓ Like trust, *respect* is earned over time.

How does a child learn respect? Respect is a result of appreciation, not a skill. Therefore, it is hard to teach. A child must come to believe that he is worthy of respect himself. He must realize that others care about him, appreciate his qualities and strengths, accept his weaknesses, and believe in him as an individual. This is a difficult concept for a child to understand. Preschool children are easily confused when others approve or disapprove of their behavior. It is hard for a young child to understand that an adult respects him, even though the adult does not like seeing him kick his toys or hear him swear. But respect can be felt, can be demonstrated and can be given to others.

A child who feels loved and respected can extend that sense of caring and respect to others. Children learn to value the adults in their world if those adults:

✓ Consistently try to meet her basic needs.

✓ Let her know that she is important to them.

✓ Let her know that she is loved.

The child will learn that he is respected and to respect others when

✓ adults are attentive and fair.

✓ adults take the time to talk about what behavior is acceptable and unacceptable and why.

✓ adults take the time to work with him to improve unacceptable behavior.

As with respect, developing a sense of personal responsibility comes from interacting with people who help us feel capable and sensitive to the feelings and expectations of others. For a child to accept responsibility for her behavior, she must first be able to

✓ understand what is expected of her.

✓ be able to act independently to make choices.

✓ understand the reactions of other people to her behavior and feelings (such as disappointment and pride).

✓ connect rules and expectations with her own actions and choices.

Preschool children begin to demonstrate responsibility in concrete ways. He can be expected to

✓ put away his toys.

✓ handle classroom materials appropriately.

✓ follow clear and age- appropriate rules.

✓ understand the consequences for breaking rules.
✓ understand there are ways to make amends when a mistake is made.

For example, he can understand that

✓ if he plays roughly with toys or rides the bike through the sand box, he might not be allowed to use those toys or bikes for a period of time. (Do not extend consequences to the next day, because young children will not connect consequences to yesterday's behavior).
✓ if he accidentally knocks over a cup of milk, he can use paper towels to wipe up the spill.

Preschool children can also learn to take responsibility for their words and social interactions. As a child begins to identify her own feelings and recognize the emotions of others, she learns that what she says affects how others feel. She learns that if she calls someone a name, criticizes a drawing, or makes fun of someone's appearance, she is being unkind and is hurting someone's feelings. She can also learn that such behavior is inconsiderate of others and is not permitted. She learns that when she accidentally bumps into a block tower, she should apologize and offer to help rebuild the structure.

To help children be self-respecting, respectful of others, and develop a sense of personal responsibility, teachers:

✓ demonstrate respect for children and other teachers, thereby creating an atmosphere of respect, and
✓ encourage the use of manners.

Strategies for promoting respect and personal responsibility are at the end of this lesson.

Summary

Learning kindness, self-control, cooperation, respect, and empathy are important tasks for young children. The role of teachers in facilitating the learning of these behaviors has four components:

1. Modeling prosocial behavior in interactions with other adults and with children.
2. Coaching, encouraging, and praising positive behavior.
3. Creating opportunities for children to strengthen their interpersonal skills through daily play.
4. Teaching specific skills, such as problem-solving, how to state one's feelings, use of manners.

Prosocial learning occurs throughout the day as children and teachers model, teach skills, coach children and create opportunities for learning. In essence, teachers are both stage managers and actors: they set up and create the right stage for prosocial play to occur and also take an active role in playing with children and modeling desired behavior.

- ✓ Specific activities to teach children KINDNESS, including manners and helpfulness are found in the Appendix (pp 293).
- ✓ Specific activities to teach children to understand and express EMOTIONS are found in the Appendix (pp 304).
- ✓ Specific activities to teach children to be RESPECTFUL and responsible are found in the Appendix (pp 316).
- ✓ Specific activities to teach children COOPERATION and sharing are found in the Appendix (pp 333).
- ✓ Specific activities to teach children SELF CONTROL, problem solving, and anger management are found in the Appendix (pp 350).

The next lesson discusses strategies to foster relationships between staff and parents.

References

Shure, M. B. & DiGeronimo, T. F. (1994). *Raising a Thinking Child*. New York: Henry Holt.

Strategies for Setting the Tone in a Prosocial Classroom

Teacher Behavior	*Acknowledge each child's arrival and departure.*
For Example	✓ Each day upon arrival, greet each child warmly and help her to settle in. Ask about her morning, or anything special that might have happened the previous evening. Notice changes in appearance or demeanor and comment positively about them, such as a new haircut. Acknowledge new personal belongings and briefly discuss them with the child. Ask if she is willing to share the new toy/book/game with the other children or if it is something that she feels will be safer in her cubby until she goes home.
	✓ As children leave for the day, smile and say "Goodbye" to each child. Make positive comments about his day, or his efforts to have a good day and his continued efforts for the next day. Follow up on comments he made about

	his plans for activities outside of the center (such as having pizza for dinner) and tell him you are looking forward to his return the next day.
Because	Such comments let him know that his efforts were appreciated, his conversations throughout the day were important, and that his teachers care about him.
Teacher Behavior	*Be expressive.*
For Example	With positive facial expressions, words, and tone of voice, convey interest, pleasure and excitement over the discoveries, classroom activities, and general behavior of the children.
Because	Children generally respond positively to smiles and adults who listen to their concerns and comments.
Teacher Behavior	*Be available.*
For Example	Join the children in their activities. For example, sit on the floor and engage in block play, join her at the computer, get involved in the dramatic play center, join the play at the sensory table and comment on the process, etc. Bend down to her eye level. If involved with Maria, and Anthony requests teacher attention, ask Anthony to wait a minute, finish with Maria and give undivided attention to the second child. Save paper work and lesson preparation for rest time or a scheduled planning time.
Because	✓ Teachers can prevent unwanted behavior by encouraging negotiation and facilitating the problem solving process. ✓ Joining children in their play sends a message that teachers care. ✓ Acknowledging a child in need shows respect and kindness. ✓ Gives teachers more opportunity to recognize, acknowledge, and reinforce appropriate behavior.
Teacher Behavior	*Moderate noise level.*
For Example	Consciously moderate the volume and pitch of environmental sound. This includes voices of adults and children as well as music, computer and electronic games, outdoor sounds such as lawn mowers and emergency vehicles, etc. Encourage children to use loud "outside" voices outdoors and quieter "inside voices" when indoors.
Because	✓ A loud environment encourages children to be louder in order to be heard.

✓ When the noise level is high, children and adults find it more difficult to focus on an activity. Environments that are too loud or busy inhibit opportunities for children to focus on their own thoughts, feelings and ideas, and make it difficult for him to learn how to express himself in appropriate ways.

✓ An appropriate volume allows him to hear others and be heard without raising his voice. When children can hear each other they can learn and use negotiation techniques. When he cannot think through the process of conflict resolution, the easiest response to a situation may be to respond by hitting.

Teacher Behavior	*Speak calmly and softly.*
For Example	When speaking to a group of children, teachers may need to project their voice without raising their voice to an inappropriate level. If the noise level during group time starts to increase because children are continuing to talk, stop speaking, take a deep breath, and look expectantly around at each of the children. Wait for them to quiet down. When ready to speak, do so in a whisper. Whispers are dramatic and children, intrigued by drama, quiet down to focus on what is being said. Yell across the room only if her safety is threatened. When unable to go to another part of the room to speak to her 1. Choose an appropriate child to be a messenger and have her come to you, or 2. Call her name once or twice and ask her to come to you so you may speak with her.
Because	✓ Modeling an appropriate voice sets a good example for the children and shows respect for classroom rules. ✓ An appropriate voice allows others to be heard and allows others to continue to play uninterrupted.
Teacher Behavior	*Seeing eye-to-eye.*
For Example	When talking to an individual child, sit or kneel close to him and make eye contact. Keep eye contact as he responds.
Because	Adults are much taller than preschool children and standing over the children creates a barrier and may appear threatening to the child. Being at eye-level with him creates a strong, positive connection and sends the message that you care about him.

Teacher Behavior	*Use signals.*
For Example	When children are noisy or occupied and the attention of the group is required, use signals to gain their attention. Children must be aware of what the signal is and what it represents, such as "Stop and listen," "Stop and go to group meeting," "Stop and prepare for next activity or transition." Some children may also need a "reminder" such as a gentle hand on the shoulder, or a personal, direct and quietly spoken reinforcing message. Possible signals include: ✓ Turn the lights off until the children are quiet and ready to listen. ✓ Flick lights on and off. ✓ Clap hands. ✓ Ring a bell or specific musical instrument. ✓ Raise one finger to the lips and the other hand is raised into the air. ✓ Sing a specific song.
Because	✓ Children are able to hear and see each time a teacher needs the attention of the whole group because there is a consistent signal used only for the purpose of gaining their attention. ✓ Individual reminders help children who do not respond to group signals.
Teacher Behavior	*Mind your manners.*
For Example	When talking with children and adults use words like "Please," "Thank you," "Excuse me," and "I'm sorry," when making a request, acknowledging what someone has done, interrupting an activity or conversation, and acknowledging a mistake.
Because	Modeling these simple courtesies teaches children basic manners and creates an atmosphere of respect and appreciation for others. These words help him understand that everyone is important and is to be treated with respect. An apology from the teacher sends him the message that the teacher 1. Recognizes her words or actions had an impact on him. 2. That she cares enough to correct the situation. 3. Takes responsibility for her words and behaviors and she cares about his feelings. 4. Makes mistakes.

When teachers model good manners such as offering apologies children learn how to acknowledge their own errors and admit they might be wrong, or are sorry about an inconsiderate behavior. Children also learn that it is important to consider the feelings of others and to try to correct mistakes.

Teacher Behavior	*Moderate the noise and energy level of your classroom.*
For Example	✓ Moderate the energy level using a signal if needed. ✓ Offer less active choices or do structured movement activities.
Because	To prevent children from becoming over-stimulated, overly excitable, or distressed.
Teacher Behavior	*Provide cozy, comfortable nooks away from the major activity areas.*
For Example	Keep the corners simple, with a small couch or a few comfortable beanbag chairs or pillows as well as books and magazines. A tape player and drawing materials might round out the area.
Because	This is a place for children to retreat to when they are feeling quiet, tired, or overwhelmed.
Teacher Behavior	*Offer appropriate choices whenever possible.*
For Example	Early childhood programs offer many opportunities for free choice activities throughout the day. Also offer choices when a child becomes angry or combative. For example, when Maria throws blocks: "Maria, it looks like you're not really interested in playing blocks right now. Do you want to spend a few minutes in our quiet corner until you're feeling calmer or do you want to go over to the puzzle table?"
Because	By offering appropriate choices, he will learn to make appropriate choices before inappropriate behavior occurs.
Teacher Behavior	*As a teaching team, decide what options to make available to children who have a difficult time participating in group or rest time.*
For Example	Encourage children to participate in large group activities and convey the expectation that group time is for everyone and that it will be fun. However, some children may not be able to sit for more than three minutes. If the teaching team plans for children who are unable to sit through a group time or who may no longer need a

two-hour nap, inappropriate behavior from boredom may be avoided. Plan quiet, non-distracting, easily supervised activities as alternatives. For example:

✓ resting in the quiet corner,

✓ reading a book at a table or on the cot, and

✓ playing quietly at a table with puzzles or markers.

Because	By planning alternatives, the remainder of the group can participate in group time or rest time with less interruption.

Teacher Behavior	*Help children manage transitions.*
For Example	To help children anticipate standard transitions between activity periods, snacks and meals, and departure, provide visual as well as environmental cues. For example: ✓ Post a chart or picture time line. ✓ Throughout the day remind children of the routines. ✓ Keep the routine consistent. ✓ Give five minute warnings such as specific songs or physical cues such as flicking lights and singing a clean up song. ✓ Give quiet individual reminders to children who are engrossed in their play or who have a hard time shifting their attention from one activity to the next. ✓ A teacher's physical presence may help children move forward: a gentle arm on the shoulder with a reminder that "in three minutes we will be washing hands for lunch," or simply kneeling beside the child engrossed in racing cars and stating, "This race track will be closing for lunch. I'll put away the wall pieces if you'll put away the cars."
Because	Children are more likely to comply when they are informed about and expect transitions.

Teacher Behavior	*Play soothing music.*
For Example	In a peaceful corner of the room, such as the book corner or at the Peace Table, provide classical lullabies at a serene volume.
Because	This reinforces the fact that his mood or state of mind (his feelings) is acceptable.

Teacher Behavior	*Spend time with small groups of children.*
For Example	✓ Read quietly with two or three children. ✓ Play a quiet table game or do puzzles with two or three children.

✓ Listen to music and talk about how the music feels.
✓ Lay on the grass and watch clouds pass by; talk about their shapes.
✓ Watch the birds feeding or building nests from a window or on the playground.

Because

✓ He may be more likely to express himself verbally in a smaller group.
✓ The smaller the group, the less stimuli there is, creating a more relaxing environment for him.

Teacher Behavior	*On enrollment, plan with parents ways they can help their child through challenging days.*
For Example	Have each child's parent or special relative record on audiotape a favorite story and store the cassettes in a teacher cupboard. When a child is feeling tired or lonely or out of sorts, he can listen to the recording of his parent reading a story. Ask each parent to record on audiotape a letter they have written to their child.
Because	This creates a home to school connection that helps him adjust to the new situation.

Teacher Behavior	*Be alert.*
For Example	During arrival, be alert for the child who arrives irritable, easily annoyed, or especially unresponsive to staff. Keep demands to a minimum and encourage him to become involved in activities which do not require much interaction with other children such as computer, puzzles, playdough, reading books, etc.
Because	His attitude and behavior are letting us know that he is not in a position to handle many demands. As with children who are overwhelmed by stress or fear, the angry child has fewer of his normal coping resources available to help him deal with his world.

Teacher Behavior	*Be observant.*
For Example	Throughout the day carefully observe her for continued irritability and over-reaction. If she begins to become loud or physically agitated, gently try to redirect her to a safer outlet. This might include throwing beanbags at a target or pounding clay with a clay mallet or fist.
Because	Preventing a full-scale escalation of inappropriate behavior is much easier than helping her calm down once she is out of control.

Strategies for Developing Emotional Understanding

Teacher Behavior	*Use "I statements" to express personal feelings, opinions, hopes.*
For Example	"Hello, Jacob. I'm so glad to see you are back!" "I've never eaten noodle cakes before. I wonder what they taste like." "I am worried you might fall when you climb on the cubbies." "That beautiful blue picture you painted makes me feel so peaceful." "I wish we could stay outside a little longer too, but it's time to go inside for lunch." "I'm sorry that scrape on your knee has been bothering you today, Carlos. I hope it feels better tomorrow."
Because	Modeling appropriate ways to handle feelings provides children with an opportunity to consider what they are feeling and how to express those feelings.
Teacher Behavior	*Help children identify their own feelings.*
For Example	Ask them about their feelings: ✓ "How are you feeling?" ✓ "How does that make you feel?" ✓ "How do you feel when Maria pushes you away? John tears your paper? Devon helps you pick up the toys?" Comment on the emotion expressed in conversation or demonstrated in an activity by telling her what you think she is feeling or by making a sympathetic statement. For example: ✓ "You've been really quiet today, Zach. Are you feeling a little tired?" ✓ "I noticed that you don't sit next to the other children in circle, Amanda. Are you feeling a little shy?" ✓ "Jake, you look angry. Are you mad about something?" ✓ "Michael, you're walking so fast I think you must be very eager to get outside, but please be careful not to bump into anyone." ✓ "Sometimes when people move into a new home (apartment), they feel a little scared about who their new friends will be." ✓ "Look at you dancing, Tony! You look so happy!"

Because	✓ Children will learn that it is okay to experience these feelings and there are appropriate ways to demonstrate them.
	✓ When he can express himself with words, he will be less likely to use aggression or violence to express his feelings.
Teacher Behavior	*Help children recognize feelings in other children.*
For Example	Encourage children to try to understand what another child is feeling by asking questions such as:
	"How do you think Bobby is feeling right now?"
	and offering simple interpretation of the behavior of other children.
	For example:
	✓ "Mary is walking over to the reading corner with a book. I think she doesn't want to play right now."
	✓ "I heard Reggie say he hates you. Why do you think he said that? He seems pretty upset that you smashed into his robot."
	✓ "Maria has gone to get more paper. Maybe she's feeling bad that she spilled a cup of juice on your picture."
	✓ "Yes, I see that Reggie keeps following both of you. Do you think he wants to play trucks with you?"
Because	When he can recognize verbal and physical cues, he is building the foundation for the development of empathy and compassion for others.
Teacher Behavior	*Help children make connections between actions and feelings.*
For Example	Ask specific, direct questions and interpret the emotions behind the behavior. For example:
	✓ "When you kicked over the castle Gina was building, how do you think she felt?"
	✓ "That's a very special card you made for your dad, Sylvie. I think he will be happy to get it."
	✓ "Reggie, Maria, and Bobby have been waiting quietly for several minutes. How do you think they would feel if you use the computer before they do?"
	✓ "I can see you are very angry right now, so angry you want to throw that block at Juan. How will Juan feel if it hits him?"
	"Jonathan, you noticed that Maria was standing there watching you play with the magnets. She looked so happy when you invited her to play with you."
	✓ "You worked so hard on that collage, Reggie. I think you are very proud of your work."

Because	Being able to anticipate the emotional consequences of certain actions is a very important skill for effective problem solving and the development of empathy.
Teacher Behavior	*Let the children know that all feelings are acceptable and valid.*
For Example	Help the children distinguish between their emotions and how they express them. For example:

  ✓ "I see you are not happy to put the puzzle away right now. It's okay to be frustrated, but you may not kick the cabinet doors."
  ✓ "I know you are excited that we have a new bike, but Jamal and Reggie have been waiting to use it and you may not push ahead of them. You must wait for your turn."
  ✓ "If you don't want to sing with us, that's okay. You can just sit and listen."
  ✓ "I know you like to listen to the rain, Reggie, but Maria feels a little scared when it rains hard. Sometimes we feel different things."

Because	Validating her feelings gives her the confidence to express herself again in similar situations. Providing acceptable choices when necessary will give her options for similar situations.
Teacher Behavior	*Encourage children to state their own opinions and feelings with simple "I statements."*
For Example	Remind him that:

1) each person has his own feelings and interests.
2) he doesn't have to feel the same as others.
3) he doesn't have to do the same thing as others.
4) it is not acceptable to deliberately hurt the feelings of others.

For example:

"Reggie, when Tina asked you to play store with her and you said, 'Playing store is stupid;' how do you think Tina felt? *(Give him time to answer.)* It's okay not to want to play store, but how can you tell her you don't want to play in a way that will not hurt her feelings? (*"No thanks, I don't want to play store now."*)

"Jamal, instead of shoving Reggie, can you tell us what is making you angry?" (*"I wanted that book."*)

"I can see that lots of things are annoying you today, Maria. Would you feel better if others didn't try to play with you right now?"

> "Reggie, what can you say to Maria when she starts to touch your hair? ("I don't like people touching my hair. Please don't.")

Because   This gives him power and control of his own thoughts and feelings.

This creates a situation in which there is no right and no wrong.

Strategies to Help Children Manage Impulsive Outbursts and Angry Emotions

Teacher Behavior	*Stay close to him.*
For Example	Identify those times that will be challenging for the child. Sit or stand near him during transitions, meals, rest time, large group times and those times predicted to be most challenging for him.
Because	Teachers can often predict those times during the day when children need additional support to maintain self-control. By staying close to him, teachers can: ✓ prevent inappropriate behavior by intervening before behavior is out of control. ✓ take advantage of opportunities to reinforce anger management skills and support him through difficult times.
Teacher Behavior	*Encourage her.*
For Example	Reinforce every time she appropriately deals with a situation by telling her specifically what she did. For example, " Maria, I noticed that you used your words to let Juan know you want to be alone. Good for you."
Because	Encouragement and reinforcement of appropriate behavior promotes more appropriate behavior.
Teacher Behavior	*Provide art activities such as easel painting and coloring.*
For Example	Check in with him and ask him to tell you about his work as he paints or colors. If he begins to describe an event, dream, or feeling, listen carefully and offer feedback such as, "And then what?" "I see," or "Hmmm." Give him an opportunity to talk about what is on his mind without asking too many questions. If he is describing an entire event or story, ask if he would like you to write down his words. If you are

	concerned about his ability to use paint appropriately while feeling so upset, limit choices to markers or tactile collage materials.
Because	Children who are frustrated, angry, or easily annoyed have a need to work out their feelings in verbal and non-verbal ways.

Teacher Behavior	*Offer opportunities to release physical energy.*
For Example	✓ Provide large mounds of clay, play dough, or goop. Pounding the play dough, rolling out snakes, mounding up volcanic mountains are great ways to channel that energy. Consider keeping a specific color of play dough that she can ask for when she is having a "very angry" day. ✓ Provide a hammer and golf tees to be pounded into a thick piece of hard foam board. ✓ Provide a diagonal cut of a tree for pounding nails. ✓ Besides climbing apparatus and riding toys, have a variety of balls to bounce on the playground. ✓ If it is too cold to go outdoors, set up an area of the room or hallway where children may throw the paper airplanes, bean bags or foam balls at targets. The target might be an empty wastebasket, plastic bowling pin, or empty dishpan. ✓ Engage the children in their own contests of "physical fitness." Count the number of hops, jumps, sit-ups, toe touches, or push-ups they can do.
Because	Children who are angry often need to physically release their energy. Providing acceptable opportunities helps children avoid responding physically to others (hitting, punching, pushing, etc.).

Teacher Behavior	*Develop an "Angry Energy Burn" routine.*
For Example	For example, the following is a rocket ship exercise. ✓ Have the children quickly march in place. ✓ While marching in place, have the children hum loudly. ✓ Lean over from the waist, letting arms dangle down. ✓ While humming and marching place, slowly straighten up to a standing position with arms outstretched. ✓ Slowly lower hands, stop humming, and slowly stop marching. End exercise with voice command, "Control, we are now clear."
Because	When she is feeling so volatile that she cannot enter into verbal problem solving, this activity will expend some built-up physical tension.

Teacher Behavior	*The Garbage Pail for Garbage Words*
For Example	Use this strategy when children are unable to control particularly offensive verbal language and swearing. Provide a small plastic container with lid that looks like a garbage can. When a child is unable to stop using foul language, quietly take him to a place that is private: the hallway, the director's office, and an unoccupied part of the classroom. Tell him that such words are not allowed in school and they must be "thrown out." Have him speak the offensive words into the miniature garbage pail, then put the lid on it. Before returning to the classroom, have him brainstorm other ways he could express the same ideas. Help him identify a substitute phrase that is acceptable to use.
Because	This reinforces the fact that certain words are not acceptable and gives the child a chance to problem solve.

Teacher Behavior	*Bear Hug*
For Example	First demonstrate a Bear Hug: ✓ Stand still. ✓ Cross your arms over your body. ✓ Place your right hand on your left shoulder and your left hand on your right shoulder in a "hug." ✓ To complete the bear hug, take a deep breath and let your head drop down. Explain to her that the Bear Hug is a way to love herself and calm herself when she is feeling upset or angry. Explain that when she gives herself a Bear Hug, it also gives her time to stop and think about what she wants to say or do next. Explain that whenever someone is giving herself a Bear Hug, the others must not bother her or talk to her: The Bear Hug is a signal to stop and leave the hugger alone.
Because	She will learn to stop and close out the stimuli in the environment, thereby calming herself.

Strategies to Develop Conflict Resolution Skills

Strategy	For Example
Make conscious choices about when to intervene.	Children need to develop negotiation and problem-solving skills at their own pace, and they need to try different approaches and practice what they've been taught. If the conflict seems minor and no one is in danger, watch to see how the children resolve the issue on their own. If the situation continues to escalate or another child is being victimized, intervene and lead them through the A-B-C-D-E steps.
Remain non-judgmental as children state their views, feelings, and ideas.	Even when you are repeating back to a child his negative emotions or wishes ("I hate Juan. I wish he didn't come here!"), you can do so without criticizing the child: "You are really angry at Juan right now and it would feel easier for you if he wasn't here in this room." This allows the teacher and the children to continue to define the real problem — what behaviors caused such strong feelings in the first place — then consider solutions.
Avoid offering solutions.	This is particularly difficult when working with children who have no personal experience thinking through problem situations. Gently encourage him with a simple, "What else could you do?" If he truly cannot respond, restate the problem and the behavior that was NOT working, then say, "So that didn't seem to help. I wonder what else you could do." Encourage each suggestion, knowing that, with time and experience, children will be able to brainstorm more possibilities and consider their likely consequences with greater understanding.
Do not tolerate bullying.	In cases where a child consistently pushes, hits, or picks on other children, define the situation as the problem of the aggressive child, not a case of two conflicting viewpoints. The aggressive child needs to learn how to appropriately handle his frustrations and anger. Work with the aggressive child to define his problem, brainstorm more acceptable options, and consider the emotional consequences on other children.

Strategies for Creating Respectful Environments

Teacher Behavior	*Listen attentively to what each child says.*
For Example	Kneel or bend close to him, make eye contact, and listen without interrupting what he says.
Because	Listening attentively tells the speaker that you value him and value what he is saying. You do not have to agree or even like what you hear, but you must listen first before you can form an opinion or response.
Teacher Behavior	*Ask the children what they think.*
For Example	Ask her what she thinks about the activity, event, situation, etc.
Because	This simple process lets her know that you recognize that she has her own thoughts and opinions and that you do not expect everyone to think or feel the same. It lets her know that you appreciate her as unique individual.
Teacher Behavior	*Provide opportunities for win-win decision making.*
For Example	Offer safe, appropriate choices frequently throughout the day.
Because	This encourages him to consider what he feels like doing, what he prefers to eat, whether he wants to play with others or play alone, etc. Giving choices conveys the awareness that you recognize he is unique and that you respect his right to think and decide for himself. Choices give him the chance to express his own preferences and convey respect for all.
Teacher Behavior	*Acknowledge children's efforts and achievements.*
For Example	✓ Let her know that you recognize how hard she has worked on a project or how hard she worked at being patient as she waited for her turn. ✓ Let her know that you've noticed her efforts at self-control and kindness, even if her behavior wasn't completely successful. For instance, Maria may have pushed Jonathan away, but only after she twice told him to stop touching her. When you problem solve with her, you can acknowledge her attempts to use her words, then help her consider what other options were open to her when it didn't work.

Because	By praising her good intentions and efforts, you show your respect for her, not just your appreciation of what she created (in a drawing, song, etc.).
Teacher Behavior	*Create leadership opportunities for the children.*
For Example	Identify those classroom tasks that children can help with and assign rotating responsibility. For example: helping to prepare snack setting the table for meals carrying the first aid kit to playground selecting the book for story time, etc
Because	This emphasizes the importance of taking responsibility in ways that are very concrete and meaningful.
Teacher Behavior	*Model the use of good manners.*
For Example	✓ Use "please," and "thank you "and "excuse me" appropriately with the children and other adults. ✓ Say "I'm sorry" when you have accidentally disturbed a situation or hurt someone. ✓ Encourage him to use good manners; prompt him when necessary. ✓ Acknowledge with a smile, a "thumbs up", and/or with words when he uses good manners.
Because	You are modeling the way you like to be treated and you are letting him know that you are respecting him. Apologizing for hurting someone else, or disturbing their efforts, is a very important step toward taking personal responsibility, and a hurtful conflict is not resolved until apologies have been made.

	Pretest				*Posttest*	
1.	T	F	Children learn prosocial skills by simply imitating adults.		T	F
2.	T	F	Typically four-year-olds tend to act on impulse, tend to be reactive, and have feelings and emotions that change rapidly.		T	F
3.	T	F	Many behavior issues in a preschool classroom are the result of the child's inability to manage her emotions in a positive manner.		T	F
4.	T	F	A child's temperament has no effect on how children respond to stimuli.		T	F
5.	T	F	Teachers of young children are seldom able to recognize when children are overwhelmed, overstressed, or feeling afraid.		T	F
6.	T	F	When a child has a disruptive outburst, it most likely reflects impulsive behavior and lack of self-control and does not necessarily imply anger.		T	F
7.	T	F	Learning how to negotiate interpersonal conflicts is key to the development of overall social competence.		T	F
8.	T	F	Before children can engage in effective problem solving, they need to comprehend opposites, understand consequences, and verbalize their feelings.		T	F
9.	T	F	Respect is taught through concrete activities.		T	F
10.	T	F	Children demonstrate responsibility when they put away their toys, handle materials appropriately, and follow rules.		T	F

PRACTICE MAKES PERMANENT

Identify 2 specific activities you will use to teach children prosocial skills.
1.

2.

For each activity, complete the following:

1st Activity:	2nd Activity:
The goal is to teach	The goal is to teach
☐ Kindness	☐ Kindness
☐ Empathy	☐ Empathy
☐ Cooperation/Sharing	☐ Cooperation/Sharing
☐ Respect	☐ Respect
☐ Self-control	☐ Self-control

Specific children to benefit from   Specific children to benefit from
this activity: this activity:
1. _____   1. _____

2. _____   2. _____

3. _____   3. _____

4. _____   4. _____

☐ Entire Group   ☐ Entire Group
Dates to implement: Dates to implement:

Time of day or activity   Time of day or activity
  period to implement: period to implement:

Special Considerations: Special Considerations:

LESSON 5: FOSTERING POSITIVE
HOME–CENTER PARTNERSHIPS

This lesson discusses the importance of fostering positive relationships with families of children enrolled in the program. Teaching prosocial skills to children in partnership with their parents results in greater success for the adults and increased skills for the children. Several concrete, easy to implement strategies are offered. When parents feel welcomed and valued by teachers, partnerships develop: partnerships that are mutually supportive of childrens' learning.

At the end of this lesson is a series of Tips for Parents. Each *Tips* is two pages: the first page is an article, the second is a questionnaire. The first five *Tips* articles each discusses a different Bingham principle: kindness, understanding and expressing emotions, respecting self and others, fostering cooperation and sharing, and self control. Each article ends with a fill-in-the-blank statement. This gives teachers an opportunity to share with parents a positive example of how their child has demonstrated one of the Bingham principles. The questionnaires are to be sent to parents a few days after the article and promptly returned. The questionnaires ask parents to think about how their child has demonstrated one of the principles and share it with teachers. The topic of the last *Tips* is *Guiding Your Child's Use of the Media*. It, too, is a one page article with corresponding questionnaire.

While the childcare community is comprised of on-site staff, support personnel, and the children they serve, teachers are aware of the extended community, which includes their children's families. The beliefs and values children hold, their coping styles and interests, even their daily moods or levels of energy and fatigue are all strongly influenced by their family environment. Children who are up late, exposed to frightening situations or constant change come into our childcare centers with greater needs and concerns. Children who are part of a family system which respects and cares for all family members come into our centers with a sense of being loved and some ability to show kindness to others.

Yet, all children must experience the transition from home to preschool and back to home again on a daily basis. Even with the most positive childcare center and loving home, there are shifts and changes within the child's day. The smooth coordination of these transitions becomes a very important factor in the child's feelings of security and success.

Preschool teachers are establishing vital partnerships on behalf of the children in their care when they

✓ work with parents to create open channels of communications.

✓ provide parents with information and support.

✓ and encourage family participation in school and community.

Each day preschool teachers share important information regarding the child's health, concerns, and needs, and communicate news of upcoming events, center expectations and requirements. Equally important, when there are strong home-school partnerships, teachers and parents have the chance to share a child's new discoveries, funny moments, and triumphs. And the child knows that both sets of important adults in his life—parents and teachers—care about him, know him, appreciate him, and are working hard to make his life whole and happy, at home and at school.

Fostering positive relationships between parents and teachers requires a genuine appreciation of the importance of this partnership and a commitment to making the effort to strengthen those bonds. Teachers convey their respect for the children's families and desire to include the families in their community when they

✓ are at ease and communicate with parents about their children.

✓ demonstrate interest in getting to know parents.

✓ and are physically available to speak with parents on arrival and departure.

Parents who feel free to speak with a teacher, call her from work, or send in a note are parents who

✓ are likely to feel a closer connection to their children's preschool program.

✓ and are more likely to take an active, participatory role in the preschool program.

Setting the tone of an inclusive childcare community by welcoming and appreciating parents and families is an essential foundation. Below are several specific ways teachers can develop the home-school partnership even further.

1. *Warmly greet and acknowledge the adults who bring in and/or pick up their children each day.* Welcome them by name, ask how they are. Just as with their children, it is vital to set a tone of welcome and caring, one that invites the parents into your center without judgment or discomfort. While teachers greet the children and help them settle, being available to parents for a few minutes at beginning and end-of-day transition times is crucial: opportunities to connect with parents are more limited.

2. *Create a physical space where parents can chat for a few minutes with each other* at arrival and departure times. Suggestions include:

✓ Reserve "parent space" in an adjacent office, alcove, or corner of the preschool room or hallway.

✓ Provide a couple of chairs and a table with information for parents.

✓ If the space is comfortable and inviting, parents are more likely to feel welcome.

✓ Label the area *Family Place* or *Parent Corner.*

✓ Post important parent information along with additional artwork, photographs of the children at play, and reminders of deadlines and upcoming events.

✓ If possible, have coffee, hot water for tea, or juice available for parents to encourage them to stay a few minutes and socialize with each other.

3. *Create a parent resource area,* preferably in your Parent Corner.

✓ Hang a bulletin board to display all essential notices (emergency procedures, center schedule, fee payment deadlines, etc.) and also to post information regarding community events, adult education, social services, free community activities for children and families, etc.

✓ Leave a corner of the board available for parents to post *SWAP* lists of items needed and items for sale or trade.

✓ Provide a box for parents to leave and take shopping coupons.

✓ Provide a basket to trade winter coats and boots.

✓ Provide a basket for parents to leave food to donate to a local food bank or for other parents to take.

4. *Develop a parent lending library,* which includes a variety of books on parenting and child development. Many parents find it extremely helpful to have a teacher recommend a specific book or article on parenting issues such as children's sleep problems or how to help a child cope with divorce. This kind of library not only enhances a parent's knowledge of the topic, it also fosters improved communication between parent and teacher around the issues affecting children.

5. *Develop a child lending library,* which includes a variety of children's stories and simple nonfiction books concerning the world in which children live. Creating a simple system for borrowing books overnight or over the weekend serves a number of purposes:

✓ It promotes reading as an important life skill and an activity to enjoy.

✓ It encourages parent-child interaction through reading.

✓ It provides an opportunity for children to share with their parents stories or subjects of interest from their school day.

✓ It provides a bridge between home and school.

Include some *Books on tape*. These often appeal to children who spend lots of time alone and are also very helpful for encouraging reading in families where adult literacy may be a concern.

6. *Introduce parent breakfasts on a periodic basis*, perhaps once a month. To encourage parents to take a few moments to visit and socialize, have coffeecakes, rolls, or donuts available in the Parent Corner. Try to schedule teaching staff to be available to parents as much as possible, perhaps rotating classroom coverage in order to free up a teacher to talk with parents. Some centers hold this breakfast in the classroom, allowing parents and children to mingle, play, and socialize with each other. This arrangement facilitates family relationships and allows teachers to be easily available to children and their parents. If this arrangement is your choice, set up the refreshment area in a part of the room where extended parent-parent conversations will not disrupt the flow of children's activities.

7. *Hold monthly family events*. The purpose of family events is to help parents develop a sense a community and build relationships with and between families. Family events may take many forms such as

- ✓ suppers or breakfasts at the child care center.
- ✓ weekend projects or outings.
- ✓ interactive educational/craft activities for parents and children.

Frequently these are seasonal, perhaps celebrating a holiday or seasonal transition. Family events may celebrate a special theme such as literacy. Successful events adhere to two basic principles: (1) Be sure that at least part of the event includes both parents and their children, and (2) Plan the timing of the event to accommodate busy working families who often have other children. For example, more families are likely to attend a special pumpkin carving night if it begins with a light supper at 5:30 followed by the carving activity. Once they have picked up their children and given them dinner, most parents will not be eager to return to the child care center for a 7:00 p.m. activity, no matter how exciting.

Occasionally, centers offer a combined educational/entertainment event: parents and a speaker discuss a particular issue such as discipline, while the children are led in an activity of their own. Afterwards, parents and children come together to do a craft, make cookies, etc. This kind of activity is more likely to be successful if the parent topic is one which they have requested (perhaps how to help children dealing with the loss of a loved one or how to channel a very active child's energies in positive ways) and if the children and parents' activities are related.

8. *Offer special, small group activities when several families in your center are facing a similar situation*. For instance, if several parents are expecting another child or have just had another baby, you might consider

holding a *Baby Night*. For this event, a speaker may facilitate parent discussion around parent questions and concerns while a teacher leads activities dealing with babies and what it means to be a big brother or big sister. Afterward, parents and children together create a *Big Brother/Big Sister and Baby Bag*, which might include a few basic baby supplies and a couple new storybooks for the older child. As a follow-up, teachers could provide space to display photographs of the new big brothers/big sisters and their little siblings. Similar events can be planned if several children are experiencing parental divorce, or similar loss, or anticipate a special event such a trip to the zoo.

9. *Encourage parent participation throughout the day*. Find out about special skills, interests, or history of family members and invite them to come in and share it with the class. Parents or other relatives might be eager to come on a regular basis to read stories or play and sing music with the children. Even parents who work a typical eight hour day can sometimes make arrangements to visit once a month to join the children for lunch or story time.

10. *Encourage family participation and support of your social curriculum through the* Tips for Parents *pages* (see pp. 273). These one-page hand-outs serve two purposes:

1. They let parents know the particular social skills and topics their children have been focusing on at school.
2. They include suggestions for ways parents can encourage these same behaviors at home.

Provide an area in your *Parent Corner* or right next to the sign in-out book where parents can drop off the handout with their own comments. Sometimes parents forget to return the completed pages. The following ideas have been found to be helpful in assuring the rate of the completed pages:

✓ Hand the *Tips for Parents* directly to the parents. Tell the parent what the topic is and ask them to return it the next day. This could take as little as 30 seconds, yet it provides an opportunity for staff to connect with parents on a positive topic.
✓ The next morning, ask each parent for the completed *Tips for Parents*. This, too, could take as little as 30 seconds.
✓ Have extra *Tips for Parents* available and hand them directly to parents who have forgotten to return them.
✓ Highlight the theme of the *Tips for Parents* with special posters, mobiles, etc. to emphasize the subject and the parents' participation at home.

✓ Keep a record of all returned *Tips for Parents* and have the children graph their family participation.
✓ Offer incentives for completion of *Tips for Parents* activities—weekly stickers, bulletin board graphs, a grab bag or small quarterly prizes for 100% participation.
✓ Provide parents with magnets so the *Tips for Parents* can be posted on the refrigerator.

11. *Routinely send parents brief written notes or memos to share highlights of their child's day.* All parents love to hear of their children's triumphs, special moments, and funny comments. When teachers have been communicating with parents in an appreciative and supportive way, it is easier to establish a working partnership to address the issue when a child demonstrates concerning behavior.

12. *Provide parents with short memos where they can tell YOU about a highlight or funny comment their child made at home.* Home-center communication should work both ways, and it is wonderful to have a mechanism for sharing positive information and appreciation for the children in your care. The child then receives the extra acknowledgement of both teacher and parent. This two-way communication then allows the parent to more comfortably discuss any questions or concerns which may arise.

13. *Hold periodic parent-teacher conferences* at least twice a year to (1) discuss parents' observations concerning their children's needs and growth and (2) to share classroom observations.

These conferences are opportunities to share developmental accomplishments and strengths as well as to note areas where more help might be needed. With the parents, develop one or two common goals, which both family and center will work toward on behalf of the child. For example, a common goal might be for the child to become a better listener or learn how to play cooperatively with one or two friends.

Conferences SHOULD
✓ feel comfortable to both parent and teacher and support a parent / teacher partnership.
✓ cover areas which have been informally discussed in daily interaction or notes between home and school.

Conferences SHOULD NOT
✓ be an opportunity for teachers to challenge parenting skills.
✓ list complaints and concerns which either teacher or parent has been "saving up" for the conference.

14. *Responding quickly to situations of concern and maintaining good home-center communication* is critical to helping children grow in healthy ways.

Ask for a parent meeting immediately if a behavior causes significant concern. Also, encourage parents to contact you immediately if they have concerns which involve their child's behavior or an incident which occurred at the center. For example, parent meetings are helpful when a child

- ✓ begins to bite others or is frequently the victim of biters.
- ✓ is unable to sit for as little as five minutes.
- ✓ has revealed a strong fear of someone in his environment, etc.

Parent meetings must be held if there are behaviors which present significant safety concerns or indicate that the child requires more care than your preschool environment can offer. For example, a child who

- ✓ consistently hurts himself until he is bruised or bleeding.
- ✓ hurts other children throughout the day despite teacher's interventions.
- ✓ identifies a specific child to hurt.
- ✓ uses vulgar or other inappropriate language.

It is important to hold a parent meeting when there are less serious, but still troubling behaviors. This allows the teacher and the parent to work together to address the concern. In these meetings, it is important to

- ✓ describe classroom observations and concerns.
- ✓ find out what the parents have noticed about particular behavior at home.
- ✓ find out how parents have handled this behavior successfully at home.
- ✓ discuss with parents other strategies that might be helpful.
- ✓ decide on and give the parent a copy of a plan for responding to this behavior at home and school.
- ✓ plan a time to meet again to consider whether or not the behavior has improved and what else may need to be done.

Summary

For a child to have successful preschool experiences, parents must feel confident of the care their children are receiving. When teachers welcome and encourage parent participation, communication, and planning, and when teachers respect parents' needs and knowledge of their children, parents are more likely to trust and appreciate their children's child care world, and a true home-center partnership can grow.

TIPS FOR PARENTS

Raising a Kinder, Gentler Child

Carol had a splitting headache. She slumped down in her chair with her head in her hand. Her son, Tony, came over and asked if Carol was sick. He patted her arm, and a few minutes later, came back with his stuffed bunny. "Here, Mommy" he said. "Sit with Bunny. He always helps me feel better." At one time or another, we all have been touched by a child's simple, heartfelt gesture of caring or concern for another child, an adult or a pet. It is wonderful how a child with so little experience can offer so much with a pat, a hug, or an offer of help. Caring about others and taking time and energy to consider someone else's feelings and needs are key qualities in a healthy family and a strong community. This instinct needs to be nurtured in children if we want them to grow into considerate, responsible adults who are good friends and good neighbors. Here are some ideas you can try.

Give your child an important job to do. Children need a sense of belonging. One way to get it is to contribute to the family by helping with the daily chores. With coaching, even children as young as three or four can help to set the table, pick out the groceries, water the plants, feed the pets, pack a lunch—the list is endless! Be sure to let them know how much you appreciate their efforts, even if they need some help to get the job done.

Encourage your child to be a good friend. If a classmate, a friend or a relative is ill or in difficulty, talk to your child about what he can do to help that person feel better. Perhaps you could make a card together, or bake some cookies, or plan a visit. Sometimes helping your child to make a thoughtful phone call is enough to make a difference.

Help your child to find good "heroes." There are lots of books and videos about famous people who committed their lives to helping others. Ask your local children's librarian for suggestions. There are probably many people right in your family and community who are good role models for helping others. Make sure your child gets to know some of them.

Remember that the apple doesn't fall far from the tree! What may work best in teaching your child to care about others is to show him how you live by this principle in your own life. If you do volunteer work for your church, school or community—bring your child along some day. If you're going out to assist a sick neighbor, let your child help you to get ready. If you're not involved in any volunteer activities, think about what you might have to offer. Nothing makes you feel quite as good as helping someone who needs a hand. Ask any child—he'll tell you!

During the past three weeks we have been talking about Kindness at school. There are many opportunities for children to show kindness and consideration of others. _____ can be very kind and helpful. One example we have seen at school is:

_____

_____

_____

Your child must have a good role model at home!

BINGHAM EARLY CHILDHOOD PROSOCIAL BEHAVIOR PROGRAM

Kindness

During the past three weeks we have been talking about *Kindness* in our classroom. You received *Tips for Parents*, which included ideas to support your child's learning about kindness.

Please check one box for each question.

1. Have you noticed a change in the acts of *kindness* (words or acts of kindness, consideration, helpfulness) your child shows at home in the past three weeks?

   ☐ same number of acts of kindness
   ☐ more acts of kindness
   ☐ fewer acts of kindness

2. I tried *Tips for Parents* on *Raising a Kinder, Gentler Child*. They:

   ☐ helped a lot
   ☐ helped some
   ☐ helped a little
   ☐ did not help at all   or
   ☐ I did not try *Tips for Parents* this week.

3. Are you satisfied with how things are going in your child's preschool classroom?

   ☐ very satisfied
   ☐ mostly satisfied
   ☐ mostly unsatisfied
   ☐ not satisfied at all

Please give your comments about what is going well or concerns about what is not going well:

_____
_____
_____
_____
_____

Do not sign your name on this questionnaire.

Thank you for your help. Please return this questionnaire to your child's teacher. An envelope is provided for confidentiality.

TIPS FOR PARENTS

Helping Children to Identify and Express Emotions

When David arrived at school this morning, he was very quiet and did not want to play with the other children. He roamed around the room, unable to find an activity to hold his interest. His teacher asked him if he was O.K. but David just sucked this thumb and didn't say anything. David's grandmother had moved away over the weekend and he was feeling very sad. He wanted a hug and to sit in his teacher's lap but he didn't know how to ask or to explain how he was feeling.

Learning to identify and express emotions helps children to take care of themselves because it helps them to tell others what they need. Children who do not understand their feelings or who are not allowed to express their feelings in appropriate ways may get depressed or act their feelings out in ways that are unsafe for themselves or others.

Children need to know labels for their emotions: sad, happy, angry, afraid, and they need to know that their feelings are accepted. This is important for both boys and girls. Boys who are not allowed to express sadness or fear may not learn to respect others' feelings. Girls who are not allowed to be angry may not learn to stick up for themselves. Here are some things you can do to help your child learn about emotions.

1. Use emotion words yourself. For example "I'm feeling very happy right now because your Grandma is cooking my favorite dinner." Or "I'm angry that I will be late for work because you hid your shoes in the toy box."
2. Play games about likes and dislikes. For example, everyone in the family can name her most favorite and least favorite foods, animals or book characters.
3. Notice and respond to your child's emotions. It will help him to understand what is happening in his body and to know that his feelings are O.K. If your child has to go to the doctor for shots, for example, and becomes very quiet because he is afraid, you might say "You're looking kind of worried. It can be scary to get a shot because it hurts a little. I'll be right here with you and it will be over very quickly and will help to keep you healthy."
4. Talk with your child about how characters in books and on TV may feel and ask how she would feel in the same situation. Discuss *how* you know what someone is feeling. Is the person frowning,

smiling, stomping her feet? How would your child express that feeling?

If your child is acting on an emotion in a way that is unsafe or disrespectful, try to be clear that you understand his feelings; at the same time, you need to correct his behavior.

During the past three weeks we have been talking about *Understanding and Expressing Emotions.* Your child's feelings are important to us. With so many children in class, each with different interests, strengths, and experiences, it is important for him/her to know how to tell us and the other children what he's/she's feeling so we know what he/she needs.

Here is an example of how _____ shared how he/she was feeling:

_____

_____

_____

We'd like to hear about your experience at home! A questionnaire will be coming!

BINGHAM EARLY CHILDHOOD PROSOCIAL
BEHAVIOR PROGRAM

Emotions

During the past three weeks we have been talking about *Emotions* in our classroom: Understanding and Expressing Emotions. You received *Tips for Parents*, which included ideas to support your child's learning about feelings.

Please check one box for each question.

1. Have you noticed a change in your child's *understanding of feelings* at home in the past three weeks?

   ☐ seems to understand feelings about the same
   ☐ seems to understand feelings more
   ☐ seems to understand feelings less

2. Our last unit was about *kindness*. Have you noticed further changes in *acts of kindness at home* (kind words, consideration, helpfulness)?

   ☐ same number of acts of kindness
   ☐ more acts of kindness
   ☐ fewer acts of kindness

3. I tried *Tips for Parents* on Helping Children to Identify and Express Feelings. They:

   ☐ helped a lot
   ☐ helped some
   ☐ helped a little
   ☐ did not help at all   or
   ☐ I did not try *Tips for Parents* this week.

4. Are you satisfied with how things are going in your child's preschool classroom?

   ☐ very satisfied
   ☐ mostly satisfied
   ☐ mostly unsatisfied
   ☐ not satisfied at all

Please give your comments about what is going well or concerns about what is not going well.

_____

_____

_____

Do not sign your name on this questionnaire.

Thank you for your help! Please return this questionnaire to your child's teacher. An envelope is provided for confidentiality.

TIPS FOR PARENTS

Respecting Self and Others

One day Tamara and her mother were grocery shopping. As they turned into the next aisle they passed an over-weight woman. Tamara exclaimed in a loud voice, "Mommy, look at that fat, fat, lady!"

This situation shows that preschool children are beginning to notice differences in people. It is natural for children to be curious about differences and ask questions or make comments. Sometimes we may find these comments rude, embarrassing or hurtful. However, this can be an opportunity to help your child learn to treat others with respect.

Respecting yourself and others is important in a healthy family and to build a strong community. Being respectful must be nurtured in children if we want them to grow into responsible and respectful adults. Here are some ideas you can try to help your child learn to respect herself and others.

Talk about differences in people. Look at a family picture together. Talk about the differences among your family members. Some of us are tall and some short, some are thin and others heavy, your child is young and his grandparents are older, some of us have lighter skin while others are darker, Aunt Millie uses a cane to help her walk, etc. Look at books, magazines and newspapers together and talk about differences in physical characteristics: skin color, eye color, hair color and texture, and body size. Some people have differing abilities. For example, some people are born with legs that aren't very strong, so they need a wheelchair or brace to help them move from place to place. Also talk about differences in national origin and language. If we respect others, we must allow and appreciate differences.

Teach your child to be proud of who she is. Talk to her about where she was born, where her ancestors were from, what physical characteristics she has. Help her understand her strengths, abilities, and what she may need help with. For example, "You were born with very, very strong legs so you can run fast. Your eyes are not quite so strong, so you need glasses to help you see clearly."

If your child says or does things that are disrespectful or that show prejudice toward others talk to him about it right away. Make it clear that it is not right to be mean or treat people poorly. For example, calling an over-weight person fat might hurt his feelings. Talk about what makes him sad or angry. Words can make others sad or angry so we should choose our words carefully. Talk about words that are kind and unkind and write them down.

Help your child learn to respect all living things. Have her help care for plants and pets in your home. Talk about responsibility and what would happen if we did not take care of living things.

Be a good role model. Children are learning how to treat others by what adults do or say. If we all treat people with respect and kindness that is what children will learn!

During the past three weeks we have been talking about respect at school. There are many opportunities for children to show respect for him/herself and others. _____ can be very respectful. One example we have seen at school is:

_____

_____

Your child must have a good role model at home!

BINGHAM EARLY CHILDHOOD PROSOCIAL
BEHAVIOR PROGRAM

Respect

During the past three weeks we have been talking about *Respect* in our classroom: *Respecting Self and Others.* You received *Tips for Parents*, which included ideas to support your child's learning about respect.

Please check one box for each question.

1. Have you noticed a change in your child's *respectful behaviors* at home in the past three weeks?

   ☐ same amount of respectful behaviors
   ☐ more respectful behaviors
   ☐ less respectful behaviors

   Comment about what your child did or said to show respect:

   _____
   _____
   _____
   _____

2. I tried *Tips for Parents* on *Respecting Self and Others.* They:

   ☐ helped a lot
   ☐ helped some
   ☐ helped a little
   ☐ did not help at all   or
   ☐ I did not try *Tips for Parents* this week.

   What are the ways we can make these *Tips* more useful to you?

   _____
   _____
   _____
   _____

3. Our first unit was about *Kindness.* Have you noticed further changes in your child's acts of kindness (words of acts of kindness, consideration, helpfulness)?

   ☐ same number of acts of kindness
   ☐ more acts of kindness
   ☐ fewer acts of kindness

4. Our second unit was about *Understanding and Expressing Emotions.* Have you noticed further changes in your child's understanding and expressing emotions?

☐ seems to understand and express feelings about the same
☐ seems to understand and express feelings more
☐ seems to understand and express feelings less

5. Are you satisfied with how things are going in your child's preschool classroom?

☐ very satisfied
☐ mostly satisfied
☐ mostly unsatisfied
☐ not satisfied at all

Please give your comments about what is going well or concerns about what is not going well:

_____

_____

Do not sign your name on this questionnaire.

Thank you for your help! Please return this questionnaire to your child's teacher. An envelope is provided for confidentiality.

TIPS FOR PARENTS

Fostering Cooperation and Sharing

How many times do we say to children, "I want you to share your toys?" Most of us agree that this is very hard for children, and that it is too much to expect a child to share their brand new doll or puzzle with others. However, we all hope that children will learn to cooperate and share with others as they get older. Through cooperation, children learn to compromise, negotiate and share.

Here are some ways you can teach cooperation and sharing at home:

- Talk about the many things your family does together. Do you grocery shop or put groceries away together? Do you all gather laundry and go to the aundromat together? Point out the differences in doing things alone and working together as a family. What jobs do you do at home that someone helps you with?
- Having your child help with chores around the house can help him learn to cooperate. Sorting laundry, wiping the table and cooking are ways your child can work with you and learn to cooperate. Talk about what would happen if one person had to do all the jobs. Pick a room at home to clean together. (Children are good at dusting and sweeping floors!) While you work, talk about how nice it is to have cooperation and sharing of chores.
- Plant a family garden of flowers or vegetables, or plant seeds or bulbs in a pot. Decide together who will water, weed and pick flowers or vegetables. Talk often about how the garden or plant is growing, how it belongs to everyone, and how everyone is sharing the work of caring for plants.
- When your child has to wait for a turn with a toy, you can help her find another way to continue her play. For example, if your child and her cousin are arguing over a shovel, you can point out that she could move sand with the rake until it is her turn to use the shovel.
- Bake cookies or bread together and share some with a neighbor. Talk about cooperation and sharing in the neighborhood. Have your child go with you to deliver the treats.
- Go for a walk together and gather leaves, flowers, small sticks, acorns, etc. Explain to your child that you are going to cooperate in making a nature collage. When you come home, work together gluing items to cardboard or thick paper. Put both your names on the

paper and point out that it took cooperation to make such a lovely picture!

Here is an example of how _____ cooperated or shared at school.

_____
_____
_____

We would like to hear about your experience at home! A questionnaire will be coming!

BINGHAM EARLY CHILDHOOD PROSOCIAL BEHAVIOR PROGRAM

Cooperation

During the past three weeks we have been talking about *Cooperation and Sharing* in our classroom. You received *Tips for Parents*, which included ideas to support your child's learning about cooperation.

Please check one box for each question.

1. Have you noticed a change in your child's *cooperation and sharing* at home in the past three weeks?

   ☐ same amount of cooperation
   ☐ more cooperation
   ☐ less cooperation

   Comments about what your child did to show cooperation:
   _____
   _____
   _____

2. I tried *Tips for Parents* on **Cooperation and Sharing**. They:

   ☐ helped a lot
   ☐ helped some
   ☐ helped a little
   ☐ did not help at all   or
   ☐ I did not try *Tips for Parents* this week.

   What are the ways we can make these *Tips* more useful to you?
   _____
   _____

3. Our first unit was about *Kindness*. Have you noticed further changes in your child's acts of kindness (words of acts of kindness, consideration, helpfulness)?

   ☐ same number of acts of kindness
   ☐ more acts of kindness
   ☐ fewer acts of kindness

4. Our second unit was about *Understanding and Expressing Emotions*. Have you noticed further changes in your child's understanding and expressing emotions?

☐ seems to understand and express feelings about the same
☐ seems to understand and express feelings more
☐ seems to understand and express feelings less

5. Our third unit was about *Respect for Self and Others*. Have you noticed further changes in your child's respectful behaviors?

☐ same amount of respectful behaviors
☐ more respectful behaviors
☐ less respectful behaviors

6. Are you satisfied with how things are going in your child's preschool classroom?

☐ very satisfied
☐ mostly satisfied
☐ mostly unsatisfied
☐ not satisfied at all

Please give your comments about what is going well or concerns about what is not going well:

_____

_____

_____

Do not sign your name on this questionnaire.

Thank you for your help. Please return this questionnaire to your child's teacher. An envelope is provided for confidentiality.

TIPS FOR PARENTS

Helping Children with Self-Control: Anger Management

Handling children's anger can be puzzling, draining and distressing for adults. Parents of preschoolers are often challenged by their children's anger. Because young children have difficulty understanding someone else's point of view and often don't know how to talk about their anger, these children may exhibit aggression as a kind of natural response to being angry. Such is the case with Maria in the example below.

> Four-year-old Maria is sitting at the kitchen table drawing with her crayons. Amber, Maria's two year-old sister, is seated across the table, drinking a cup of juice and watching Maria at work. "I want crayon!" Amber demands. "I'm using them now," Maria replies. Amber reaches across the table for a crayon and spills her juice on Maria's picture. Maria slaps Amber's hand and screams "I hate you, Amber! You always ruin my things!"

As Maria and Amber's parent, you would most likely be upset by how Maria reacted. How might you help her to manage her emotions without being aggressive? We can help children to manage anger in the following ways:

- Naming the emotion
- Accepting the anger as a normal feeling
- Helping her to channel her anger appropriately

Maria's parent might want to say "Maria, I can see that you are feeling very angry with Amber right now. Amber ruined your picture and you have a right to be mad, but it's not okay to hit her. Tell Amber "I don't like it when you take my things and ruin them."

Depending on how upset Maria is, she may need a cooling off period before talking it out. Some children need to be directed to a cooling off area such as their bedroom. For Maria, as for most children, anger can be a scary and overwhelming emotion. Both hurting her sister and disappointing her parent are actions that make Maria feel out of control and unsafe. Having her help take care of Amber and then helping her to get started on a new picture in a place where she won't be disturbed might make Maria feel less afraid of her actions and reassure her that she is still loved.

Bingham Early Childhood Prosocial Behavior Program

We work hard at school to help children use their words to express their anger and to work out conflicts with other children. Here is a recent example of how _____ was able to talk about being angry instead of hitting or fighting.

_____

_____

_____

We would like to hear about your experience at home. A questionnaire will be coming!

BINGHAM EARLY CHILDHOOD PROSOCIAL BEHAVIOR PROGRAM

Self-Control

During the past few weeks we have been talking about *Self-Control and Anger Management* in our classroom. You received *Tips for Parents*, which included ideas to support your child's learning about anger management.

Please check one box for each question.

1. Have you noticed any change in the way your child *manages anger* at home in the past three weeks?

   ☐ manages anger in about the same way
   ☐ manages anger more appropriately
   ☐ manages anger less appropriately

   Comment about how your child manages anger:

   _____

   _____

2. I tried *Tips for Parents* on *Helping Children Manage Anger*. The *Tips*:

   ☐ helped a lot
   ☐ helped some
   ☐ helped a little
   ☐ did not help at all   or
   ☐ *I did not try Tips for Parents this week.*

3. Our first unit was about *Kindness*. Have you noticed further changes in your child's acts of kindness (words of acts of kindness, consideration, helpfulness)?

   ☐ same number of acts of kindness
   ☐ more acts of kindness
   ☐ fewer acts of kindness

4. Our second unit was about *Understanding and Expressing Emotions*. Have you noticed further changes in your child's understanding and expressing emotions?

   ☐ seems to understand and express feelings about the same
   ☐ seems to understand and express feelings more
   ☐ seems to understand and express feelings less

5. Our third unit was about *Respect for Self and Others*. Have you noticed further changes in your child's respectful behaviors?

   ☐ same amount of respectful behaviors
   ☐ more respectful behaviors
   ☐ less respectful behaviors

6. Our fourth unit was about *Cooperation and Sharing*. Have you noticed further changes in your child's cooperation and sharing at home?

   ☐ same amount of cooperation
   ☐ more cooperation
   ☐ less cooperation

7. Are you satisfied with how things are going in your child's preschool classroom?

   ☐ very satisfied
   ☐ mostly satisfied
   ☐ mostly unsatisfied
   ☐ not satisfied at all

Please give your comments about what is gong well or concerns about what is not going well?

_____

_____

Do not sign your name on this questionnaire.

Thank you for your help. Please return this questionnaire to your child's teacher. An envelope is provided for confidentiality.

TIPS FOR PARENTS

Guiding Your Child's USE of the Media

Watched any good TV lately? Many TV programs, videos and computer games are giving children the wrong messages about violence. It is important that we understand the impact of media on children.

Research shows that too much TV, video or computer use can negatively affect young minds.

- Too much viewing is associated with lower school performance, especially reading scores.
- Some children develop attention problems from watching too much TV.
- If children watch too many violent acts on TV movies, or computer games they may behave more aggressively or violently. They may become fearful and see the world as a mean and scary place.

Here are some suggestions to make television a more positive family experience.

- *Set limits on how much screen time your child spends each day.* The American Academy of Pediatrics recommends no more than two hours per day total viewing time, including TV, videos, and computer games, for young children.
- *Choose programs and games carefully.* Check the rating of TV, movies and computer games. Do not allow your child to watch shows, movies, or play computer games with too much violence, sexual content, bigotry or where people treat others in a mean or unkind way.
- *Make TV watching a family event.* Watch with your children whenever possible. Talk to your child about what you are seeing and hearing. "That man was angry so he hit the other man. What else could he do if he is angry that doesn't hurt others?"
- *Know when to say "No!"* "This is not a good program for us to watch. I am turning it off (or changing channels) now and we will find something else to do."

There are many choices of fun things to do other than watching TV. Here is an idea that your child _____ suggested instead of watching

TV:_____

_____

_____

_____

BINGHAM EARLY CHILDHOOD PROSOCIAL
BEHAVIOR PROGRAM

Media

During the past few weeks we have been talking about the media: T.V., videos and computer games. You received *Tips for Parents,* which included ideas to support your child's learning about the media.

Please check one box for each question.

1. Have you noticed any changes in how much time you spend together with your child watching TV or playing computer games?

   ☐ no change
   ☐ spend more time lately
   ☐ spend less time lately

2. How much time do you and your child usually spend watching TV or playing computer games together?

   ☐ less than an hour a day for most weeks
   ☐ between one hour and two hours a day for most weeks
   ☐ more than two hours a day for most weeks

3. How much time do you and your child usually spend watching TV or playing computer games alone?

   ☐ less than an hour a day for most weeks
   ☐ between one hour and two hours a day for most weeks
   ☐ more than two hours a day for most weeks

4. How much time do you and your child usually spend watching TV or playing computer games with siblings?

   ☐ less than an hour a day for most weeks
   ☐ between one hour and two hours a day for most weeks
   ☐ more than two hours a day for most weeks

5. I tried *Tips for Parents* on *Guiding Your Child's Use of the Media.* The *Tips*:

   ☐ helped a lot
   ☐ helped some

☐ helped a little
☐ did not help at all   or
☐ I did not try *Tips for Parents* this week.

6. Our first unit was about *Kindness*. Have you noticed further changes in your child's acts of kindness (words or acts of kindness, consideration, helpfulness)?

   ☐ same number of acts of kindness
   ☐ more acts of kindness
   ☐ fewer acts of kindness

7. Our second unit was about *Understanding and Expressing Emotions*. Have you noticed further changes in your child's understanding and expressing emotions?

   ☐ seems to understand and express feelings about the same
   ☐ seems to understand and express feelings more
   ☐ seems to understand and express feelings less

8. Our third unit was about *Respect for Self and Others*. Have you noticed further changes in your child's respectful behaviors?

   ☐ same amount of respectful behaviors
   ☐ more respectful behaviors
   ☐ less respectful behaviors

9. Our fourth unit was about *Cooperation and Sharing*. Have you noticed further changes in your child's cooperation and sharing at home?

   ☐ same amount of cooperation
   ☐ more cooperation
   ☐ less cooperation

10. Have you noticed any change in the way your child *manages anger* at home?

    ☐ manages anger in about the same way
    ☐ manages anger more appropriately
    ☐ manages anger less appropriately

11. Are you satisfied with how things are going in your child's preschool classroom?

    ☐ very satisfied
    ☐ mostly satisfied
    ☐ mostly unsatisfied
    ☐ not satisfied at all

Please give comments about what is going well or concerns about what is not going well:

_____

_____

_____

Do not sign your name on this questionnaire.

Thank you for your help. Please return this questionnaire to your child's teacher. An envelope is provided for confidentiality.

APPENDIX

The following pages include activities for each Bingham concept. While the activities have been categorized by theme, many can be used to teach more than one Bingham concept. The five themes are: Kindness, Emotions, Respect, Cooperation, and Self-Control. Labels on the bottom right hand corner of each page easily identify themes. Each theme contains the following sections: Changes to the Environment, Group Time Discussions, Books, Small and Large Group Activities: Art, Sensory, Games, Science, Movement, and Miscellaneous, Parent Participation: Prop Bag and Weekly Tips. The last theme is the Effect of Media on Young Children. It is set up differently: Group Time Discussions, Book Lists for Children and Parents, Classroom Activities, Parent Participation: Prop Bags, Fun Activities and Weekly Tips.

These activities have been used in several classrooms. The Helpful Hints section in some of the activities was created when changes needed to be made in order to benefit different groups of children. It is important to continue to modify these activities when necessary.

The Weekly Tips for Parents are to be photocopied at the beginning of each theme and handed out to parents on the first day of each week. Designate part of a bulletin board for parent feedback. Staple blank paper and attach a marker. Encourage them to write about their experiences.

Suggestions are made for Prop Bags. These are cloth sacks or shopping bags that contain items related to one particular activity. Some Prop Bag activities include a Feedback Form for parents to complete and return to the center. It is important to display the completed forms immediately to show that the hard work of the parent is respected and appreciated.

At the end of the activities is a complete list of the books and useful Internet websites. The Early Childhood websites are a great source for songs, poems, and finger plays to accompany these themes. For example, the themes "community helpers" and "friendship" contains songs that promote kindness, cooperation, and respect. The Internet Web sites are current as of October 2002.

CONTENTS

KINDNESS

Changes to the Environment

Dramatic Play

- ✓ Doctor's Office: dolls, clipboards, paper, pencils, doctor kit, real bandages, gauze, cloth bandages, and telephone.
- ✓ Grocery Store: empty food boxes (real), paper/plastic grocery bags, cash register, money, purses, wallets, grocery cart (play), grocery basket (real-most grocery stores are nice enough to let you borrow one or two), paper, pencils, coupons.
- ✓ Flower Shop: plastic flowers, notepads, pencils, telephone, cash register, money, flower catalog/magazines, and cardboard cones to hold flowers (check recycling center).

Sensory

- ✓ Washing baby dolls: multicultural dolls, soapy water, sponges, clothes, and towels.
- ✓ Fresh flowers
- ✓ Potting soil, plastic or real flowers, plastic planting containers.
- ✓ Flower seeds, cups, scoops, spoons, and funnels.

Art

- ✓ Large paper that children can draw on together if they choose to.
- ✓ List of children's names with matching photos (so children can give their art to another child and attempt to write the child's name).
- ✓ Heart shaped stencils in various sizes.

Writing

- ✓ List of children's names with matching photos.
- ✓ Picture dictionary: photos of kind acts and corresponding words (helping, sharing, listening, caring, kindness, friendly, etc.)

Science/Discovery

- ✓ Planting: plastic cups, potting soil, seeds, and watering cans.

Manipulatives/Math

- ✓ Heart shapes of different sizes and colors for sorting and classifying.
- ✓ Flower memory game: either create your own flowers or use stickers on $1/2$ an index card to make this game.

Blocks

> ✓ Add road map, vehicles and signs to encourage community kindness.

Group Time Discussion Ideas

1. Kindness questions:
   - ✓ What does being kind mean?
   - ✓ How do you feel when you are kind to someone?
   - ✓ How do you feel when someone is kind to you?
   - ✓ Can you be kind to someone you do not know?
   - ✓ Can you be kind to someone you do not like?
2. Kindness vocabulary: nice, manners, polite, favors, friendly, kind, help
3. *Photographs*: show photos (clip from magazines/newspaper) of acts of kindness and ask kindness questions. Share our own stories with each other.
4. Introduce kindness bulletin board. In advance prepare a card for each child with an act of kindness written on it. Read the cards as you staple them to the board. Add to the display daily. At group time each day read all or at least new additions. Variation: kindness tree or kindness jar.
5. Discuss opportunities to demonstrate kindness in dramatic play. Ask the children to help with preparation.
   - ✓ Cut paper to fit on clipboards
   - ✓ Cut out coupons
   - ✓ Bring in materials from home (coupons, bags, empty food boxes)
   - ✓ Create cards for flower shop
6. *Who Is It?* Activity.
7. *What is a hero?* Define heroes and identify several from the community (newspaper or TV segments) and from our culture. Identify local roles of people who perform heroic acts like nurses, doctors and firefighters. Compare and contrast with the "heroes" that children see on their television shows: how are they alike or different? Discuss ways that children can be heroes to others. Plan and execute an activity that the children can do to be "heroes" in some way to someone else in their class or community (i.e., a neighborhood cleanup, making pictures for residents of a nursing home, etc). Guide a discussion about what activities are considered in the classroom. Design badges or ribbons to reward "heroic deeds" in

the classroom. Create a system for recognizing "heroic deeds" in the classroom.

8. *Good deeds*: This strategy helps children to understand what goods deeds are as they are reinforced throughout the day.

   ✓ Create several sets of badges or computer generated stickers for the following behaviors:

   Sharing: a picture of two hands holding a ball
   Kindness: a picture of a heart
   Cooperation: a picture of two smiling faces
   Respect: a picture of two hands shaking, each a different skin tone.
   Self-control: a picture of an angry face that is counting to ten
   Empathy: a picture of an angry face and a smiling face

   ✓ Initially choose one behavior to recognize and define it with the children at group time. Each week add another behavior or emphasize a different behavior each week or month.
   ✓ Throughout each day, as children, demonstrate these behaviors, give them a badge/sticker recognizing the behavior. Periodically ask the children what they did to receive the badge.
   ✓ Each child must receive at least one badge each week.
   ✓ One alternative to the badges/stickers is a kindness/sharing/cooperation tree. This might be a small branch supported in a bucket of sand or a paper tree on a bulletin board. As the identified behavior is recognized, a new leaf is added to the tree with a brief description of the behavior.

Kindness Book List

Aliki *Manners*
Ancona, George *Helping Out*
Carle, Eric *A House For Hermit Crab*
Carrick, Carol *Mothers Are Like That*
Cazet, Denys *Born in the Gravy*
Erickson, Karen and Roffey, Maureen *I Like To Help*
Fox, Mem *Wilfrid Gordon McDonald Partridge*
Hafner, Marilyn *Mommies Don't Get Sick*
Henderson, Kathy, *Newborn*
Janowitz, Marilyn *Can I Help?*
Keister, Douglas *Ferdando's Gift*
Keller, Holly *Island Baby*
Novak, Matt *Jazzbo and Googy*

Roe, Eileen *With My Brother/Con Mi Hermano*
Russo, Marisabina *When Mama Gets Home*
Shaw, Charles Green *It Looked Like Spilt Milk*
Smalls, Irene *Kevin and His Dad*
Steig, William *Amos and Boris*
Torres, Leyla *Liliana's Grandmothers*
Turner, Ann Warren *Through Moon and Stars and Night Skies*
Urdy, Janice May *Is Susan Here?*
Wenninger, Brigette *Will You Mind the Baby, Davy?*

For You

Theme: Kindness
Targeted Skills: kindness, friendship, generosity
Materials: paper, crayons, markers, pencils or paint
Vocabulary: kind, generous, help, present
Group Size: 5
Process

1. Gather the children at the art table.
2. Talk about what it means to be kind.
3. Brainstorm ways to be kind to the people in your family.
4. Explain that they will make presents for their families. They will decorate cards and teachers will write the children's sentiments on them.
5. Send kindness cards home with a note asking family members to use a card each day.
6. Encourage family members to tell you (or write down) their children's acts of kindness and how the kindnesses made others feel.

Helpful Hints

1. Add your own ideas when brainstorming. "If I were a Dad, I would love for my child to help me do the dishes."
2. Index cards work well.
3. Talk about the cards being presents.

Kindness Tree

Theme: Kindness
Targeted Skills: kindness, community awareness, togetherness

Materials: Butcher block paper, water soluble brown paint, large paintbrushes, reliable smocks, leaf shaped construction paper in various colors (the children can trace and cut these out while others are painting.)
Vocabulary: kind, thoughtful, appreciate, compliment
Group Size: 6
Process

1. Draw a tree trunk (large enough for bulletin board) on butcher-block paper.
2. Have the children paint it brown.
3. Pair the children. Have them decide who will be the first painter.
4. The painter gets a paintbrush and brown paint and paints the fingers, palm, and inside forearm of the other child.
5. The painted child then makes a print at the top of the tree trunk.
6. Switch roles and repeat.
7. Have each child say something kind about his partner. Write this on a leaf and hang on the tree after it dries.
8. Add to tree daily and read at group time.

Kindness Caterpillars

Theme: Kindness
Targeted Skills: kindness, creativity, sharing
Materials: pom-poms, clothespins, glue, googly eyes, pipe cleaners, and magnetic strips
Vocabulary: kind, magnet, share
Group Size: 5
Process

1. Put all of the materials out on the table.
2. Have each child help you attach the magnetic strip to one side of the caterpillar (either self-sticking or glue on).
3. Let the children decorate their caterpillar any way they would like. Ask them to leave the magnetic side empty so it can hang on the refrigerator.
4. Allow to dry and send home with "Kindness, Tips for Parents"

Kindness Art Ideas

1. When children are at the art area, encourage them to make something for someone else. It could be a friend, teacher or family member. Encourage the children to think about the things this person

likes and enjoys. Ask the child if she would like to dictate a letter or note to this person.

2. If two or more children are at the art area, encourage them to make things for each other.
3. Join children at the art area and casually talk about a child that feels sad or does not feel well.

Who Is It?

Theme: Kindness
Targeted skills: friendship, listening, kindness
Materials: nothing
Vocabulary: familiar, describe, listen, kind
Group Size: whole class
Process

1. Invite the children to join you for a game called "Who Is It?" Explain that you are going to describe a child in the class and they will try to guess who it is.
2. Describe a child based on likes, dislikes, appearance, and family members.
3. Then describe how the child was kind that day.
4. After several clues tell them you are ready for some guesses.
5. If they do not guess correctly, give clues that will alert the child you are describing to the fact that it is she.
6. Repeat with another child.

Helpful Hints

1. This works well as a transition activity.
2. Before the activity, during free play, make comments to the children about what the others are doing. Use these as clues in the game.
3. When children have played the game several times, allow them to describe another child for others to guess.

Every Day is Earth Day

Theme: Kindness
Targeted Skills: cooperation, kindness, gentleness
Materials: tree, buckets/watering cans, fertilizer, mulch, and various garden tools

Vocabulary: teamwork, fertilizer, mulch, name of tree, trunk, branches, leaves
Group Size: whole group
Process

1. Gather the children for an outdoor group time.
2. Tell the children that you would like their help. Ask them to find a few small trees in or near the playground. Explain that in order for the trees to grow bigger, they need to be taken care of. Point out the benefits of full-grown trees such as shade and animal habitats.
3. Brainstorm ways to take care of trees/plants.
4. Show the children the tools you brought to group time.
5. Let each child help care for the tree.
6. Make a chart with different tasks and allow children to carry the tasks out each day.

Helpful Hints
If many children regularly show interest:

1. Have them care for other plants on the playground.
2. Plant seeds for indoor plants or an outdoor garden.
3. Create an indoor garden with donated plants.

Musical Hugs

Theme: Kindness
Targeted Skills: kindness, gentleness
Materials: music, floor space
Vocabulary: kind, gentle
Group Size: any
Process

1. Turn music on and begin to dance.
2. Pause the music
3. The children have to find a partner to hug. Often 2, 3, or more children hug each other.
4. Start the music and repeat until children are done

Kindness Quotes

"No act of kindness, no matter how small is ever wasted"

AESOP

"Even the smallest act of kindness says 'I care', says, 'you matter', says, 'I thought of you.'"

SIR ARTHUR HELPS

"If someone is too tired to give you a smile, leave one of your own, because no one needs a smile as much as those who have none to give.

RABBI SAMSON RAPHAEL HIRSCH

"Kindness in words creates confidence. Kindness in thinking creates profoundness. Kindness in giving creates love"

LAO-TZU

"One of the most difficult things to give away is kindness, for it is usually returned."

MARK ORMAN

"The unkind voices that surround us are loud and shrill, demanding our thoughtful and truthful attention. All the more reason then to listen for the soft breath of friendship and carry our reassuring stories above the din."

VIVIAN GUSSIN PALEY

"Guard well within yourself that treasure, kindness. Know how to give without hesitation, how to lose without regret, how to require without meanness."

GEORGE SAND

"Kind words can be short and easy to speak, but their echoes are endless."

MOTHER TERESA

"Never look down on anybody unless you're helping him up."

JESSE JACKSON

"When I was young, I admired clever people. Now that I am old, I admire kind people."

ABRAHAM JOSHUA HESCHEL

"You cannot do a kindness too soon, for you never know how soon it will be too late."

RALPH WALDO EMERSON

"Wherever there is a human being, there is an opportunity for kindness."

SENECA

Teacher Preparation for Prop Bag

Materials
   Crayons
   Markers
   Glue
   Scissors
   Tissue paper
   Construction paper
   Any other art materials
   Instruction Sheet
   Feedback Form

Prop Bag

Activity for Parents and Children; Estimated Time of Activity: 30 minutes

   1. Take the materials out of the bag.
   2. Let your child explore the materials
   3. Invite your child to start creating anything she would like
   4. Ask her what she is making
   5. Ask her if she is making it for herself or for someone else. IF she says herself, encourage her to make another for someone else. You can do this by giving your creation to her.
   6. Talk about how it feels to give her something and ask her how it feels to receive.

Feedback Form

Please take a few minutes to answer the following questions so we can continue to create activities that suit your needs as well as strengthen the bond between home and school.

1. How did you and your child use the materials in the bag?

2. What did you and your child like about the activity?

3. Please add any other comments or questions, including what you would change about this activity.

Weekly Tips for Parents (cut these apart and send home on Monday of each Kindness week)

✂ ---

With Your Family

1. Bake cookies together, and take them to a neighbor.
2. Walk to a nearby park and pick up trash, then have a picnic there.
3. Shovel snow or rake leaves for a neighbor.

At Work

1. Create a "You Are So Kind!" box where staff can leave notes about the kind acts of their coworkers. Hang them in your workplace. If you have customers, provide them with access to the "You Are So Kind" box. They can write kind things about staff. Hang these in a prominent area for customers to see.

✂ ---

With Your Family

1. Go to a children's zoo or a park where feeding animals is allowed. Bring extra food and share with another family.
2. Bake a treat and take it to a police or fire station.

At Work

1. Arrange to plant flowers or a tree at a school or park on a Saturday morning.
2. Leave flowers on a neighboring business's front step.
3. Clean up trash on a stretch of road near your work.

✂ ---

With Your Family

1. Clean up the yard of a neighbor or clean up a common area of your apartment complex.
2. Plant flowers at a neighborhood school or park.

At Work

1. Create "Pass it on" cards. The card should include the kind act and a reminder to pass it on. Start one yourself and give a friend another to start. Acts of kindness can include arranging for a parent to eat lunch at her child's school, filling an employee's desk drawer with snack food, bringing someone a coffee, etc.

✂ ---

With Your Family

1. Bring a neighbor's garbage cans in at the end of garbage day.
2. Volunteer with your children to help at a soup kitchen.

At Work

1. Pick up trash in the parking lot and on the grounds.
2. Organize spring and fall clean-up projects.

EMOTIONS

Changes to the Environment

Dramatic Play

- ✓ Costume Shop: masks, costumes, mirrors, face paint.
- ✓ Flower shop: plastic flowers, notepads, pencils, cash register, money, flower catalog/magazines, telephones, cardboard cones (to hold flowers)
- ✓ Housekeeping: clothing for different family roles, food and accessories, broom, mop, tool kit, telephone, baby dolls, etc.

Sensory

- ✓ Sand, sticks, unsharpened pencils, paintbrushes: draw faces in the sand
- ✓ Paper mache paste (see pp. 345–346)
- ✓ Play dough and hammers
- ✓ Potting soil, flowers, shovels, and buckets

Art

- ✓ Paper with different textures: tissue paper, copy paper, construction paper, wallpaper, sand paper, etc.
- ✓ Many different drawing tools: oil pastels, crayons, markers, chalk, colored pencils, charcoal (untreated), watercolors, etc.

Writing

- ✓ Picture Dictionary: facial expressions and situations with corresponding words; children's photos and names
- ✓ Greeting cards and envelopes

Science/Discovery

- ✓ Plastic cups, water, salt, eye droppers, tissue paper
- ✓ Mirrors for self discovery

Manipulatives/Math

- ✓ Photograph sorting (happy, sad, angry, frustrated)
- ✓ Feelings patterning: create happy, sad, angry faces on 6" paper plates (at least four of each emotion). Using roll paper, start a pattern: trace 6–10 plates in a row and add facial features (that match the plates) to the first 3–4. Leave the rest blank for the children to continue the pattern with the plates. Make a few different patterns.

Blocks

✓ Add people: ask questions regarding how they might feel if they were on top of the building, under the blocks, etc. Ask again when they use other dollhouse people: would the Mom feel the same way?

✓ In the following weeks, add jungle animals and/or dinosaurs. Pose the same questions.

Group Time Discussion Ideas

1. Identify emotions
   ✓ By name: happy, excited, lonely, sad, angry, frustrated, proud, bored, surprised, scared, afraid, disappointed, nervous, worried, grumpy, anxious . . .
   ✓ Using facial expressions: let the children watch your face as you say and show each emotion. Then have them watch each other or themselves in the mirror.
   ✓ By watching body language: use whole body to portray emotion (include tone of voice)
   ✓ By example: start to talk about specific incidents that occurred that day (or recently). Label the emotions by name. See if the children can remember the incidents and connect specific body language or facial expressions.
   ✓ Make a large cardboard picture frame and hold it up to your face. Make an emotional expression and ask children to identify the emotion and then copy it using the frame. That child can then make a new expression.
   ✓ Talk about your own emotions using real (appropriate) examples.
2. Appropriate expression of emotions and empathy for others.
   ✓ Ask the following questions and insert various emotions

   What do you do when you feel_____?
   What would you want your friend to do if you feel_____?
   What are some things that make you feel_____?

   ✓ Reinforce the importance of keeping yourself and others safe when you express emotions.
   ✓ Ask a child to show any emotion. Ask the following questions to the group. Repeat with different emotions. Record what is said and refer to it in real situations.

How does she feel?
How can you tell?
Why do you think she feels _____?
What could she do to make herself feel better?
How could YOU help this person feel better?
Did you feel_____today at school?
What do you do when you feel _____?

✓ Photograph games

Book List

Aaron, Jane *When I'm Afraid*
Aaron, Jane *When I'm Angry*
Amos, Janine *Feelings: Brave*
Amos, Janine *Feelings: Confident*
Bang, Molly *Delphine*
Bang, Molly *When Sophie Gets Angry, Really, Really Angry*
Bunting, Eve *Going Home*
Carr, Jan *Dark Day, Light Night*
Crary, Elizabeth *I'm Excited*
Crary, Elizabeth *I'm Frustrated*
Crary, Elizabeth *I'm Furious*
Crary, Elizabeth *I'm Mad*
Crary, Elizabeth *I'm Proud*
Crary, Elizabeth *I'm Scared*
Da Costa Nunez, Ralph *Our Wish*
DeGroat, Diane *Roses Are Pink, Your Feet Stink*
DiSalvo-Ryan, Dyanne *Uncle Willie and the Soup Kitchen*
Freymann, Saxton *How Are You Peeling?*
Havill, Juanita *Jamaica's Blue Marker*
Havill, Juanita *Jamaica's Find*
Johnston, Tony *Uncle Rain Cloud*
Kreiner, Anna *Let's Talk About Being Afraid*
Lewis, Kim *Friends*
Lewis, Kim *One Summer Day*
Lionni, Leo *It's Mine*
Markel, Michelle *Gracias Rosa*
McCain, Becky Ray *Nobody Knew What To Do*
McCormick, Wendy *Daddy, Will You Miss Me?*
McCourt, Lisa *I Miss You Stinky Face*
McCourt, Lisa *I Love You Stinky Face*

Moncure, Jane Belk *I Never Say I'm Thankful, But I Am*
Pfister, Marcus *The Rainbow Fish and the Sea Monster's Cave*
Smith, Miriam *Annie and Moon*
Weninger, Brigette *Why Are You Fighting, Davy?*
Weninger, Brigette *What's the Matter, Davy?*

Masks

Theme: Emotions
Targeted Skills: empathy, understanding emotions
Materials: paper bags (large), markers, crayons, yarn, and paper
Vocabulary: happy, sad, afraid, surprised, angry
Group size: 4–5
Process

1. Suggest to the children that they make masks that have feelings. Give examples of different feelings.
2. Let the children decorate their masks.
3. Help cut out eyeholes.
4. Have children wear masks and try to guess others' emotions.
5. Have children act out how they feel.

Helpful Hint
    If a child wants to make a non-human mask—encourage her to still give it a feeling (sad lion, happy monster, angry alien, etc.).

Shaving Cream Emotions

Theme: Emotions
Tageted skills: listening, expressing
Materials: shaving cream, table
Vocabulary: angry, sad, happy, feeling, scared, frustrated, other feelings words
Group Size: 5
Process

1. Give each child a squirt of shaving cream.
2. Let them play with it for a few minutes.
3. Ask them to listen to your story and draw how the person would feel.
4. Tell stories of children in conflict. Ask how one child involved would feel and then ask how the other child involved would feel.
5. See if they can offer solutions that would make both children happy.

Photograph Games

Theme: Emotions
Targeted Skills: observation, interpretation, empathy
Materials: Photographs of people showing all different kinds of emotions and a hat. Attach Velcro (rough side) to the back of each photo for flannel board use. (optional)
Vocabulary: upset, sad, happy, excited, angry, frustrated any emotion that matches photos.
Group Size: any, depending on the number of photos.
Process: The following activities can be done with these photographs.

1. Memory: match emotions (photos will be different, emotion will be the same.) Do not label the photos with emotion because children have different ideas about what emotions look like.
2. Find the emotion that is different from the rest: Place 4 photos on the table or flannel board. 3 should show the same emotion and the 4th should be different. Have the children pick out the one that does not belong.
3. Sorting emotions: place many photos on a table or on the flannel board. The children will sort according to their view of each person's emotion. (Some children may see someone crying and think it is happy tears, another child may see the same photo as showing sad tears.)
4. The Hat Game: Put several photos in a hat. One at a time, ask the children to pick a photo out and then pose the following questions: Why do you think this person is _____? How could you make this person feel better? What do you do when you feel _____? Record their answers and use as suggestions when children experience these emotions.

Helpful Hints

1. These photographs will last a lot longer if they are laminated or covered in contact paper. Mount each one on plain paper first to keep the children's attention focused on the appropriate side.
2. The newspaper is the best source for photographs. The photos are of people from all around the world and have a wide variety of emotions. Magazines tend to have photos of happy people.

Photograph Games 2

Theme: Emotions
Targeted Skills: acceptance
Materials: Photographs of objects or activities that elicit different emotions from different people. (Clowns, tigers, dogs, roller coaster, skyscrapers, airplanes, bumblebee, snake, astronauts in space shuttle, rodeo, swimming pool, etc.)
Vocabulary: Opinion, fact, acceptance, different, similar
Group Size: any, depending on the number of photos.
Process: The following activities can be done with these photographs.

1. The Hat Game: Put several photos in a hat. One at a time, ask the children to choose a photo and then pose the following questions: Pretend you are close to this or involved in this (name specific item or activity). How would that make you feel? Would anyone else feel the same as (insert name)? Would anyone feel differently? How? Explain that the same object can make some people scared and some people happy. Encourage the children to use "I" when describing their feelings: "I am afraid of dogs" instead of "Dogs are scary". This will help teach them the difference between opinion and fact.
2. Sorting game: place several photos on the table or flannel board. Children will sort according to what makes them happy, sad, afraid, etc.

Dr. Emotions

Theme: Emotions
Targeted Skills: understanding physical changes and emotions
Materials: stethoscope
Vocabulary: stethoscope, heartbeat, rhythm
Group Size: any
Process

1. Introduce a stethoscope to the classroom.
2. Explain that a stethoscope is used to hear heartbeat. Let them know that it makes quiet sounds much louder, and loud sounds VERY loud. It is not safe to yell into a stethoscope!
3. Let the children listen to their heartbeats.
4. Talk about the changes that happen to our bodies when we become upset, excited, angry, etc.

5. Leave the stethoscope out and encourage the children to use it when they experience different feelings.
6. If they are willing, let others listen to their heartbeat. Compare between someone who is happy and someone who is excited.

Move Me

Theme: Emotions
Targeted Skills: cooperation
Materials: music, open space, different kinds of music
Vocabulary: movement, tempo, beat, body language
Group Size: whole group
Process

1. Play slow music first and dance with slow exaggerated movement. Encourage the children to join you.
2. Change music and dance a little faster.
3. Surprise the children with varying tempos.
4. Turn the music off.
5. Talk about body language and how to identify feelings by looking at someone's body language.
6. Show them what your body looks like when you are sad, angry, happy etc.
7. Encourage the children to walk like they feel sad etc.

Snack Ideas: Faces and Expressions

1. *Pizza Faces*

   You will need:

   Pizza dough (use pre-made dough or follow directions on a boxed mix)
   Pizza sauce
   Shredded mozzarella cheese
   Assorted toppings such as sliced green and black olives, sliced green peppers, sliced pepperoni, mushrooms, orange and yellow cheeses, sliced tomatoes, cubed or sliced tofu, etc.

Either make one large pizza for the class or give each child a small ball of dough to make their own individual pizza.

Form dough into a traditional (circular) pizza shape. Spread sauce on it and then sprinkle cheese over sauce. Use the toppings to make a face. Be creative!

Place pizzas on lightly greased pan (or as directed by dough recipe). Depending on size of pizza, bake at 350 to 400 degrees for 8 to 15 minutes.

2. *Cracker Faces*

You will need:

> Crackers in a variety of shapes (circle, rectangle, square) or sliced bread (white, Italian, wheat, party rye, etc).
> An assortment of spreads such as peanut butter, yogurt, cream cheese.
> An array of toppings such as raisins or other dried fruit, chocolate chips, pretzels, sliced cheese, tomatoes, sliced bananas, orange sections, etc.

Allow the children to apply a spread to their crackers or bread and then decorate with toppings. Ask the children to make happy, sad, angry, and excited snacks.

Teacher Preparation for Prop Bag

Materials

> ✓ Photographs of people expressing many different emotions. The best place to find these is the newspaper. It is a good idea to laminate or enclose in contact paper so they can be reused.
> ✓ Newspapers: make sure you scan them first and remove any inappropriate material.
> ✓ Paper: several sheets for emotions collages and drawings
> ✓ Assorted markers or crayons: every time a bag is returned, replace missing, worn out or broken crayons and markers.
> ✓ Glue sticks
> ✓ Scissors
> ✓ Instruction Sheet
> ✓ Feedback Form

Be sure to include extra materials for families of more than one child even if that child is not in your program.

Prop Bag

Activity for Parents and children; estimated time of activity: 30 minutes

Before you start, read through the whole activity so you will feel more comfortable and know what to expect.

1. Let your child explore the photographs. Talk about the emotions that the people might be feeling.
2. Sit down with your child and tell him or her about an emotion that you experienced today. Ask your child to find a photo that matches your emotion.
3. Ask your child the following questions: insert the same feeling for each question.

   Why do you think this person feels _____?
   What could this person do to feel better?
   How could you help this person feel better?
   Did you feel _____today at school?
   What do you do when you feel _____?

4. Then talk about your experience. Share with your child how your body felt as you experienced the emotion. Share with your child what you did to feel better. Did anyone help you to feel better? You could also share ways that you help others to feel better. Feel free to share emotions that make you feel good! (See example on the next page.)
5. Have your child draw a picture. It can be a face showing the emotion or an example of how or what they would draw if they felt this way. For example, an angry child may use a bold color and press down very hard on the paper using wild strokes. A sad child may draw very lightly or draw a picture of her Mom to make her feel better.
6. Look through the newspaper and cut out photographs of people showing emotion. Sort them into different feelings and glue them on the paper. As you do this talk about the feelings using the questions above.
7. Bring these back to school to be shared at group time and then hung on an emotions bulletin board. Please also return the photos.

For example, in reference to questions 2 on the previous page, here is a story about emotions that a parent may have experienced:

I felt nervous at work today. I had to tell my friend / boss / etc. (use words that your child is familiar with) Tanisha that I lost an important paper. Before

I told her, my tummy hurt and my body felt very warm. My hands got sweaty, too. This is how my body feels when I am nervous. To feel better, I told my other friend Julie what happened. Julie said the same thing happened to her! Julie told me I would feel better if I told Tanisha right away. Before I told Tanisha, I was very nervous! After I told her, Tanisha told me she was disappointed that I lost the paper, but happy that I told her right away. This make me feel proud that I had the courage to tell her right away. Then she helped me to find a way to get my important paper back.

This story involves many different feelings that can be explained in more detail, especially if you think your child may be experiencing these same feelings. Ask your child about her body feels when she is happy, scared, angry, etc. Explain that this is normal.

Activities for Parents and Their Children

1. What emotion did you choose?
2. Did your child find a photo to match?
3. How did your child answer the questions about the photo?
   a. Why do you think this person feels _____?

   b. What could this person do to feel better?

   c. How could you help this person feel better?

   d. Did you feel _____ at school today? Tell me about it.

   e. What do you do when you feel _____?

Feedback Form

Thank you for taking your time to share your emotions with your child. The more we brainstorm healthy ways to deal with our emotions, the more choices our children will have when they encounter different situations.

Please take just a few more minutes to answer the following questions so we can continue to create activities that suit your needs as well as strengthen the bond between home and school.

1. What did you enjoy about this activity? What did your child enjoy about this activity?

2. Were you surprised by anything your child said?

3. How did you use the materials? Which activities did you try?

4. Please add any other comments or questions, including what you would change about this activity.

Tips of the Week

Take ownership of your feelings. Use "I" messages.
"*I* explain that it is time to go and you continue to play with the toys."

Avoid blaming your emotions on others (*You* make me feel _____ when *you*_____.)

✄ --

Validate your child's emotions.
"I know that you really wanted me to buy you that toy. When I said 'no' that made you very upset. It's okay to feel upset and it is okay to tell me you are upset."

✄ --

Set limits and give options.
"I can tell that you are still very upset about not getting that toy, but it is never okay to hit people. You can talk to me about how you feel or you can hug your teddy bear (squeeze a pillow, hold my hand, draw a picture, stomp your feet, etc.)"

✄ --

Be flexible. Do what is best for your child.
You may think that "stomping your feet" does not sound like an acceptable solution, especially if you are in the middle of a store, however, if you give this as an option it allows for a physical outlet without anyone getting hurt. If people look at you funny, all you have to do is say to your child (loudly enough for your audience to hear), "Thank you for showing me you feel angry in a way that does not hurt anyone." Hopefully anyone watching has just learned a valuable lesson from you. If your child is more out of control, go to the car and read a magazine until she has settled then ask her if she is ready to go back into the store.

RESPECT

Changes to the Environment

Dramatic Play

- ✓ Restaurant: choose an ethnicity and gather appropriate props (i.e. Chinese restaurant: real menus, chop sticks, uniform-ask to borrow one, plastic foods, plates, money, cash register, purses, wallets)
- ✓ Grocery Store: include ethnic food boxes
- ✓ Dress Up Clothes from different cultures

Sensory

- ✓ Dirt and earthworms
- ✓ Potting soil with real flowers, shovels, buckets
- ✓ Skin Tone Dough (see recipe p. 328)

Art

- ✓ Multicultural paints, crayons, and markers.
- ✓ Stencils of bodies (all types).
- ✓ Stencils of face shapes (heart, oval, round, squared oval).

Writing

- ✓ Premade books for storytelling

Science/Discovery

- ✓ Add skin tone bags after doing the Story Enhancer: *The Colors of Us* (p. 333)
- ✓ Plastic cups, spoons, containers with white flour, wheat flour, cinnamon, ground coffee, curry powder and other skin tone spices (NO HOT PEPPER SPICES!)

Manipulatives/Math

- ✓ Multicultural dolls: sorting, patterning.

Blocks

- ✓ Add dollhouse and people. Each week try different kinds of families (one parent, two parent opposite sex, two parent same sex, multicultural mix, etc.).
- ✓ Use the dramatic play refrigerator and turn it into apartments. Use ladders from fire trucks or create your own with Popsicle sticks.

Group Time Discussions

1. What does respect mean? To show consideration for yourself, all other people, all living things, your belongings and the belongings of others.
2. All people have similarities and differences. Brainstorm and list these. Some ideas are: body type, age, accent, language, skin color, hair color/texture, clothing, accessories (glasses, turbans, canes, seeing eye dogs), geographic location, type of housing, type of food, amount of money, physical differences, religious beliefs and the like.
3. Kindness and respect: It is okay to like anyone who is different from you. It is also okay not to like everyone you meet. However, all people should be treated kindly and with respect. Children are usually told, "We are all friends at school" and this may not be the case. (There must be someone that you work with that you do not consider a friend.) Instead tell the children "You do not have to be her friend, but you do need to treat her with respect."
4. Respect can be introduced at group time using almost any traditional theme: themes about living creatures, plants, and anything that is found in different parts of the world (transportation, people, clothing, food, families, games, toys...)
5. Introduce the idea of respecting the ideas of others, ways of expressing opinion, and the right to disagree without anyone being right or wrong.
6. Puppet role-playing: Teachers use puppets to act out typical, recently occurring classroom conflicts. Provide several variations of each situation. In a group discussion, children decide which puppets were respectful, how the respect was demonstrated, and how the situation made each puppet feel.

Book List

Ajmera Maya and Ivanko, John D. *To Be a Kid*
Ajmera, Maya and Versola, Anna Rhesa *Children from Australia to Zimbabwe*
Aliki, *Manners*
Aliki, *We Are All Alike, We Are All Different*
Burnes, Laura T. *Teeny Tiny Ernest*
Carlson, Nancy *ABC I Like Me*
Cohen, Miriam *So What?*
Cooper, Melrose *I Got a Family*

Hammanaka, Sheila*All the Colors of the Earth*

Havill, Juanita *Jamaica's Find*

Hoffman, Mary *Amazing Grace*

Hollyer, Beatrice *Wake Up, World! A Day in the life of Children Around the World*

Katz, Karen *The Color of Us*

Katz, Karen *Over the Moon*

Keller, Holly *Horace*

Morris, Ann *The Daddy Book*

Orr, Katherine Shelley *Story of a Dolphin*

Parr, Todd *It's Okay to Be Different*

Pinkney, Sandra *Shades of Black*

Rotner, Shelley *Faces*

Rotner, Shelley *Lots of Moms*

Rotner, Shelley Pick a Pet

Ryder, Joanne *Each Living Thing*

Ryder, Joanne *My Father's Hands*

Stevenson, James *Wilfred the Rat*

Van Dort, Evelien *Am I Really Different?*

Trace Me

Theme: Respect
Targeted Skills: respect, cooperation
Materials: pencils, markers, crayons, roll paper
Vocabulary: cooperative, trace, similar, different
Group Size: whole group, depending on floor space
Process

1. Pair the children and give each a variety of writing tools and 2 large body size pieces of newsprint or roll paper.
2. Explain that you would like them to take turns tracing each other's bodies.
3. As you walk around helping, talk about the differences and similarities between their bodies.
4. Decorate and add detail.
5. Hang up around the room.

Helpful Hint
Encourage cooperation if the first child traced does not want to trace her partner. Teacher can enthusiastically offer to trace the child and perhaps the child will change her mind. If not, facilitate problem solving by asking the child (who wants to be traced) what his options are.

Story Enhancer: *Faces* by Shelley Rotner and Ken Kreisler

Theme: Respect
Targeted Skills: respect, kindness
Materials: *Faces* by Shelley Rotner and Ken Kreisler, various shaped buttons, multicultural paper, mirrors, glue, yarn, crayons.
(Optional: instant camera, photo of each child)
Vocabulary: different, alike, similar
Group Size: 6
Process

1. Read the story *Faces*. Find similar facial features of each child.
2. Using mirrors, photo or close up facial photo have the children look at the shape of their eyes, nose and mouth.
3. Give the children the buttons and encourage them to choose shapes that they think match their features. Also give them the choice of paper to glue their features on.

4. Have the children add ears, hair, mouth etc.
5. Display pictures of faces and encourage children to examine differences and similarities.

Source: S. Rotner, (1994). *Faces.* Macmillan Publishing Company, Incorporated.

Respect Art Activities

1. *I Am Special posters*: Children create collages of their favorite things.
2. *People-Colors*: Each child makes a set of handprints in shades of
   skin tones. Once each child has completed the project, bring all
   the projects to a group discussion. Talk with the children about the
   differences in colors. Emphasize that all are different, but also the
   same: children may have different color skin, but each is a child,
   each is a member of the class, each is accountable for their own
   behavior, each follows the same classroom rules, each is a good
   person.
3. *Family Portraits*: Provide the children with materials to compose
   a family portrait. Materials may include photos or magazine
   pictures, paper cutouts of people to identify and dress, and paints,
   markers, and colored pencils to complete drawings. When the
   children have completed their family portraits, encourage them to
   talk about their families, their customs and their heritage.

Skin Tone Dough Recipes

Cinnamon Dough
   2 cups flour
   1 cup salt
   5 tsp. cinnamon
   $\frac{3}{3}$ cup water

Coffee Dough
   2 cups flour
   1 cup salt
   $\frac{1}{2}$ cup instant coffee dissolved in $\frac{3}{4}$ cup warm water

Flour Dough
   3 cups flour
   1 cup salt

2 tsp cornstarch
1 cup water
2 tsp. oil

For each dough, the process is the same:

- ✓ Mix dry ingredients on the table
- ✓ Form mountain shape with a well in the middle
- ✓ Slowly, pour ½ wet ingredients into well
- ✓ Mix with hands
- ✓ Add remaining wet ingredients
- ✓ Add more flour or water as needed
- ✓ Store dough in an airtight container in the refrigerator for up to a week.

Skin Tone Dough Activity

Theme: Respect
Materials: Skin tone doughs
Vocabulary: shade, tone, similar, different
Group Size: 5–8
Process

1. Let the children explore the different colors, textures and smells of the doughs.
2. Find one that matches someone's skin color and point this out.
3. Take a small piece of one color and a small piece of another color and blend them together. Encourage the children to do the same.
4. Try mixing different combinations to come up with many different colors.
5. Show the children that they can make a face with eyes, nose, and mouth by flattening out a ball and pinching bits of different colors for the features. Add scissors to the table to cut the dough into strands of hair.

Surprise!

Theme: Respect
Targeted Skills: acceptance, risk taking, manners
Materials: assorted exotic fruits or other unusual foods, plastic knives, napkins

Vocabulary: risk, different, exotic, opinion, descriptive words based on food
           selected
Group Size: 4–6
Process

1. Have the children wash their hands.
2. Tell the children that you have brought some food to share with them. Explain that they may not have ever seen or tasted this food before. Ask them how they could learn more about this food. (Encourage using 5 senses.)
3. Allow children to cut, smell, touch, look at, and taste food.
4. Ask open-ended questions about this new food. For example: "What if I decided that this food looked yucky and left the table?" "What if a toddler did not want to try an apple for the first time?" "What have you tried that you liked (or didn't like)?"
5. Talk about what you might miss out on if you do not try new things.

Helpful Hints

1. Expand this idea of risk taking to other areas like playing with a new friend, jumping off the climber, painting with fingers, etc.
2. Teach children polite ways to express dislike. Instead of "that's gross" say "I do not like the way that tastes." Teach them that it is okay to have different opinions.
3. Extend to home by asking parents to supply an unusual food.

The Day No One Listened to Harry

Theme: Respect
Targeted Skills: Active Listening
Materials: Tongs or big spoon, frying pan, stack of papers, television guide, eyeglasses, headphones, and drumsticks. (All are optional.)
Vocabulary: Listen, Respect
Group Size: Any
Process:

1. Read the following story. If possible have another teacher pantomime the various family members. Follow through with role-playing exercises.

   It had been gray and cloudy all day, but now, as Harry looked out the window of his bedroom, he saw the sky growing darker and darker. He stuck his head out the window and felt the wind blow strong and cool. The heard the air whoosh as it rushed past his ears and messed up his hair. "Yep," thought Harry. "It's going to rain any minute. I'd better bring Buster inside."

Harry ran outside into the yard and unhooked the leash holding his big brown dog. "Come on, Buster," he said. If you stay out here you're going to get all wet." Buster licked Harry happily and raced him back into the house.

As Harry came through the kitchen, he saw his dad cooking dinner on the stove. "Dad," said Harry, "you better . . .". But before Harry could finish what he was saying, his father waved him off, explaining, "Not now, Harry. I have to keep my eye on this fried chicken. Tell me later."

Harry sighed and ran out of the room to find his mother. She was in the dining room, hunched over a pile of papers on the table. "Mom," exclaimed Harry, "you only have a few minutes. . .". But she just shook her head, and without even looking up, told him, "I'm sorry, Harry, but I have to get these bills straightened out. Wait until after dinner."

Harry sighed an even bigger sigh and went to find his grandfather. There he was, just where Harry thought he'd be: sitting in his favorite chair, watching the news on TV. "Grandpop," Harry began, "You'd better come outside. . .". But his grandfather just smiled at him and cut him off, saying, "That's a good boy, Harry." We can play after the news is over," and turned his head back to the TV.

"Gee, Buster," Harry muttered to his faithful dog. "No one is listening to me." He trudged upstairs, where he heard loud music blasting from his older brother's room. "Hey, Jason!" yelled Harry. But his brother just ignored him, playing imaginary drums to the music blaring from his radio.

Harry didn't even try to talk to him anymore and turned toward his own room. Buster followed and lay down with a thump as Harry flopped on his bed. For several minutes, Harry lay still, listening intently. Then, a smile spreading over his face, he turned to look out the window.

"Here it comes, Buster," Harry said softly. Sure enough, a gentle burst of raindrops splattered lightly on his windowpane. Moments later, the rain was falling harder, rattling noisily on the roof and splashing wildly on the street out front.

"Oh no!" Harry heard his mother cry. "My laundry!" and she ran to the kitchen door, gazing in frustration at the clean sheets hanging on the clothesline, dripping now with fresh rain.

As Harry's mother cried out, his father ran to the kitchen window, shaking his head in dismay. "I knew I should have rolled up the car windows!" he muttered to himself. "It'll take days to air those seats off," and he returned to take the chicken off the stove, his hunger gone.

"Tarnation!" Grandpop spluttered, as he struggled to get out of his armchair. "It took me all morning to paint those shelves, and now the paint's going to run all over. Why didn't I set them inside the garage to dry...?"

Moments later, Harry heard footsteps racing down the stairs. "Why didn't someone say something?" Jared demanded. "Don't you know that rain will rust my new bike?" He flew out the door, grabbed his bright blue, very wet bike, and pushed it into the garage. Then Jason hopped around, looking for a rag to soak up the raindrops beading up on the blue fenders.

Dinner that night was very quiet, everyone but Harry looking down at his or her food. Just as Harry was about to say, "Great fried chicken, Dad," Harry's mother, father, grandfather, and brother all said at once, "Why didn't someone tell me it was going to rain?!" Buster sat up on the floor, alarmed by the sound of everyone talking at once. But Harry just sighed a huge sigh, saying, "I tried to tell you, really I did. But no one would listen." Silence filled the room, and Buster crept over to lie on Harry's feet.

1. When you've finished reading the story, ask the children what was Harry's problem (no one would listen to him). Ask them why Harry tried to warn each family member that it was going to rain (Dad's car windows were down, Mom's laundry was hanging on the line, Grandpop's painted shelves were outside, and brother Jason's bike would get wet and rusty).
2. Explain, "Being a good listener isn't always easy, but listening is very important. Sometimes another person is trying to warn us, like Harry did, or tell us how to do something. Being a good listener is a very special part of being a friend. Does anybody know HOW we can be good listeners?" Allow children to respond.
3. Tell the children the following three ways to show we are good listeners.

   ✓ Look at the person who is talking to you.
   ✓ When you are listening, be quiet.
   ✓ When you are talking to a friend, use a soft voice.

4. Role-play each of the above with another teacher, having him or her demonstrate good and poor listening skills (have the teacher look at you one time, look around the room another time, listen attentively one time, start playing with something nearby during the next interaction, etc.). Have the children identify whether the other teacher is being a good or poor listener. Then select students to role play listening, and have the rest of the class decide if that student is showing good listening skills.

5. Review with the class the three ways to be a good listener. Then say, "There's one other thing that is pretty important, something Harry found out: You have to get your listener's ATTENTION first. How should we do that?" Let children respond, guiding the discussion to ways which are respectful, such as:

   ✓ Coming close to a person before talking to him (rather than shouting from a distance).
   ✓ Tapping another lightly on the arm or shoulder.

6. Waiting a minute if he's already talking, then saying, "excuse me".
7. This is also 'a fun exercise to role-play' (Julian, personal communication).

Play, Play, Give It Away

Theme: Respect
Targeted Skills: Respect for different cultures and turn taking
Materials: various instruments from different cultures
Vocabulary: new, different, pass, share
Group Size: dependent on number of instruments
Process

1. Give each child an instrument to play.
2. Talk about how the instruments come from all around the world. Talk about instruments that are common in your area.
3. Walk around the classroom, building or playground marching band style.
4. Play for a few minutes then say "play, play, give it away" and pass your instrument to the person behind you. (THEY WILL NEED HELP WITH THIS!)
5. Continue until each child has a chance to play each instrument.

Helpful Hint
Some children will not want to pass their instrument. Just skip over the child in the exchange process and keep a few extra instruments near by.

Planting a Garden

Theme: Respect
Materials: planting trays (size dependent upon number of children per group), planting soil, various seeds for planting and comparing, gardening tools, Rebus* poster of steps. (Optional: camera/film to photographically record process/growth)

Various Processes

1. Encourage children to draw their prediction of how their garden will look. Display their picture behind the garden to compare as it grows.
2. Fill sensory table with potting soil, nuts, and pinecones (things from nature) and tools and planting cups. Engage the children in discussions about the materials and what they are doing.
3. Examine and discuss the qualities of various seeds such as pinecones, acorns, pumpkin, carrot, apple, etc. Chart differences and similarities.
4. Discuss how the plants will grow, what they will look like, and what will happen as the plants grow. In the Writing Center record comments and predictions.
5. Do seed rubbings and trace seeds. Sort and classify seeds by size.

*A Rebus is a picture story. In this example, a Rebus poster would include a series of pictures detailing step by step, how to plant the garden.

Story Enhancer: *The Color of Us* by Karen Katz

Theme: Respect
Targeted Skills: respect, kindness
Materials: *The Color of Us*, by Karen Katz, various skin tone colored foods (for example: soy sauce, syrup, peach yogurt, spices, honey, bread) each in a separate zip lock bags
Vocabulary: different, same, alike, shade, tone
Group Size: less than 10
Process

1. Read the *Color of Us*.
2. Encourage the children to interact while listening. They may look for and compare their own skin tone with that of their friends.
3. Show the children the zip lock bags filled with the food items.
4. Pass around the bags and have children find a close match to their skin tone and the children in the book.

Helpful Hints

1. Be sure to have a close match for each child.
2. Recreate the page in the book with all of the different legs. Compare skin tones, count legs, etc.

K. Katz, (2002). *The Color of Us*. New York: Henry Holt Books for Young Children.

Whale Watch

Theme: Respect
Targeted Skills: kindness, respect, feelings, cooperation, emotions
Materials: Pictures of whales from newspapers or books
        Whales figurines or stuffed animals
        Whale video (optional)
    Mural paper and art medium of choice: paint, paper and glue, markers,
    crayons, etc.
Vocabulary: whale pod, family, togetherness, rescue, saving, nurturing, car-
ing, volunteer, team work, sympathy, news (current events), stranded
Group Size: can vary according to class size as well as class interest.
Process

1. Initiate a group discussion around recent news such as stranded
   whales, a new whale at the aquarium, whale sightings, etc.
2. Pass picture around the group.
3. Open up discussion regarding children's knowledge and experiences with whales.
4. Teacher gives *simple* explanation about the story such as why whales
   became stranded, where the new whale came from, why is the
   whale sighting newsworthy.
5. Give each child the opportunity to express their feelings about the
   stranding, new arrival, and sighting.
6. Encourage group discussion.
7. Encourage children an opportunity to explore materials.
8. Encourage children to create a mural.

Helpful Hints

1. Continued use of vocabulary.
2. Continued follow-up on events as they unfold in newspaper.
3. Adapt this activity to other current events. For example:
   • Have a "Rain Dance" during a drought
   • Have an art show during the local annual art festival.
   • Have a "Snow Ball" after a large snowfall

Miscellaneous

1. *Care of plants/animals in the classroom*: Children take turns caring for
   animals and plants. Group time discussions involve responsibility

and what the consequences are if they do not take care of living things.

2. *Charts and Graphs*: Group discussions about children's and teacher's physical attributes (such as hair and eye color and skin tone), likes and dislikes (such as food, animals, weather), and families (such as number and gender of siblings, town of residence, and number and type of pets) can be charted and graphed. These activities show children that they are alike and different at the same time.

Stuffed Animal Sleepovers

Theme: Respect
Targeted Skills: respect, responsibility, creativity, story telling
Materials: stuffed animal, tote bag, notebook, crayons, and large piece of paper (to list possible names and chart voting results)
Vocabulary: responsible, respect, sleepover
Group Size: whole group
Process

1. Introduce a cuddly stuffed animal. Together children and teachers brainstorm ideas for a name, vote on a name and take turns bringing the stuffed animal home for "sleepovers."
2. Provide a "home" for the stuffed animal in a tote bag. Include the stuffed animal, the story notebook, crayons, markers, pens, and pencils.
3. When they take the tote bag home, parents and children are asked to write a story about what they did with the stuffed animal. The child may dictate the story and draw a picture of their adventure with the stuffed animal.
4. Remind parents that this is also a lesson in responsibility: the family is expected to do the project and return the animal the next day.
5. The child and teacher tell/read the story aloud to everyone.
6. To set an example of what is expected (notebook story), a teacher may be the first to take the stuffed animal home.
7. It may be helpful to outline what is expected and place it in the front of the notebook.

Teacher Preparation for Prop Bag

Materials
Construction paper in multicultural colors
Markers or crayons
Scissors
Glue
Paper plates.
Instruction Sheet
Feedback Form

Prop Bag

Activity for parents and children; estimated project time: 30 minutes

Before you start, read through the whole activity so you will feel more comfortable and know what to expect. Included is a piece of paper to jot down any comments your child makes as you are doing this project. The hands wreath is part of this project, but the real project is open discussion about how people have similarities and differences. We talk about how everyone is important, no matter what they look like.

1. Get the materials out of the bag and let your child comment on them. We have been talking a lot about how people can be similar and different. Ask your child to find a color that matches (or comes close to matching) her own skin tone. Find matches for anyone else involved in this project with you.
2. The following is a Suggested activity idea. Before you suggest it to your child, see what he may like to do with the material.
3. Trace each person's hand on the matching paper. You may offer to trace your child's hand and then he can do the same for you or your child may prefer to trace her own hand.
4. Each person should cut his own hand out. If your child wants help, hold the paper for her, turning it to make cutting easier. For beginning cutters, draw a circle around the hand and have your child cut the circle out.
5. One at a time, glue the hands on the edge of the paper plate, so the fingers hang off the edge.
6. Look at the remaining colors of paper and talk about people you know that may match those colors.

7. Trace, cut and glue the other hands on until hands go all the way around the plate. (if your child is satisfied with just your hands on the plate that's fine. This is about the process, not the end product!)
8. If you want, label the hands with the names of the people they match.
9. Included with this project is a book about children from around the world. What similarities and differences can you and your child find? Add these to your discussion paper.
10. Return the discussion paper and feedback forms as well as the prop bag with the scissors, glue, left over paper and book to a teacher.

Feedback Form

Please take a few minutes to answer the following questions so we can continue to create activities that suit your needs as well as strengthen the bond between home and school.

1. How did you and your child use the materials in the bag?

2. What did you and your child like about the activities?

3. Please add any other comments or questions, including what you would change about this activity.

Weekly Tips For Parents

Talking

Be a good role model by showing respect in your daily interactions with others. It is important for parents to remember that children are **constantly** watching and imitating adults. It is important to make sure that the language you use and the television shows you watch are examples of what you would want you children to imitate. If you speak in a disrespectful tone or use disrespectful words like "stupid" or "brat," your child will think it's okay to speak that way to friends and family members.

Doing

Make up special weeks this month dedicated to polite words. Week one: please, week 2: please and thank you, week 3 please, thank you and your welcome, week 4: please, thank you, your welcome and excuse me. Give your child something meaningful (a hug, a high-five, a note that says 'I was polite today!') each time she uses a phrase. When she forgets you can say, "That would have been a great chance to use the words 'your welcome.'"

✂ ---

Talking

Talk to your child about showing respect for individual differences and preferences. Help your child learn that everyone has different likes and dislikes. There is no right or wrong because it is an opinion. You can introduce this at the dinner table.

Doing

Fun ways to help your child learn about how people are different include going to museums, listening to a variety of music styles, and tasting foods from different cultures. Try a new exotic fruit that no one in your family has ever had. Let everyone try a piece and chart who likes it and who does not. You can also try this with different kinds of bread, cheese, ice cream, vegetables and many other foods. Keep a running list and try the same thing every once and a while to see whose tastes have changed.

✂ ---

Talking

Talk to your child about respecting her environment and belongings. Talk about what each family member is currently responsible for. Thank each other when responsibilities are carried out.

Doing

Play "What Would Happen If. . . " "What would happen if I stopped taking out the garbage?" "What would happen if Dad stopped doing the laundry?" "What would happen if we both decided not to cook dinner?" Then start to focus on your child. "What would happen if you never picked your toys up off of the floor?" "What would happen if you stopped brushing your teeth?" Brainstorm new ways your child can take responsibility. Write it down with clear expectations. Add more when he is ready.

✂ ---

Talking

Reinforce your child's politeness as much as possible. But be specific: "Thank you for saying please when you asked for a turn on the bike," or "Thank you for saying excuse me when you wanted my attention." Remember, it's just as important to **kindly** remind the child who forgets. Do not compare your child to another, even if it is a sibling. Each child should receive positive reinforcement. You are teaching **disrespect** if you say something like, "See, your sister remembers to say 'thank you', why can't you?"

Doing

Make a specific list of all the ways your child has shown respect in the past month. Hang it on the refrigerator so you can add to it and read it frequently. Make a copy for your child's teacher, grandparents, and your workplace. (You should feel proud; after all she learned it by watching and listening to YOU!)

COOPERATION

Changes to the Environment

Dramatic Play

- ✓ Any occupation and appropriate props
- ✓ *Sports team*: include matching outfits, duffle bags, sports equipment, water bottles

Sensory

- ✓ *Sand and water*: start in two separate containers, put scoops, buckets, funnels in each.

Art

- ✓ Pair painting: Tie two children's arms together, loosely with a bandana or tie. Put paint and two paintbrushes on the table (or easel) with the paper. Children will work together to create a picture.

Science/Discovery

- ✓ *Mixing colors*: plastic cups: 3 filled with water and food coloring (red, yellow, blue), eye droppers (if you do not have eye droppers, dip coffee filters instead), empty cups (not needed if using coffee filters). Encourage the children to share the colors and work together to see how many other colors can be made from the three provided. Record what they think might happen as well as what does happen.
- ✓ Magnet wands with combination of magnet and nonmagnetic items.

Manipulatives/Math

- ✓ *Yardsticks, rulers, and tape measures.* Children can get clipboards and pencils from the writing area. If possible, take photographs of various classroom items. Children can measure and record findings.
- ✓ Tweezers, sorting trays, and many different shapes of (uncooked) pasta.

Writing

- ✓ *Picture Dictionary*: photos and corresponding words (together, cooperate, help, teamwork, partner, share, etc.)

Blocks

> ✓ Teachers trace blocks to make a design. Make several different ones. Leave in the block area and children can work together to match block designs.
> ✓ Cars, tubes (wrapping paper) and large pieces of cardboard (sides of boxes) for creating ramps.

Group Time Discussion

1. Cooperation questions
   - ✓ What does it mean to cooperate?
   - ✓ What kinds of things do you like to do with your friends?
   - ✓ What activities are more fun to do with a friend?
   - ✓ What are some things you cannot do alone?
   - ✓ How do you cooperate at home? At school?
2. *Cooperation vocabulary*: together, listen, communicate, teamwork, compromise, goal
3. Grown ups and cooperation
   - ✓ How do parents cooperate with each other? With children?
   - ✓ How do teachers cooperate with each other? With parents? With children?
   - ✓ Think of other occupations and how workers would cooperate (fast food, toy store, zoo/aquarium, fire station). What might happen if they did not cooperate?
4. *Puppet play*: use a typical classroom scenario. Demonstrate puppets that will not cooperate. Invite children to give ideas about how to cooperate. Do scenarios for each area of the classroom. Post the children's cooperation ideas in each area. Catch the children cooperating and add to the lists.

Book List

Brown, Marcia *Stone Soup: An Old Tale*
Burton, Virginia Lee *Katy and the Big Snow*
Burton, Virginia Lee *Mike Mulligan and His Steam Shovel*
Cowen-Fletcher, Jane *It Takes a Village*
Ernst, Lisa Campbell *Zinnia and Dot*
Galdone, Paul *The Little Red Hen*
Gelsanliter, Wendy *Dancin' in the Kitchen*

Hoban, Russell *Best Friends For Frances*
Kubler, Susanne *The Three Friends*
Lionni, Leo *Alexander and the Wind Up Mouse*
Lionni, Leo *Swimmy*
Lyon, George Ella *Together*
Merrifield, Margaret *Come Sit By Me*
Pfister, Marcus *Penguin Pete and Little Tim*
Pfister, Marcus *The Rainbow Fish*
Williams, Vera *A Chair For My Mother*

Community Centerpieces

Theme: Cooperation
Targeted Skills: cooperation, sharing, teamwork
Materials: play dough, anything that can be found on a nature walk, paper bags
Vocabulary: share, cooperate, everyone, participate, centerpiece
Group Size: 5–6, # that fit at a table
Process

1. Go on a nature walk with a group of 5–6 children.
2. Gather the same group of children at a table and ask if anyone knows what a centerpiece is. (Give description if necessary.)
3. Place a ball of play dough in front of one child and ask him to shape it (offer ideas such as poking with finger, squeezing a section, flattening with palm or fist).
4. Pass it around until each child has had a chance to give it shape, making sure that it is wide enough to hold objects without tipping over.
5. Explain that the play dough is the base and they are going to add their nature items as decoration.
6. Pass the dough around and let each child add one item at a time. Explain that they must push their object in deep so that it will stay standing when the dough dries.
7. When no one else chooses to add something, the centerpiece is done. Allow it to dry and then put in the center of each table during lunch and snack.
8. Initiate and encourage conversation about cooperation and teamwork.

Helpful Hints
Some children may want to keep certain items for individual projects.

Piñata

Theme: Cooperation
Targeted Skills: cooperation, gentleness
Materials: newspaper, balloons, flour, water, burner, pot, spoon, and large mixing bowls: one per two children, paint, paint brushes
Vocabulary: Piñata, paper mache, strips, paste, smooth, rough
Group Size: 5–6

Process

1. Make paper mache paste by heating water and adding flour until you reach a boil and paste like consistency. Use about 5 cups of water and 3 cups of flour, but it's easier just to estimate and add flour as needed.
2. Tell children you are going to make a piñata. Ask them if they know what a piñata is. Have they played with one before?
3. Have them begin by ripping newspaper into long strips.
4. When the paper mache paste is at a temperature that is comfortable, pour into plastic bowls.
5. Blow up the balloon and have children dip the strips of paper into the paste and put them on the balloon.
6. Repeat this process until the balloon has been covered several times, keeping the tied end in sight.
7. Hang the balloon and allow it to dry for several days.
8. When it is dry, pass it around and let the children feel it. Talk about the differences in texture before and after the glue dried.
9. Paint when dry.
10. When paint has dried, pop the balloon and pull it out.
11. Using the opening, fill with treats: small toys, notes with special messages, materials for art and writing centers (no sharp objects).
12. Gather the children in an area away from the piñata, but where they can still see.
13. One at a time, have children try to break piñata with a long block or bat.

Helpful Hints

1. Start this project on a Friday so it can dry over the weekend.
2. Do not use a blindfold with preschool age children.
3. The first children to hit the Piñata should be those that you think will not break the piñata. This will allow all children to have a turn.
4. More than likely they will use so much paste that a teacher will have to break the piñata!
5. Liquid starch can be substituted for paper mache paste.

Cooperative Story Stretcher

Theme: Cooperation
Targeted Skills: cooperation, creativity

Materials: various art materials
Vocabulary: cooperate, together, section
Group Size: depends on story
Process

1. Read a book with clearly divided sections such as *The Very Hungry Caterpillar* by Eric Carle or *Going On a Bear Hunt* by Michael Rosen.
2. Introduce the idea of recreating the story through art. Those who are interested can choose a section and decide how to create it. When each child has finished, display as a story.

Helpful Hints

1. *The Very Hungary Caterpillar* idea: Each child chooses a fruit or other food. Give the child several choices on how to make this. Offer paints, glue, tissue paper, scrap paper, etc. Use small paper to be put together as a book or large paper to be displayed on the wall.
2. *Going on a Bear Hunt* idea: Each child chooses a scene. Provide charcoal (untreated) for black and white pages and watercolors for the color pages.

Wildflower Field

Theme: Cooperation
Targeted Skills: belonging, cooperation
Materials: construction paper, roll paper, glue, photos of flowers, scissors, crayons
Vocabulary: group, together, individual, different
Group Size: 3–4 at a time; include all children in one 'field'.
Process

1. Explain to children that together they will make a field of wildflowers to hang in the classroom.
2. Encourage the children to look at photos of all the different kinds of flowers and wildflower fields.
3. Encourage the children to cut or rip petals, stems, and leaves out of construction paper.
4. Glue flower parts onto butcher-block paper.
5. Hang the field of wildflowers on the wall and initiate conversation about how each flower is different and important. (You can't have

a field of wildflowers without lots of flowers!) Talk about how the child is different and important. (You can't have a class without lots of children!)

Helpful Hints

1. When a new child joins the class, have her add a flower.
2. Try creating flowers on individual papers and then plant them onto the butcher-block paper.

Group Sculpture

Theme: Cooperation
Targeted Skills: cooperation, belonging, friendship
Materials: scrap wood pieces, tempera paint, paintbrushes, glue
Vocabulary: sculpture, important, together, cooperate
Group Size: 5–6 at a time (be sure to include all children)
Process

1. Lay materials out on the table. Allow each child to choose his own piece of wood.
2. As they paint the wood, explain what they will be able to do with their pieces when they dry.
3. Start with two children and have them decide how they want their pieces glued together.
4. As children finishing gluing their piece on, invite more to glue. Always have at least two children gluing at the same time. Initiate conversation about how they can work together to place their pieces on the sculpture. Encourage them to share ideas and help each other if necessary.

Helpful Hint

1. Use stiff cardboard, cut into various shapes and sizes if scrap wood is not available.

Create a Story

Theme: Cooperation
Targeted Skills: cooperation, listening
Materials: tape recorder, blank audiotape, pencils, paper
Vocabulary: teamwork, listen, contribute, patient

Group Size: 6
Process

1. Gather children in a group and have them sit on the floor or at a table.
2. Explain that together you are all going to tell a story and record it on audiotape. The teacher begins the story by introducing characters, location, etc. She stops midsentence and lets the child next to her continue.
3. Encourage each child to tell a bit of the story.
4. Transcribe tape and read aloud.
5. Encourage each child to make a picture and put them together in a book.
6. Play tape and look at book.

Helpful Hints

1. Tell the children you are creating the beginning of the story from your imagination.
2. When you leave the story midsentence make it easy for the child to continue. For example "... and out of the box jumped a ... "
3. Story idea: This is a story about Jack. Jack lived in his apartment with his Dad and Grandmother. One day they all went for a walk in the park. As they crossed the street, a police officer told them that all of the animals from the zoo had escaped! She warned them to be careful and off they went. At first, Jack, his Dad and his Grammy thought that the officer was joking. Could all of the animals really be loose? Then they heard a roar and out from the bushes jumped a great big ...

Decorate Cupcakes

Theme: Self Control
Targeted Skills: kindness, sharing
Materials: cupcakes, assorted toppings
Vocabulary: share, remaining, enough
Group Size: 5
Process

1. Give each child $1/2$ of what she will need to decorate cupcake (i.e. cupcake and plastic knife to one child, icing and raisins to another child).

2. Have each child find a partner; someone who has the other things that she needs.
3. Encourage the children to use language to get what they need, to problem solve (what do they do if they both need the knife), and have fun!

Group Dough

Theme: Cooperation
Targeted Skill: Cooperation, sharing
Materials: ingredients to your favorite play dough recipe, measuring cups/spoons, bowl
Vocabulary: cooperation, ingredients, experiment, measure, contribute
Group Size: one person per ingredient
Process

1. Explain that you would like to work together to make play dough and that each child may contribute one ingredient. Give the children time to discuss which ingredient they would like to add. Help them problem solve when necessary. Discuss what could happen if 2 children want to add the flour and no one wants to add the salt. If there are enough ingredients experiment when there is a conflict. For example, make the dough without the salt.
2. Take turns mixing the dry and then wet ingredients by hand. Lump the dough together and encourage the children to discuss ways of splitting the dough evenly.

Story Enhancer: *Stone Soup* by Marcia Brown

Theme: Cooperation
Targeted Skills: cooperation, sharing
Materials: assorted vegetables, spices, large pot, large spoon, ladle, knives (that are safe for children to use), bowls, spoons, hot plate or stove, *Stone Soup* by Marcia Brown
Vocabulary: cooperate, participate, donate, prepare, raw, cooked, chop, grate
Group Size: whole class (or 2–3 small groups)

Process

1. Read *Stone Soup* and talk about the idea of making a soup together. Discuss what kind of vegetables the children like and might want to donate.
2. Post a note to parents asking for FRESH vegetable donations. Tell them you would like the child to choose the vegetable.
3. When group soup day arrives, have the children wash their hands and bring their vegetables to group time. Discuss the names and characteristics of each vegetable.
4. Have the children wash and cut up their vegetable and add it to the soup. (Add water, chicken broth, or other liquids to make the broth.)
5. When the soup has finished cooking, serve as afternoon snack. Share with parents at pick up time if there is enough.

Helpful Hint

Bring a variety of fresh vegetables to school with you on the day of the activity. They can be used if children forget to bring a donation or if you get several of the same vegetable.

Story Enhancer: *The Little Red Hen* by Paul Galdone

Theme: Cooperation
Targeted Skills: cooperation, sharing
Materials: *The Little Red Hen* by Paul Galdone, bread ingredients (see recipe below)
Vocabulary: cooperate, share, recipe
Group Size: 8 including teacher (one ingredient per person)
Process

1. Read *The Little Red Hen* and discuss cooperation and sharing. Did the Little Red Hen want to share when no one would cooperate? Why not? How did she feel when no one would help her?
2. Recreate the book for the children by telling them that you would like to eat Lemon Bread for snack. (This is your goal). Talk about the tasks that need to be done in order to reach your goal. (the room must first be cleaned, the tables wiped down, the materials gathered, and hands washed.) Encourage them to help you and reinforce their attempts at cooperation.

Lemon Bread Recipe and Directions
   $1/4$ cup plus 2 tablespoons margarine, softened
   2/3 cup sugar
   $1/4$ cup egg substitute
   1 teaspoon grated lemon rind
   $1/2$ teaspoon vanilla extract
   2 $1/4$ cups flour
   $3/3$ teaspoon baking powder
   $1/4$ teaspoon salt
   8 oz. Low fat lemon yogurt
Glaze
   $1/2$ cup sugar
   $1/2$ cup fresh lemon juice

Cream margarine; slowly add sugar while beating at medium speed, continue until light and fluffy; add egg substitute, vanilla and lemon rind; beat until blended; in a separate bowl, mix flour, baking powder, baking soda and salt. Begin beating egg mixture on low speed. Alternate adding flour mixture and yogurt, starting and ending with the flour.

Transfer batter to a greased loaf pan and bake at 350 degrees for 55 minutes or until toothpick inserted in center comes out clean. Cool on a cooling rack.

Mix $1/2$ sugar and lemon juice in a saucepan. Bring to a boil and cook for 1 minute. Remove from heat.

Poke the top of the bread with a serving fork in several places. Pour sauce on top and allow cooling for 15 minutes.

Enjoy!

Blanket Toss

Theme: Cooperation
Targeted Skills: cooperation
Materials: child size blanket, balls
Vocabulary: toss, teamwork, spread out, cooperation
Group Size: 4–6 (per blanket)
Process

1. Lay blankets on the ground.
2. Ask them to pick up the edges of the blanket and wave it. Make a connection to parachute play.
3. Place a ball on top and have the children practice tossing the ball in the air. As the children become skilled at tossing and catching the ball, add more balls.

4. Put 2 groups next to each other and encourage the groups to toss a ball between the blankets

Helpful Hints

1. With the children engage in experiments:
   - ✓ What would happen if one person lets go of the edge of the blanket?
   - ✓ What would happen if children held on to the same side of the blanket?
   - ✓ Acknowledge the children's cooperation.

Cooperative Musical Chairs

Theme: Cooperation
Targeted Skills: cooperation, problem solving, creativity
Materials: chairs, large floor space
Vocabulary: creative, communicate, cooperate, gentle
Group Size: any
Process

1. Place chairs on two rows, back to back.
2. Have children stand around them
3. Start the music and begin walking (or dancing) around the chairs. Do this with them and help them to walk in the same direction.
4. When the music stops, everyone must sit in a chair.
5. Take one chair away and repeat.
6. From now on, everyone must sit in a chair or on the lap of someone in a chair.
7. Continue until it is not possible to get everyone on a lap or chair.

Sharing Box*

Theme: Cooperation
Targeted Skills: cooperation, sharing
Materials: large box, small toys (dinosaurs, farm animals, cars, trucks, etc)
Vocabulary: share, borrow, responsibility, consideration
Group Size: 8

---

*This idea was contributed by Shirley Robbins at Pfizer Kids, New London, CT.

Process

1. Collect small toys from promotions, etc. Store in "sharing box" to be used at special times: at the end of the day, rainy days, nap time when only a few children are awake.
2. The sharing box is taken out only a few times a week or at the end of the day. Children are encouraged to share one toy at a time. Toys can be taken home and returned the following day.
3. Encourage responsibility by asking children to return the toy promptly so other children can share it.
4. The main idea is that this is a special community "sharing" collection. Children are encouraged to cooperate and show consideration of others by thinking about the feelings of others, and caring for and returning the toys (responsibility) so that others may enjoy them.

Teacher Preparation for Prop Bag*

Materials for *The Very Hungary Caterpillar*
  Book
  White construction paper
  Colored construction paper
  Watercolors
  Tissue paper
  Felt
  Glue
  Markers
  Crayons
  Scissors
  String
  Instruction Sheet
  Feedback Form

Materials for *Going On a Bear Hunt*
  Book
  White construction paper
  Watercolors
  Untreated charcoal (find at grocery stores in summer or hardware/home stores)
  Substitute black chalk, markers, and crayons for charcoal if necessary.

*Highlight the appropriate book on each instruction sheet.

Hole puncher
String
Instruction sheet
Feedback Form

Cooperation Prop Bag

Cooperation: Activity for Parents and children Estimated Time: 30–60 minutes

1. Read the book with your child. Then introduce the idea of recreating
   the story through art.
   ✓ *The Very Hungary Caterpillar* idea: Each family member chooses
   a fruit or other food to recreate using the materials provided in
   the bag. Create as few or as many as your child is interested
   in. For more fun, ask her to create a small caterpillar and a big
   caterpillar.
   ✓ *Going on a Bear Hunt* idea: Each family member choose either
   to do all black and white pages or all colors pages OR one person does the grass, one does the river, etc. Use charcoal (untreated) for black and white pages and watercolors for the color
   pages.
2. When each family member has finished, punch matching holes in
   the left side of each paper and use the string to lace together like a
   book. "Read" the story with your child by looking at the pictures
   you made together. Talk about cooperation. What would have happened if one of you had not done your part? Would the book have
   ended up the same way? Bring it to a relative or friend's house to
   read.

Feedback Form

Thank you for taking your time to model cooperation for your child. The more we participate in activities that promote cooperation, the more your child will learn about cooperating.

Please take just a few more minutes to answer the following questions so we can continue to create activities that suit your needs as well as strengthen the bond between home and school.

1. What did you enjoy about this activity? What did your child enjoy about this activity?

2. How did you use the materials? Which activities did you try?

3. Please add any other comments or questions, including what you would change about this activity.

Tips of the Week

Give each person in your family a "dinner preparation job." They can include clearing the table, setting out plates and glasses, setting out silverware and napkins, washing vegetables, cooking the food, bringing food to the table or putting food on the plates. Each job should have clear expectations. Start by letting the child or children choose the job they want. Let them do it for a week and then have them choose a different job for the following week. This will teach them cooperation as well as the importance of sitting down to dinner each night. Thank them each night for their contribution to dinner.

✂ --

Start a game night
Ask your child's teacher about borrowing a game from the classroom if you would like to try something new. Establish rules at the beginning of the game. They do not necessarily have to be the rules on the box. If they are different, write them down so you can refer to them if necessary. Modify games to suit your child's developmental level. For example, play memory with half the given pairs or play card games with fewer cards in hand. Reinforce turn taking, patience, cheering others on, and any other positive behaviors. Most importantly, play until everyone has finished. If you are playing a game in which someone typically "wins," tell the players "nobody wins until everybody finishes, and then everyone wins."

✂ --

Share a snack
Make fruit salad or veggie salad with your family. Let each person choose a fruit/vegetable, cut it up (cut your preschool child's fruit/veggie in half and let her do the rest with a dinner or plastic knife). Put a bowl in the middle of the table and pass it around until each person's food is inside. Then each person can scoop out a bowlful for someone else, until everyone has a snack. Talk about the how they feel about the difference between eating one fruit and eating many different fruits together.

✂ --

Play balloon games
Take a balloon and blow it up. Move potential hazards out of the way (tables with sharp corners, breakable items). Gather the family in the room. The object is to keep the balloon in the air for as long as possible. After playing

for a few minutes, set some goals and restrictions. Examples are: try to keep the balloon up for 2 minutes, try to keep the balloon up for 25 touches, try to keep it up using only your feet, or left hand or right hand, or head, only two touches in a row for any person, try to move into the next room (make it hazard free also) and anything else you can think of.

SELF-CONTROL

Changes to the Environment

Dramatic Play

- ✓ *Family life*: Clothing suitable for moms, dads, or grandparents. Baby dolls, food, dishes, telephone, magazines, paper, pencils, "bills", envelopes, money, purses, wallets, etc.
- ✓ Puppets and puppet stage

Sensory

- ✓ Play dough and tools
- ✓ Warm water and citrus extract (optional)

Art

- ✓ Bold colored paper
- ✓ Bright colored markers and paints
- ✓ Precut paper in drastic shapes
- ✓ Magazine pages showing item that children may find comforting

Writing

- ✓ Problem solving steps written out, numbered and posted
- ✓ Greeting cards and envelopes

Science/Discovery

- ✓ Magnet wands, pipe cleaners in half pieces, table with thin top or large cardboard box. (Cut a hole in the side of the box near the bottom. Turn the box upsidedown.) Put the pipe cleaners on top of the surface and use the magnet wands underneath to make the pipe cleaners move.
- ✓ Water with food coloring in primary colors, eye droppers, and empty plastic cups.

Manipulatives/Math

- ✓ Parquetry blocks with shape cards. Include several large shapes that require more than one block to fill the space.
- ✓ Beads in various colors, shapes, sizes, lacing strings and pattern cards.

Blocks

> ✓ Have the children create labels for the block shelf (trace each shape block onto paper and cut out. Let them decide where each shape should go. This will help them remember where certain blocks are. If they see another child with a block they want to use, they can look for the shape. Do this activity even if you already have labels. The children will be more apt to use the system if they help create it.

Group Time Discussion

1. *Emotions photos*: Use the photos of people who are angry. Ask the following questions:
   ✓ What made her so angry?
   ✓ What do you think she did when she got angry?
   ✓ What makes you angry?
   ✓ What do you do when you get angry?
2. Use stuffed animals to act out a situation in which one becomes angry. Ask the children "what would you do?" Then ask, "what would your mom do? What would your older sibling do? What would your younger sibling do? What would a teacher do? What would a police officer do? What would your dad do? What would your grandparent do?" Write down all of their responses and sort them into safe choices and unsafe choices. Add the safe choices to you list.
3. Talk about ways to get help. When children have trouble with self-control they need a fast, consistent method of seeking help in the heat of the moment. Suggest different ideas and let each child choose what works best for her. One idea is yelling "I need help" or "help me." This works best for the child that is physically aggressive. It is useful because the child does not need to attach a teacher's name. Since most classes combine in the early morning and late afternoon, and use floaters and substitutes the child may react before figuring out whose name to call for help.
4. That Makes Me Mad discussion
5. What If discussion
6. Puppet play
7. I Can Problem Solve (pp. 356–357) Discuss in detail using specific, recent events. Keep the steps of the process posted around the classroom for easy reference.
8. Elizabeth Crary problem solving books (see book list)

Book List

Agassi, Martine *Hands Are Not For Hitting*
Bang, Molly *When Sophie Gets Really, Really Angry*
Blumenthal, Deborah *The Chocolate-Covered-Cookie Tantrum*
Couric, Katie *The Brand New Kid*
Crary, Elizabeth *I Can't Wait*
Crary, Elizabeth *I'm Frustrated*
Crary, Elizabeth *I'm Furious*
Crary, Elizabeth *I'm Lost*
Crary, Elizabeth *I'm Mad*
Crary, Elizabeth *I Want It*
Crary, Elizabeth *I Want To Play*
Crary, Elizabeth *Mommy, Don't Go*
Crary, Elizabeth *My Name is Not Dummy*
Everitt, Betsy *Angry Arthur*
Fox, Mem *Harriet, You'll Drive Me Wild*
Lachner, Dorothea *Andrew's Angry Words*
Oram, Hiawyn *Mean Soup*
Simon, Norma *I Was So Mad*

Story Enhancer: *When Sophie Gets Angry, Really, Really Angry* by Molly Bang

Theme: Self-Control
Targeted Skills: anger management
Materials: book, paper, crayons/markers
Vocabulary: angry, choices, safety, alone, comfort
Group Size: any
Process

1. Read book and talk about what different children do when they are angry. Write down what they say and have them draw a picture to go with their words.
2. Make into a book.

Story Enhancer: *The Doorbell Rang* by Pat Hutchins

Theme: Self-Control
Targeted Skills: Problem solving
Materials: the book *the Doorbell Rang*, play dough, play dough tools
Vocabulary: sharing, self-control, problem solving, cooperation

Group Size: 4 to 6 children
Process

1. Read *The Doorbell Rang* by Pat Hutchins.
2. Talk about how the Characters in the story solved the problem.
3. Ask the children if they think they could solve a problem like that.
4. Recreate the story using play dough: Give the 1st child at the table all of the play dough and see if they can solve the problem as more children join the group.

Listening Games

These games will enhance the children's listening skills, a very important part of problem solving.

1. Lie down and close your eyes. Listen to sounds for a minute. Sit back up and ask children to share what they heard. Try this outside, in the classroom, in a hallway, etc.
2. Animal game: teacher names animal and children respond with animal sound. Try patterning, fast, slow, etc. (cow: moo, cow: moo, cat: meow, cat: meow, cow: moo, cow: moo).
3. What Am I? Describe a familiar object, person or place and let the children guess what it is. (I can be green, yellow or red, I grow on tress, I am crunchy when raw and soft when cooked, I can be made into sauce and pie . . .)

Teamwork

Theme: *Self-Control*
Targeted Skills: problem solving, cooperation
Materials: large bins, beanbags
Vocabulary: cooperate, together, teamwork, accomplish, goal
Group Size: whole group: depends on space, number of bins and number of beanbags
Process

1. Divide the children into teams of three. Explain that teams are groups of people that work together to accomplish a goal.
2. Give each team one bin and a few beanbags. Ask them to decide who will hold the bin (2 children) and who will throw the beanbags. Help them through this process if necessary.
3. Explain that their goal is to try to get the beanbag in the bin.

4. Ask them to find a space in the room that is not too close to another group.
5. Encourage the children to communicate their ideas with each other. Stress the importance of listening to all ideas and then choosing one to try first.
6. Let them try for a few minutes and then ask them to share with the group how they accomplished their goal. Did they stand close together? Did they move the bin to catch the beanbag?
7. After they have shared their ideas, let them try again, switching roles, until everyone has had a chance to throw.
8. At the next group time, talk about they way they worked together. Ask if anyone used someone else's idea to accomplish the team's goal.

Together We Can

Theme: Self Control
Targeted Skills: problem solving, cooperation
Materials: heavy object
Vocabulary: cooperation, together, alone, group, individual
Group Size: dependant on object
Process

1. Choose a heavy, large object for the children to move. Make it something that several children can move together, but no one child can move alone. Make it meaningful if possible (hose on water day, full sensory table, classroom furniture)
2. Allow children to try one by one to move the object. Then explain that you will need their help and cooperation.
3. Keep children safe and encourage them as they try different ways of moving the object.

What Can We Do?

Theme: Self-Control
Targeted Skills: problem solving, creativity
Materials: Paper bags (one for each child), twigs children collect, play dough, paint, and paper.
Vocabulary: creative, unique, different
Group Size: 10

Process

1. Take several children at a time to a safe area with trees, and offer each child a paper bag. Encourage children to pick up sticks they find on the ground that fit in their bag. Explain that they can take the sticks back to the classroom and explore different ways to use them. Try to include a variety of sticks that are different sizes, textures, and shapes.
2. Offer paint at one table, play dough at another and put sand and water in the sensory table. Invite children to bring their bag of twigs to the center of their choice.
3. Help children discover ways to use the sticks. For example, at the sensory table, talk about mixing, separating, and stirring, and drawing. At the play dough table, children can use the sticks to make impressions, cut, poke, and roll the dough. At the painting table, encourage them to experiment using the twigs as paintbrushes. Talk about the different marks that each stick makes.

Helpful Hints

1. Monitor children's play with sticks and twigs closely. Remind them to use their sticks safely.
2. Look for other ways children can use the sticks and twigs as tools in the classroom.

What If . . . ?

Theme: Self-Control
Targeted Skills: understanding consequences
Materials: none
Vocabulary: consequences
Group Size: any
Process

1. Start a story about a situation that you have seen in the classroom where someone could become angry or upset. Give several endings and talk about how they affect the people involved.
2. For example:

> Dominick is wandering around the classroom. He cannot decide what to do. Just then his friend Andre walks in the door. Dominick wants to give Andre a hug as fast as he can, but there is a big block building in front of him that Sam has been working on all morning.

Rachel is also on the other side of the easel with her painting, trying to find a place for it to dry.

What if: he knocks over the building on his way to hug Andre?
he runs around the block building and collides with Sam?
he walks around the building?
How will Sam feel? How will Rachel feel? How will Dominick feel?
Will Dominick get to hug Andre right away like he wanted to?

3. Discuss which option works best for everyone and which solution gets Dominick where he wants to be the fastest.

Helpful Hint

Use this game while children are playing if you see a child that is going to make a decision without thinking about the consequences.

I Can Problem Solve

Theme: Self-Control

1. Define the problem.
   What happened?
   Help me understand the problem better.
2. Elicit feelings.
   How do you feel?
   How does _____ feel?
3. Elicit consequences.
   What happened when you did that?
4. Elicit feelings about consequences.
   How did you feel when _____?
   (For example: *He took your toy/she hit you?*)
5. Encourage the child to think of other solutions.
   Can you think of a DIFFERENT way to solve this problem so _____?
   (For example: *You both won't be angry/she won't hit you.*)
6. Encourage evaluation of the solution.
   Is that a good idea or NOT a good idea?
   If a good idea: *Go ahead and try that.*
   If not a good idea: *Oh, you'll have to think of something different.*
7. Reinforce the child's act of thinking.

If the solution works: *Oh, you thought of that all by yourself. You're a good problem solver!*

If the solution does not work: *Oh, you'll have to think of something different. I know you're a good thinker!*

Note: I can Problem Solve (ICPS) teaches children *how* to think, rather than *what* to think. It is not necessary for the adult to ask each question every time there is a dialogue.

Source: Myrna B. Shure (1992). *I Can Problem Solve. An Interpersonal Cognitive Problem-Solving Program*, 2nd ed., pp. 8 and 9. Champaign, IL: Research Press. Copyright 1992 by Myrna B. Shure. Reprinted by permission.

The first message is that "Your anger is okay, anger is natural and it's an expected feeling." At the same time, how we express that anger has to be appropriate. So it's not okay to act on that anger in hurtful ways, by hitting, by screaming, by being out of control, by name-calling. Those are two very different messages and they need to be put together in skillful ways by adults.

That Makes Me Mad!

Theme: Self-Control
Targeted Skills: Problem solving, identifying feelings, self-awareness
Materials: Easel paper, markers
Vocabulary: Anger, angry, mad, acceptable, unacceptable
Group Size: Whole group
Process:

This is a series of activities to be completed over a span of several days or a couple of weeks.

- ✓ With a group of children, define anger. Ask the children "What is Anger" and record their responses on an experience chart. This can be done as a small group (four to five children) or a large group (12–15 children). The ability of the children to sit and participate in groups should determine the size of the group. Review the completed list and post it for parents and children to see.
- ✓ Review the definition of "anger." Make a list of what makes the children angry. Ask them, "What makes you angry/mad?" and record their responses on an experience chart. Post it for the parents and children to see.
- ✓ Review previous definition and list of what triggers anger for the children. Ask them "What makes parents angry?" and record their

responses on an experience chart, posting it for the parents and children to see.

✓ Review previous definition and lists of what triggers anger. Ask the children "What makes teachers angry?" and record their responses on an experience chart, posting it for parents and children to see.

✓ Review previous definition and lists of what triggers anger. Ask the children "How do you know when *other people* are angry?" Record their responses and post them. You may need to prompt them with other questions such as "What do people do/say when they are angry?" "How do people look/sound when they are angry?" Record the responses and post them.

✓ Review previous lists and ask the children "How do you know when you are angry?" You may need to prompt with additional questions such as; "What do you do/say when you are angry?" "How do you look/sound when you are angry?" Record the responses and post them.

✓ Ask the children "When you are angry, what do you do?" Record the responses and post the list. The list will most likely include *acceptable* and *unacceptable* behaviors (such as "hit someone" and "run away").

✓ With the children, review the lists of acceptable and unacceptable behaviors and evaluate them. Decide as a group what behavior is okay and what behavior is not okay. Edit the lists and post them.

✓ Ask the children, "When you are at school and you get angry, what should you do?" You may need to be more specific such as, "When someone hits you/takes your clay/pushes you off the bench, and you get angry, what should you do?" and "If you get angry because you want to paint and the paints are put away because it is lunch time, what should you do?" Make a list of responses. If the children become stumped, you may need to provide further guidance such as, "Is it okay to push/hit/bite/scratch/yell/walk away/sit in a quiet corner/tell a teacher?"

✓ Follow up these group discussions with personal and individual talks with children when they become angry.

Using all of the experience charts developed, create a book and have the children illustrate it. Make copies for the children to take home and keep several copies for the classroom.

Puppet Play

Theme: *Self-Control*
Targeted Skills: Problem Solving, identifying feelings
Materials: Puppets
Vocabulary: problem solving, feelings words such as happy, sad, etc.
Group Size: less than 10
Process

   1. Use puppets to act out daily problems.
   2. Have children brainstorm situations.
   3. Act out solutions that children suggest and talk about how each character felt.

Teacher Preparation Prop Bag

Materials
   More than 2 cups of baking soda
   More than 1 cup of cornstarch
   Measuring cups 1 cup, 1/3 cup
   Saucepan (if you think the family may not have one)
   Stirring spoon—large (wood or metal)
   Large plastic bag that can be sealed
   Put cornstarch and baking soda in sealed, labeled bags. Put more than enough in so that each family can measure out amount rather than just add what is in the bag.
   Instruction Sheet
   Feedback form

Prop Bag

Activity for parents and their children; estimated time: 30 minutes

When children become upset or angry, they often need to calm down before they are able to express their emotion in a safe way. This can be accomplished by offering sensory experiences such as soothing music, back rubbing, or play dough. This prop bag includes all the necessary ingredients for play clay. It is extremely smooth and soothing. When your child becomes angry or upset he can squeeze, squish, punch and tear the dough. When he has calmed, he can take a small piece and make an object. If left in the open air, it will dry. It can then be painted (or sealed with clear nail polish) and used as a reminder to always find appropriate ways to express anger. This is also a good tool for parents and teachers. When you become angry, take a small chunk in your hand and just squeeze it before you speak (or while you're counting to ten in your head!) It is a great stress reliever!

Soothing Clay
2 cups baking soda
1 cup cornstarch
1 1/3 cup water

1. Mix baking soda and cornstarch in a saucepan.
2. Add water
3. Mix with hands
4. Place saucepan over medium heat and bring to a boil.
5. Stir constantly (with a spoon this time!) until it looks like mashed potatoes.
6. Remove from pan and place on the table.
7. Let it cool until it is not too hot to handle (5–10 minutes)
8. Knead the dough until it is smooth
9. Have Fun!
10. Create an object using rollers, plastic utensils, and your hands.
11. Find things around the house to make imprints in the dough (pens, paperclips, bottles, spoons, forks, be creative!)
12. The dough will dry quickly when exposed to the air.
13. The dough will last for several weeks in a sealed bag or other airtight container

Feedback Form

Please take a few minutes to answer the following questions so we can continue to create activities that suit your needs as well as strengthen the bond between home and school.

1. How did you and your child use the materials in the bag?

2. What did you and your child like about the activity?

3. Please add any other comments or questions, including what you would change about this activity.

Weekly Tips for Parents

✂ ---

When your child has a problem, follow these steps with your child:

1. What is the problem: ask every person involved.
2. What are some solutions?
3. For each solution ask:

   Is it safe?
   How might people feel?
   Is it fair?
   Will it work?
4. Choose a solution and try it.
5. Is it working? If not, what else can we try?

✂ ---

Problem-solving hints
Listen to your child's ideas. Accept it even if it seems unreasonable. If your child suggests kicking or hitting, write it down and it will be evaluated in the next step. Ask your child if he would like more ideas. If so, add yours to the list. Do not insist that your child choose one of your ideas. Repeat the problem every time you ask for a solution.
✂ ---

Practice while children are cooperating
Children are more likely to solve the problems of others when they are not directly involved. Write down their ideas and save them for when similar problems arise with your child.

Puppet problems
Ask your child to act out two puppets (or stuffed animals) having a problem waiting for a turn on a bike. Help him to have the puppets follow the problem solving process.

Let's pretend
Give your child a problem scenario, such as, one child is sitting at the art table, another approaches and says, "Hey, I was sitting there. I got up to give Miss Maria a hug. I was coming right back." Act out different possible endings with your child.
✂ ---

Recognize and reinforce positive behavior
When your child exhibits self-control, point it out and talk about feelings. For example, "Wow! I can tell that you are feeling angry. You are doing a great job keeping your hands to your self! Stomping your feet and walking away was a great choice. How do you feel when you keep yourself and others safe?"

MEDIA

Group Time Discussion Ideas to Promote Media Awareness

1. TV Rules: Discuss different rules the children have for the television. Post a large piece of paper in a prominent area. Ask parents to write a TV rule on the paper.
2. Brainstorm alternatives to television. Post, send home and ask parents to add their own ideas to a class list.
3. TV Talk Activity
4. Is That Real?
5. Talk about appropriate television for preschoolers: PBS programs, certain Nickelodeon programs. Research programs and offer suggestions to children and parents.

Book List

For Parents

Canter, Lee *Couch Potato Kid: teaching kids to turn off the TV and tune in to fun*

Cantor, Joanne *Mommy, I'm Scared: how TV and movies frighten children and what we can do to protect them*

Greenfield, Patricia Marks *Mind and Media: the effects of television, video games, and computers*

Fox, Roy F. *Harvesting Minds: how TV commercials control kids*

Levine, Madeline.*Viewing Violence: how media violence affects your child and adolescent*

Moody, Kate. *Growing Up On Television: the TV effect : a report to parents*

Robie, Joan Hake *Teenage Mutant Ninja Turtles Exposed!*

Singer, Dorothy G. *Teaching Television: how to use TV to your child's advantage* Walsh, David Allen *Dr. Dave's cyberhood: making media choices that create a healthy electronic environment for your kids*
Steyer, James P
The Other Parent: the inside story of the media's effect on our children

For Children

Berenstain, Stan *The Berenstain Bears and Too Much TV*
Brown, Marc Tolon *Arthur's TV Trouble*

McCoy, Glenn *Penny Lee and Her TV*
Miller, Sara *Better Than TV*

Is That Real?

Theme: Media
Targeted Skills:
Materials: magazines, catalogs, toy brochures, scissors, media awareness poster board or bulletin board with three sections labeled "real", "pretend", and "not sure"
Vocabulary: real, pretend, make believe, character
Group Size: 3–10
Process

1. Have the children cut out pictures of their favorite TV characters, costumes, and real people in costumes/uniforms.
2. Start a discussion about what they watch on TV. Explain the difference between real and pretend. (Many children this age cannot distinguish between real and pretend, even after it is explained.)
3. Talk about the characters that they have chosen. Start with ones that you think the children will agree on, and then move on to harder ones. Let each child voice his opinion. If a consensus is reached, place the character on the appropriate side of the board. If consensus is not reached, put the character in the "not sure" category.
4. Return to the board as children feel the need to move characters around or add additional characters.

TV Talk

Theme: Media
Targeted Skills: language, listening
Materials: paper, markers
Vocabulary: violence, real, pretend, scared, rules
Group Size: 2–10
Process

1. Discuss children's television viewing habits.
   ✓ What TV shows do you watch?
   ✓ Do you like them?
   ✓ Why or why not?

✓ When do you watch TV?

✓ Where do you watch TV (in the kitchen, bedroom, Grandma's)?

✓ How many TV's do you have?

✓ Do you have a TV in your bedroom?

✓ What would you do if your TV broke?

✓ What else do you do at home?

2. Record what the children say.
3. If violence is mentioned, invite children to discuss other non-violent action that characters could use.
4. Discuss appropriate programs for children.
5. Provide parents with the list of non-TV activities that the children generated.

Working with Parents to Limit, Censor, and Find Alternatives to Watching TV and Playing Video Games

✓ Challenge parents to turn off the TV for at least a day. Have them write a paragraph about what they did instead and how their child reacted.

✓ Encourage parents to watch television with their child and discuss both appropriate and inappropriate behaviors of characters.

✓ Inform parents of the detrimental effects of violent television shows, movies and video games

✓ Provide a bulletin board for parents to share their ideas.

✓ Offer a list of free or low cost community activities, such as the library, fire houses, children's museums, parks, zoos, etc. Provide all necessary information including cost, directions and hours of operation. If possible, obtain coupons for discounts and distribute to parents.

✓ Provide the following ideas, prop bags and Tips of the Week to get parents started.

Turn Off the TV Prop Bags: Feedback Form
Prop Bag Name:_____

Please take just a few more minutes to answer the following questions so we can continue to create activities that suit your needs as well as strengthen the bond between home and school.

1. What did you enjoy about this activity? What did your child enjoy about this activity?

2. How did you use the materials? Which activities did you try?

3. Please add any other comments or questions, including what you would change about this activity.

Teacher Preparation for Science Prop Bag

Materials
Magnets of different shapes and sizes
Magnetic objects
Non-magnetic materials and objects
Magnet wands
Note pad
Pencil/crayon
Cardboard (from cereal box or cracker box)
Instruction sheet
Feedback form

Turn Off the TV Prop Bag

We teach science to preschoolers by providing materials, asking questions and encouraging the children to ask questions as they use the materials. Daily science experiments include baking, making play dough, mixing paint, water and sand play, and exploring the world around us. Exploring magnets is an area of science that children are intrigued by. Included in this prop bag are items to help you explore magnetism with your child.

1. Put all of the materials on a table.
2. Give your child a magnet wand and ask her to find the items that stick to the magnet.
3. Sort item into two piles: items that stick and items that do not.
4. Ask your child to try slowly pulling one of the magnets off of the wand. What does it feel like?
5. Find two magnets that stick together. Then turn one magnet over and try to stick them together again. What happened? What did it feel like?
6. Take the piece of cardboard and tape the ends to two chairs (like a bridge). Put the pipe cleaner bits on top and have your child rub the magnet wand under the board. What happens?
7. What else will the wand stick to? Walk around your house and see. Have your child try to guess before trying each object. (DO NOT put magnets anywhere near a computer!!)
8. Write down your guesses and observations.

Teacher Preparation Prop Bag

Materials
Construction paper
Tissue paper
Aluminum foil
Felt
Scrap materials
Recyclable materials
Glue
Markers
Crayons
Oil pastels
Watercolors
Instruction sheet
Feedback form

Prop Bag

Art is a process, not a product. We encourage children to make what they want with available materials. We do not expect their projects to look alike or mimic a teacher's project. In this bag you will find all sorts of art materials. Here are some ways to encourage your child to be creative with them.

1. Let your child empty the bag of materials and explore what they have. You can ask:
   ✓ What can we do with this?
   ✓ What color would you like to use first?
   ✓ Do these pieces of paper feel the same?
2. As your child begins to make something, ask thought provoking questions like:
   ✓ What are you making?
   ✓ Why did you decide to make that?
   ✓ Who are you making it for?
   ✓ Can I help you?
   ✓ Can I use some of the materials to make my own art?
3. As you begin to create your art describe what you are doing so your child will learn to describe her actions.
4. After you and your child complete your projects, talk about what you made and how you feel. Hang it on your refrigerator or give to the person it was created for.

Teacher Preparation for Literacy with Puppets Prop Bag

Materials
   Any quality book (look through Bingham book list at the end of the
   activity section)
   Puppets—animals or people, depending on the story
   Instruction sheet
   Feedback form

Literacy with Puppets Prop Bag

To help children develop reading skills, we read to them and with them.
We encourage children to read by telling a story about what they see in the
illustrations. The use of puppets enhances the story by giving the child a
chance to learn about the feelings and perspectives of others. Below are a
few ways to use the materials in the bag.

1. Let your child explore the contents of the bag.
2. Ask him if he would like to pick a book to read.
3. Let him know he can use the puppets as you read.
4. Ask questions like, "What do you think is going to happen next?"
   "How did that make her feel?" "What could she have done differently?" "Why do you think he did that?"
5. Follow your child's lead while reading. It is perfectly okay to reread
   certain pages, skip over others or finish before the story is over.
6. Talk about the book when you are done. Use a puppet and
   pretend to be one of the characters, see if your child will do this
   also.
7. Ask your child to read one of the books to you. Encourage her to
   look at the pictures and describe what she sees.
8. Use the puppets to act out your own story. It could be something that
   happened at school that day, a book from home or a favorite story.

Teacher Preparation for Math Fun Prop Bag

Materials
   Beads of different shapes, sizes and colors
   Lacing string (thin shoe laces)
   Instruction sheet
   Feedback form

Math Fun Prop Bag

Math happens all around us. It happens in the classroom even when it is not a planned activity. We see children measure water and sand, organize art materials, and build in the block area. Math skills for preschoolers are sorting, patterning, and creating categories. Here is a fun way for you to explore math with your child at home.

1. Let your child empty the bag of materials and start exploring.
2. Let your child lead you to your first activity. She may begin by sorting into different colors, sizes or shapes, she may start a pattern card or she may start stringing the beads.
3. Stringing ideas:
   - ✓ Point to each bead and label it by shape and color
   - ✓ Point out any pattern he may have made.
   - ✓ You can string a pattern and say the characteristic of each bead (green, yellow, green, yellow, green or square, circle, square, circle . . .) Alternate the tone of your voice so they can hear the pattern as well.
   - ✓ Ask your child which color or shape she is going to use next.
4. Sorting ideas:
   - ✓ Offer your child different cups, bowl or plates to put each color or shape in.
   - ✓ If your child sorts by color, ask her to then sort by shape.
   - ✓ Talk about other things that you could sort (like laundry, silverware, etc.)
5. Patterning ideas:
   - ✓ Use the cards to start patterns.
   - ✓ Make up your own patterns.
   - ✓ Let your child pick the first bead and you pick the next bead in the pattern.
   - ✓ Alternate the tone of your voice to prompt your child about what comes next.
   - ✓ Create harder patterns for more of a challenge.

Fun Activities (Using Household Items) to Do Instead of Watching TV

1. *Letter Writing:* With your child, write a letter to a friend or family member. Ask your child what she would like to say in the letter. Read the letter to your child after writing it. Ask your child if she would like to draw a picture to go with the letter. Explain to your child that letters must be sent in envelopes and then address the envelope reading the address as you write. Take a trip to the post office to buy stamps and let your child mail the letter.

2. *Sorting Chore:* Involve your child in a sorting game. Have her sort the forks and spoons, light and dark laundry, canned and boxed food, paper and plastic recyclable goods, etc.

3. *Counting Groceries:* Have your child help you put the groceries away. At the same time, ask, "How many potatoes did I buy? How many bars of soap? How many oranges? How many cans of dog food? How many boxes of crackers?"

4. *Sort and Count Activities:* Pick two different items (pens and pencils, cars and trucks, pennies and quarters, etc.) and place them on the table. Mix them up. Have your child sort the items and then count them. Ask, "Which group has more? Which group has less? How are these items different? How are they the same?"

5. *Bowling:* Collect 2 litter bottles until you have ten. (You can play this with any number of bottles). Set them up in a triangle formation with a point pointing toward you. Your child can help with this; half the fun is trying to keep them upright! Take a small inflated ball (or orange, kickball, beach ball, etc.) and roll it to the bottles. Have your child count how many bottles fell down and mark that number on a pad of paper. "Writing the number" will mean different things to different children. It can range from scribbling, to slash marks for each pin, to the actual number. Older children can add the total number of pins knocked down at the end of the game.

6. *Treasure Hunt:* Send your child on a treasure hunt to see if she can find the objects on your list. Draw pictures or ask for each item out loud. When she finds the item, then ask for the next, or go on the hunt with her, reading each item as you go. Some ideas are:

- ✓ Bar of soap
- ✓ Laundry basket
- ✓ Large serving spoon
- ✓ Telephone book
- ✓ A pot with a lid
- ✓ Something red (or green, purple)
- ✓ Something round
- ✓ Something smooth (or rough)

- ✓ A coin
- ✓ A pen or pencil
- ✓ Something longer than her arm
- ✓ Something shorter than his finger
- ✓ Something with words on it
- ✓ Something with numbers on it
- ✓ Something with her name on it
  Anything else that is safe for him to find

7. *Recipes:* Measuring, pouring and mixing, and observing ingredients provide your child with math and science experiences.

No Cook Play Dough
1cup water with food coloring
3 cups flour
1 cup salt
2 tbsp. cooking oil

In a large bowl, mix ingredients dry ingredients (mix with your hands) then slowly add the wet ingredients. Mix until it reaches dough like consistency. Add more flour if it is too sticky, more water if it is too dry. Store in an airtight container.

Cooked Play Dough
3 cups flour
1/2 cup cream of tartar
1 cup water
2 tbsp. cooking oil

Mix 1 cup flour and cream of tartar together in a large saucepan. Add water and oil and cook over medium heat until the mixture begins to stiffen. Remove from the pan and allow cooling. Mix an additional 1 or 2 cups of flour into the mixture. Store in an airtight container.

Goop
2 cups cornstarch
water

Pour the cornstarch in a bowl and let your child explore with her hands. Give her a cup of water and let her add it when she wants. If it gets too runny, add more cornstarch.

8. *Science in Your Tub:* You will need: Sponges, meat baster, boats, squeeze bottles, tubes, plastic pitchers, soap bubbles and rubber animals. Ideas for science activities:

- ✓ Ask your child to find out which items sink/float (have her predict first what she thinks will happen)
- ✓ Float a plastic container in the water. Start adding rubber animals. Count the number of animals your child can put into the "boat" before it sinks.
- ✓ Use small pitchers for pouring and measuring.
- ✓ Fill a variety of bottles with water. Talk about which has more, which has less.
- ✓ Fill one container with soap bubbles and another container with water. Talk about heavy and light.

Weekly Tips for Parents

Turn Off the TV and:

Play a board game.
Write a letter.
Clean out a desk or messy drawer.
Make cookies.
Build a fort in the living room with
    cushions and blankets.

Play with shaving cream on the
    kitchen table or in the bathtub (no
    water needed until cleanup).
Start a journal or diary.
Use scrap art material to make
    a collage.

✂ --

Turn Off the TV and:

Play Simon Says.
Find shapes in the clouds.
Make an obstacle course.
Make puppets out of paper bags,
    socks or cardboard with Popsicle
    sticks.

Make vanilla and chocolate
    pudding: put a spoonful of each
    in a bowl and swirl with a spoon.
Go to the library.
Paint rocks; hide them around the
    house for a scavenger hunt.

✂ --

Turn Off the TV and:

String pasta or cereal to make a
   necklace.
Fly a kite.
Read a book.
Build a tower with food boxes.
Look at the stars.
Play freeze tag.

Cut pictures out of a magazine and
   make a collage.
Play a card game.
Put on a puppet show.
Go through belongings, make a
   give-away pile to give away .

✂ --

Turn Off the TV and:

Have a taste test and chart the
   results.
Make a paper bag mask.
Go to the zoo (or pretend with
   stuffed animals).
Draw with sidewalk chalk.

Cut letters out of a magazine and
   glue them on paper to make
   familiar words.
Go for a walk around the
   neighborhood.
Pack a picnic lunch.

BOOKS FOR PROSOCIAL DEVELOPMENT

Kindness

Title	Author	Publisher/City/Year	ISBN/ASIN
A House For Hermit Crab	Eric Carle	Simon & Schuster Children's Publishing, NY, 1991	0887081681
Born in the Gravy	Denys Cazet	Scholastic Inc., NY, 1997	0531070964
Fernando's Gift	Douglas Keister	Sierra Club Books for Children, San Francisco, 1995	0871564149
Is Susan Here?	Janice May Urdy	HarperCollins Children's Book Group, Toronto, 1993	0060261420
Island Baby	Holly Keller	Mulberry Books, NY, 1995	
It Looked Like Spilt Milk	Charles Green Shaw	Harper Collins Children's Book Group, NY, 1988	0064431592
Jazzbo and Googy	Matt Novak	Hyperion Books for Children, NY, 2000	0786803886
Kevin and His Dad	Irene Smalls	Little-Brown & Company, NY, 1999	0316798991
Liliana's Grandmothers	Leyla Torres	Ferrar, Straus & Giroux, NY, 1998	0374351058
Mommies Don't Get Sick	Marilyn Hafner	Candlewick Press, Cambridge, 1995	08335559788
Mother's Are Like That	Carol Carrick	Houghton Mifflin Company, Boston, 2000	0395883512
Newborn	Kathy Henderson	Dial Books for Young Readers, NY, 1999	0803724349
Through Moon and Stars and Night Skies	Ann Warren Turner	Harper & Row, NY, 1996	0660261897
When Mama Gets Home	Marisabina Russo	HarperCollins Children's Book Group, NY, 1998	0688149855
Will You Mind the Baby, Davy?	Brigette Weninger	North-South Books, Incorporated, NY, 2001	0735813094
With My Brother/ Con Mi Hermano	Eileen Roe	Aladdin Paperbacks, NY, 1994	0689718551

Emotions

Title	Author	Publisher/City/Year	ISBN/ASIN
Annie and Moon	Miriam Smith	Gareth Stevens, Inc., Milwaukee, 1988	1555329284
Daddy Will You Miss Me?	Wendy McCormick	Simon and Schuster, NY, 1999	068981898X
Dark Day, Light Night	Jan Carr	Hyperion Books for Children, NY, 1996	0786800186

(*Continued*)

Title	Author	Publisher/City/Year	ISBN/ASIN
Delphine	Molly Bang	Morrow Junior Books, NY 1998	0688056369
Feelings: Brave	Janine Amos	Steck-Vaughn Company, Austin, 1994	0811492281
Feelings: Confident	Janine Amos	Steck-Vaughn Company, Austin, 1999	081149229X
Friends	Kim Lewis	Candlewick Press, Cambridge, 1998	0763603465
Going Home	Eve Bunting	Harper Trophy, NY, 1998	0064435091
Gracias Rosa	Michelle Markel	Albert Whitman Co., Morton Grove, 1995	0807530247
How Are You Peeling?	Saxton Freymann	Scholastic Limited, NY, 2000	0439104319
I Love You, Stinky Face	Lisa McCourt	Troll Communications, LLC, Mahwah, 1998	0816744599
I Miss You Stinky Face	Lisa McCourt	Bridge Water Books, Mahwah, 1999	0816756473
I Never Say I'm Thankful, But I Am	Jane Moncure	Children's Press, Chicago, 1979	0895650231
I'm Excited	Elizabeth Crary	Parenting Press, Inc., Seattle, 1996	0943990912
I'm Frustrated	Elizabeth Crary	Parenting Press, Inc., Seattle, 1992	0943990645
I'm Furious	Elizabeth Crary	Parenting Press, Inc., Seattle, 1996	0943990939
I'm Mad	Elizabeth Crary	Parenting Press, Inc., Seattle, 1992	0943990629
I'm Proud	Elizabeth Crary	Parenting Press, Inc., Seattle, 1992	0943990661
I'm Scared	Elizabeth Crary	Parenting Press, Inc., Seattle, 1996	0943990890
It's Mine	Leo Lionni	Knopf, NY, 1996	0679880844
Jamaica's Blue Marker	Juanita Havill	Houghton Mifflin Company, Boston, 2003	0618369171
Jamaica's Find	Juanita Havill	Houghton Mifflin Company, Boston, 1987	0395453577
Nobody Knew What To Do	Becky Ray McCain	Albert Whitman & Company, Morton Grove, 2001	0807557110
One Summer Day	Kim Lewis	Candlewick Press, Cambridge, 1996	1564028836
Roses Are Pink, Your Feet Really Stink	Diane DeGroat	HarperCollins Children's Book Group, NY, 1997	0688152201
The Rainbow Fish and the Sea Monster's Cave	Marcus Pfister	North-South Books, Inc., NY, 2001	0735815364
Uncle Rain Cloud	Tony Johnston	Charlesbridge Publishing, Inc., Watertown, 2001	0881063711

(Continued)

Title	Author	Publisher/City/Year	ISBN/ASIN
Uncle Willie and the Soup Kitchen	Dyanne DiSalvo-Ryan	Mulberry Books, NY, 1997	0688152856
What's the Matter Davy?	Brigette Weninger	North-South Books, Inc., NY, 2001	0735814910
When I'm Afraid	Jane Aaron	Golden Books, NY 1998	0307440575
When I'm Angry	Jane Aaron	Golden Books, NY 1998	0307440192
When Sophie Gets Angry, Really, Really Angry	Molly Bang	Scholastic, Inc., NY, 1999	0590189794
Why Are You Fighting Davy	Brigette Wenninger	North-South Books, NY, 1999	07358810737

Respect

Title	Author	Publisher/City/Year	ISBN/ASIN
All the Colors of the Earth	Sheila Hamanaka	Morrow Junior Books, NY, 1994	0688111319
Am I Really Different	Evelien Van Dort	Floris Books, Edinburgh, 1998	0863152724
Amazing Grace	Mary Hoffman	Dial Books for Young Readers, NY, 1991	0803710402
Children From Australia to Zimbabwe	Maya Ajmera and Anna Rhesa Versola	Charlsbridge Publishing, Watertown, MA, 1996	088106999X
Each Living Thing	Joanne Ryder	Harcourt Children's Books, San Diego, 2000	0152018980
Faces	S. Rotner/ K. Kreisler	MacMillan Publishing Company, Inc., NY, 1994	0027778878
Horace	Holly Keller	Mulberry Books, NY, 1995	0688118445
I Got a Family	Melrose Cooper	Henry Holt and Co., NY,1993	0805019650
It's Okay to Be Different	Todd Parr	Little, Brown and Co., NY, 2001	0316666033
Jamaica's Find	Juanita Havill	Houghton Mifflin Company, Boston, 1987	0395453577
Lots of Moms	Shelley Rotner	Dial Books for Young Readers, NY, 1996	0803718926
Manners	Aliki	Mulberry Books, NY, 1997	0688045790
My Father's Hands	Joanne Ryder	Harper Collins Children's Book Group, NY, 1994	068809189X
Pick a Pet	Shelley Rotner	Scholastic, Inc., NY, 1999	0531301478
Shades of Black	Sandra Pinkney	Scholastic Trade, NY, 2000	0439148928
So What?	Miriam Cohen	Greenwillow Books, NY, 1982	0613087755
Teeny Tiny Ernest	Laura T. Burnes	Barnesyard Books, Sergeantsville, 2000	0967468116
The Color of Us	Karen Katz	Henry Holt Books for Young Readers, NY, 2002	0805071636
The Daddy Book	Ann Morris	Silver Press, Parsippany, 1996	0382246950

(Continued)

Title	Author	Publisher/City/Year	ISBN/ASIN
To Be a Kid	Maya Ajmera	Charlesbridge Publishing, Watertown, 1999	0881068411
Wake Up World!	Beatrice Hollyer	Henry Holt and Co., NY, 1999	0805062939

Cooperation

Title	Author	Publisher/City/Year	ISBN/ASIN
A Chair for My Mother	Vera Williams	Pearson K-12, 1984	0688040748
Alexander and the Wind Up Mouse	Leo Lionni	Bantam Doubleday Dell Books for Young Readers, NY, 1974	0394829115
Best Friends for Frances	Russel Hoban	Harper CollinsChildren's Book Group, NY, 1976	0064430081
Dancin' in the Kitchen	Wendy Gelsanliter	Putnam, NY, 1998	0399230351
It Takes a Village	Jane Cowen-Fletcher	Scholastic, Inc., NY, 1993	0590465732
Katy and the Big Snow	Virginia Lee Burton	Scholastic, Inc., NY, 1971	0590047922
Mike Mulligan and His Steam Shovel	Virginia Lee Burton	Scholastic, Inc., NY, 1967	0395066816
Penguin Pete and Little Tim	Marcus Pfister	North-South Books, Inc., NY, 1997	15585773X
Swimmy	Leo Lionni	Knopf, NY, 1992	0394826205
The Little Red Hen	Paul Galdone	Houghton Mifflin Co., NY, 1973	0395288037
The Rainbow Fish	Marcus Pfister	North-South Books, Inc., NY, 1996	1558585362
The Three Friends	Susanne Kubler	MacMillan Publishing Co, NY, 1985	0027511502
Together	George Ella Lyon	Orchard Books, NY, 1994	0531070476
Zinnia and Dot	Lisa Campbell Ernst	Dial Books for Young Readers, NY, 1992	0670830917

Self-Control

Title	Author	Publisher/City/Year	ISBN/ASIN
Andrew's Angry Words	Dorothea Lachner	North-South Books, Inc., NY, 1997	1558587691
Angry Arthur	Hiawyn Oram	Farrar, Straus & Girous, LLC, NY, 1997	0374403864
Hands Are Not For Hitting	Martine Agassi	Free Spirit Publishing, Minneapolis, 2000	1575420775
Harriet, You'll Drive Me Wild	Mem Fox	Harcourt Children's Books, San Diego, 2000	0152019774
I Can't Wait	Elizabeth Crary	Parenting Press, Inc., Seattle, 1996	1884734227
I Want It	Elizabeth Crary	Parenting Press, Inc., Seattle, 1996	1884734146

(Continued)

Title	Author	Publisher/City/Year	ISBN/ASIN
I Want To Play	Elizabeth Crary	Parenting Press, Inc., Seattle, 1996	1884734189
I Was So Mad	Norma Simon	Albert Whitman & Company, Martin Grove, 1991	0807535192
I'm Frustrated	Elizabeth Crary	Parenting Press, Inc., Seattle, 1992	0943990645
I'm Furious	Elizabeth Crary	Parenting Press, Inc., Seattle, 1996	0943990939
I'm Lost	Elizabeth Crary	Parenting Press, Inc., Seattle, 1996	1884734243
I'm Mad	Elizabeth Crary	Parenting Press, Inc., Seattle, 1992	0943990629
Mean Soup	Betsy Everitt	Harcourt Children's Books, San Diego, 1992	0152531467
Mommy, Don't Go	Elizabeth Crary	Parenting Press, Inc., Seattle, 1997	1844734200
My Name is Not Dummy	Elizabeth Crary	Parenting Press, Inc., Seattle, 1996	1884734162
The Brand New Kid	Katie Couric	Doubleday, NY, 2000	0385500300
The Chocolate-Covered-Cookie Tantrum	Deborah Blumenthal	Houghton Mifflin Company, Boston, 1999	0395700280
When Sophie Gets Really, Really Angry	Molly Bang	Scholastic, Inc., Seattle, 1999	0590189794

Media

Title	Author	Publisher/City/Year	ISBN/ASIN
Harvesting Minds: how TV commercials control kids	Roy F. Fox	Praeger, Westport, CT, 2000	0275971015
Couch Potato Kids: teaching kids to turn off the TV and tune in to fun	Lee Canter	Lee Canter & Associates, Santa Monica, CA, 1996	0939007762
Mommy, I'm Scared: how TV and movies frighten children and what we can do to protect them	Joanne Cantor	Harcourt Brace, NY, 1998	0151004021
The Other Parent: the inside story of the media's effect on our children	James P Steyer	Atria Books, NY, 2002	074340582X
Viewing Violence: how media violence affects your child and adolescent	Madeline Levine	Doubleday, NY, 1996	0385476868

(Continued)

Title	Author	Publisher/City/Year	ISBN/ASIN
Teenage Mutant Ninja Turtles exposed!	Joan Hake Robie	Starburst, Lancaster, PA, 1991	0914984314
Mind and Media: the effects of television, video games, and computers	Patricia Marks Greenfield	Harvard University Press, Cambridge, 1984	0674576209
Penny Lee and her TV	Glenn McCoy	Hyperion Press, NY, 2002	0786806613
Better than TV	Sara Swan Miller	Bantam Doubleday Dell, NY, 1998	0385323255
Arthur's TV Trouble	Marc Tolon Brown	Bt Bound, 1999	0613036182
The Berestain Bears and Too Much TV	Stan Berenstain	Random House, NY, 1984	0394685707

INTERNET WEB SITES

Organization	Site
FastCounter by b Central FC 77259	http://www.coe.iup.edu/worldofkindergarten/
New York University Child Study Center	http://www.aboutourkids.org/books/index.html
Education Research Consumer Guide	http://www.ed.gov/pubs/OR/ConsumerGuides/cooplear.html
Winning Strategies for Classroom Management, Teaching Inc.	http://www.ascd.org/readingroom/books/cummings00book.html
Office of School Readiness, The Ford Foundation & Harvard University in Partnership with Council for Excellence in Government	http://www.osr.state.ga.us
Public Broadcast System	http://www.pbs.org/wholechild/providers/getting.html
Northwest-Shoals Community College	http://www.nncc.org/Guidance/cc21_learn.kindness.html
National Parent Information Network, Virtual Library	http://npin.org/library/2000/n00135.html
Cambridge, MA: Harvard University Press, The Kindness of Children	http://www.gse.harvard.edu/~hepg/HER-BookRev/Articles/1999/2-Summer/Paley.html
Moozie's Kindness Foundation, Inc.	http://www.moozie.com/mk.pdf
The Center for Nonviolent Communication	http://www.cnvc.org/grabbing.htm
Zero to Three, The Nation's Leading Resource on the First Years of Life	http://zerotothree.org
Educators for Social Responsibility, The Counter.com	http://esrnational.org/
Teachers Resisting Unhealthy Children's Entertainment	http://www.truceteachers.org/
Google	http://www.google.com
American Academy of Pediatrics	www.pediatrics.org
Gayle's Preschool Rainbow	www.preschoolrainbow.org
Perpetual Preschool	www.perpetualpreschool.com
Preschool Education	www.preschooleducation.com

About the Editors

Martin Bloom obtained a PhD in social psychology from the University of Michigan and a diploma in social study from the University of Edinburgh. He has been teaching in schools of social work for most of his career, and is currently editing *The Journal of Primary Prevention*. He coedited the *Encyclopedia of Primary Prevention and Health Promotion* (with Tom Gullotta, 2003), and coauthored *Evaluating Practice: Guidelines for the Accountable Professional* (with Joel Fischer & John Orme, 4th Ed., 2003).

Elda Chesebrough, LCSW, is the Coordinator of the Bingham Program at the Child and Family Agency of Southeastern Connecticut. She has 28 years of experience in early childhood programs including family childcare, non-profit and for-profit childcare, young parents programs, and family centers. Her work includes child and family counseling, home based therapy, and parent education. She is the coach and primary developer of the Bingham program and coeditor of The Bingham Early Childhood Prosocial Behavior Program.

Thomas P. Gullotta is Chief Executive Officer of Child and Family Agency of Southeastern Connecticut and is a member of the psychology and education departments at Eastern Connecticut State University. He is the senior author of the fourth edition of *The Adolescent Experience*, coeditor with Martin Bloom of *The Encyclopedia of Primary Prevention and Health Promotion*, and is editor emeritus of the *Journal of Primary Prevention*. He is the senior book series editor for *Issues in Children's and Families' Lives*. He holds editorial appointments on the *Journal of Early Adolescence, The Journal of Adolescent Research, and the Journal of Educational and Psychological Consultation*. He serves on the Board of the Asperger Coalition of the United States and has published extensively on adolescents and primary prevention. He was honored in 1999 by the Society for Community Research and

Action, Division 27 of the American Psychological Association with their Distinguished Contributors to Practice in Community Psychology Award.

Patricia King, MS, is the Director of Early Childhood Services at Child and Family Agency of Southeastern Connecticut. She has a 29 years experience in early childhood programs with 25 years in administration. Her experience has included teaching children birth to 12 years old, directing child care programs and Family Resource Centers, curriculum specialist, and consultation. She is cochair of two school readiness councils and past president of the Connecticut Family Resource Alliance. She is an NAEYC validator and has presented at local and national conferences.

About the Contributors

Susanne Denham received her PhD in 1985, after serving 11 years as a school psychologist. Her research involves social-emotional development, particularly in preschoolers. She is following a longitudinal sample of children she has known since age 3, examining their emotional competence, its socialization, and its contribution to social competence, and is also studying a little-studied aspect of children's development—forgiveness. Finally, she is the mother of three grown children who taught her much of what she knows about development.

Joseph A. Durlak is Professor of Psychology at Loyola University Chicago. He has always been interested in community and child psychology, particularly in prevention, and is now focusing attention on the impact of positive youth development programs.

Paul Flaspohler is completing his doctorate in clinical-community psychology at the University of South Carolina. A graduate of Xavier University (Ohio), Paul has conducted therapy, applied research, and evaluation with children and families and has worked in education and community development in the Peace Corps in West Africa. He recently received a National Research Service Award from NIMH to support his dissertation investigating young children's coping-response patterns.

Alice Sterling Honig is Professor Emerita of Child Development at Syracuse University. Courses taught include Language and Cognitive Development; Infancy, Parenting, Cross-cultural Study of the Child and Family, Eriksonian Theory, Prosocial and Moral Development, Observation and Assessment, Programs and Models in Early Childhood Education, and Theories of Child Development. She has published hundreds of articles and book chapters, more than a dozen books, and narrated videos for care-givers and parents. She is Director of the National Quality Infant/Toddler Caregiving Workshop held annually at Syracuse University for 27 years. Her books include *Playtime Learning Games for Young Children, Behavior guidance for Infants and Toddlers, Prosocial Development in Children* (with D. Wittmer), *Talking with Your Baby: Family as the First School* (with H. Bro-phy) and *Secure Relationships: Nurturing Infant/Toddler Attachment in Early Care Settings*. Among Dr. Honig's awards are the Chancellor's Citation for Academic Excellence, and the Onondaga Woman of Achievement Award. As a licensed psychologist and therapist, she is a volunteer in leading groups on divorce and custody for the Mental Health Association.

Doré R. LaForett is a doctoral student in Clinical Psychology at Temple University. She received her B.A. from the University of Denver with a dou-ble major in Psychology and Spanish, and her M.A. in Clinical-Community Psychology from the University of South Carolina. She is presently a project coordinator with the Head Start Quality Research Center at Temple Uni-versity in Philadelphia, Pennsylvania. Her areas of interest include early childhood, school readiness, and language and literacy development. She is specializing in the study of sociocultural issues related to child develop-ment, including linguistic factors and poverty.

Julia L. Mendez is an Assistant Professor of Psychology at Temple Uni-versity and the director of the Head Start Quality Research Center. She received her PhD in School, Community, and Clinical Child Psychology from the University of Pennsylvania in 1999. Dr. Mendez studies peer play, culture, and school readiness with children from low-income and ethnic minority backgrounds. She is also developing preventive interventions for promoting parent involvement and family-school relations.

Jennifer C. Messina is a senior at Villanova University in Pennsylvania majoring in Human Services. Interested in after-school activities that pro-mote the well-being of youth, she intends to work with young people after graduation prior to attending graduate school.

Margaret M. O'Shea has been an educator since 1969, teaching at every grade level from kindergarten through the graduate level. After graduating from Hunter College in New York with a double major in Political Science and Education, she began her career as a preschool teacher in a Head Start program in New York City. She then moved to Connecticut, where she taught third grade.

After receiving her Masters Degree in Reading from the University of Rhode Island and becoming certified as a reading consultant for the State of Connecticut, she became a remedial reading teacher. Following that, she began work as a teacher of gifted and talented students in a special program for such students.

While teaching and directing the gifted program, she continued her studies at Southern Connecticut State University to become certified as an administrator and supervisor in the State of Connecticut by receiving a Sixth Year Degree. Her next position employed her administrative certification, as she became the Director of Reading and Language Arts for the Lyme-Old Lyme School System. She then became the principal of Lyme Consolidated School, where she started Higher Order Thinking Skills through the Arts Program (HOTS) and various instructional approaches that used the multiple intelligences. She also worked with the University of Connecticut to pilot a training opportunity for teachers to learn how to differentiate instruction for all learners in the classroom. She then became the Director of Curriculum and Professional Development for the Lyme–Old Lyme School System.

She received her PhD in 1998 in Educational Leadership from the University of Connecticut, where her dissertation topic was focused on high-ability women and math achievement. She then became a Professor in the Education Department at St. Joseph College in West Hartford, where she was responsible for training teachers aspiring to teach at the secondary level. Presently she is also working for the Connecticut State Department of Education as a consultant in various school districts in Connecticut, including many urban districts.

She serves as a trustee for Mitchell College and is also Chairperson of the Board of Directors of Child and Family Agency in New London. She was a founding member of the Women and Girls Fund at the Community Agency in New London. She is also a trustee of the Florence Griswold Museum in Old Lyme and Chairperson of the Education Committee of the Florence Griswold Museum.

Jessica M. Ramos, B.A. Psychology, is a Research Assistant at Child and Family Agency of Southeastern Connecticut. She has served as a research assistant, editing, undertaking library research, and supporting the work of the editors Thomas Gullotta and Martin Bloom on the *Encyclopedia of Primary Prevention and Health Promotion.* She has also assisted in the editorial process in the *Asperger Syndrome: A Handbook for Professionals and Families,* and is involved in child observations and research for the Bingham Early Childhood Prosocial Behavior Curriculum.

Jen Seager is working toward her B.A. in Early Childhood Education. She has over 10 years of experience in early childhood programs. She has taught children six weeks old through fourteen years old in a variety of settings, including childcare, nursery school, afterschool programs, camps, and nonrecurring care programs. She has worked for The Child and Family Agency since 1998 first as a preschool teacher and most recently as a research assistant for the Bingham Early Childhood Prosocial Behavior Program.

Lindsey Stillman is a doctoral student in clinical-community psychology at the University of South Carolina. She received her B.S. in Anthropology and Psychology from Emory University. She has worked with evaluation teams on such projects as South Carolina's First Steps to School Readiness and Parent University in Spartanburg. Her interests include family support, parent education, and school readiness programs in impoverished communities.

Abe Wandersman is a Professor of Psychology at the University of South Carolina. He is a coauthor of *Prevention Plus III* and a coeditor of *Empowerment Evaluation: Knowledge and Tools for Self Assessment and Accountability*. In 2000, he was elected president of Division 27 of the American Psychological Association, The Society for Community Research and Action. Dr. Wandersman recently collaborated with the governor's statewide initiative for improving school readiness in South Carolina.

Roger P. Weissberg is a Professor of Psychology and Education at the University of Illinois at Chicago. He is Executive Director of the Collaborative for Academic, Social, and Emotional Learning (CASEL), an organization committed to advancing the science and practice of social and emotional learning (www.casel.org). He has published 150 articles, chapters, and books on school-based prevention and positive youth development.

Issues in Children's and Families' Lives

Series Editors:
Thomas P. Gullotta, *Child and Family Agency of Southeastern Connecticut, New London, Connecticut*
Herbert J. Walberg, *University of Illinois at Chicago, Chicago, Illinois*
Roger P. Weissberg, *University of Illinois at Chicago, Chicago, Illinois*

Series Mission

Using the collective resources of the Child and Family Agency of Southeastern Connecticut, one of the nation's leading family service agencies, and the University of Illinois at Chicago, one of the nation's outstanding universities, this series focuses attention on the pressing social and emotional problems facing young people and their families today.

Two publishing efforts are to be found within these volumes:

The first effort from the University of Illinois at Chicago Series on Children and Youth draws upon the multiple academic disciplines and the full range of human service professions to inform and stimulate policymakers and professionals that serve youth. The contributors use basic and applied research to uncover "the truth" and "the good" from such academic disciplines as psychology and sociology as well as such professions as education, medicine, nursing, and social work.

The second effort belongs to the Child and Family Hartman Scholars program. More than a decade in existence, this chosen group of scholars, practitioners, and advocates is formed yearly around a critical study area. This honored learning group analyzes, integrates, and critiques the clinical and research literature as it relates to the chosen theme and issues a volume that focuses on enhancing the physical, social, and emotional health of children and their families in relationship to that issue.

University Advisory Committee for
The University of Illinois at Chicago Series on
Children and Youth

LASCELLES ANDERSON
College of Education

CARL C. BELL
Department of Psychiatry

SUZANNE K. CAMPBELL
Department of Physical Therapy

BARRY R. CHISWICK
Department of Economics

VICTORIA CHOU
Dean, College of Education

JUDITH A. COOKSEY
Health Research and Policy
  Centers

SUZANNE FEETHAM
College of Nursing

STANLEY FISH
Dean, College of Liberal Arts
  and Sciences

BRIAN R. FLAY
School of Public Health

RACHEL A. GORDON
Department of Sociology

CREASIE FINNEY HAIRSTON
Dean, Jane Addams College of
  Social Work

DARNELL F. HAWKINS
African-American Studies

DONALD HELLISON
College of Kinesiology

CHRISTOPHER KEYS
Department of Psychology

JACK KNOTT
Institute of Government
  and Public Affairs

DAVID PERRY
Director, Great Cities Institute

OLGA REYES
Department of Psychology

SUSAN C. SCHRIMSHAW
Dean, School of Public Health

GERALD S. STROM
Department of Political
Science

JAMES J. STUKEL
President, University of
Illinois

CHARLOTTE TATE
Provost and Vice Chancellor for
  Academic Affairs

PATRICK H. TOLAN
Institute for Juvenile Research

WIM WIEWEL
Dean, College of Urban Planning
  and Public Affairs

National Advisory Committee for
The University of Illinois at Chicago Series on
Children and Youth

Index

Head Start, 130–133
  Early, 132–133, 150–151
  eligibility requirements for, 150–151
  Family and Child Experiences Survey
      (FACES) evaluation of, 131
  in high-crime communities, 123
  Izard's program for, 33, 35
  PATHS (Promoting Alternative Thinking
      Strategies) program, 33, 35, 37
  performance standards for, 131
  social-emotional learning basis for, 33
  teacher-parent collaborative training in,
      41
Health
  of children
    effect of community resources on,
        121
    as parental goal, 127–128
    maternal, effect on children's
        development, 102, 104–106
Health care services, access to
  social network-based access to, 124
  socioeconomic factors in, 121
Health insurance, universal, 186
Health promotion, 96
Heart of Parenting, The (Gottman and
    Declaire), 39
Hedgehog's Balloon (Butterworth), 50–60
Helpfulness. *See also* Kindness
  reciprocation of, 52, 146
  required, 65–66
Helping behavior, 52
"Helping coupons," 75, 147–148
Help-seeking behavior, 351
Heroes, identification of, 294–295
Hiawatha's Kind Heart (Walt Disney),
    59
High/Scope curriculum, 37
Hispanic children, residence in
    impoverished neighborhoods,
    126–127
Holiday celebrations, 76
  as family events, 269
Home owner occupancy, 118
Home visiting programs, 104, 106
Homicide, gun-related, 187
Horton Hears a Who (Dr. Seuss), 60
Housing, substandard or vacant, 119–120,
    123, 124, 135, 150

Hugs
  Bear Hug, 260
  Musical, 299

I

"I Can Problem Solve" (ICPS) curriculum,
    67–68, 243, 245, 351, 356–357
Image-making, 9
"I" messages, 315
Impulse management, 185, 195–196,
    198–201, 238, 258–260
Increased appetite effect, of violence, 71
Independence, development in toddlers,
    175–176
Inductive guidance, 24–25
Infant-caregiver relationship, 144
Infant Health and Development Program
    (IHDP), 117
Infant mortality, 121
Infant-parent relationship, 174–175
  attachment in, 145
Infants
  prosocial behavior in, 51–52
  temperaments of, 175
  trust development in, 174–175
Inheritances, symbolic and behavioral,
    128
Innocence, of children, 186
Intelligence, "Flynn effect" in, 10
Intelligence quotient (IQ), effect of
    neighborhood socioeconomic
    status on, 117
Interest centers, 220
Internalizing behavior
  neighborhood factors in, 117–118, 119
  as self-regulation coping strategy, 19
  violence-related, 52–53
Internet Web sites, as prosocial
    development resources, 291,
    381
*Interpersonal Cognitive Problem Solving
    program*, 67
Interpersonal relationships. *See also* Peer
    interactions; Positive interactions
  responsible decision making about, 146
Involvement, parental, 98
Irritability, teachers' awareness of, 254
"I" statements, 254–255, 257–258
Is That Real? activity, 364

Printed in the United States
58620LVS00001B/79-96